Power and Urban Space in Pre-Modern Holland

POWER AND URBAN SPACE IN PRE-MODERN HOLLAND

ARENAS OF APPROPRIATION IN THE NETHERLANDS, 1500–1850

Clé Lesger

BLOOMSBURY ACADEMIC
LONDON • NEW YORK • OXFORD • NEW DELHI • SYDNEY

BLOOMSBURY ACADEMIC
Bloomsbury Publishing Plc, 50 Bedford Square, London, WC1B 3DP, UK
Bloomsbury Publishing Inc, 1385 Broadway, New York, NY 10018, USA
Bloomsbury Publishing Ireland, 29 Earlsfort Terrace, Dublin 2, D02 AY28, Ireland

BLOOMSBURY, BLOOMSBURY ACADEMIC and the Diana logo are trademarks of
Bloomsbury Publishing Plc

First published in Great Britain 2024
Copyright © Clé Lesger 2024

Paperback edition published 2025

Clé Lesger has asserted his right under the Copyright, Designs and Patents Act, 1988,
to be identified as author of this work.

Cover image: View of houses in Delft, known as 'The Street', Johannes Vermeer,
ca. 1658, oil on canvas, Gift of H.W.A. Deterding ©Rijksmuseum

All rights reserved. No part of this publication may be: i) reproduced or transmitted in any form, electronic or mechanical, including photocopying, recording or by means of any information storage or retrieval system without prior permission in writing from the publishers; or ii) used or reproduced in any way for the training, development or operation of artificial intelligence (AI) technologies, including generative AI technologies. The rights holders expressly reserve this publication from the text and data mining exception as per Article 4(3) of the Digital Single Market Directive (EU) 2019/790.

Bloomsbury Publishing Plc does not have any control over, or responsibility for, any thirdparty websites referred to or in this book. All internet addresses given in this book were correct at the time of going to press. The author and publisher regret any inconvenience caused if addresses have changed or sites have ceased to exist, but can accept no responsibility for any such changes.

Every effort has been made to trace the copyright holders and obtain permission to reproduce the copyright material. Please do get in touch with any enquiries or any information relating to such material or the rights holder. We would be pleased to rectify any omissions in subsequent editions of this publication should they be drawn to our attention.

A catalogue record for this book is available from the British Library.

A catalog record for this book is available from the Library of Congress.

ISBN: HB: 978-1-3504-1237-8
PB: 978-1-3504-1236-1
ePDF: 978-1-3504-1238-5
eBook: 978-1-3504-1239-2

Typeset by Deanta Global Publishing Services, Chennai, India

For product safety related questions contact productsafety@bloomsbury.com.

To find out more about our authors and books visit www.bloomsbury.com and
sign up for our newsletters.

To Yona and to the students who over the past decades have made teaching in the History Department an inspiring and always enjoyable experience

Contents

List of Figures	ix
List of Maps	xi
List of Tables	xiv
Preface	xv
Acknowledgements	xvii

Introduction: Resources, power and the appropriation of urban space in pre-modern Holland ... 1

1 Inequality and power relations in the cities of Holland ... 11
   1.1. Inequality ... 11
   1.2. Views on the social hierarchy and self-image of the elites ... 14
   1.3. A web of alliances ... 19
   1.4. Images of the working classes and the poor ... 22

2 Residential appropriation of urban space in the first half of the nineteenth century ... 29
   2.1. The field of housing and residential differentiation: Theory and spatial models ... 29
   2.2. Residential differentiation in the pre-modern cities of Holland ... 34
   2.3. Residential appropriation of urban space around 1830: The summary picture ... 49

3 Resources, power and residential appropriation of urban space ... 53
   3.1. Previous history: Residential patterns in the cities of Holland, fourteenth–nineteenth centuries ... 53
   3.2. Resources, power and residential appropriation of urban space ... 55
      3.2.1. Residential appropriation of urban space: Macro-level ... 56
      3.2.2. Residential appropriation of urban space: Meso-level ... 74
      3.2.3. Establishment and continuity of patterns of urban residential appropriation in pre-modern Holland: Explanations ... 80

	3.3. Urban elites and the desire for a socially homogeneous and exclusive residential environment	83
	3.4. Residential appropriation and the continuity of power relations in the cities of Holland	95
4	Power, theatrical violence and ephemeral appropriation of urban space	97
	4.1. Violence and the appropriation of space in the urban arena	97
	4.2. Execution of public punishments	98
	4.3. Presence of middle-class militias	108
	4.4. Working-class riots and revolts	122
	4.5. Collective violence as a communicative act in urban space	137
5	Discursive appropriation of urban space	139
	5.1. The proximity and yet limited visibility of 'the other'	139
	5.2. Power relations and the limited visibility of 'background people': Texts	140
	5.3. Power relations and the limited visibility of 'background people': Maps and cityscapes	147
	5.4. Smothering and the discursive appropriation of urban space	163

Conclusion: Power relations and appropriation of urban space in pre-modern Holland — 165

Appendix: Patterns of residential differentiation in the cities of Holland, fourteenth–nineteenth centuries — 173
Notes — 207
Bibliography — 263
Index — 290

Figures

AM: Amsterdam Museum
HHM: Haags Historisch Museum
KMSKA: Koninklijk Museum voor Schone Kunsten Antwerpen
RMA: Rijksmuseum Amsterdam
SAA/Bb: Stadsarchief Amsterdam, Beeldbank (image collection)
UBL: Universiteitsbibliotheek Leiden

1.1	Carousing beggars, first half of the seventeenth century (RMA, RP-P-OB-59.480)	24
4.1	Harness for corpses of persons broken on the wheel, 1764 (SAA/Bb, 010001000143)	99
4.2	The public display of a bigamist in Amsterdam, 1805 (SAA/Bb, 010095000031)	101
4.3	Penny print depicting scaffold punishments, third quarter of the eighteenth century (RMA, RP-P-OB-200.378)	105
4.4	A subdivision (*rot*) of the Amsterdam militia-guild of the Kloveniers, 1534 (AM, SA 7300)	110
4.5	*Optrek* of five regiments of the Amsterdam civic militia, 1683 (SAA/Bb, 010094008258)	113
4.6	Commemorative print of the Aansprekersoproer in Amsterdam, 1696 (SAA/Bb, 010097000004)	116
4.7	Marching militiamen in The Hague, c. 1750 (RMA, RP-P-OB-83.712)	119
4.8	*Exercitiegenootschap* (drill club) De Palmboom in Rotterdam, 1785 (RMA, RP-P-OB-85.398)	121
4.9	Plundering of the house and storehouses of tax-farmer A. M. van Arssen on Singel in Amsterdam, 1748 (SAA/Bb, 010097007332)	125
4.10	Riot on Dam square during the Aansprekersoproer in Amsterdam, 1696 (RMA, RP-P-OB-82.871)	127
5.1	Courtyard of the Rasphuis in Amsterdam, 1614 (SAA/Bb, ANWK00203000001)	143
5.2	The outskirts of The Hague, mid-seventeenth century (UBL, Coll.BN. P304_2N027)	152
5.3	Dam square in Amsterdam by Gerrit Berckheyde, 1668 (KMSKA)	155
5.4	Plein in The Hague, 1750 (HHM, 1-1875)	156
5.5	Bricklayer and assistant at work on Oudezijds Achterburgwal in Amsterdam, 1796 (SAA/Bb, 010001000775)	157
5.6	A fishmonger selling turbot on Bierkade in The Hague, 1780 (HHM, 3-1960)	158

5.7	Beggar with children in Kalverstraat near Muntplein in Amsterdam, 1778 (SAA/Bb, 010001000582)	159
5.8	Beggar woman with child at the Gasthuis gate in Amsterdam, 1793 (SAA/Bb, 010001000524)	159
5.9	Image of the Elandsgracht/Elandsstraat area in Amsterdam, 1690 (SAA/Bb, 010094005360)	160
5.10	The Mennonite church in Bloemstraat in Amsterdam, 1729 (SAA/Bb, 010055000098)	161
5.11	Decay and demolition of houses in the Jordaan district, 1816 (SAA/Bb, 010097013640)	162
5.12	Goudsbloemgracht in Amsterdam, 1816 (SAA/Bb, 010055000242)	162

Maps

AHN: Actueel Hoogtebestand Nederland
BDH: Biblioteca Digital Hispánica
EL: Erfgoed Leiden en omstreken
KB: Koninklijke Bibliotheek The Hague
MPD: Museum Prinsenhof Delft
SAA/Bb: Stadsarchief Amsterdam, Beeldbank (image collection)
SAD: Stadsarchief Delft
All remaining figures were made by the author.

2.1	Distribution of the six selected cities across the area of Holland	36
2.2	Residential differentiation in Edam, c. 1830	37
	Inset map: Location of industries (tannery in red)	
2.3	Residential differentiation in Alkmaar, c. 1830	39
	Inset map: Location of industries (tanneries in red)	
2.4	Residential differentiation in Alkmaar by block face, c. 1830	40
2.5	Residential differentiation in Delft, c. 1830	41
	Inset map: Location of industries (tanneries in red)	
2.6	Residential differentiation in Delft by block face, c. 1830	42
2.7	Residential differentiation in Leiden, c. 1830	43
	Inset map: Location of industries (tanneries in red)	
2.8	Rental values in the block of houses around Olieslagerspoort in Leiden, c. 1830	44
2.9	Residential differentiation in The Hague, c. 1830	46
	Inset map: Location of industries (tannery in red)	
2.10	Rental values in the block of houses east of Lange Houtstraat and Plein in The Hague, c. 1830	47
2.11	Residential differentiation in Amsterdam, c. 1830	48
	Inset map: Location of industries (tanneries in red)	
3.1	Street names in Delft	58
3.2	Current ground level in Delft (AHN)	60
3.3	Current ground level in The Hague (AHN)	64
3.4	Current ground level in Alkmaar (AHN)	65
3.5	Current ground level in Leiden (AHN)	66
3.6	Current ground level in Edam (AHN)	68
3.7	Current ground level in Amsterdam (AHN)	71
3.8	Delft: Oosteinde and adjacent houses, 1536 (MPD, detail Stadsbrand Delft)	76
3.9	Amsterdam: block formation on Kalverstraat, 1544 (SAA/Bb, 010094007921)	77

3.10	Amsterdam: block formation in the Jordaan district, 1625 (SAA/Bb, UZFA00002000001)	78
3.11	Edam: map by Jacob van Deventer, *c.* 1560 (BDH)	79
3.12	Edam: blocks of houses between Voorhaven and Nieuwehaven, *c.* 1665 (KB, Stedenatlas De Wit)	79
3.13	Residential differentiation in Amsterdam, 1562	84
3.14	Residential differentiation in Amsterdam, 1733–42	85
3.15	Residential differentiation in Leiden, 1561	86
3.16	Residential differentiation in Delft, *c.* 1730	87
3.17	Residential differentiation in The Hague, 1561	88
3.18	Residential differentiation in Alkmaar, 1561	90
3.19	Residential differentiation in Alkmaar, *c.* 1630	90
3.20	Residential differentiation in Edam, *c.* 1630	91
4.1	Route of the Leiden militia during the 1646 *optrek* (EL, PV_PV351A)	111
4.2	The eight districts of Leiden and the (numbered) location of *loopplaatsen*, *c.* 1675 (EL, PV_PV371.8)	115
4.3	Alkmaar *c.* 1830: to-movement potential at a radius of 200 metres	130
4.4	Leiden *c.* 1830: to-movement potential at a radius of 200 metres	131
4.5	The Hague *c.* 1830: to-movement potential at a radius of 200 metres	132
4.6	Amsterdam *c.* 1830: to-movement potential at a radius of 400 metres	133
4.7	Spatial distribution of rental values around 1830 and plunder route of the rioters during the Damoproer in Amsterdam, 1848	136
5.1	Bird's-eye view of Amsterdam by Cornelis Anthonisz., 1544 (SAA/Bb, 010094007921)	148
5.2	The western city wall on the bird's-eye view of Amsterdam by Cornelis Anthonisz., 1544 (SAA/Bb, 010094007921)	149
5.3	Bird's-eye view of Amsterdam by Johannes de Ram, 1691–3 (SAA/Bb, KOKA00098000001)	150
5.4	The *Kaart Figuratief* of Delft, 1678 (SAD, TMS 133555)	151
5.5	Map of The Hague, 1657/1698 (KB, Stedenatlas De Wit)	152
A.1	Residential differentiation in Delft within the city walls, *c.* 1730	174
A.2	Highest and lowest rental values in Delft within the city walls, *c.* 1730	176
A.3	Residential differentiation and dwellings with weekly rents in Delft, 1543	177
A.4	Residential differentiation in Edam, *c.* 1630	181
A.5	Residential differentiation in Edam, 1569	182
A.6	Residential differentiation in Edam based on the *schotgeld* tax, 1569	184
A.7	Residential differentiation in Edam based on the *schotgeld* tax, 1514	185
A.8	Residential differentiation in Edam based on the *schotgeld* tax, 1462	185
A.9	Residential differentiation in Alkmaar within the city walls, *c.* 1730	187
A.10	Residential differentiation in Alkmaar within the city walls, *c.* 1630	188
A.11	Residential differentiation in Alkmaar inside and outside the city walls, 1561	189
A.12	Residential differentiation in The Hague, 1711	191
A.13	Residential differentiation in The Hague, 1561	193

A.14 Rental values in the *verponding* tax and percentage of poor households per *bon* in Leiden, 1748–9   195
A.15 Streets with an average tax above (red) and below (blue) the city average and location of the top-100 most prosperous inhabitants in Leiden, 1674   196
A.16 Residential differentiation in Leiden, 1561   197
A.17 Average wealth and percentage of impecunious households per *bon* in Leiden, 1498   198
A.18 Coefficients of variation of wealth per *bon* in Leiden, 1498   199
A.19 Assessments in the 1733 *verponding* tax and location of the top-250 incomes in 1742 in Amsterdam   201
A.20 Goudsbloemgracht in Amsterdam and surroundings, 1775 (SAA/Bb, ANWK00017000001)   202
A.21 Residences of the wealthiest inhabitants of Amsterdam, 1631   203
A.22 Residential differentiation in Amsterdam, 1562   205
A.23 Houses along alleys and blind alleys in Amsterdam, 1562   206

Tables

1.1	Gini Coefficients Based on Rental Values for Selected Cities in Holland, c. 1560 and 1832	12
1.2	Spatial Distribution of the 250 Largest Fortunes of Residents of the Dutch Republic in the Seventeenth and Eighteenth Centuries	14
2.1	Population Size and Built-Up Area in Hectares of Selected Cities in Holland, c. 1500–1850	36
4.1	Built-Up Area in Hectares of Selected Cities in Holland, 1500–2010	128
4.2	Population Density in Number of Inhabitants per Hectare of Selected Cities in Holland, 1500–2010	129
A.1	Population of Amsterdam, Leiden and The Hague, c. 1398–1830	190

Preface

Gentrification has changed the Jordaan district of Amsterdam beyond recognition. Today, it is an extremely popular residential area and tourist attraction, with sky-high real-estate prices to go with it. But when I grew up there in the 1950s and 1960s, it was an impoverished working-class neighbourhood, destined for demolition and total reconstruction (which, incidentally, never took place). But this impoverished working-class neighbourhood bordered directly on Amsterdam's famous ring of canals. The contrast between the two could hardly have been greater. It is this contrast, which I was confronted with daily while going to school and also during long evening walks with my brother, that may have contributed to my interest in social inequality and how it is expressed spatially. This interest was given a more academic foundation when, around 1980, as a junior history student I attended classes by the Amsterdam social geographers Rob van Engelsdorp Gastelaars and Michiel Wagenaar. At the time, Michiel was doing research that would result in his now classic study of the spatial transformation of Amsterdam in the decades around 1900.[1]

In the present book, too, urban space takes centre stage, but here it functions primarily as an arena in which the power relations between social classes are expressed in the physical and discursive appropriation of that space. During my research into this theme, I have benefited from the excellent library of the University of Amsterdam and from the research facilities in archives and museums in Dutch cities. Special mention should be made of the efforts made by many archives, museums and libraries to digitize the visual material they keep and make it available on their websites. In the present study, the accessibility of visual material proved to be of great importance. Equally important was the HisGis data collection, housed at the Fryske Akademy and containing data from the first national land register, which dates from around 1830. Speaking of the land register, I am also much obliged to the Amsterdams Universiteitsfonds, whose generous financial support enabled HisGis to digitize and make accessible the oldest land register of The Hague.

In addition, I am indebted to persons at home and abroad. It is impossible to name them all, but I do want to mention that in the past years I have received a great deal of support in collecting and processing data from Willem van den Berg, Corrie Boschma-Aarnoudse, George Buzing, Reinout Klaarenbeek, Hans Mol, Herman Rijswijk, Arie van Steensel, Gabri van Tussenbroek, Gerrit Verhoeven and Bart Vissers. Teaching in the Master's programme Urban History/Architectural History was not only very enjoyable, but it also broadened my horizon and steered me in the direction of the perspective chosen in this study. Also inspiring were the discussions with fellow urban historians and architectural historians at the University of Amsterdam and with visiting scholars at the meetings of the Amsterdam Centre for Urban History (ACUH).

Special thanks go to Marco van Leeuwen, Richard Yntema and Danielle van den Heuvel. I have known Marco since my student days and was fortunate to find in him a fellow student and later also a fellow historian with a similar interest in residential segregation in early modern Dutch cities. In some chapters of this book I build on our common interest and publications, and I think back with pleasure to our first introduction to and struggle with geographical information systems. I have also known Richard for decades, and over the years I have often benefitted from his keen observations and suggestions. This book bears the marks of that too. Danielle and I have been colleagues in the History Department at the University of Amsterdam for several years now, and we share an interest in the spatial aspects of pre-modern urban life. I am very grateful to her for taking time out of her busy life to thoroughly read an earlier version of this study in its entirety. Her critical comments, questions and suggestions have in many ways benefitted the final result. And last but not least I would like to thank Rhodri Mogford, Gabriella Cox and other staff at Bloomsbury for their efforts in publishing this book.

The contribution of all these people and institutions can hardly be overestimated, but according to good academic practice, I would like to stress that they should not in any way be held responsible for any shortcomings of this study.

Haarlem/Amsterdam, 2023

Acknowledgements

The research for this book was supported by a financial contribution from the Amsterdams Universiteitsfonds.

Introduction

Resources, power and the appropriation of urban space in pre-modern Holland

Individual views on the nature of society vary widely, but when seen from some distance, most can be grouped under the two fundamental models of society in the social sciences: the consensual model and the conflictual model. The consensual model of society emphasizes the inherent order, harmony and consensus in societies, which are rooted in common values and norms. In the conflictual model of society, on the other hand, the emphasis is on contradictions of interest, tensions and conflicts. Power and power inequality play an important role in this model. Clearly, both models describe a part of social reality and complement rather than exclude each other, for although conflict occurs in all societies, societies can only exist (and continue to exist) if there is at least some consensus and social cohesion.[1]

In the Netherlands, the consensual model of society is at the heart of what is known as the 'polder model', a societal model characterized by broad consultation of organized interest groups and aimed at achieving consensus and compromise through negotiation.[2] Interestingly, the term itself is a direct reference to the (alleged) deep historical roots of this consultative model. It is said to have its origins in medieval water management, in which the inhabitants of the wet and low-lying lands found out that they could only keep the water under control by consensus, cooperation and making generally accepted agreements on the construction and maintenance of water works. In popular literature and in some historical studies as well, this gave rise to the idea that Dutch society from the Middle Ages onwards has been characterized by a culture of consultation and the search for consensus and harmony.[3] For the Middle Ages and early modern period, this implies that much attention is paid to corporative interest groups such as guilds, neighbourhoods, militias, charitable institutions and water boards. These functioned as a pre-modern civil society and fulfilled a bridging function between governments and individual citizens. In this way, they gave a part of the population some influence on policy.[4]

This corporatist interpretation of Dutch history has produced a number of important studies, but it is worth emphasizing that the focus on consultation, consensus and compromise implies that contradictions of interest, conflicts and power relations almost automatically take a back seat in corporatist-inspired historiography. Their existence is not denied, of course, but they do not play a prominent role in the argument. The present study of the pre-modern cities in Holland focuses on precisely this underexposed part of social reality. Cities are not analysed and presented here as societies sustained by consultation, consensus and harmony, but as arenas where power relations between social classes are expressed in a more or less permanent appropriation of physical space and through discursive strategies.[5] The continuity of the power relations in the cities of Holland, spanning centuries, makes it urgent to look not only at the appropriation of urban space as an expression of power relations within society, but also at the contribution of this appropriation to the acceptance and continuity of the power relations. In summary, this study seeks to understand *how the power relations between social classes in pre-modern Holland were expressed in the physical and discursive appropriation of urban space, and how this appropriation in turn affected the continuity of these power relations.*

Within this broad area, extensive attention will be paid to the very prominent and enduring appropriation of urban space in the field of housing, the less permanent, but violent appropriation of urban space during the public execution of punishments, the maintenance of public order by civic militias, and during riots and revolts, and finally attention is called for the discursive appropriation of urban space in city descriptions and on maps and pictures of the pre-modern cities in Holland. These themes each have an extensive historiography, but to my knowledge they have never been brought together in the conceptual framework of the appropriation of urban space and the effect of this appropriation on the continuity of power relations.

The emphasis on power relations obviously requires a clear picture of what is meant here by power and by power relations.[6] That clear picture can perhaps best be sketched by first making clear what power is not. Power is not a thing that can be collected, stored and kept for use at will. Nor can people or institutions own power and move it to another location. The fact that we often think of power as a 'thing', as an almost tangible substance, is consistent with everyday speech, in which we talk about people who 'possess' power, and about 'powerful' countries, companies or institutions. But these persons, countries, companies and institutions do not possess power, they possess resources that enable them to exercise power. These resources include money, land and weapons, but also less tangible things like (technological) knowledge, status and influence.[7]

Now that it is clear what power is not, the question remains what it is. Haugaard places power among the concepts referred to by Wittgenstein as family resemblance concepts. It is a concept that has several related meanings and whose precise interpretation depends on the discipline or scientific tradition in which it is applied. It is therefore not surprising that there is no generally accepted definition of the concept of power, nor a generally accepted theory in which the concept is embedded.[8] For this study, the work of the British geographer John Allen proved particularly relevant.[9] In his *Lost Geographies of Power* he defines power as 'a relational effect of social interaction'.[10] In doing so, he is in keeping with earlier work by Giddens and Kilian, among others.[11]

This interpretation of the concept of power has several important implications. The first one is related to the distinction between power and resources. When, in the context of this definition, it is said that an actor (either human or institutional) is powerful, it is meant that it can call on sufficient resources to cause an effect. The latter is crucial. Power is exercised only when there is an actual effect. The possession of resources alone is not sufficient to speak of power. These resources can remain unused and not be used to achieve a specific effect, or they can be used but prove to have no effect.[12] In line with this, *power relations* in this study are therefore seen as *relationships between social classes in which power based on the possession and use of resources causes an effect*. For this study, the emphasis on resources and the effect of the use of resources is important because these have left traces in historical records and therefore offer the possibility to study power relations and the appropriation of urban space in the past. Moreover, the emphasis on resources prevents power from functioning as an abstract and more or less autonomous force that can be invoked at will to explain observed forms of appropriation.

A second implication of this definition of power is in line with the aforementioned view that power is neither a thing nor a property of actors. Power, after all, comes about in social interaction and it is the context in which this interaction takes place that determines the balance of power. Power or powerlessness are therefore not properties that are attached to certain (groups of) actors.[13] This observation is not unimportant because, as we will see later in this study, in Holland's cities those with few resources were often the underlying party in interactions, but in some interactions they were indeed able to exercise power. In line with this, it can be argued that in power relations there are never completely powerless actors, that is, actors without any resources. Giddens points out, for example, that all actors have some resources at their disposal, but that for those with few means of power, the use of those resources often comes at a high price. The most extreme example of this, according to Giddens, are prisoners who go on hunger strike, thereby using their own lives as resources and putting them at risk. It can also be argued that there is no point at all in deploying the means of power if the 'receiving' party has nothing to offer, even if it is only social stability.[14] The conclusion must be that power is a complex phenomenon and that a division of the urban population into 'the powerful' and 'the powerless' contributes little to an understanding of how power relations in Holland's cities were expressed in the appropriation of urban space.

Although we now know that power is a relational effect of social interaction, in everyday life we think of power primarily as actors who impose their will on others. This association ties in with the work of Weber, who defines power as 'jede Chance, innerhalb einer sozialen Beziehung den eignen Willen auch gegen Widerstreben durchzusetzen, gleichviel worauf diese Chance beruht'.[15] With Weber and in everyday speech, power is therefore actually seen as dominance, as exercising power over others. This limited interpretation of the concept of power has been the subject of many objections. In line with the work of Arendt in particular, it has been pointed out, for example, that alongside the interpretation of power as dominance, there can also be power derived from cooperation. In *On Violence*, Arendt states: 'Power springs up whenever people get together and act in concert'.[16] So in that case it is not about domination, but about empowerment and power to achieve something together with others.

These two visions of power are grouped by Allen under the denominators of 'instrumental power' (power exercised over others) and 'associational power' (power exercised with others) respectively.[17] For this study, it is important that Allen places a series of manifestations (modalities) of power under these headings. By doing so, he succeeds in finding a middle ground between the simple equation of power with dominance on the one hand, and an almost infinite series of expressions of power on the other. In concrete terms, he refers to negotiation and persuasion as associational power, and for instrumental power we have to think of domination, authority, seduction, manipulation, coercion and inducement.[18] Allen rightly remarks: 'A world of difference separates dominant relationships which restrict choice and close down possibilities from those which, for instance, secure assent, manipulate outcomes, impute threats or seduce through suggestion and enticement.' The essence of his argument, then, is that power is not undifferentiated, but has specific manifestations, and, he adds, these manifestations can overlap and merge into one another.[19]

It has been emphasized earlier that power and the possibility of exercising power are rooted in the possession of resources. This emphasis on resources places this study in a context that ties in with Bourdieu's work and more specifically with his use of the term 'capital'. By 'a capital' Bourdieu means 'any resource effective in a given social arena that enables one to appropriate the specific profits arising from participation and contest in it'.[20] Characteristically, unlike in common parlance, he distinguishes several forms of capital that can be grouped into three principal species. The first of these three principal species of capital is economic capital. This has the usual meaning of financial and material resources (money and possessions). Under cultural capital Bourdieu includes matters such as knowledge, abilities and (social) skills of an individual. Social capital refers to a person's social network and the social position of the people within that network.[21] At the same time, however, all these forms of capital can also be considered symbolic capital and contribute to a person's prestige and status.[22] Symbolic capital differs from the three forms of capital mentioned earlier in that it has a higher degree of 'concealment'. In other words, prestige and status are often not recognized as rooted in the possession of economic, cultural and social capital and this gives a person an aura of legitimate competence that makes that individual's position in society almost self-evident and not open to discussion.[23]

An important feature of Bourdieu's concept of capital is that the various forms of capital are convertible. This applies in particular, but not exclusively, to economic capital. According to Bourdieu, economic capital is often at the basis of cultural and social capital, which therefore both function in a certain sense as disguised forms of economic capital.[24] And although money does indeed make it possible, for example, to get a good education (cultural capital) and to make contacts in influential circles (social capital), the conversion of economic capital into cultural and social capital usually takes a long time; an investment that is only possible for those who have sufficient economic capital.[25] If, through acquisition or inheritance, cultural and social capital is available it can of course in turn be helpful in acquiring more economic capital, for example, by providing access to a lucrative job or a financially attractive marriage. These are things that, especially in pre-modern times, were not easy to achieve without the possession of cultural and social capital.

The link between the possession of capital by individuals and the power relations within society as a whole is established by two other central concepts in Bourdieu's work: field and habitus. Fields are the social arenas in which power relations come to expression. Swartz summarizes Bourdieu's extensive description of fields as follows: 'Fields denote arenas of production, circulation, and appropriation of goods, services, knowledge, or status, and the competitive positions held by actors in their struggle to accumulate and monopolize . . . different kinds of capital.'[26] People thus function within society, 'social space' in Bourdieu's terminology, in a series of fields, for example, politics, science, art, religion, fashion and economics.[27] In each of these fields, people strive to accumulate capital in order to gain access to the benefits and privileges that characterize that field. Their position within a specific field is determined by the amounts and type of capital they possess.[28] The latter is important because in some fields a specific form of capital (economic, cultural or social) is 'worth' more than in others. Hence the attempts of actors to transform capital into a form that strengthens their position in a specific field.[29] Although each field has its own ratio between the various forms of capital and its own rules, fields also reflect and perpetuate the power relations within society as a whole. Habitus plays an important role in this.

By habitus, Bourdieu means a mental framework established during childhood through socialization in a specific social environment that shapes the way individuals tend to perceive the world, appreciate it and act within it.[30] Fields are the social environment in which habitus is shaped and, as a result, an individual will tend to take that social environment and his or her position within it for granted, thus contributing to the continuity of existing power relations.[31] But not everyone has the same opportunities within the various fields. The elites, through their habitus and the wide availability of capital in its various guises, occupy a dominant position within the fields and are therefore able to leave their mark on the rules, values and standards within those fields and thus within society as a whole. The convergence of social rankings within the various fields is reinforced by the central position of economic capital in the acquisition of cultural and social capital.[32]

In combination, habitus and the dominant logic of the economic field make Bourdieu's theoretical framework useful also for analysis at the level of groups. Bourdieu uses the term 'classes' for these groups and understands it (in Thompson's words) as 'sets of agents who occupy similar positions in the social space, and hence possess similar kinds and similar quantities of capital, similar life chances, similar dispositions, etc.'.[33] With this, Bourdieu clearly and deliberately distinguishes himself from Marxist theory in which classes are after all defined exclusively by their relationship to the means of production. And unlike Marx, with Bourdieu classes are not concrete groups involved in class struggle, but theoretical constructions which allow for a certain type of analysis.[34]

In the present study, the theoretical notions of power and Bourdieu's model of society discussed earlier function as a heuristic tool and interpretative framework. The emphasis on power relations and the appropriation of urban space, however, does not imply that I believe cities function exclusively as arenas of conflicting interests, nor does it imply that the behaviour of individuals and social groups should be seen exclusively in terms of power and power relations.[35] It is worth emphasizing again that societies can be studied from different perspectives and scientific traditions and that the consensual and conflictual views both describe a part of social reality and complement each other in this sense.³⁶ The latter will become apparent, for example, in the description in Chapter 1 of the alliance between urban elites and middle classes in Holland. Corporative interest groups such as guilds and militias played an important role in this alliance, but the relationship between these middle-class interest groups and the elites was not only about consultation and cooperation, and the corporatist quest for consensus and harmony, but also about the deployment of resources and the associated potential for exercising power.

In a spatial sense, this study is limited to the cities in Holland, a region in the west of the Netherlands. This choice is obviously related to my familiarity with these cities and the source material available for them. But apart from that, Holland is an interesting case. The fact that at the beginning of the sixteenth century, 44 per cent of the population lived in urban settlements with more than 2,500 inhabitants shows that, economically speaking, Holland was by then already one of the more advanced regions in Europe.³⁷ From the end of the sixteenth century until the second half of the seventeenth, this area experienced a period of exceptionally rapid economic growth, followed by a long period of economic stagnation and, in some sectors, decline until around the middle of the nineteenth century. This development is reflected in the size of the cities. During the period of economic expansion, the population of the cities increased spectacularly and the degree of urbanization rose to 61 per cent. After that time, the total size of the urban population decreased, but due to a similar population decline in the countryside, the degree of urbanization remained high. Thus, throughout the early modern period (and beyond), cities were a dominant factor in the regional economy and society.

A typical feature of Holland, and one that makes this an interesting case study, is that within an area of limited size, cities with very different population sizes were found.³⁸ In the period of rapid economic growth, the population of Amsterdam increased from about 30,000 inhabitants in 1560 to about 200,000 to 220,000 inhabitants in the third quarter of the seventeenth century and about 240,000 inhabitants in 1740.³⁹ This growth made Amsterdam one of the largest cities in Europe. Only London, Paris and Naples had (considerably) more inhabitants in 1700.⁴⁰ In addition, Holland had a series of medium-sized cities with several tens of thousands of inhabitants and also relatively small cities such as Edam with 4,000 inhabitants around 1670 and only a few hundred more in the middle of the nineteenth century.

Besides the predominance of the urban sector and the diversity in the size of cities, the case of Holland in a study of power relations and appropriation of urban space is also interesting because of the comparatively limited role of the nobility in society. Around 1500, the nobility held positions in the regional administration, performed military services for the sovereign lord and functioned as representatives of the lord in the countryside, but they did not dominate society. Moreover, as a political elite, the nobility lost importance in the sixteenth century. It is tempting to associate this loss of political influence with the Dutch Revolt and the establishment of the decentralized and bourgeois Dutch Republic, but research by Van Nierop has shown that even before the Revolt the nobility withdrew from government offices which, to their dismay, were increasingly becoming a profession instead of a position of honour due to the bureaucratization of the central administrative apparatus.⁴¹ At the time of the Dutch Republic, the nobility continued to function as owners of seigneuries in the countryside and as representatives of the countryside in the States of Holland and other governing bodies, but in the cities they played no significant role, not as residents, not as administrators and not as urban landowners. Thus, the situation in Holland differed greatly from that in, for instance, England, where the nobility did own lands in the cities and where in the early eighteenth century no less than 4,000 landed families and their servants lived in London.[42]

In a temporal sense, the focus here is on the period from the sixteenth to about the middle of the nineteenth century. The sixteenth century is the time when the sources necessary for this research started to flow more abundantly in Holland, but this does not alter the fact that when necessary, attention is also paid to the preceding period. Especially when analysing and explaining the patterns of residential appropriation, it proved necessary to pay attention to the origins and medieval history of the cities in Holland. The middle of the nineteenth century is in many ways a logical end for this study. After that time, newly constructed railway lines and later tramways made it possible for the well-to-do inhabitants of Holland to live in exclusive residential villages such as Heemstede, Bloemendaal, Baarn and Wassenaar and to commute to the city. By then the residential appropriation of space by the urban elites took place on a different geographical scale.

This was also the period when the Dutch state started to play a more prominent role and Dutch cities lost their independence. In time, moreover, the traditional elite families were pushed out of urban politics by newcomers who acquired influence on urban policy through (census) voting rights.[43] This resulted in a fundamentally different power structure.[44] Women and the working classes would have to wait a long time for the right to vote, but the new social movements that emerged from the middle of the nineteenth century gave those without direct political influence a voice and, where the socialists were concerned, an emphatic presence in urban space, for example in the forms of parades, demonstrations and, from the end of the century, May Day celebrations.[45]

Finally, in the second half of the nineteenth century the economic stagnation of the preceding period came to an end and ideas that prevailed among middle classes and elites about the social order and the position of 'the common people' slowly began to change. The practical consequences of these new ideas were still a long time coming, but many ideas that had been taken for granted during the previous centuries were now being called into question.[46] It is because of the radical changes that took place in the second half of the nineteenth century that I refer to the whole period up to the middle of the nineteenth century as the pre-modern period.

In this study a distinction is made between elites, middle classes and working classes, and just as with Bourdieu, these terms should also be regarded as theoretical constructs that refer to the unequal distribution of resources and the related positions of groups of actors within society.[47] The plural forms used here, emphasize the diversity of positions within these broad categories.[48] In pre-modern Holland the working classes included domestic servants, sailors, soldiers and the large numbers of skilled, semi-skilled and unskilled wage earners. This broad class also included the poorest part of the urban population, those who had to support themselves and their families with casual jobs, itinerant trade and begging.[49] Recent migrants and minorities were generally overrepresented in the working classes. More resources were available to the middle classes, including self-employed craftsmen, shopkeepers and owners of pubs, inns and lodges, permanent staff employed by private entrepreneurs and in the public sector, as well as skilled workers in clerical jobs, education and health care. Those who possessed the most economic, cultural and social capital are collectively referred to here as the elites. Among them, of course, are the administrative elite of regents and their families, as well as successful entrepreneurs in trade and industry, high-ranking civil servants, senior officers and a number of liberal professions such as lawyers and public prosecutors. The size of these three classes varied according to time and place, but in the period from the seventeenth to the mid-nineteenth century, roughly 45–60 per cent of the urban population in Holland belonged to what are here referred to as the working classes, 32–50 per cent to the middle classes and 5–8 per cent to the elites.[50]

The first chapter outlines the context in which the physical and discursive appropriation of urban space took place. It will show that throughout the period from the sixteenth to the mid-nineteenth century, urban society in Holland was characterized by a degree of inequality that was extreme by modern standards, and by the existence of strong views among literate elites and middle classes about the social hierarchy and about the working classes with whom they shared urban space. The chapter also discusses the complex web of alliances between elites, middle classes and working classes that contributed to the long-term continuity of existing power relations.

Chapter 2 reconstructs the patterns of urban residential appropriation in Holland in the 1830s on the basis of empirical research in the oldest national land register and also confronts them with Sjoberg's and Vance's views on the residential structure of pre-modern cities and with Bourdieu's work on the benefits to be gained in the field of housing. The distribution of social classes across urban space reflected the unequal distribution of resources and related power in the field of housing, but the reconstructed residential patterns also raise the question of when and by which factors these patterns came into being.

These questions could only be answered on the basis of extensive research into the residential history of Holland's cities, reported in the appendix. Chapter 3 summarizes the most important findings and shows that the patterns of residential differentiation remained essentially the same for hundreds of years and had their roots in the medieval period of city formation and the physical-geographical environment in which the cities developed. From an early stage, the patterns of residential appropriation were not only an expression of the power relations within society, but through their physical permanence in the urban landscape they created the impression that they were self-evident and of all times. This suggested that the social hierarchy was also self-evident and not open to discussion. In this way, residential appropriation contributed to the acceptance and continuity of the power relations in the cities of Holland.

In Chapter 4, the focus shifts to the less permanent, but very pronounced ways in which power relations were expressed in the explicit and violent appropriation of urban space during the public execution of punishments, the maintenance of public order by armed middle-class militias, and during riots and revolts. In this context, judicial punishment and the monitoring of public order functioned as theatrical and ritualistic demonstrations of the existing power relations and, as will become clear, in subtle and less subtle ways they promoted and enforced acceptance and continuity of the power relations. The equally theatrical and ritualistic riots and revolts of the working classes and middle classes were expressions of discontent, but they rarely if ever questioned or rejected the existing social relations in principle.

Chapter 5 then examines the discursive appropriation of urban space in texts and on maps and cityscapes. By bringing some matters prominently to the attention of readers and spectators and keeping others in the background or ignoring them, these texts and images also reflect the power relations between social classes. In the context of this study, the discursive appropriation of urban space is also important because on paper and canvas a world was created that matched the views and prejudices of their readers and observers. In their turn, these same texts, maps and pictures confirmed and reinforced these views and prejudices. This gave the existing power relations a self-evident character that made it easier for those who could get acquainted with these texts and pictures to accept the existing power relations, and this acceptance obviously contributed to their continuity.

This study concludes with a summary and a conclusion in which the age-long continuity of the power relations in the cities of Holland is linked to the values, opinions and ideologies stored in the habitus of social classes. In addition, attention is called for the dynamic character of habitus and its relevance in finding an answer to the question of what caused the age-old power relations to come under pressure after the middle of the nineteenth century.

At the end of this introduction, I would like to emphasize that I am aware of the danger in a study such as this, which focuses on inequality, power and appropriation of space, of presenting society as a conspiracy of the rich against the poor, of the 'powerful' against the 'powerless' and of those with the right social skills and contacts against those who lack them. In what follows, an attempt has been made to avoid this pitfall by doing justice to the agency of all social classes, without ignoring the, by today's standards, extreme degree of inequality in the pre-modern cities of Holland and the negative consequences thereof. Chapter 1 will substantiate this inequality with some figures and will also focus on the literate elites' vision of the social hierarchy, on the web of alliances that bound social classes together, and on the stereotypical images of the working classes and the poor who populated the cities. This outlines the societal context within which social classes appropriated urban space and from which the appropriation derived its function.

1

Inequality and power relations in the cities of Holland

1.1. Inequality

In 1658, an astonished English traveller wrote: 'The Dutch behave as if all men were created equal.'[1] This traveller's amazement about the manners in Holland does not alter the fact that pre-modern Dutch society too was characterized by a large degree of economic, cultural and social inequality, which left its traces everywhere in society. It is not easy to capture this inequality in figures. For the period that is the focus of this study, no information is available about the income and wealth of the entire population. We will therefore have to make do with data that indirectly reveal something about the extent of inequality in Holland's cities. Rental values are the most appropriate. Such data are available in relative abundance from the sixteenth century onwards. Moreover, their use as an indicator of the socio-economic position of the inhabitants is easily defensible. After all, the choice of a particular dwelling reflects the income and wealth of its inhabitants, that is the economic resources available to them.

The use of rental values also has disadvantages. One of these disadvantages is that rental values are sensitive to population growth and decline, which influence the price level of housing through supply and demand on the housing market.[2] This problem is particularly relevant to the study of long-term developments in the extent of inequality, which is not what is intended here. For this study, a more important disadvantage is that the distribution of rental values underestimates the degree of inequality in income and wealth. This underestimation is a consequence of the phenomenon known as Engel's Law, that expenditure on housing (and other necessities) above a certain income level does not keep pace with the increase in income. In the first instance, an increase in income will lead to a desire for greater home comfort and a different home environment, but after a while, the housing preferences will be satisfied, even if the income continues to rise. These higher incomes will then give rise to other forms of luxury consumption or the purchase of a second home outside the city rather than the occupation of an even larger, more luxurious and more expensive home within the city. As a result, in the words of Van den Berg and Van Zanden, 'the top of the urban rental value pyramid is usually flatter than the top of the income pyramid'.[3] With this caveat in mind, it is nevertheless worth taking a look at that rental value pyramid.

In order to express the degree of inequality in a society in terms of a number, the Gini coefficient is often used. This is a measure that varies from 0 for complete equality to 1 for complete inequality. In the context of this study, rental values were collected for a number of cities and for several points in time. These are used in the following chapters to map residential differentiation, but here they serve as the basis for calculating Gini coefficients. We will discuss the sources and their possibilities and limitations in detail in the next chapter and in the appendix, but for now it is worth emphasizing that the cities studied here were selected on the grounds of their diversity in terms of geographical location, size of the built-up area and population size. On the basis of these considerations, the cities chosen are in ascending order of population size during the first census of 1795: Edam, Alkmaar, Delft, Leiden, The Hague and Amsterdam. Table 1.1 presents the Gini coefficients for the 1560s and for the time of the first national land register (1832).

The Gini's for the cities in Holland in the sixteenth century correspond well with those for cities in Brabant and Flanders. In 1584, the Gini coefficient based on rental values in Antwerp was 0.48; in Den Bosch in the sixteenth century it varied between 0.40 and 0.49, and Bruges in 1583 had a Gini of 0.46.[4] In some cases, it is possible to compare these Gini's based on rental values with Gini coefficients based on the income distribution. For instance, we know that the income Gini in Den Bosch in the sixteenth century was 0.69 to 0.73 and in Amsterdam around the middle of the nineteenth century it was 0.65 to 0.70.[5]

The comparison of Gini coefficients based on rental values with those based on incomes is important because the latter can be better interpreted in terms of economic inequality. Gini coefficients in the range of 0.65 to 0.75 indicate an extreme degree of income inequality by today's standards. In the Netherlands, in the previous decade (2011–18), the value of the Gini coefficient after income redistribution through taxes and income transfers was consistently around 0.28 to 0.29.[6] This figure is slightly higher than, for example, in Belgium (0.27 in 2018) and Norway (0.28 in 2018), but lower than in Germany (0.32 in 2016), the United Kingdom (0.35 in 2017) and the United

Table 1.1 Gini Coefficients Based on Rental Values for Selected Cities in Holland, *c.* 1560 and 1832

	c. 1560	1832	Inhabitants per house, 1832
Edam	0.39	0.37	4.59
Alkmaar	0.34	0.44	4.58
Delft	0.45	0.49	5.29
Leiden	0.39	0.54	5.31
The Hague	0.47	0.54	6.85
Amsterdam	0.52	0.47*	8.23

* The relatively low Gini coefficient for Amsterdam in 1832 is due to the fact that in Amsterdam many houses contained several independent residential units and the land registry only recorded the total rental value of the entire house. The large number of inhabitants per house supports this interpretation.
Source: See Chapters 2 and 3 and the appendix. The average number of inhabitants per house is calculated on the basis of J.D. Hoeufft and J.C.R. van Hoorn van Burgh, *Kadastrale uitkomsten van Noord- and Zuid-Holland 1832*. Reissue with an introduction by W.J. van den Berg and Ph. Kint (Dordrecht: Historische Vereniging Holland, 1993).

States (0.41 in 2018). Countries with Gini coefficients higher than 0.5 are rare these days. In this category, we should mainly think of countries where a small top layer appropriates a large part of society's wealth. The highest Gini among the countries for which information is available, and thus the greatest degree of income inequality, is found in South Africa where the World Bank recorded a Gini of 0.63 for 2014.[7]

Extreme caution is required when making such comparisons in time and space, but one thing is certain: urban societies in pre-modern Holland were characterized by a very high degree of economic inequality. This is confirmed by what we know about the contrast between the small and very wealthy upper classes in the cities of Holland and the large numbers of people who lived in poverty and were occasionally or structurally dependent on charity. To start with the latter group; throughout the first half of the nineteenth century, about a third of Amsterdam's population lived below the poverty line by the standards of the time, and a quarter regularly received assistance in the form of money and/or goods.[8] In a small city like Alkmaar, the situation was less unfavourable, but even there, at the end of the eighteenth century and in the beginning of the nineteenth century, 15–18 per cent of the population received poor relief.[9] In the more distant past, too, the number of poor people could be very high. Orlers mentions in his description of the city of Leiden published in 1614 that in those years about a quarter of the population were 'poor and needy persons'.[10] In Delft the Chamber of Charity supported 12–15 per cent of the city's population in the seventeenth century, but during the political and economic crisis of 1672 this quickly increased to a quarter of the population. In years of high food prices, too, many were unable to make ends meet and the number of people supported increased considerably, in 1740 even to 30 per cent of the Delft population.[11]

For the entire period from the mid-seventeenth to the end of the eighteenth century, the poverty threshold lay at an annual family income of approximately 200 guilders. In the mid-nineteenth century, Amsterdam's poor relief committees applied a limit of 250 guilders for a family with four children.[12] The households that had to make ends meet on this income formed the base of the income pyramid. In 1742, a year for which detailed information is available, the top of the income pyramid in Amsterdam consisted of 102 people with an estimated annual income of at least 16,000 guilders. The highest incomes were recorded for the widow of the merchant, insurance broker and banker Andries Pels on Herengracht, with an estimated annual income of 70,000 guilders, and the burgomasters Dirk Trip and Jan Six, also on Herengracht, with estimated annual incomes of 50,000 and 45,000 guilders respectively.[13] In the smaller cities of Holland, the top incomes were not as high as in Amsterdam, but even there income inequality was extremely high by today's standards. The latter also applies to the period before the middle of the seventeenth century when both the top incomes and the lowest incomes were at a lower level than after that time.[14]

The contrast is, of course, even greater when we look at wealth. Wealth inequality was already considerable at the beginning of the sixteenth century and increased particularly sharply in the period of rapid economic growth between around 1580 and 1670. Van Zanden calculated on the basis of wealth taxes that in the seventeenth century the richest 10 per cent of households owned virtually all the taxable wealth in Holland's cities, and the richest per cent of households owned around 40 per cent of the total taxable wealth. More than 70 per cent of the population was too poor to contribute to the wealth taxes.[15] Zandvliet's study confirms that the wealthy residents of the Dutch cities did indeed possess very considerable fortunes. In the seventeenth century, 198 of the 250 wealthiest residents of the Dutch Republic were to be found in the province of Holland. The average size of these 198 fortunes was slightly more than 555,000 guilders. In the eighteenth century, Holland counted 202 of the 250 largest fortunes with an average size of almost 958,000 guilders.[16]

Table 1.2 Spatial Distribution of the 250 Largest Fortunes of Residents of the Dutch Republic in the Seventeenth and Eighteenth Centuries

	Seventeenth century		Eighteenth century	
	Number	Average wealth	Number	Average wealth
Amsterdam	113	557,889	121	1,003,649
The Hague	46	688,250	28	922,554
Elsewhere in Holland	39	389,744	53	872,274
Holland total	*198*	*555,056*	*202*	*957,938*
Elsewhere in the Dutch Republic	35	372,086	20	827,900
Outside the Dutch Republic*	13	609,462	26	1,145,731
Orange and Nassau	4	8,881,250	2	9,365,500
Total	250		250	

* This concerns residents of the Dutch Republic who resided, temporarily or more permanently, in Asia, South Africa, America and elsewhere in Europe.
Source: Calculated on the basis of Kees Zandvliet, *De 500 rijksten van de Republiek. Rijkdom, geloof, macht & cultuur* (Zutphen: Walburg Pers, 2018), 42.

The table also shows that in the seventeenth century the highest average wealth was registered in The Hague and in the eighteenth century in Amsterdam. By then in Amsterdam the average was more than 1 million guilders, but this average conceals the very large fortunes of among others the Amsterdam merchant banker Henry Hope II (11,600,000 guilders), the Amsterdam merchant Jeronimus de Haze de Georgio (4,912,500 guilders) and the Amsterdam city secretary Nicolaes Geelvinck I (4,000,000 guilders).[17] In the seventeenth century, the fortunes were less substantial, but in Amsterdam in particular there were already fortunes in excess of 1 million guilders.[18]

If we look at the aforementioned data, we may indeed conclude that in the premodern cities of Holland the distribution of economic resources was extremely unequal.

1.2. Views on the social hierarchy and self-image of the elites

Gini coefficients, percentages of the population receiving poor relief, incomes and the extreme inequality in wealth give an impression of the very unequal distribution of economic resources, but to get a full picture of the power relations in the cities of Holland, it is important to also look at the views of contemporaries on society and on the classes that constituted society. Of course, these are almost exclusively the views of the literate middle classes and elites, but that is not insurmountable in this context. After all, it was they who, through their use of economic, cultural and social capital, left their mark to a significant extent on social relations and – as we shall see in the following chapters – also on the socio-spatial structure of cities and the image of those cities as we still know it today from texts and pictures.

Before delving into the views of contemporaries, a single word should be devoted to the relationship between texts and power. The work of Foucault and Bourdieu has had a great influence on our thinking about this relationship. Both authors see texts (and statements) not primarily as the expression of the ideas of a specific individual but as part of an entire repertoire of texts. Foucault summarizes that repertoire with the term 'discourse'. By this, he means the entire body of statements and reasoning with which a group or society constructs a certain theme and implicitly or explicitly determines what is 'true' and 'correct'.[19] According to Foucault, the content of discourses is a reflection of power relations within those discourses, and by establishing what is true and correct, discourses also form the basis for the legitimation and reproduction of those power relations.

For Bourdieu, texts and statements are in fact acts, concrete interventions in social reality that contribute to the construction of that social reality. Talking and writing about a hierarchy of social classes, to give an example appropriate to this chapter, is therefore not 'innocent' because it contributes to the construction and continuity of that hierarchy and the distinction between social classes. And so, for Bourdieu too, words are connected with power and power inequality. After all, one person's words have more influence than another's, and one audience has more influence than another.[20] Having said this, let us now look at contemporaries' views on the social hierarchy in the pre-modern cities of Holland.

The tripartite division of the population into elites, middle classes and working classes proposed in the introduction to this book is in line with an old tradition.[21] In the second half of the thirteenth century, Thomas Aquinas wrote in his *Summa Theologiae*:

> Even though there are many orders in a single city, they can nonetheless be reduced to three, since every complete multitude has a beginning, a middle, and an end. Hence, in cities there are three orders of men. For some are the highest, viz., the aristocrats (*optimates*), whereas others are the lowest, viz., the common people (*vilis populus*), and still others are in the middle, viz., the 'respectable' people (*populus honorabilis*).[22]

In doing so, he adhered to a threefold division of society that had been expressed much earlier by Aristotle but rejected his view that the middle class should be at the heart of the political community.[23] The division of society into an upper class, a middle class and a lower class remained the most common during the Middle Ages and early modern period, but from the seventeenth century onwards, city descriptions (chorographies) and treatises were published in which this division was refined and adapted to the situation in Holland. This is not surprising, since, from the sixteenth century onwards, the nobility no longer played a significant role there and the growth of the urban population and economy called for differentiation within the broad middle classes and the working classes.

In his description of Haarlem, Theodorus Schrevelius (Dirk Schrevel), humanist, poet and former rector of the Latin schools in Haarlem and Leiden, provides us with one of these more elaborate stratifications.[24] At the top of the 'corpus' of the city, according to him, is the magistrate (city government). Below the magistrate, but listed as part of the government, are high-ranking officials such as the bailiff and the pensionaries. Book VI of his *Harlemias* then deals with the subjects. The scholars are at the top: the theologians, the jurists and the doctors of medicine.[25] Then follow in the stratification of Schrevelius 'those who are excellent in the arts' and in particular painters and poets. Below them are the merchants, who are themselves ranked by status and who also include the brewers. Still lower in the hierarchy are the craftsmen and shopkeepers organized in guilds. And finally, at the base of the pyramid, there are the 'ordinary people', about whom more later in this chapter. Schrevelius does not consider them part of 'the society of citizens', but they are indispensable to the proper functioning of society and therefore do belong to the 'corpus' of the urban republic.[26] Schrevelius thus used a global threefold division of society, but within this, he introduced a certain degree of differentiation: an upper class consisting of the magistrate and high officials, a middle class comprising the liberal professions, merchants and guild-organized craftsmen and shopkeepers, and an undifferentiated working class of day labourers in unskilled and unattractive professions.

Almost half a century later, the Amsterdam broker Joris Craffurd also gives us his vision on society. He does so in an extensive and detailed account of the Aansprekersoproer, a revolt that held Amsterdam in its grip for several days in 1696. The revolt was triggered by the introduction of a tax on burials and especially by the attempt of the city government to turn the free profession of *Aanspreker* (undertaker) into a municipal office. This would be to the detriment of the *Aansprekers* who would not be appointed by the city and who would therefore become penniless. And the working classes, and especially the poor among them, were outraged because they feared that for those who were unable to contribute to the new tax on burials, the provisions of the new ordinance would make their burial a public demonstration of financial insolvency.[27] Craffurd's account is important to us because in describing the revolt, he mentions *en passant* the composition of the population of Amsterdam. He distinguishes four kinds of people, namely: the gentlemen of the government and their families; the 'very eminent, distinguished and rich merchants'; the 'shopkeepers . . . among whom must also be counted many master craftsmen and artisans'; and finally 'the commoners', or 'the lowest class of people'. But then he actually further differentiates within this class of people and makes those who worked in the city service a separate group. Craffurd explicitly mentions the official carriers of corn, beer and peat and also the appointed bargemen. Because they were often not 'van de discreetste en civielste', that is not civilized enough, they did not fit in with the decent middle classes and are placed between the middle classes and working classes.[28]

Broadly speaking, the division outlined by Schrevelius and Craffurd for the seventeenth century would be seen as valid until well into the nineteenth century.[29] Only after the middle of the nineteenth century were some new views heard in the wake of new political and economic dynamics, but even these often remained close to the older view. In *Amsterdam en de Amsterdammers*, for example, published in 1875, the aristocracy was placed at the top of the social pyramid.[30] It consisted of 'the descendants of the former kings of the Republic' (the former members of the city governments) and those whom the anonymous author refers to as the money aristocracy. Next in rank to the aristocracy was the upper middle class of traders, higher officials and practitioners of liberal professions. Then there are various groups that belong to the middle classes and working classes. The author has less to say about these than about the aristocracy and upper middle classes, but it is clear that there are fine distinctions within the middle classes based on profession, ethnicity and wealth.[31] The working classes, still referred to as *het gemeen* (the common people, mob) in 1875, do not appear in the stratification, but elsewhere in the booklet, their behaviour during the Amsterdam fair is characterized as disgusting.[32] And in one of the fictitious dialogues between the Amsterdam resident and his friend from The Hague, it is stated that it will take a lot of time and effort to civilize the common people, especially since social movements have stirred up resentment against capital.[33] Not to the author's delight, the new era shows its influence, but despite the greater dynamism, much remained the same.

The three authors discussed here belonged without doubt to the (higher) middle classes. Schrevelius was the rector of the Latin school, Joris Craffurd was a broker in securities and the anonymous Amsterdammer also revealed to which class he belonged by his critical remarks about the elites, lower middle classes and working classes.[34] Their texts, and the treatises from the Middle Ages and Antiquity to which they relate, are part of a discourse among literate people about the social order. In this discourse, society is presented as a hierarchy with a marked distinction between social classes. At the same time, the texts underline which classes are considered most important within the corpus of society and which are (much) less important. This is evident from the order in which the social classes are listed and it is also evident from the terminology used: gentlemen for those at the top of the hierarchy and *volk* (populace) or *gemeen* for those at the bottom.[35] In line with the ideas of Foucault and Bourdieu, these texts can be considered an expression of power, the power of literate groups to assign themselves and others a place in a society that was presented as a hierarchy. This hierarchy of social classes was a social reality created and also sustained in part by the texts, and which, as will become apparent, affected the appropriation of urban space in pre-modern Holland.[36]

The views of the higher middle classes and elites on the social hierarchy are, of course, linked to the self-image of those classes. In the context of this study, the self-image of the ruling elites is particularly important. After all, it was they who had a bearing on the development and use of urban space through their grip on policy, urban finances and civil service departments. It is also worth remembering that in social, economic and cultural terms, the *regenten* (administrative elites) were closely linked to the upper layers of society in Holland's cities.[37]

We have already seen that Schrevelius referred to the city – in his case Haarlem – as a 'corpus' and he was certainly not alone in comparing the urban community to a body. Within this metaphor, the *regenten* formed the head of the urban body and the other inhabitants the limbs.[38] And, of course, it was the head that took charge. Democracy or popular government was equated by the *regenten*, and not only by them, with anarchy since in that case, the unity of government would be broken and disputes, conflicts of interest and selfishness would plunge society into chaos.[39] Therefore, it was of the utmost importance that the discussions and contradictions within the urban government did not become public.[40] The *magistraat* had to present itself to the outside world as a united force, for only then could it properly fulfil its role of guardian of unity and custodian of order in the municipal body.

Who were these administrators who had to guard the unity and order of the urban corpus? To begin with, they were exclusively men. By definition, women were not considered suitable for administrative posts. The 'natural order', in which women are subordinate to men, would then be jeopardized. The Grand Pensionary and poet Jacob Cats referred to the book of Genesis, in which it is written that woman was created after man, from a rib of man and for the benefit of man. In his *Inleijdinghe tot de Hollandsche rechts-geleerdheijdt* (1631) Grotius (Hugo de Groot) derived his arguments from the classical (Galenic) theory of humours, in which the temperament of women (cold and moist) was contrasted with that of men (warm and dry). De Groot put it like this: 'Since the female gender, being colder and damper, usually has less suitability for affairs requiring reason, than the male gender, so the male gender has been endowed with a certain supremacy over the females.'[41]

But not all men were eligible. In the fourteenth and fifteenth centuries, an oligarchy of ruling families had developed in the cities of Holland, which collaborated with the monarch and excluded other families and institutions, such as guilds, from political power as much as possible.[42] With the Dutch Revolt, the monarch disappeared from the scene in Holland and power increasingly concentrated with the urban *regenten*. This situation continued formally until the end of the Republic and in fact until the Municipalities Act of 1851. This does not mean, however, that the same families were pulling the strings all along. Political crises, such as during the Dutch Revolt and the foreign invasions in 1672, interference on the part of the stadtholders and the absence of male descendants led to the renewal of (part of) the ruling elites. But the principles of *regenten* rule remained unchanged. Van Deursen rightly states that the most important change brought about by the emergence of a Protestant Republic was probably not 'that the formerly inconsiderable now came to the fore, but that a number of already wealthy families now entered the patriciate more quickly and easily'.[43]

Prestige, good pedigree and reputation were important conditions for access to administrative positions. They were supposed to be a guarantee against undesirable behaviour. After all, in doing so, one would not only put one's own reputation at stake but also that of the entire family. And if one came from humble origins, it was possible to acquire sufficient cultural and social capital through a good marriage, the purchase of seigniories, the drawing up of (often partly fictitious) family trees or through an aristocratic lifestyle. The possession of an ample amount of economic capital was indispensable since it was relatively easy to convert this into the other forms of capital and together with this cultural and social capital it contributed to the symbolic capital – prestige and status – of the person in question. But having sufficient financial resources was also seen as a precondition for holding high administrative positions.[44] Being financially independent would prevent administrators from being tempted to enrich themselves at the expense of the community. In practice, corruption and self-enrichment among the ruling elites were an ineradicable evil, but without ample financial means, a high administrative career was out of the question.[45]

The *regenten* considered themselves eminently qualified for their task. In the case of Jacob Cats, who was appointed Grand Pensionary of Holland in 1636, this was not only because of his family relations, social status and wealth but also, according to Cats himself, because of his God-given qualities, as 'God Almighty, who in accordance with his fatherly benevolence is accustomed, where he lawfully gives an office, also to give qualities to carry out the office in an appropriate manner.'[46] Nevertheless, these self-satisfied urban elites were strongly aware that they depended for the survival of their regime on at least the passive support of a broader section of society than their own class. As we will see in the next section, this support was part of a complex web of power relations and alliances between the social classes in the pre-modern cities of Holland.

1.3. A web of alliances

The elites usually sought and found support for the existing social relations and for their dominant position in urban society among the middle classes and more specifically among those who owned formal citizenship.[47] After all, these citizens were bound to the city and thus to the city government by an oath, which, according to the Amsterdam burgomaster C.P. Hooft, obliged them to warn the city in case of danger and to promote the common good to the best of their ability.[48] In other cities the same commitment was expected. Among the citizens we find craftsmen and retailers organized in guilds, for whom being a citizen was usually a requirement for joining the guild and practising their profession. And the citizens of the city were – as far as they were wealthy enough to buy armour and were capable of fighting – included in the city militia. There, under the leadership of the officers of the militia, they had to prepare themselves to defend their city against enemies from outside the city and against attacks on public order by groups within the city. With the latter, the elites and middle classes thought of the large working classes who, they believed, were mutinous and easy to incite to rioting (see the next section).

For elites, the situation became especially precarious when the armed militia turned against the city government. This happened, for example, in Alkmaar at the turn of the year 1609–10 and in Enkhuizen in 1653. In both cases it concerned protests against the (current or future) *magistraat*.[49] But even in the aforementioned Aansprekersoproer in Amsterdam, the ruling classes could not be sure of the unconditional support of the middle classes.[50] Nevertheless, the alliance between the elites and the part of the middle classes that was bound to the city by an oath was generally close and contributed to the continuity of the *regenten* regime and the relative stability of urban society in Holland.

The support of the middle classes, which except for a few short periods had no direct influence on the administration of their city, did come at a price.[51] According to McCants, institutionalized social care in the Dutch Republic was primarily intended to protect middle classes as much as possible from the consequences of loss of income and, in the case of orphanages, the premature death of parents. These welfare arrangements were the cement that bound the middle classes to a political system in which they had no say, but which imposed heavy taxes upon them.[52] On the subject of taxation, William Temple, the British ambassador to The Hague, reported in 1673 that the inhabitants of the Republic were 'oppressed with the most cruel Hardship and variety of Taxes, that was ever known under any Government'.[53] According to McCants, the high literacy rate (the highest in Europe), the degree of urbanization and the good infrastructure created a situation in which ideas, and thus also political discontent among the middle classes, could easily spread. This was another reason for the elites to cherish the alliance with the middle classes.[54]

The guilds, which directly and indirectly united large parts of the middle classes, also played a role in the implicit alliance between elites and middle classes. In the cities of Holland, with the exception of Dordrecht, they had no political influence. They functioned as an instrument that protected guild members and their employees against competition from outsiders. At the request of the guilds, municipal authorities issued by-laws which prohibited craftsmen and retailers who were not members of a guild from practising their profession and which severely restricted the activities of country folk and other strangers in the city.[55] In Amsterdam and The Hague, it was not only the working classes and strangers who suffered from these restrictions but also the large Jewish communities in those cities.[56] Transfer of economic insecurity and crisis to rural areas and to urban dwellers who were not registered with a guild was thus the flip side of the corporatist guild system.

In the alliance between elites and middle classes, corporative interest groups such as guilds and militias thus played an important role, but it is worth emphasizing that the aforementioned exchange of political support and livelihood security was not only supported by corporative consultation and cooperation, and the pursuit of consensus and harmony, but also by the resources these groups had at their disposal and the potential power based on these resources. By supporting the middle classes and their children in bad times and thus preventing them from becoming part of the working classes, and also by limiting economic competition by 'outsiders', elites exercised power in the form of seduction. They could entice the middle classes to support them because they had some crucial resources at their disposal. For instance, political elites had control over urban policies on social care, they made the by-laws that protected citizens from economic competition from those who were not considered to be part of the urban community, they managed the authority apparatus that could enforce laws and they decided on the use of the financial resources of the city. In addition, members of the elites often held administrative positions in social care institutions specifically aimed at their co-religionists and, to a large extent determined the policy and the use of the financial resources of these institutions.

The availability and use of all these resources supported the status and prestige of the elites and thus created, in their relationship with the middle classes, both power in the form of seduction and power in the form of authority. This authority was linked to what Bourdieu calls symbolic capital and it promoted acceptance by those who did not belong to the elites, of the dominant role of the elites in society and the hierarchical structure of society in general.[57]

In the introduction, power is defined as 'a relational effect of social interaction'. This implies that the exercise of power is not a one-way street and indeed, the urban middle classes also exercised power over the elites. Their size and especially the presence of considerable numbers of armed militiamen in the cities made the middle classes an indispensable, but also dangerous ally. If they were dissatisfied with their position in society, they could turn against the elites, or they could join the working classes when they rose up against the city government or the wealthy elites.[58] In this way, the middle classes exercised power in the form of implicit threat, a form of coercion that was not consciously brought about but that did have an effect. And when the middle classes actually turned against the elites, it was of course power in the form of domination.

The working classes were the third party in the web of alliances that is at the centre here. They lacked the resources that elites and middle classes had at their disposal, but the working classes were not without means of power. Those with few resources derived power from their numbers and presence in the cities. The effect they produced (mostly unconsciously) was to make the middle classes and elites fear that the social peace and stability of existing relations would be broken. In other words, they exercised power in the forms of implicit threat and of domination when unrest actually arose. In the relationship of the elites with the working classes, power in the forms of seduction and authority once again played an important role since members of *regenten* families often had a part in managing institutions for the care of the poor and the urban governments in Holland never completely abandoned their 'own' poor (see the next section). They thus created a situation in which the working classes, periodically affected by poverty and want, were, as it were, indebted to the elites. This condition of indebtedness, as the symbolic power of prestige and status, also supported the elites' claims to authority among this part of the urban population. Insofar as they were part of the armed militias, the middle classes exercised power in the form of dominance over the working classes because the latter could be confronted with the violence of armed and trained militiamen.[59] In short, power played a major role in the relationships between social classes in the cities of Holland, but it was power in various forms and not just dominance of the 'powerful' over the 'powerless'.[60]

Now that we have a better understanding of this complex web of alliances, and of the role of (fear of) the working classes in the relation between elites and middle classes, it is time to take a closer look at the views on these working classes. And also for the texts presented in the next section, it is true that they should be seen mainly as part of a discourse that was conducted by the literate middle classes and elites *about* the working classes. Like the texts on social structure, these texts too reflect the existing power relations and they also contribute to the legitimation and reproduction of these power relations.

1.4. Images of the working classes and the poor

In what is undoubtedly his best known and most widely read work, *Psychologie des foules*, Gustave Le Bon writes: 'It will be remarked that among the special characteristics of crowds there are several – such as impulsiveness, irritability, incapacity to reason, the absence of judgement and of the critical spirit, the exaggeration of the sentiments, and others besides – which are almost always observed in beings belonging to inferior forms of evolution – in women, savages, and children, for instance.'[61] The picture that Le Bon sketches here of the crowd, and of women and children, fits in perfectly with the views that the literate sections of society had held for hundreds of years about the working classes or *het gemeen*. In 1114–15, Rudolf, abbot of the monastery of Saint Truiden, wrote in his chronicle about the common people attached to the monastery as 'our riotous people, who easily give in to disorder'. The common people were unbalanced and dangerous, characteristics that Rudolf also said they shared with women and youth.[62] Centuries later, the poet Vondel spoke of 'wispeltuurigh volck' (the fickle folk).[63] That fickle folk would also be easily stirred up. This partly explains the aversion that the burgomaster of Amsterdam, C.P. Hooft, had in the decades around 1600 against the orthodox Protestant ministers who, in his opinion, incited the people against the city government.[64] The idea that the common people are easy to stir up led to a tough existence and appears also in the aforementioned description by Joris Craffurd of the Aansprekersoproer of 1696. In this revolt, the common people are said to have been 'stirred up by evil and ill-intentioned people, who envy the common peace and prosperity and who at any incident of discord or tumult or change of circumstances seek to satisfy their own advantage'. And Craffurd, too, emphasized the role of women and boys in the revolt.[65]

In a following chapter, we will discuss riots and revolts in more detail. For now, it is important to note that in the views of contemporaries, the working classes and the poor often coincided.[66] This is not surprising, since from the Middle Ages until well into the nineteenth century, a slow but unmistakable process of proletarianization took place in Europe, that is more and more people became dependent on income from wage labour.[67] Tilly estimates that by the middle of the sixteenth century, almost a quarter of the European population (excluding Russia) was already dependent on wage labour. That proportion would rise to 58 per cent by the middle of the eighteenth century and 71 per cent in 1843.[68] Of course, wage labour is not synonymous with poverty, but especially when these wage workers were dependent on work in export industries, they were vulnerable to what was characteristic of this sector: periodic crises and fierce competition from other production areas. Consequently, wage labourers often had to cope with periods in which the available quantity of paid labour was insufficient to make ends meet.[69] Begging could then provide additional income and migration to places where one knew or hoped there was sufficient work could also offer a way out of misery. Lis and Soly emphasize that this process of proletarianization, which did not occur everywhere at the same time and to the same extent, was impossible to recognize by contemporaries. What they did see were its effects, such as the wandering poor in search of work or other sources of income.[70] There are no comparable figures for

Holland, but in France in the seventeenth century a quarter to a third of the population was destitute and without a permanent home.[71]

These poor people evoked mixed feelings among the geographically and socially established citizenry. In the late Middle Ages, the idea of a special bond between the poor and Christ was widespread. Sometimes the metaphor of the body of Christ was used. Its head was in heaven, but on earth the poor were the living limbs of his body.[72] Whoever did good to the poor therefore did good to Christ himself. This also made the poor intermediaries between this world and the next. So, in Gouda, during the monthly mass of the Sint-Joris militia-guild, a table was laid for thirteen poor people. A similar ritual took place during the Christmas celebrations of the Haarlem Holy Christmas guild. In both cases, the thirteen invited poor obviously represented Christ and the twelve apostles at the Last Supper.[73] In addition to the special bond between Christ and the poor, the unity of the Christian community was underlined by the late-medieval church as an incentive to support the poor. In this context, Boele quotes from *Des conincs summe*, printed in Haarlem in 1484. In it, the faithful are told that 'we are all the sons of God and of the Holy Church. And the one brother should always help the other in his need'.[74]

Strictly speaking, all (Christian) poor should therefore be eligible for assistance, including itinerant beggars. In practice, however, a distinction was made between the various degrees of proximity. One's own parents, children and other relatives came first, followed by friends, neighbours, guild brothers and fellow citizens in general. Finally, at the very back of the list were the strangers, those who came from elsewhere and were not considered part of the community. This differentiation was not a late-medieval invention but can be traced back to Ambrose and other Church Fathers. They had also argued that the way of life and morals of the poor should certainly be taken into account when providing support. Giving to '. . . guaden lieden, Alse speellieden ende hyrauden, Riesen wiuen ende ribauden' was not recommended.[75] That would only encourage these street musicians, frivolous women and vagabonds in their sinful way of life. The fact that street musicians were explicitly mentioned here is significant because they belonged to the most mobile groups in medieval and early modern society.[76] And because the behaviour and morals of strangers were not easy to assess, it was the wandering poor and newcomers in the cities who were most easily and frequently excluded from poor relief.

The distinction between 'true' and 'false' poor, which was made in medieval texts and most probably also in daily practice in the cities of Holland, became sharper in the sixteenth century. The countless people who, due to hunger and want, had to wander around in search of work and income had a hard time of it. Lis and Soly argue that they appeared in four different discourses and that each of these discourses reinforced the negative image of the group. The church, for instance, emphasized the difference between the 'true' and 'false' poor; high secular authorities expressed their fear of groups of people who did not have a customary hierarchical relationship with a superior (landlord, master, employer, officer), while local authorities were suspicious of strangers; humanists wrote with contempt about those who, in their eyes, were guilty of idleness; and writers served the public's graving for sensation with elaborate treatises on the tricks, disguises and deception of beggars.[77] In the texts from that time

Figure 1.1 Carousing beggars, first half of the seventeenth century.

(and also in texts from later centuries) we see an endless variety of disqualifying terms for beggars, 'false poor' and the working classes in general: vagabonds, thieves, sloths, good-for-nothings, cheats, lazy scum, rabble and riff-raff.[78] Illustrative is Figure 1.1, which shows false beggars who forget their feigned ailments and squander the day's proceeds in Inn D'Laserusclep. The accompanying verses speak of 'pleysters sonder Wondt' (plasters without wound) and 'Windels sonder Loch' (bandages without cavity) to entice compassionate people to give generously.[79]

In the context of this study, the views of Dirk Volkertsz. Coornhert (1522–90), born in Amsterdam and living for a long time in Haarlem, are particularly interesting. This is all the more so because his views influenced the policy towards beggars and criminals throughout Holland. In his publications on charity, the late-medieval notions of the unity of society and the responsibility of the rich for the poor still clearly prevailed. Even the body metaphor is not lacking.[80] But at the same time he complains about 'Doverheyts slapheyt' (slackness of the authorities) when it comes to combating begging. In doing so, he aligned himself with the ideas of the Bruges-based Spanish humanist Juan Luis Vives (1493–1540), who in 1526 published an influential treatise on poor relief and argued for centralization and a strict distinction between 'true' and 'false' poor.[81] Only then could charity flourish in the cities; charity which thus excluded the 'unworthy' poor from support. And although there was never any real centralization of poor relief in Holland, institutions providing support did take greater care not to 'indiscriminately' give, and city councils issued decrees against begging.[82]

In Delft, for example, we indeed see that the policy towards beggars tightened in the course of the seventeenth century.[83] Collectively, they were seen as 'false' poor and were excluded from the support that was available for the 'true' poor. Not much is known about the size of the group that was placed outside the urban community in Delft in this way. However, their numbers must have been considerable, for between 1626 and 1650, almost 500 beggars were prosecuted by the city. Among them were very few of the poor supported by the Chamber of Charity, who would lose their support if caught begging.[84] The closure of the Baaierd (shelter for passers-by) of the Gasthuis in 1661 is also evidence of the city's attitude towards the poor from other places. The trustees of the Gasthuis referred to these passers-by as beggars and vagabonds. This labelled them as 'false' poor, which meant that the city no longer had a duty to provide them with shelter.[85]

It is remarkable that Coornhert in his *Boeventucht* (1587 edition) appears to realize that the circumstances of war during the Dutch Revolt and the ensuing economic disruption were at the root of the beggar problem.[86] Because, according to Coornhert, these had turned 'naerstige broodwinners' (diligent breadwinners) into 'verderflycke ledigh ghangers' (pernicious good-for-nothings), compassion was out of the question. In *Boeventucht* roaming beggars are even dehumanized by describing them as sluggish donkeys, ferocious bears, wolves bent on money and blood, and annoying wasps. For Coornhert and many contemporaries, labour was the cure for what they saw as a threat to the urban community. It is partly on the basis of their ideas that Amsterdam, as the first city on the European continent, established a house of correction for men (the Rasphuis) in 1596 and later also one for women (the Spinhuis).[87] In 1609 Haarlem was the second city in Holland to get such an institution. The underlying ideology was clearly articulated by the Haarlem clergyman Samuel Ampzing in 1628: 'So we prune the tree that gives bad fruit / Yes, we even bend the branch that has reached maturity.'[88]

By this time, therefore, there was a clear distinction within the cities of Holland between their own 'true' poor and the large group of poor who were not considered part of the urban community, who were stigmatized with terms such as 'gespuys' (rabble) and for whose well-being the urban community bore no responsibility. Only by forced labour and severe discipline could they be cured of their 'onsturigheyd' (unruliness). Even someone like Coornhert saw them more as source of their own misfortune than as victims of the unpredictable whims of the economy and their weak position as wage-dependent labourers.

In the long period up to the middle of the nineteenth century, poverty remained a real threat to the working classes, and the views of the elites and middle classes on the working classes did not change much either. The rebelliousness and unrestraint of the working classes were still feared. In 1830, it was noted that among the many residents of Amsterdam there are always those who 'at the slightest concourse of a certain number of people . . . take the opportunity to indulge in the worst excesses'. And in the economically difficult years around 1800, boards of trustees feared looting by the poor people in well-to-do neighbourhoods.[89]

As in earlier centuries, the elites and middle classes still believed that poverty was primarily a consequence of the moral shortcomings of the working classes themselves.

Thus, in 1841, Luttenberg wrote in his *Proeve van onderzoek omtrent het Armwezen in ons Vaderland* (Investigation into poverty and the poor in our fatherland): 'All investigations into the real causes of poverty and crime, which have been carried out both in our Fatherland and in other countries, especially in Great Britain, have led to the following conclusion: idleness and vice are the real causes of poverty and crime.'[90] The image of the 'unworthy' poor also appears to have lost none of its attraction: 'the first cause of poverty is the ill will of the poor' was noted in 1843.[91] In his *Gedachten over armoede, overbevolking en kolonisatie* (Thoughts on poverty, overpopulation and land settlement), published in 1845, Van den Berg stated: 'They live on carefree, seldom save for tomorrow and when they are without earnings, they immediately fall back on poor relief.'[92]

Poor relief was a thorn in the flesh of many writers, for it would provide an alternative source of income for all those who were too lazy to work. Therefore, objections to what the middle classes and elites considered to be generous and uncritical almsgiving were frequently raised. According to them, this was a relic from the days of the Republic. As a remedy, at the end of the eighteenth century the Patriots advocated government intervention and centralization in the fight against poverty. Not very different from the measures advocated by humanists in the sixteenth century. Liberals, on the other hand, saw greater benefit in government abstinence and the free operation of supply and demand on the labour market.

The excited tone that can be heard in many of the writings about the poverty problem was out of all proportion to the practice of caring for the poor. Van Leeuwen's research into poor relief in Amsterdam and Pot's research into the care of the poor in Leiden have made it abundantly clear that the practice of almsgiving in these cities was in keeping with what was customary in pre-industrial Europe. Poor relief was neither generous nor uncritical. In the first half of the nineteenth century, poor relief in Amsterdam never amounted to more than 12–14 per cent of the subsistence minimum and it was therefore impossible to live on it. Poor relief was only a small supplement to an insufficient income, and it was not uncritical either.[93] In fact, only a limited number of groups were eligible for almsgiving: the elderly, the sick and disabled and families with many small children.[94] Moreover, the poor from outside the city usually only received support after a number of years. In the first half of the nineteenth century, therefore, strangers still had fewer rights than those born in the city.[95] They were probably also strongly represented among those who left the city in bad times to seek refuge elsewhere. In Leiden, this outflow played an important role in the decline of the city's population between 1735 and 1749. And also it is no coincidence that in Amsterdam between 1795 and 1829, a time of economic malaise, the population declined most in poor working-class areas such as the Jordaan district (henceforth referred to as the Jordaan).[96]

An exception to the small amount of the alms and the public humiliation of going to public charitable distributions were the so-called *schaamsarmen* (shamefaced poor), or, as they were called in Leiden, *pauvres honteux*. These were individuals and families from the middle classes who had fallen into poverty and were therefore in danger of dropping out of their own social class.[97] In Amsterdam they received considerably more support than the other poor, they were not registered in the alms books, and they could collect the alms by appointment from the poor relief institution or from an administrator of that institution at home.[98] In Leiden, they did not receive more support, but they were spared the humiliation of public almsgiving.[99] These *schaamsarmen* are a convincing illustration of the previously discussed alliance between the elites and middle classes. Consistent with this is also the fact that the mass of the poor received nothing (strangers) or were very poorly provided for ('own' poor).

The four aforementioned discourses in which beggars figured and the very negative views on the poor and the working classes in general that were still prevalent in the first half of the nineteenth century, have – as far as I know – not led to large-scale violence against this group.[100] Indeed, as early as the first half of the seventeenth century, the indispensability of this 'lower class of people' was pointed out. In his social stratification of the urban community in Haarlem, Schrevelius refers to the working classes in his city as 'schuym van volck, gheboeft' (scum, rabble) and then mentions among others cooks, old-clothes dealers, cobblers, coffin bearers, garbage collectors, chimney sweeps, cesspit cleaners and dredgers. And then he continues: 'whose help and service the community and society of citizens cannot do without, they cannot do without each other . . .'.[101]

Schrevelius was not alone in this. For the sake of the city's economy the government of Amsterdam, for example, never decided to actively keep out the many thousands of migrants who sought work and income in the city. This theme also emerged in discussions about the care of the poor. In 1826, for instance, the trustees of one of Amsterdam's poor-care institutions opposed the city council's intention to end all assistance to able-bodied workers and to transfer them to the agricultural settlements of the Maatschappij van Weldadigheid in the east of the Netherlands. The trustees argued that poor relief made it possible for craftsmen and others to get through the winter period when there was too little work available. If they were to leave the city, it was inevitable that in summer there would be a shortage of labour in the city. And in 1815, in a similar argument, it was noted that those who were supported 'could not possibly be taken out of society without causing it . . . substantial damage and . . . paralyzing if not destroying it'.[102]

This emphasis on the usefulness of the destitute classes for society and the economy did not exclude compassion for the fate of the poor. We can find expressions of this among city administrators, trustees of social institutions and private individuals. But that compassion was always accompanied by the conviction that everyone should remain in his or her own class. And so it was emphasized that education at the city schools for the poor was certainly not meant to give children the opportunity and ambition to climb up from the class they were born into. 'The hallmark of a good upbringing must be that it turns everyone in his particular rank and class into a good and useful member of the state', wrote the Parnassim of the Ashkenazi Jewish community in 1807.[103] And they were certainly not alone in this opinion.

The texts written by middle classes and elites about the behaviour and lack of morals among the working classes have their own dynamics and should not be seen as a reliable representation of reality. They are part of a discourse that can be characterized as 'othering'. In his study of ethnic minorities in contemporary Denmark, Jensen defines othering as 'discursive processes by which powerful groups . . . define subordinate groups into existence in a reductionist way which ascribe problematic and/or inferior characteristics to these subordinate groups. Such discursive processes affirm the legitimacy and superiority of the powerful . . .'.[104] That is exactly what also happens in this pre-modern discourse. The texts are intended for consumption by the literate elites and middle classes of Dutch society and they repeat time and again the message that the poor, and the working classes in general, are different and above all less than themselves: less civilized, less moral, less virtuous and less industrious. With this discourse, the literate classes defined themselves and also confirmed and legitimized the existing social hierarchy.

The texts do not tell us much about the poor and the working classes, but they do reflect the views and obsessions of the established middle classes and elites. That makes them relevant. After all, their views on 'the other' also had a bearing on the decision-making processes at individual (choice of housing) and collective (zoning) levels that shaped the residential patterns in the pre-modern cities of Holland. In the next chapter, these residential patterns will be presented as an expression of the appropriation of urban space that was based on the unequal distribution of resources and the related potential for exercising power in the field of housing.

2

Residential appropriation of urban space in the first half of the nineteenth century

2.1. The field of housing and residential differentiation: Theory and spatial models

It is no coincidence that the residential appropriation of urban space plays an important role in this study. Indeed, it is in the residential distribution of social classes across urban space that the social structure and the power relations within society clearly come to the fore, or, in Bourdieu's words: 'Though *social space* is not a physical space, it tends to realize itself in a more or less complete and accurate fashion in that space.'[1] And that is not all. The residential distribution of social classes had a major influence on the daily lives of all city dwellers. It determined who their neighbours were, who they met in the street, how much or how little they suffered from polluting industries and other nuisance, and it also determined the image people formed of them on the basis of the location and nature of their dwellings. This chapter reconstructs for the first half of the nineteenth century the residential patterns in selected cities in Holland, but not before taking a moment to discuss housing in the context of Bourdieu's model of society, and the work of Sjoberg and Vance, both of whom have commented on the residential structure of pre-modern cities.

In line with what was argued in the introduction, we can consider housing as one of the many fields that together constitute social space. Within the field of housing, individuals and social groups compete for maximum control over and access to the benefits associated with living in a particular location. According to Bourdieu, actors individually and collectively strive to keep unwelcome people and things at a distance and to attract desirable people and things.[2] The degree to which they are successful in this depends on the amount of economic, cultural and social capital they have at their disposal. If capital is plentiful and of the right composition, then a socially homogeneous, clean, beautiful and safe residential environment in the vicinity of suppliers of attractive – usually scarce – goods and services is possible. Lack of capital in its various forms 'brings the experience of social finitude to a climax: it chains one, ties one down to a despised locale'.[3] According to Bourdieu, a well-to-do, prestigious residential neighbourhood functions as a club that keeps undesirable people out and allows its members to share, as it were, in the capital at the disposal of the collective of all members. A poor neighbourhood, on the other hand, functions as a ghetto that degrades and stigmatizes its residents. The stigma of residence also makes it virtually impossible for residents to acquire sufficient capital to escape poverty and deprivation, just as the status of an upscale residential location contributes to the accumulation of capital of the privileged upper classes.[4] Between these extremes of ghetto and club, of course, are the residential locations of those with more capital than disadvantaged groups, but less than the residents of affluent neighbourhoods. In short, the relative position of individuals and groups in social space which is based on the possession of resources/capital, corresponds to their relative position in the physical space of the city.

The question of how we should concretely envisage the spatial distribution of those individuals and groups in pre-modern cities falls outside the scope of Bourdieu's work. Two influential studies do make statements on this subject: *The Preindustrial City. Past and Present*, published in 1960 by the Swedish sociologist Gideon Sjoberg, and 'Land Assignment in the Pre-capitalist, Capitalist and Post-capitalist City' by the North American geographer James E. Vance Jr., published in 1971.[5] Let us start with Sjoberg's study.

The Preindustrial City was referred to in 1976 by Abu-Lughod as 'perhaps the most influential book to have come out in comparative urbanism during the present generation'.[6] In spite of the criticism, which there was, the book has remained very influential. This is partly due to the fact that the author establishes a relationship between social structures and residential land use in pre-industrial cities, and of course also because Sjoberg was the first to devote an extensive study to this. In his book, Sjoberg uses the terms 'preindustrial' and 'feudal' as synonyms. Because he believes that the social order results in the last instance from the level of technological development, for him the Industrial Revolution is the great watershed and the entire preceding period is placed under a single denominator. That denominator is feudalism and he gives the following description of it: 'the feudal order has a well-defined and rigid class structure and a clear-cut division of labour according to age, sex, and occupation. A small, privileged upper class commands the key positions in the political, religious, and educational structures and exercises rather autocratic rule.'[7] According to Sjoberg, this 'feudal order' was not only found in Europe but all over the world, and his book gives numerous examples from urban civilizations in China, Japan, India, the Middle East, America and Europe. What is important for us is that according to the author, this feudal order generates a residential pattern that is similar for all pre-industrial cities, irrespective of time or place and that corresponds to the characteristic 'rigid class structure', consisting of an elite, lower class and outcasts.

Regarding that residential pattern Sjoberg states the following: 'The preindustrial city's central area is notable . . . as the chief residence of the elite. Here are the luxurious dwellings, though these often face inward, presenting a blank wall to the street – a reflection of the demand for privacy and the need to minimize ostentation in a city teeming with "the underprivileged". In contrast: 'The disadvantaged members of the city fan out towards the periphery, with the very poorest and the outcastes living in the suburbs, the farthest removed from the centre. Houses toward the city's fringes are small, flimsily constructed, often one-room, hovels into which whole families crowd.'[8] The reason why the elite preferred the centre, he argues, had to do with the limitations of pre-industrial transport technology. Since means of transport were primitive and uncomfortable, the elite lived in the centre, that is, in the immediate vicinity of the administrative, religious and educational institutions from which they derived their high social position.[9] In turn, a central place of residence raised one's status and, moreover, in the centre of the city one faced less danger from shelling and military attacks on the city.

The lower class was internally differentiated and included the lower officials in the political and religious bureaucracies as well as merchants, artisans and the unskilled.[10] Their homes were located outside the centre and they therefore had to put up with longer journey times and other inconveniences. And finally, there were the outcasts or marginal groups. They performed tasks that were necessary for the functioning of urban society but were avoided by the lower class (and of course the elite). As examples Sjoberg mentions the disposal of human faeces, tanning of leather and the slaughter of animals. The outcasts mainly lived on the outskirts of the city, but in smaller numbers they could also be found elsewhere.[11] In addition to the zonal division, the first spatial characteristic of Sjoberg's pre-industrial city, the author also points to the existence of clusters and districts based on occupation and ethnicity. These form the second spatial characteristic of his model. Some of these clusters and districts were located in the lower class zone but were inhabited by people who were considered outcasts, ethnic minorities for example. According to Sjoberg, the concentration of professional peers was a result of the fact that the various guilds were located in different parts of the city, or along specific streets.[12] For that matter, domestic servants living in the houses of the elite also broke through the zonal model of the pre-industrial city.[13]

It will be clear from the above that Sjoberg's pre-industrial city was the result, in spatial terms, of processes of appropriation. The elite preferred to live in the centre because of the proximity of important institutions, because of the status a central location conferred and because of the greater safety in the face of enemy attacks and shelling. The rest of the population was therefore forced to find accommodation elsewhere. Within this large group, the same process of appropriation took place: those with more resources were better able to realize their housing preferences than those with fewer resources, who in turn had to make do with a location further removed from the centre. And those with the least resources had the least choice and ended up in the periphery, far away from the prestigious centre. The latter was also explicitly intended because the elite, according to Sjoberg, tried to avoid contact with 'low-status groups' as much as possible.[14]

At the heart of the appropriation of urban space was the willingness of social groups to use their resources and thereby exercise power. The most important resource in Sjoberg's pre-industrial city was status, which in turn was linked to the position held, the profession exercised, family background, the possession and display of desirables and 'special moral and personal attributes'.[15] The relatively low status of merchants shows that economic resources were less important. The question of how status was used as a resource to exercise power and achieve concrete results is answered by Sjoberg only for the elite. This is in line with his view that 'The upper class sets the pace for the total society'.[16] Rather than dominance and coercion, Sjoberg emphasizes authority:

a situation in which the hegemony of the elite is accepted by the rest of society and possibly even taken for granted.[17]

In contrast to Sjoberg's view, for Vance the social structure of society does not result from the level of technological development, but from the organization of production. With the rise of capitalism in the sixteenth century, the organization of production changed radically, and with it the social structure and the residential patterns that were the spatial reflection of the social structure. Vance therefore distinguishes between the pre-capitalist (medieval) city and the capitalist city. The latter would continue to exist until the period when governments began to play a greater role and legislation tackled the worst shortcomings of the capitalist housing market.[18]

Vance summarizes his argument as follows: 'the treatment of urban land as a source of income, which came in with the general conceptual baggage of the capitalist system as it developed, fundamentally transformed the morphology of the city. If land assignment had been primarily social in structure during the Middle Ages, it became primarily economic during the time of mercantilism and industrialism.'[19] According to Vance, the social aspect of land ownership and land use in the pre-capitalist city was based mainly on the corporatist organization of society and the crucial role of guilds. In the medieval city, the guild and not the property market was the institution that shaped the city's spatial structure. Guild members lived together because, according to Vance, this proximity was a prerequisite for practising their profession and also because it enabled them to benefit from the guild's social services.[20] The spatial result was that the city consisted of a number of guild districts, each with its own facilities and in some cities supplemented by districts based on ethnicity. Vance therefore speaks of the 'multi-centred city'.[21] Within these districts, and also within the city as a whole, residential differentiation was mainly expressed within a house (micro-differentiation). On the ground floor was usually the workshop or shop. Above that lived the guild master and his family, and on the higher floors journeymen and apprentices who lived in the house of the master. The attic was often used to store raw materials and trade goods.[22]

According to Vance, the sixteenth century was the period in which the pre-capitalist city made way for the capitalist city. From that time onwards, the possession of land and houses also acquired a different meaning: 'In place of the ... class-undifferentiated medieval appraisal of land value, there came the appraisal of the rent-productivity of land and a ranking of location in economic terms.'[23] The consequences were very far-reaching. In a society where wealth was an important condition for power and prestige, land ownership became a source of income and a means to achieve that wealth. To maximize revenue, it was necessary to break the old link between living and working since the spaces on the ground floor, which lent themselves well to shops or workshops because of their location on the street, could command more rent than the floors above them. The separation of living and working became possible because in these capitalist times, the traditional ties between the guild master and his resident journeymen and apprentices were broken. However, this does not mean that micro-differentiation within houses disappeared. The status of the residents still decreased at the higher floors, but these residents were no longer live-in servants, but households that competed for accommodation on the housing market. The letting of floors and rooms, which according to Vance was a limited phenomenon in the Middle Ages, now became much more common.[24]

Thus, there was a considerable degree of social mixing within houses, but also at the level of neighbourhoods. In those neighbourhoods, still associated with specific trades and ethnicities, densification took place. Especially in the most densely populated parts of the city, house owners filled up inner courtyards, creating a labyrinth of alleys and blind alleys where the poorest could find shelter.[25] Vance sees the emergence of this densification and infilling as a consequence of the capitalist system of land assignment. In segregation studies, the situations described earlier are characterized as micro-segregation, that is differentiation at the level of floors within the same house, and meso-segregation, differentiation between streets, with the well-to-do living along (main) streets, middle classes and part of the working classes along side streets and back streets and the poor in narrowly-spaced and poor-quality dwellings in the inner courtyards.[26]

The rewarding prospect of commercial exploitation of urban property, says Vance, was also felt by the owner-occupiers of the large houses along the main streets. By moving elsewhere themselves, the large house could be divided into parts that could then be rented out or sold separately. Because of its location on a main street, with all the location advantages that this offers, the ground floor was given a commercial purpose and correspondingly high price. The remaining rooms could be exploited as residential accommodation and storage. This successful transformation and exploitation of the building stimulated neighbours to do the same, and eventually a group of real estate operators emerged who themselves for housing and work no longer had to rely on a highly accessible location within the urban grid. They could therefore choose a location that separated them from their less well-off fellow citizens, and this preference could lead to the development of neighbourhoods with high-income housing.[27]

These new neighbourhoods fitted in beautifully with the second function of land ownership in the capitalist period. According to Vance, real estate was then not only a source of income but also a source of status. In the Middle Ages, when status was determined by family background and public function, it was hardly necessary for elites to present themselves as such in order to be treated with the respect they desired. In the capitalist period, 'Men were no longer self-evidently important when their distinction came mainly from the possession of money.'[28] As soon as they left the economic centre of the city, they needed symbols that demonstrated their wealth and status. The new elite neighbourhoods met that need. As the elite and other residents moved away, the city centre increasingly lost its function as a residential area. Because of its central location and the consequent excellent accessibility, it became a favourite location for commercial land users such as retailers and merchants. Competition for these locations drove up land prices and drove out land users who had fewer financial resources or who could not pass on the high location costs to their customers.[29] Since there was little incentive in the capitalist property market to build low-cost housing for the lower-income classes, they had to rely on the former wealthy houses in the old neighbourhoods adjacent to the commercial heart of the city, which were divided into numerous housing units.[30]

This brief summary of Vance's argument makes it clear that not only are the patterns of residential appropriation very different from Sjoberg's but also the underlying dynamics. Even in the medieval guild city, Vance sees residential patterns that can be traced back to the possession of economic resources and the possibility of using them to gain locational advantages.[31] For Vance, economic capital and the 'invisible hand' of the property market are the main structuring forces in the residential landscape. And as with Sjoberg, it was the elite, in his case an economic elite, that set the tone in a spatial sense. After all, this elite was best placed to realize its housing preferences, and households with fewer economic resources will have had to make do with less attractive dwellings and locations on the real estate market. Bourdieu too, argues that those with ample resources are able to appropriate the most attractive homes and locations, but more so than Sjoberg and Vance, he emphasizes the effect of the neighbourhood on the chances of its residents to improve their position in society.

So much for the views of Bourdieu, Sjoberg and Vance. In the following, their work is used as a reference in the reconstruction of the residential patterns established by appropriation of space in the cities of Holland in the first half of the nineteenth century.

2.2. Residential differentiation in the pre-modern cities of Holland

It is unfortunate, but for the long period up to the middle of the nineteenth century, the usual indicators of the socio-economic position of individuals and households – income and occupation – are not available for Holland's cities. Of course, there are sources that mention professions and/or incomes, but they never concern the entire city population and, moreover, they can hardly ever be linked to a specific location in the city. The latter is a necessary condition in a study of residential appropriation of urban space. As an alternative to income or occupation, this study makes use of (estimated) rental values of houses. These are much more widely available, can often be related to a location in the city and they give an indication of the position of the residents in the field of housing and society in general.[32]

The oldest source available for all Dutch cities, which makes it possible to establish a relationship between the rental value and an *exact* location in the city, is the *Kadaster* of 1832.[33] This national land register built on initiatives that had already been taken during the Kingdom of Holland (1806–10) and the annexation to the French Empire (1810–13). These first initiatives, as well as the 1832 land register, had a fiscal goal: an equal distribution of land tax over all tax payers. This should put an end to the shortcomings of the land tax during the *ancien régime*, which showed great regional differences and over time became a less accurate reflection of the value of land and buildings. The new land tax was based on the most accurate possible estimation of the revenue from land and buildings. Therefore, it became necessary to identify the owner of each plot, but also to accurately measure the size of the plot and to make an estimate of the annual yield. This labour-intensive work took a long time, but with the Act of 2 January 1832, the official land register was finally introduced.[34] The most important cadastral documents for this research are the *Oorspronkelijke Aanwijzende Tafels* (*OAT*) and *Minuutplans*.[35]

The *OAT* contain for each piece of land in the Netherlands an identifier, information about the owner, an indication of the type of buildings (if present), the estimated yield without buildings, deductions, the taxable yield and a series of references to other cadastral documents. The taxable yield is particularly important for this study. In the case of urban properties, this was based on a valuation of the rental value of the property in question. The rental values themselves are not included in the *OAT*, but can easily be calculated from the taxable yield.[36]

Via the plot's identifier (cadastral municipality, section and plot number), the information in the *OAT* is linked to the *Minuutplans*. These maps are the product of the large-scale surveying of all plots in the country and, like the *OAT*, they reflect the situation in 1832. This chapter makes use of the *OAT* and *Minuutplans* of a number of cities and their immediate surroundings. In many studies on residential patterns in pre-modern cities, research is limited to the city *intra muros*. Here, the choice was made to also include the area immediately outside the city limits in the analysis, because it cannot be excluded that these outlying areas were inhabited by households with a specific position in the field of housing. Sjoberg also refers to this. Specifically, this chapter and the next one look at the residential structure of the six cities mentioned in the previous chapter: Edam, Alkmaar, Delft, Leiden, The Hague and Amsterdam. These cities were selected because of their geographical dispersion across the region and the variation in population size and size of the built-up area.

The location of the cities and their distribution across the region of Holland is shown in Map 2.1.[37] It concerns three cities in the northern part of Holland (Alkmaar, Edam and Amsterdam) and three cities in the southern part (Leiden, The Hague and Delft). Table 2.1 reveals that the demographic and geographical size of these six cities varied greatly. The table also clearly shows that not all cities participated equally in the economic growth in Holland from the last quarter of the sixteenth century onwards. In 1500 the largest city (Leiden) had over six times as many inhabitants as the smallest one (Edam), but in 1670 the largest city (Amsterdam) was almost fifty-five times as large as the smallest one (again Edam). The figures also reflect the strong expansion and subsequent stagnation and decline of the Leiden textile industry, as well as the increasing importance of The Hague as an administrative centre and court town. Parallel to the development of population numbers, the geographical size of the cities increased significantly during the period of economic expansion.[38] The stagnation of the Dutch economy is reflected in the built-up areas in 1850. These are only marginally larger than those in 1750. Effectively, the period of large-scale city extensions had already come to an end in the third quarter of the seventeenth century.[39]

With their geographical dispersion across the region and variation in population size and built-up area, the six selected cities provide a good impression of the situation in Holland's cities in general. A practical consideration in the choice of these six cities was the availability of a digital version of *OAT* and cadastral *Minuutplans*.[40] These serve as the basis for what this chapter is about: a reconstruction of the residential patterns as an expression of the appropriation of space in the cities of Holland at the end of the pre-modern period.[41]

Map 2.1 Distribution of the six selected cities across the area of Holland.

Table 2.1 Population Size and Built-Up Area in Hectares of Selected Cities in Holland, c. 1500–1850

city	c. 1500 population	c. 1500 size (ha)	c. 1670 population	c. 1750 size (ha)	c. 1850 population	c. 1850 size (ha)
Amsterdam	11,394	88.4	219,000	469.9	224,035	474.1
Den Haag	5,500	53.5	20,000	180.8	72,225	199.6
Leiden	14,250	94.4	67,000	144.2	35,895	144.2
Delft	11,700	91.5	25,000	91.5	18,449	91.5
Alkmaar	4,179	38.9	13,650	56.5	10,192	62.5
Edam*	2,239	23.7	4,000	30.8	4,370	30.8

*The built-up area of Edam was calculated on the basis of contemporary maps, analogous to the method used by Rutte and Abrahamse.

Source: Reinout Rutte and Jaap Evert Abrahamse (eds), *Atlas of the Dutch Urban Landscape. A Millennium of Spatial Development* (Bussum: Thoth, 2016) tables E2, D3 and E3 for the built-up areas of the cities and for their population in 1850; Piet Lourens and Jan Lucassen, *Inwonertallen van Nederlandse steden ca.1300-1800* (Amsterdam: NEHA, 1997) for population figures around 1500 and 1670.

Let's start with the smallest of the selected cities: Edam. At the time of the 1832 land register, Edam had about 4,000 inhabitants and 869 houses.[42] The strongholds, city walls and wall towers had already been demolished in the previous period. Of the old defences, only a few city gates remained, but these too were not long-lived.[43] Nevertheless, the map also gives a good impression of the situation before the demolition, when Edam was still enclosed within its ramparts, but there were also residential buildings immediately outside these ramparts. Especially along the Oorgat waterway on the east side of the city, the number of houses was substantial.

In Map 2.2, the rental data of the individual houses are visualized in a so-called interpolation map.[44] This mode of presentation has the advantage over a map with average rental values per block of houses or district of a greater degree of detail and the advantage over a map with rental values for each individual house of a greater degree of overview.[45] The rent level and thus the socio-economic position of the occupants can be read from the colour. This ranges from bright red for the highest rental values via orange, yellow and green to dark blue for the lowest. The white areas indicate forms of non-urban land use (vegetable gardens, orchards, etc.) within the city boundaries. This was not a new phenomenon in Edam. The map by Frederik de Wit from 1698 already shows that especially on the north side of the city, large areas of land were used for agricultural purposes.[46] However, what interests us most is what the interpolation map reveals about residential differentiation in a small city like Edam.

What is immediately clear is that there was no zonal pattern around a wealthy centre. Contrary to Sjoberg's assertion, the most important public buildings were not located together in the city centre either. As that centre, Dam Square with the town hall (purple in the illustration) is the most appropriate. But the main church (black in the picture) was on the northern periphery and the other churches and the synagogue (also black) were scattered along the west-east running band of buildings.

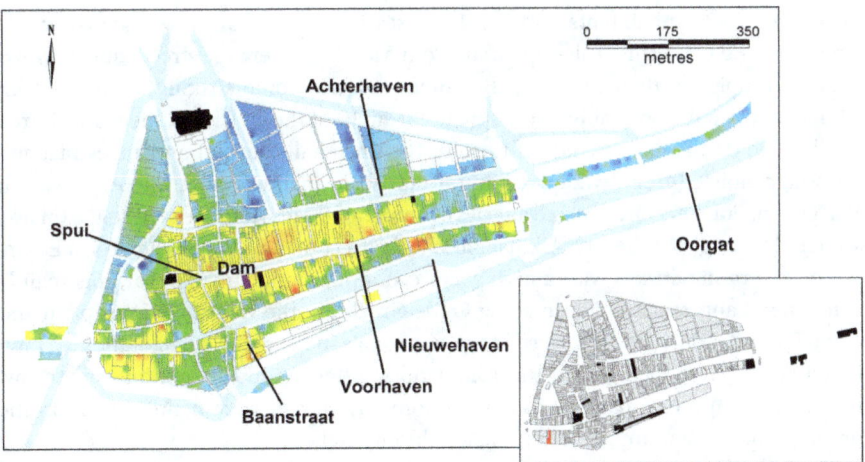

Map 2.2 Residential differentiation in Edam, c. 1830. Inset map: Location of industries (tannery in red).

Much more than appropriation and spatial differentiation in the form of concentric zones, in Edam there was differentiation at the level of streets. Judging by the rents, the wealthy elites lived on both sides of the water of Spui-Dam-Voorhaven. At the east end of this wealthy 'ribbon', however, rental values were considerably lower, a clear demonstration of the fact that rents and social positions of residents could also vary within streets. Houses outside the former eastern city gate closely matched those in the urban periphery. There, along the Oorgat, the water that connected Voorhaven to the Zuiderzee, houses had predominantly low to very low rental values and consequently they provided shelter for those with very limited financial resources. Within the former city walls, especially the streets and canals running from Achterhaven to the northern periphery had low rents, but clusters of cheap and very cheap houses could also be found elsewhere in the periphery. The lack of a compact and well-to-do city centre does not alter the fact that in accordance with Sjoberg's views, groups with a low socio-economic status were overrepresented in the periphery. And the poor houses along the Oorgat waterway are in keeping with his thesis that the outlying area is also inhabited by households with very limited resources.

The inset map shows that Edam's industry was mainly found on the edges of the city and in the eastern outskirts. There, one could find rope yards, salt works and shipbuilding yards. In pre-modern cities, an extreme degree of nuisance was caused by tanneries. The stench and dramatic pollution of the surface water must have seriously affected the living conditions of the local residents. The only tannery in operation in Edam around 1830 was located in the far southwest corner of the city, far from the well-to-do residents of houses near Dam Square and along Voorhaven.[47]

Is the socio-spatial differentiation in Edam, with the wealthy elites living along a main canal or main street and the poor living in the periphery and outside the (former) city walls unique to a small city like Edam, or is this pattern also found in larger cities? And were the homes of the least well-off in these larger cities also marked by the proximity of industries and an unattractive residential environment?

With over 9,400 inhabitants and 2,061 houses in 1832, Alkmaar was considerably larger than Edam.[48] This is also apparent from Map 2.3, where the street pattern shows greater complexity than in Edam. But there are also some striking similarities. In Alkmaar, too, public buildings were spread throughout the city. Here, the main church was located on the far west side of the city, the town hall (purple) on Langestraat and the weigh house (grey), which was important for a market centre like Alkmaar, on Waagplein. Furthermore, we find a series of churches (black) and the synagogue (black) scattered throughout the city. Alkmaar also lacked a compact elite quarter. As in Edam, there were rather streets with a high socio-economic status. In Alkmaar, this mainly concerned Langestraat, but also along Oude Gracht, in the vicinity of Waagplein and along Luttik Oudorp, the northern of the two canals in the eastern half of the city, high rental values were recorded in the 1832 land register. As in Edam, houses with low rental values and occupants with few economic resources were mainly found in the urban periphery and immediately outside the city walls.

But this overall picture needs some qualification. The interpolation map clearly shows that almost no street or canal had the same rental values over its entire length, and it is also striking that in Breedstraat, immediately south of the well-to-do Langestraat,

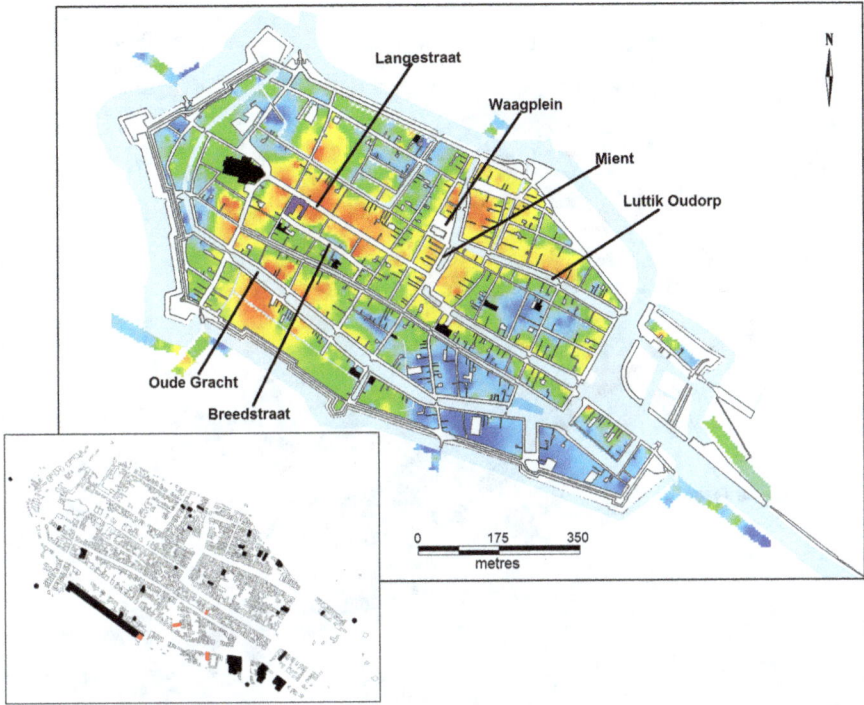

Map 2.3 Residential differentiation in Alkmaar, c. 1830. Inset map: Location of industries (tanneries in red).

rental values were generally very low. In the side streets of both Langestraat and Oude Gracht, rental values were also considerably lower than along the street and canal itself. Apparently, there was socio-spatial differentiation over very small distances in Alkmaar. This residential meso-differentiation within and between streets can be visualized more clearly in a map showing the average rental values of the four faces of each block of houses. In Map 2.4, these averages are combined into four quartiles. The fourth quartile contains the block faces with the highest average rental values, the first quartile with the lowest. Some block faces were not selected because the number of observations there was too small.[49]

The map clearly shows how the affluent block faces are strung together to form street sides along both sides of Langestraat, Oude Gracht and Mient and along the north side of Luttik Oudorp. But it also appears that houses with lower (quartiles 2 and 3) and much lower rental values (quartile 1) were located in the immediate vicinity: on side streets and back streets (meso-differentiation). This is perhaps the most characteristic difference with Sjoberg's model. In Alkmaar the elites, middle classes and working classes literally lived around the corner from each other, a situation that ties in with Vance's argument about the 'capitalist city'. According to Vance, in the 'capitalist city' the real estate market played a decisive role in the distribution of housing, and locations along the economically and socially less attractive side streets

Map 2.4 Residential differentiation in Alkmaar by block face, *c.* 1830.

and back streets resulted in lower rents and occupation by a less wealthy or even poor segment of society. Moreover, they were usually built with smaller and less comfortable houses. The least attractive, of course, were dwellings in the inner courtyards, which according to Vance were the result of real estate developers who wanted to maximize the return on their land holdings. In Alkmaar, walled-in houses in inner courtyards seem to have been virtually absent in the first half of the nineteenth century.[50]

The finely meshed residential pattern did not exclude larger-scale differentiation, however. Just as in Edam, cheap houses and residents with few resources were overrepresented in the periphery of Alkmaar. In the south-eastern quadrant of the city, there is even a relatively large concentration of cheap houses. This is also the part of the city where all the tanneries and also a number of large salt works were located (Map 2.3, inset map). Other industries were also mainly found on the city outskirts, where the least affluent inhabitants of Alkmaar found a place to live. Outside the city walls, there were a few rope yards and bleacheries, but around 1830 there was no industry of any size there.

The somewhat more complex pattern of residential differentiation in Alkmaar compared to Edam raises the question of whether this is related to the size of cities. To answer that question, it is useful to include a larger city like Delft in the analysis.

Around 1830 Delft had about 15,000 inhabitants and over 2,800 houses.[51] The interpolation map (Map 2.5) suggests that the question posed earlier must be answered in the affirmative. At the macro-level, residential appropriation of urban space in Delft seems to have resulted in a wealthy western half of the city and a much poorer eastern half. In the western half, expensive houses were mainly concentrated along two canals, one of which (Noordeinde-Oude Delft) cut through the city in its entire length and the other (Voorstraat-Koornmarkt) joined Noordeinde in the north-west.[52] Located between both canals was one of the main churches of the city: Oude Kerk. The other main church, Nieuwe Kerk, and the town hall (purple on the map) were located slightly to the east of the affluent canals at the Markt square.

The interpolation map also shows that the division between the western and eastern halves of the city was not absolute. In the north-west corner of the city, in the immediate vicinity of wealthy Noordeinde, there were houses with much lower rental values. And conversely, the eastern half of the city also contained relatively expensive houses. A map showing average rental values per block face illustrates this pattern more clearly.

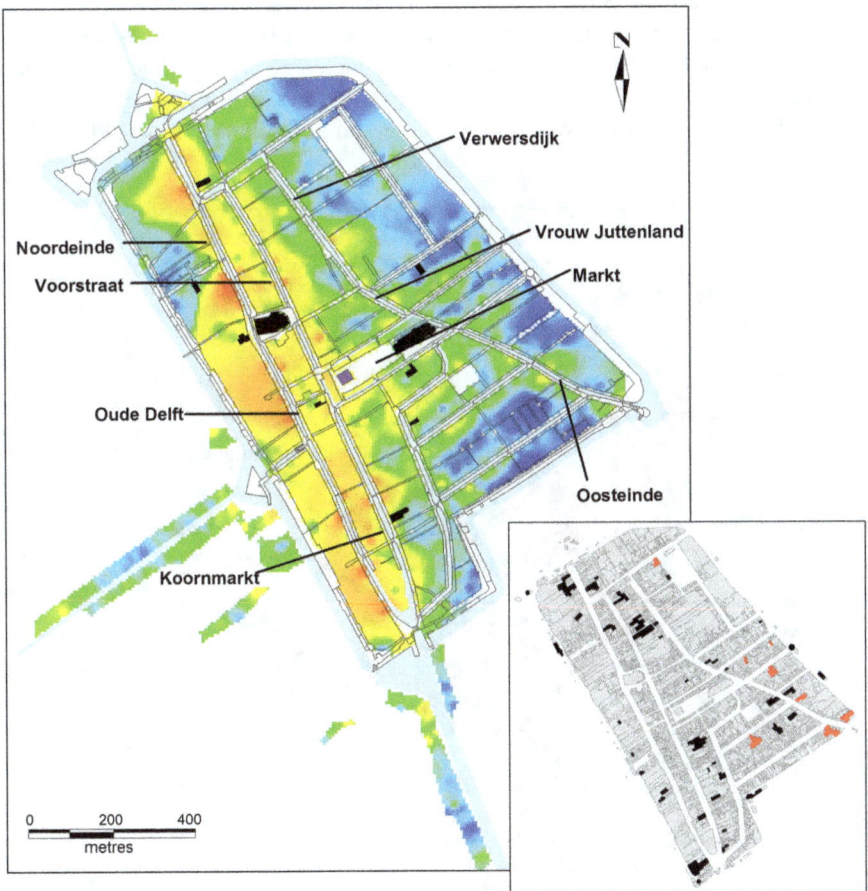

Map 2.5 Residential differentiation in Delft, *c.* 1830. Inset map: Location of industries (tanneries in red).

Map 2.6 also shows that just as in Alkmaar, the socio-spatial differentiation in Delft was expressed at the meso-level of streets. For instance, rents in the side streets of the main canals in both the western and eastern part of the city were considerably lower than those along the canals themselves. We may therefore assume that these side streets were inhabited by a (much) less affluent part of the Delft population. The map also shows that housing along this eastern main canal was not homogenous over its entire length. Especially in the south-eastern part of the canal, rents were below average and in the more central part above average. Around 1830 the poorest part of Delft's population was undoubtedly to be found in the south-eastern quarter of the city, where there was a concentration of small and very small houses with correspondingly low rents.

The inset map (Map 2.5) shows that eight of the nine tanneries in Delft were located precisely in this area. The ninth was located in the poor north-eastern part of the city. In the western part of the city, the main canals were lined with fairly large industrial buildings. These were mainly breweries and related businesses such as malt houses. This exceptional situation had its roots in a more distant past and will be discussed in more detail in the next chapter. Apart from bleacheries and the occasional glassworks, in the outlying area there was little industry to be found. People did live there, however, and just as in Edam and Alkmaar, most of them had

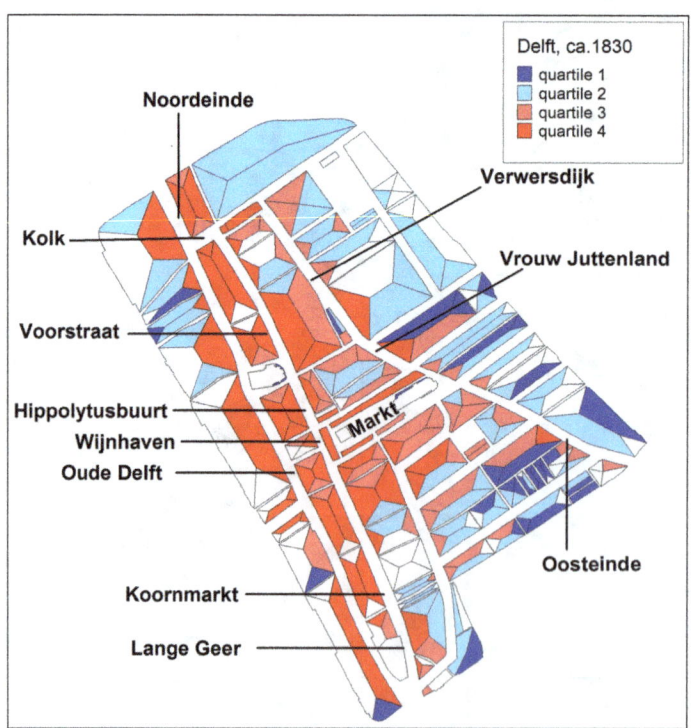

Map 2.6 Residential differentiation in Delft by block face, *c.* 1830.

limited resources and a correspondingly fragile position within the field of housing and society in general.

Although the image of macro-differentiation in the form of a global division of the city along a north-south axis retains its value, it will by now be clear that within this divide there was a much finer meso-differentiation between and within streets. For the poor in the eastern half of the city, middle-class families were never far away, and the well-to-do elites on the main canals in the western half of the city lived in the immediate vicinity of middle class, working class and even poor families. Was this also the case in Leiden, where around 1830 the population was twice the size of that in Delft and the built-up area was also considerably larger?

In the summary of the cadastral information for South Holland published in 1833 by Hoeufft and Van Hoorn van Burgh, 34,564 inhabitants and 6,503 houses are mentioned for Leiden.[53] The interpolation map of Leiden (Map 2.7) shows the now familiar pattern of houses for the wealthy elites along some canals and streets. In the case of Leiden, houses with high rental values were especially to be found along Breestraat and Rapenburg. Rents were also relatively high in the Burght area and along the south side of the river Nieuwe Rijn. This high-quality housing along a few streets and canals

Map 2.7 Residential differentiation in Leiden, *c.* 1830. Inset map: Location of industries (tanneries in red).

implies that there was meso-differentiation at the level of streets in Leiden as well. And indeed, Map 2.7 shows that rental values in side streets and back streets were generally considerably lower. Variations in rental values within streets can be clearly seen in the north and east of the city. For instance, on the north side of Oude Vest, in the vicinity of Mare, rents were considerably higher than elsewhere along this former city moat. And on the east side of the city, the same applied to the houses at the south end of Herengracht.

Although the town hall was situated on Breestraat and both main churches – Pieterskerk and Hooglandsekerk – were in the vicinity of high-quality housing, the interpolation map also shows that a compact and prosperous centre with a concentration of public buildings was lacking in Leiden. In that respect, the situation was no different than in Delft, Alkmaar and Edam. And just like in those cities, those with limited and very limited financial resources were mainly to be found in the urban periphery. Yet even there, there was no question of homogeneously poor neighbourhoods. The relatively high rents near Mare and at the south end of Herengracht have already been pointed out. The really low rents and poor inhabitants were to be found at the extreme edges of Leiden, close to the ramparts and the city moat, as well as in inner courtyards opened up by alleys and blind alleys that were scattered throughout the city.[54] The distribution of rental values in the block of houses enclosed by Lange Mare, Clarensteeg, Janvossensteeg and Marendorpse Achtergracht (present Van der Werfstraat) is illustrative of the latter situation. Rents were relatively high along Lange Mare, considerably lower along Clarensteeg, Janvossensteeg and

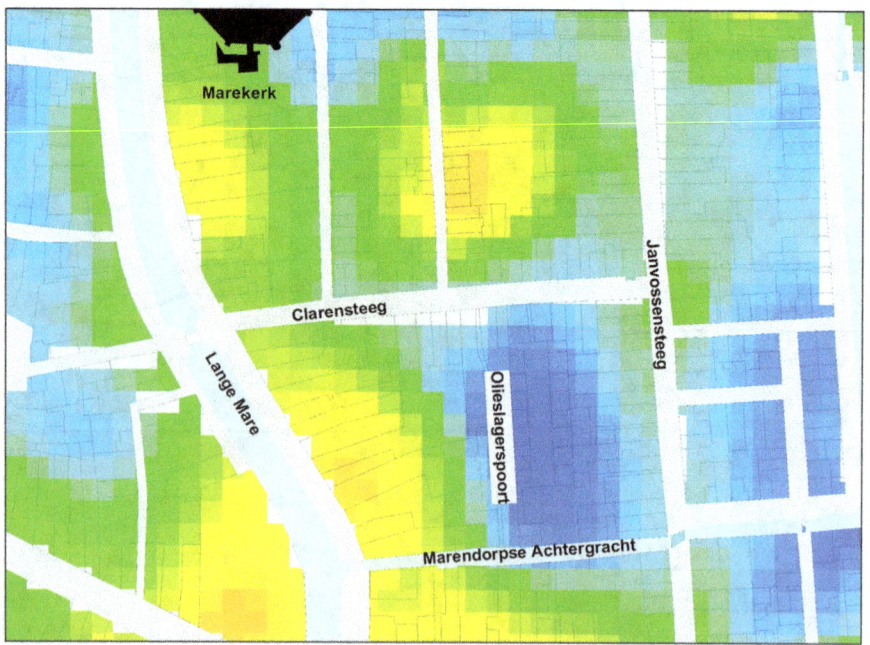

Map 2.8 Rental values in the block of houses around Olieslagerspoort in Leiden, *c.* 1830.

Marendorpse Achtergracht, but the lowest rents were recorded for the small walled-in houses east of Olieslagerspoort (Map 2.8). Wherever in Leiden there were dwellings in inner courtyards, low rental values were recorded in the land register.

The houses in inner courtyards did not usually have an industrial function. The walled-in plots were probably too small for that and, moreover, it is not obvious that nuisance-inducing industries would be tolerated in the inner courtyards behind the houses on more substantial streets and canals. Their residents had sufficient economic, cultural and social resources to prevent the quality of their environment from being affected. Industry in Leiden was mainly located in the poor northern and eastern periphery of the city (Map 2.7, inset map). There we also find twenty of the twenty-one tanneries in the city, which with their stench and pollution seriously affected the quality of their environment. The highly polluting fulling mills were also, without exception, located on the northern outskirts of the city. There, and also in the southern periphery, numerous factories without further specification are mentioned in the land register. In Leiden around 1830, we should not think of steam-powered textile production, but of manufactory, the largely manual manufacture of fabrics and yarns in a workhouse or factory house, sometimes employing considerable numbers of workers.[55]

At the time of the 1832 land register, The Hague had over 56,000 inhabitants and almost 8,200 houses.[56] This made it the third largest city in Holland in terms of population and it was the seat of the court and government. The question we must answer here is whether the presence of the court and government gave rise to fundamentally different patterns of residential differentiation. What is certain is that a court city corresponds to a greater extent to the ideal type model that Sjoberg outlined for pre-industrial cities.

Map 2.9 shows that the spatial distribution of social classes in The Hague was indeed somewhat different.[57] Much more than in the cities discussed earlier, there was a concentration of high rental values and wealthy residents in The Hague. They were mainly found in the north-eastern quadrant of the city, the area around Hofvijver and near the royal palaces (pink on the map). High rents were recorded for Lange and Korte Voorhout, Hoge Nieuwstraat, Korte Vijverberg, Lange Houtstraat and Prinsessegracht. The church (Kloosterkerk), which during the *ancien régime* was frequented by the stadtholders and their families, was also located on Lange Voorhout, and on the edge of the north-eastern quadrant were the main church (Grote Kerk, or Sint Jacobskerk) and the town hall (purple on the map). Thus, more than in other cities, there was indeed a concentration of wealth here, as well as of institutions with an administrative function: Binnenhof, town hall and palaces. Although the two main churches mentioned earlier were located in the north-eastern quadrant, churches (and synagogues) could also be found elsewhere in the city. In this respect, the situation in The Hague was similar to that in other cities.

However, the concentration of wealthy inhabitants was not complete. From the north-eastern corner of the city, houses with relatively high rental values spread out in a south-westerly direction. Low and very low rents were especially to be found in the north-western and south-eastern parts of the city, but also in the north-eastern and south-western periphery. On the map it is also easy to see that the status of houses

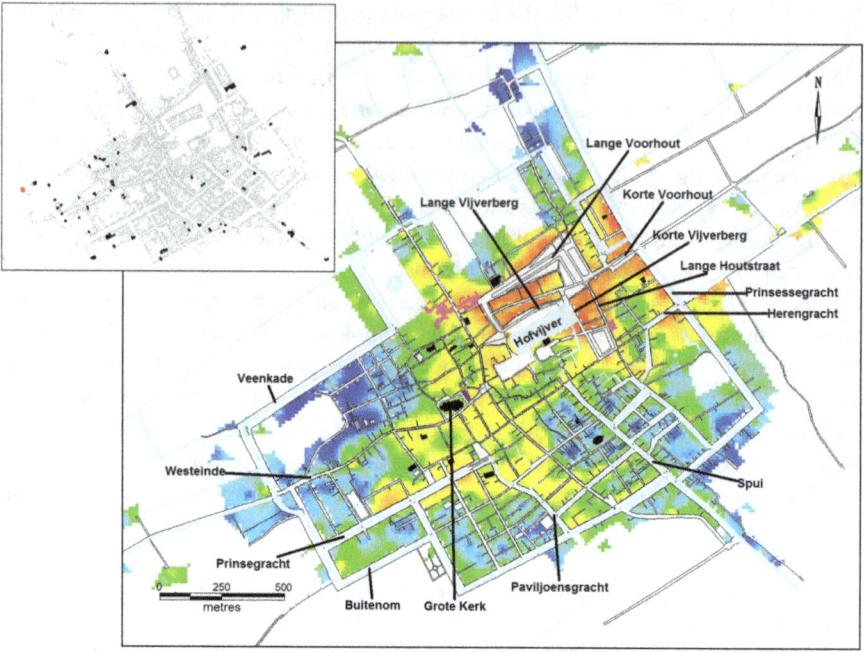

Map 2.9 Residential differentiation in The Hague, *c.* 1830. Inset map: Location of industries (tannery in red).

along the same street or canal often decreased when approaching the periphery. Prinsegracht and Westeinde are clear examples of this. The rent level and the socio-economic status of the residents in the outlying area matched the predominantly low status of the peripheral parts of the city. This pattern, too, was typical of all cities in Holland.

Nevertheless, the appropriation of urban space did not produce a homogeneous wealthy residential environment in the north-eastern quadrant of The Hague either (Map 2.10). In the blocks of houses enclosed by Korte Voorhout, Lange Houtstraat-Plein, Herenstraat-Herengracht and Prinsessegracht, the estimated rental values on Korte Voorhout, Lange Houtstraat and Princessegracht varied from around 1,000 to 2,000 guilders per year, but on Herenstraat-Herengracht the rental values were only a few hundred guilders. On the side streets Casuariestraat and Bleijenburg rents were usually even lower and in the inner courtyard between Bleijenburg and Lange Houtstraat-Plein, right behind the former *Logement van Amsterdam*, which in 1832 was used as a palace for Wilhelmina of Prussia, the wife of King William I, there was a series of small houses with rents varying from about thirty to fifty guilders per year.[58] These were rents that were also charged for walled-in houses in the much poorer north-western and south-eastern parts of the city. Meso-differentiation between streets (around-the-corner differentiation) thus also occurred in The Hague and, as in the other cities, the cheapest dwellings were generally found in the inner courtyards of blocks of houses. The large numbers of blind alleys, often referred to as *poorten* in the

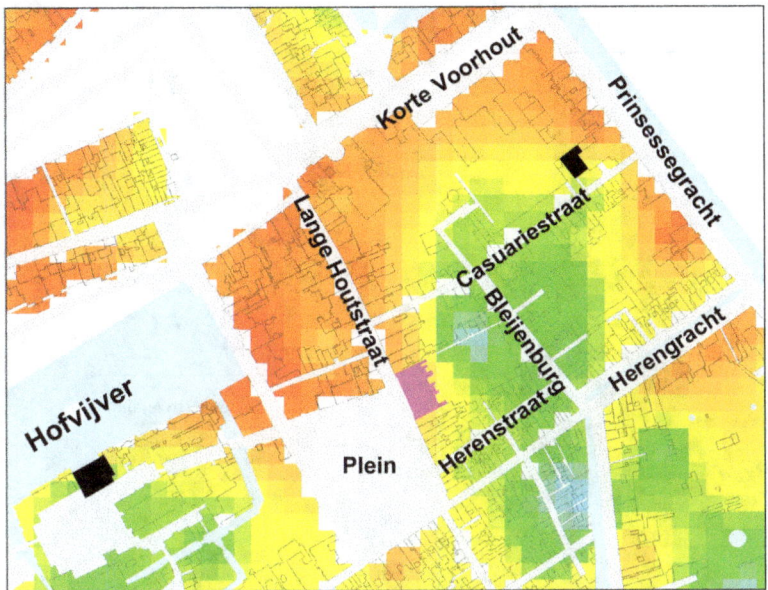

Map 2.10 Rental values in the block of houses east of Lange Houtstraat and Plein in The Hague, *c.* 1830.

sources and clearly visible on the maps shown here, give an impression of the extent of this phenomenon in The Hague.

Information on land use in the land register shows that large-scale industry was relatively rare in The Hague around 1830. The industry that did exist was mainly concentrated in the north-western quadrant of the city, which also had the largest number of houses with low rental values and poor occupants (see Map 2.9 and the accompanying inset map). The only tannery in The Hague was located at the extreme periphery of this area. The large industrial complex in the well-to-do north-eastern part of the city is the canon foundry of the War Department.[59] Outside the built-up area, The Hague also had little industry.

Around 1830, the surveyors of the land registry counted 24,408 houses in Amsterdam. In the summary published by Hoeufft and Van Hoorn van Burgh in 1833, a population of over 200,000 is mentioned.[60] Measured by the number of houses, Amsterdam was three times larger than The Hague, four times larger than Leiden, eight and a half times larger than Delft, almost twelve times larger than Alkmaar and twenty-eight times larger than Edam. From an international point of view, Amsterdam was still one of the larger European cities in these years.

The interpolation map shows a city that can roughly be divided into three parts: a city centre with a socially mixed character, a wealthy ring of canals and a relatively poor periphery to which the outlying area can also be added (Map 2.11).[61] Although Amsterdam thus bore a superficial resemblance to Sjoberg's concentric zone model, the differences with his model are considerable. Just as in Edam, Alkmaar, Delft and

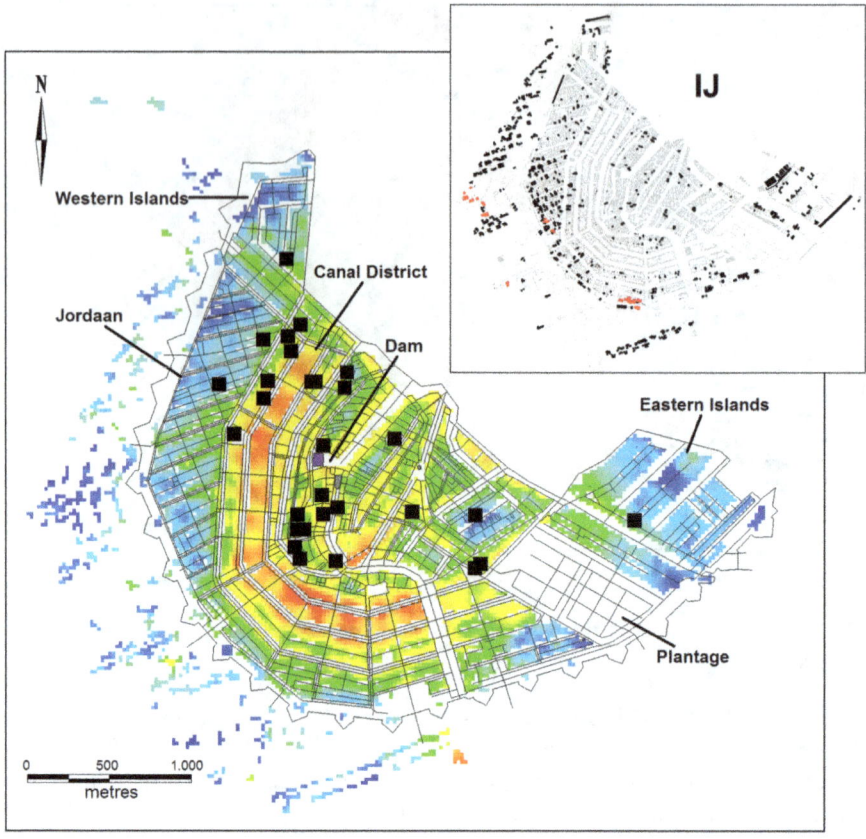

Map 2.11 Residential differentiation in Amsterdam, c. 1830. Inset map: Location of industries (tanneries in red).

Leiden, the elites did not live concentrated in the centre, in the immediate vicinity of important public buildings: the town hall (purple) and Nieuwe Kerk on Dam Square, Oude Kerk near Warmoesstraat and the Exchange (grey) across and above the water of Rokin.[62] On the contrary, the wealthiest inhabitants of Amsterdam lived relatively far from Dam Square and the city centre in the so-called *Gouden Bocht* (Golden Bend) of the southern ring of canals. And the city centre had few houses with high rental values and wealthy residents, and considerable numbers of houses in the lower rent brackets.

Although the socio-economic homogeneity of the ring of canals and the urban periphery was greater than that of the inner city, there was also mixing there (meso-differentiation). This is very clear in the ring of canals, where rents in the side streets were considerably lower than those along the canals themselves. Also on the east side of the outer canal (Prinsengracht) as well as in back streets in the southern part of the ring of canals, there were relatively many houses with low rents according to the standard of the canal ring.[63] The periphery, too, was characterized by a mixture of rental values at the level of streets. In the Jordaan, for instance, many houses on the west side of Prinsengracht and along some of the radial canals had rents comparable to the cheapest houses in the ring of canals. But elsewhere in this district, and especially close to the city walls, they were much lower. This confirms that there was also differentiation in rental levels and financial capacity of the residents within streets. As is clearly shown on the interpolation map the poorest part of the Jordaan was located in the northwest, where Goudsbloemgracht (present Willemsstraat) and its surroundings were notorious for their poverty and miserable housing conditions. There and elsewhere in the periphery, the lowest rents were recorded in the inner courtyards of blocks of houses, accessed by alleys and blind alleys.

The presence of meso-differentiation between and within streets does not alter the fact that in Amsterdam, residential differentiation at the macro-level of districts seems to have progressed much further than in the other cities. This pattern of residential macro-differentiation was matched by the distribution of industrial activities (Map 2.11, inset map). Within the city walls, the largest concentrations of industries were located in the periphery and poor parts of the city: the Eastern and Western Islands on the north near the IJ waterway, along the edge of the crescent, and especially in the southern part of the Jordaan, where a large number of sugar refineries were in operation. But in contrast to the situation in the cities discussed before, there were extensive industrial areas outside the city walls of Amsterdam. On the south side of the city, this included a series of sawmills along Zaagmolensloot (present Albert Cuypstraat), but sawmills were also prominent in the western suburbs.

The sixty-four tanneries were concentrated in three clusters: in and near Nieuwe Looiersstraat on the southern edge of the city, in the vicinity of Looiersgracht in the south of the Jordaan and in the outlying area west of the city. It should not come as a surprise that these were locations with cheap accommodations for residents with insufficient resources to avoid these polluted and unattractive residential environments.

2.3. Residential appropriation of urban space around 1830: The summary picture

To conclude this chapter, let us first summarize how the patterns of residential appropriation relate to Sjoberg's and Vance's models, and then confront those patterns with the resource-based power relations in the field of housing. The previous case studies have demonstrated that contrary to Sjoberg's argument, the pre-modern cities of Holland did not have a homogenous wealthy city centre with the presence of the working classes only in the form of resident domestic servants. The wealthy elites in the cities under study and their resident servants lived along streets and especially canals that cut through a large part of the cities. This alone implies that not all members of the elites were able to live near the institutions from which, according to Sjoberg, they derived their high social standing. Also in contrast to the model is the fact that religious institutions could also be found in the less wealthy parts of the cities. The situation in The Hague corresponds most closely to Sjoberg's model of the pre-industrial city. As seat of the court and government, it showed a clear clustering of the elites around

Hofvijver (with Binnenhof) and near the royal palaces. But even in The Hague, the spatial concentration of the elites was not complete, for houses with relatively high rental values fanned out from the area around Hofvijver in a south-westerly direction.

From the foregoing it should be clear now that there was no rigid spatial segregation between the social classes within society. However, some parts of Holland's cities did have a relatively high status. The clearest examples are the western half of Delft, the north-eastern corner of The Hague and Amsterdam's ring of canals. At the same macro-level, it is also clear that the poorest and most deprived parts of the cities were almost without exception located in the urban periphery and in the outlying areas adjacent to the city.[64] This peripheral location of poor neighbourhoods is in line with Sjoberg's argument and with what has also been established in many studies of residential patterns in pre-modern European cities.[65]

But for the affluent as well as for the less affluent and poor districts of the city, residential differentiation at the macro-level was supplemented by differentiation at the meso-level of streets. Within the context of each district, the relatively well-to-do lived along the main canals and main streets of that district, the middle classes and part of the working classes lived along side streets and back streets and the poor among the working classes lived in the inner courtyards of blocks of houses, opened up by alleys and blind alleys. Furthermore, it has become clear that rental values and the wealth of residents within streets usually diminished when approaching the urban periphery. The variation in rental values between and within streets can be clearly seen when examining the interpolation maps, and the existence of 'around-the-corner differentiation' is also emphasized with the examples of the block of houses including Olieslagerspoort in Leiden and the blocks east of Lange Houtstraat in the predominantly affluent part of The Hague. Only in Edam was this pattern less prominent, due to the relatively small number of blocks with independent housing on all sides. Walled-in houses, in the small- and medium-sized cities a phenomenon of minor importance, were common in the three largest cities: Leiden, The Hague and Amsterdam. In these cities, the rental values recorded in the inner courtyards were often in the same order of magnitude as the rental values in the outermost periphery of these cities.

This differentiation at the meso-level of streets is absent from Sjoberg's work, but it is included by Vance in the model of what he refers to as the 'capitalist city', a city where the invisible hand of the real estate market structured the residential landscape and where real estate owners strove to maximize the return on their real estate holdings through densification and infilling. And his notion that the elites moved out of the old city centres and settled in newly built elite neighbourhoods seems to tie in with the residential structure of Amsterdam. There, after all, the affluent ring of canals was located outside the old city centre. But contrary to what Vance's model suggests, the ring of canals was not on or outside the city's edges, but in the zone between the centre and the poor neighbourhoods in the urban periphery. For in Amsterdam, too, the edges of the city and the adjoining outlying areas were mainly inhabited by households with few financial resources.

Considering the foregoing, it is clear that social classes were not scattered randomly over urban space, but that residential appropriation showed clear patterns, although these were not in all respects the patterns that Sjoberg and Vance had in mind. The existence of residential differentiation can be interpreted in terms of Bourdieu's model of society. In his view, social space – society – consists of a series of fields in which actors individually and collectively strive for the right quantity and composition of their economic, cultural and social capital in order to get access to the benefits to be gained in these fields. According to Bourdieu, the struggle in the field of housing is to keep persons and things perceived as negative at a distance and to attract desirable persons and things. This is also what we would expect in pre-modern Holland, where, as was noted in the previous chapter, society was characterized by a marked hierarchy, an extremely unequal distribution of income and wealth, and negative attitudes towards those who held a lower position in the social hierarchy.

The extent to which actors in Holland's cities succeeded in realizing their housing needs and wishes depended on the resources at their disposal since the use of these resources gave them power in the form of dominance within the field of housing. In the first half of the nineteenth century, as was shown earlier, the distribution of accommodation within the field of housing was driven by the operation of the real estate market and the possession of economic capital was therefore of great importance. Those with the greatest financial resources and the associated power on the housing market had ample choice and could appropriate the most attractive locations and houses, situated along prestigious canals and streets. These were therefore no longer accessible to the other inhabitants of the cities. In a similar way, the rest of the housing stock was appropriated. Each social class occupied the part of the housing stock that corresponded to the size of the available financial resources and power, and the more limited these were, the fewer the options available and the more people had to make do with smaller and poorer-quality housing in unattractive surroundings.[66] This unattractive residential environment was mainly found on the city outskirts, which implies that a large part of the working classes lived in an environment plagued by what are known as negative externalities. Johnston defines externalities as 'aspects of the local environment which contribute to the quality of life of an individual, family or household resident there, but which are not purchased directly by them'.[67] The negative externalities at the city's edges included smells, noise, pollution and other things that detracted from the quality of the home environment. It has also been observed that tanneries, the pre-modern industry that caused extreme pollution and stench, were exclusively located in the urban periphery and poor neighbourhoods, close to those with little economic, cultural and social capital, and far from the homes of those with more resources at their disposal.

But according to Bourdieu, the struggle in the field of housing was aimed not only at avoiding locations with negative externalities but also at keeping 'undesirable persons' at a distance by the *'construction of spatially based homogeneous groupings'*.[68] And it was precisely these socially homogeneous residential areas that were conspicuously absent from Holland's cities in the first half of the nineteenth century, where meso-differentiation was common even in well-to-do districts and groups of different social status lived in close proximity to each other. Why were the socially homogeneous neighbourhoods that Bourdieu associated with the pursuit of social segregation and that Sjoberg considers characteristic of all pre-industrial cities, regardless of place and time, absent in Holland? And how important is the transition from the pre-capitalist medieval city to the capitalist city that Vance considers to be the driving force behind profound changes in the residential landscape, such as the development of walled-in housing and elite neighbourhoods? Were the residential patterns reconstructed here for the first half of the nineteenth century a recent phenomenon, or did they come about earlier, and if so, when?

These questions cannot be answered with the information presented in this chapter. The patterns of residential appropriation that have been reconstructed here on the basis of the 1832 land register are, after all, no more than a snapshot in time, that is the (temporary) result of a lengthy process in which the power relations between social classes through the appropriation of space took on a physical expression in the wood and bricks of the built environment. To get a grip on the dynamics of this process and the way in which the unequal distribution of resources and power (in its various manifestations) resulted in the residential structure of Holland's cities in the first half of the nineteenth century, we will have to chart the history of that socio-spatial structure.

3

Resources, power and residential appropriation of urban space

3.1. Previous history: Residential patterns in the cities of Holland, fourteenth–nineteenth centuries

In order to interpret the patterns of residential appropriation in the first half of the nineteenth century, it is necessary to have more insight into the genesis of these patterns. Therefore, within the framework of this study, an extensive research into residential patterns in the long period before the land register of 1832 was carried out. This is reported in detail in the appendix. This chapter will briefly summarize the results of that research and then attempt to explain the residential patterns observed and relate them to the work of Bourdieu, Sjoberg and Vance. This will also make it possible to determine how and when in Holland the unequal distribution of resources and the power relations based upon them contributed to the residential appropriation of urban space, and how that appropriation in turn played a role in the acceptance and continuity of those power relations.

A crucial finding of the research in the appendix concerns the continuity of residential patterns in the cities of Holland. We have already noted that Vance sees a clear distinction between the situation in the pre-capitalist (medieval) city and that in the capitalist city. Vance is not alone in arguing that the transition from medieval to early-modern times also manifested itself in the spatial structure of cities. Lewis Mumford, for example, in his well-known *The City in History*, sketches the following picture of the medieval guild city: 'In a sense, the medieval city was a congeries of little cities, each with a certain degree of autonomy and self-sufficiency, each formed so naturally out of common needs and purposes that it only enriched and supplemented the whole.'[1] But according to him, this would not remain so. Between the fifteenth and eighteenth centuries, partly under the influence of the rise of merchant capitalism and the development of national states, 'a new complex of cultural traits' emerged in Europe that radically changed 'both the form and the contents of urban life'.[2]

In his book, Mumford hardly pays any attention to residential patterns, but for cities in North-western Europe Hoekveld does. He characterizes the medieval city in North-western Europe as a community with limited social and cultural differences. According to him, residential differentiation took place along two dimensions: from the city centre and its access roads to the urban periphery, and within houses, where a distinction existed between lower and upper storeys, and between front and rear houses. In the 'Baroque city', on the other hand, there was – also for him under the influence of (merchant) capitalism – an increasing disparity in income and wealth, and social classes lived in 'segregated areas'.[3] A similar view can be found with De Klerk. He contrasts the medieval cities with those of the Renaissance and writes:

> The spatial organisation of the medieval city was based solely on the production of goods – the guild quarters – and everyone else lived around places of common interest, churches, town halls and markets. In the Renaissance, a division emerged between parts of the city where local government was being exercised, i.e. the control of economic activities, and parts where production took place.[4]

De Klerk leaves open where these parts of the city were located, but all these authors argue that the transition from medieval to early-modern times was also reflected in the spatial structure of cities. This assumption is usually not very well substantiated because detailed research is scarce and much knowledge is drawn from examples in very different regions.

On the basis of the present research into the period before the 1832 land register, it can now be established that in the cities of Holland there was no fundamental break between the residential patterns in the Middle Ages and early-modern period (see the appendix). On the contrary, working backwards from the nineteenth-century land register it is striking how similar residential patterns were in previous centuries, both on the macro-level of districts and on the meso-level of streets. Even the great city fires, which also regularly ravaged cities in Holland, did not fundamentally change the basic pattern. This continuity is in line with Friedrichs's view that 'the truly creative and transforming epochs in the history of the European city' did not take place during the early-modern period, but before that in the late medieval period of city formation and after that during the nineteenth century with its major changes in the economic, social and spatial spheres.[5]

Perhaps the image of a rupture between Middle Ages and the early-modern period has been influenced too much by the debate on the transition from feudalism to capitalism that exerted great influence on historiography a few decades ago and that, in studies of urban societies, may have been fed by a romantic image of a relatively egalitarian and corporatist medieval guild society.[6] Years ago, Van Uytven already suggested that the contrast felt by many between the Middle Ages and the sixteenth century as the beginning of the modern era might have been triggered by 'the self-conceit of the humanists'.[7] Whether this self-conceit of the humanists has also directly or indirectly influenced the thinking of urban historians I dare not say, but this research confirms that a critical look at the (alleged) contrast between Middle Ages and early-modern period is justified.[8]

The striking continuity across the traditional divide between the medieval and early-modern periods implies that the residential patterns reconstructed in the previous chapter for the first half of the nineteenth century also apply to earlier centuries. What is more, the research into residential patterns in the period before the 1832 land register has also revealed a high degree of similarity in the residential structure of the cities studied here. These were selected on the basis of their diversity in terms of geographical location, population size and size of the built-up area, but nevertheless the similarities are much greater than the differences. Thus, at the macro-level of districts, there was no strict spatial segregation between the different classes in society, nor had the elites appropriated a compact and socially homogeneous elite quarter in the city centre. In the pre-modern cities of Holland the elites lived along a number of streets and canals that sometimes even cut through a large part of the city. The closest thing to the situation described by Sjoberg in his model of the pre-industrial city is The Hague, where the clustering of wealthy people around Binnenhof dates back to the early years of settlement.[9] But in The Hague, too, wealthy elites could be found elsewhere in the city and socially homogenous neighbourhoods were clearly absent. The concentration of 'marginal groups' in the urban periphery and outside the city walls, which Sjoberg also assumes, was on the other hand a constant during the entire period and in all the cities studied here. However, it should be noted straight away that the urban periphery and the outlying areas were less homogenous than he claims, and that members of the working classes also lived in large numbers in the more centrally located parts of the city.[10]

This last observation takes us from the macro-level of city districts to the meso-level of streets. For all cities and for the entire period, this study found that as soon as the size of the population caused building densities to increase, around-the-corner differentiation became the usual pattern. In very general terms, and ignoring specific situations, it can be said that in the cities of Holland the well-to-do elites lived along the main streets and canals, the middle classes and part of the working classes lived in side streets and back streets and along main canals and streets in the less wealthy parts of the city, and the poor among the working classes lived in the urban periphery (*intra muros* and *extra muros*) and also in the inner courtyards in the more centrally located parts of the city, which were opened up by alleys and blind alleys. However, streets and canals were rarely homogeneous from a social point of view over their entire length. Especially when approaching the generally poor periphery, rental values decreased and, it may be assumed, so did the purchasing power and social position of the inhabitants. This pattern is clearly visible on the interpolation maps in the appendix.

A second remarkable finding of the study of residential patterns in the centuries before the 1832 land register is that in the long term within the existing residential structures at macro- and meso-level, the residences of the elites show a tendency towards clustering. This is indicative of an increasing preference on the part of the elites for a socially homogeneous and distinguished residential environment. It will become clear below that this trend manifested itself most radically in Amsterdam, but this desire for an exclusive residential environment is also clearly present in other cities. This preference of the urban elites in Holland for a socially homogeneous residential environment and the way in which it was expressed in spatial terms is the focus of Section 3.3, but first some explanations for the centuries-long continuity of the patterns of macro- and meso-differentiation will be discussed.

3.2. Resources, power and residential appropriation of urban space

The striking similarities between the residential patterns in the cities under study and their long-lasting continuity over centuries raise the question of whether these patterns were (partly) rooted in the enduring characteristics of the environment in which the cities in Holland have developed. In the following it will be argued that this is indeed the case and that the physical-geographical environment and two of the basic elements of these cities – street plan and closed blocks of houses – were of great influence on the establishment and continuity of the patterns of residential appropriation, but it is worth emphasizing that these enduring characteristics were not a force of nature and only became relevant in the context of a society in which resources and the related potential for exercising power in the field of housing were very unequally distributed.

3.2.1. Residential appropriation of urban space: Macro-level

The physical-geographical environment plays a major role in the creation and continuity of residential differentiation at the macro-level of districts. This is not the place to dwell at length on the history of the reclamation and settlement of Holland, but the broad outlines are important for the argument. In the Middle Ages, the landscape in which the cities of Holland developed was part of a broad coastal strip. On the North Sea side this consisted of elongated sandbanks (*strandwallen*), lying parallel to the coast, on top of which high sand dunes were blown up. This line of dunes formed a barrier against the sea and was only here and there broken by river mouths. East of this line of dunes were the *geestgronden*, where the dune sand had become mixed with clay and peat. The outer dune row, which was exposed to sea and wind, had sparse vegetation, but the inland dunes and adjoining *geestgronden* were woody and covered with oak, beech and birch. Deciduous forests were also found on the higher grounds along the rivers.[11] East of the forested *geestgronden* was a peat wilderness that extended to the higher sandy grounds of the Gooi area, Utrecht and Brabant.

Because the marshy peat was initially unsuitable for permanent settlement, the oldest settlements in Holland are found on the higher grounds behind the dunes and on the levees along the major rivers. In the period from the tenth to the thirteenth centuries, the settlement history of Holland underwent a drastic change. In what has become known as the *Grote Ontginning* (Great Reclamation), the wild peat bogs were cultivated and made suitable for agriculture and habitation.[12] In essence, the cultivation of the wet peat bogs was about drainage. This was achieved by digging a series of parallel drainage ditches from the low edges of the peat cushions to the higher areas. These drainage ditches then, of course, had to be connected to a natural watercourse or a dug transverse drainage channel to drain the water from the cultivated area. In order to prevent water from the higher and as yet undeveloped parts of the peat from flowing over the cultivated area, this was often closed off at the rear by a small dyke.

In the recently reclaimed peatlands, mixed farming with arable farming and cattle breeding was practised, but it was not to remain that way. Making the wet peat soil suitable for agricultural activities by draining it had major consequences. This dewatering reduced the volume of the peat, which could consist of as much as 80 per cent water, and moreover, the dry upper layer oxidized, especially when it was pulled open by ploughing. The result was a lowering of the ground level and increasing (ground)water nuisance, which in turn necessitated deeper drainage of the peat. And so began an irreversible process of drainage, subsidence, flooding, deeper drainage, further subsidence and renewed flooding. And because the ground level dropped, sometimes by as much as a metre per century, the flooding was no longer exclusively groundwater-related, but the low land was also threatened by river floods and sea tides. As early as the twelfth century, it therefore became necessary to dam up the estuaries and equip them with sluices and to protect the land from high tides by means of dykes.

It was from the thirteenth century onwards that the urban element in the reclaimed peatlands came more to the fore. And in view of the foregoing, it will come as no surprise that water played an important role in this. In Holland, according to Abrahamse et al., '. . . at all levels of scale, the water system provides structure and is visually defining. It has a huge influence on the location and shape of the cities, and on how they function'.[13] In peat areas, where dykes and dams had to protect the low-lying land from encroaching sea water, dams in the peat rivers were an obvious crystallization point for urban functions. After all, with the construction of dykes, these peat rivers became the main access to the hinterland and, at the dams that had to stop the sea water, there was a need for people who took care of the transhipment of goods, ship maintenance and shipbuilding. And, of course, these gateways were also attractive locations for merchants. Thus, the seeds of a non-agricultural urban settlement had been sown. This scenario contributed to the development of the many dam-settlements in Holland.[14] In addition, settlements with urban functions arose in this period along the numerous inland waterways in the peatlands.[15]

In the following it will become clear how the physical-geographical conditions influenced patterns of residential macro-differentiation, but at least as important is the way in which human actors dealt with these given conditions. It is not useful to map out this interplay between physical environment and human action city by city. Therefore, the situation in Delft is taken as a starting point and additional information on other cities will show that the developments that can be well documented for Delft also took place in a very similar way in the other cities of Holland.

Among the selected cities, Delft is an interesting case because, unlike the dam-cities, it is not located where sea and land meet, nor on the higher grounds at the inner dune edge or along the rivers. It is true that Delft lies on the clay cover that had filled the bed of an old creek – the Gantel – but in the course of time this had become covered with a layer of peat and in the twelfth and thirteenth centuries, when Delft developed, it was probably not visible as 'firmer' ground in the wet peat landscape.[16] But water is an important explanation for the location of Delft, deep in the peat bogs. Around the year 1000, a canal – the Delf – was dug in the peat bog, which was connected to the upper course of the Schie River and through which water from the peats was drained in a southerly direction to the Meuse River.[17] The lands on either side of the Delf formed the 'Hof van Delft', owned by the counts of Holland and administered in their name. Delft is one of the settlements that developed in the Hof van Delft and, unlike other settlements in the Hof, it was located directly on the banks of the Delf. This gave the young settlement a location advantage, as the Delf not only functioned as a drainage canal but also as a connection between the Hof van Delft and the Meuse River.

On the east side of what is now Oude Delft, in the second half of the twelfth century a settlement arose on an elongated mound, raised with soil from the then excavated Nieuwe Delft, or Voordelft (the current trajectory of Voorstraat-Hippolytusbuurt-Wijnhaven-Koornmarkt-Lange Geer; see Map 3.1).[18] This mound settlement already had a non-agricultural character. This makes it likely that Delft arose when there was a need in the peat areas for a place where agricultural production could be marketed and transported elsewhere over the water of the Delf.[19] Around this market and transport function, craft activities developed; very similar to the dynamics in the dam settlements. The central function of Delft for the surrounding area was strengthened by the construction of numerous waterways in the vicinity. In addition, the canal dug in the thirteenth century (Delftse Vliet) between the Schie River to the south and the Leidse Vliet to the north of Delft created a through route between the IJ in the north and the Meuse in the south. This gave a powerful boost to the position of the city in a wider geographical context.[20]

The Delft city charter of 1246 applied to the people living in the area on both sides of Nieuwe Delft. Two decades later, in 1268, the inhabitants of the west side of Oude Delft were granted the same rights. Subsequently, in 1347 and 1355 the area where

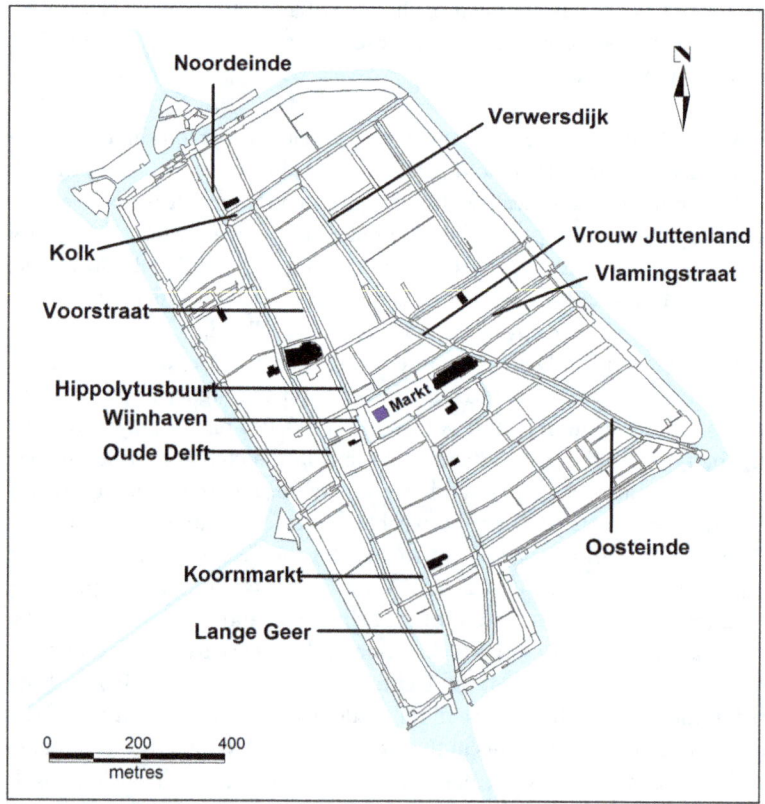

Map 3.1 Street names in Delft.

the city charter was in force, was extended again and as a result Delft got the shape and surface area that it would keep until the second half of the nineteenth century.[21] Within the city as it took shape in 1355 there were considerable differences in the level of elevation. The area around Nieuwe and Oude Delft lay on the creek ridges of the Gantel. The relatively thin layer of peat with which these creek ridges were covered could therefore only slightly subside. Moreover, in an early stage of habitation the area had already been raised with soil from the Nieuwe Delft. To the east of this oldest part of the city, the peat layer was considerably thicker, the subsidence more pronounced and because of the younger date of this part of the city, the area had been raised less often. The result was that in this eastern part of the city, the ground level was much lower than in the western part.

The difference in elevation levels is clearly demonstrated by the fact that Marktveld, the square east of Nieuwe Delft (present Markt), was raised by no less than 90 centimetres in 1484.[22] Before that time, the low-lying Marktveld was protected by a dyke (Verwersdijk-Vrouwjuttenland-Oosteinde) against water flowing in from the eastern part of the city and by (Oude) Langendijk against water from the south-eastern quadrant of the city.[23] Street names in Delft confirm the existence of considerable differences in the level of elevation within the city. For example, in 1344 the west side of Nieuwe Delft was referred to as Hoghe strate (High street). This was not surprising as its street level was about 1 metre higher than on the east side of Nieuwe Delft.[24] The name Vlouw, one of the oldest street names in Delft, refers to a low location and the same applies to Donkerstraat on the far east side of the city. The latter was referred to in 1432 as Dronckenstege, where the word *droncken* stands for submerged or flooded.[25] In fact, the eastern half of the city matched with the very low lying and wet grounds east of the city boundary. Due to subsidence of the peat, the ground there was so boggy and wet that the ramparts of 1355 did not have a wall on the east side because enemy troops could hardly approach the city from the east.[26] The contrast between the western and eastern parts of Delft still exists today and is clearly visible on a recent elevation map, where the contours of the old city are easily recognizable (Map 3.2).[27]

In short, from the middle of the fourteenth century, Delft was divided physically and geographically into a relatively high and dry western part and a low-lying and wet eastern part. The fact that this physical-geographical contrast broadly coincides with the previously observed patterns of residential appropriation and macro-differentiation of the Delft population along lines of wealth and social status is the result of a complex development in which the unequal distribution of economic, cultural and social capital is a key factor. It is to this development that we now turn.

For the fourteenth century it has been established that at least a quarter of the aldermen of Delft belonged to noble families from the surrounding countryside. These were often younger sons of noble lords who settled permanently in the city and earned an income in trade or in positions such as councillor.[28] Of course, they found a suitable place to live mainly along the two main canals of Oude Delft and Nieuwe Delft. These canals also became the location for what, from the second half of the fourteenth century, would become the dominant industry in Delft for a long time: beer brewery.[29] By the sixteenth century the city had become the most important brewing

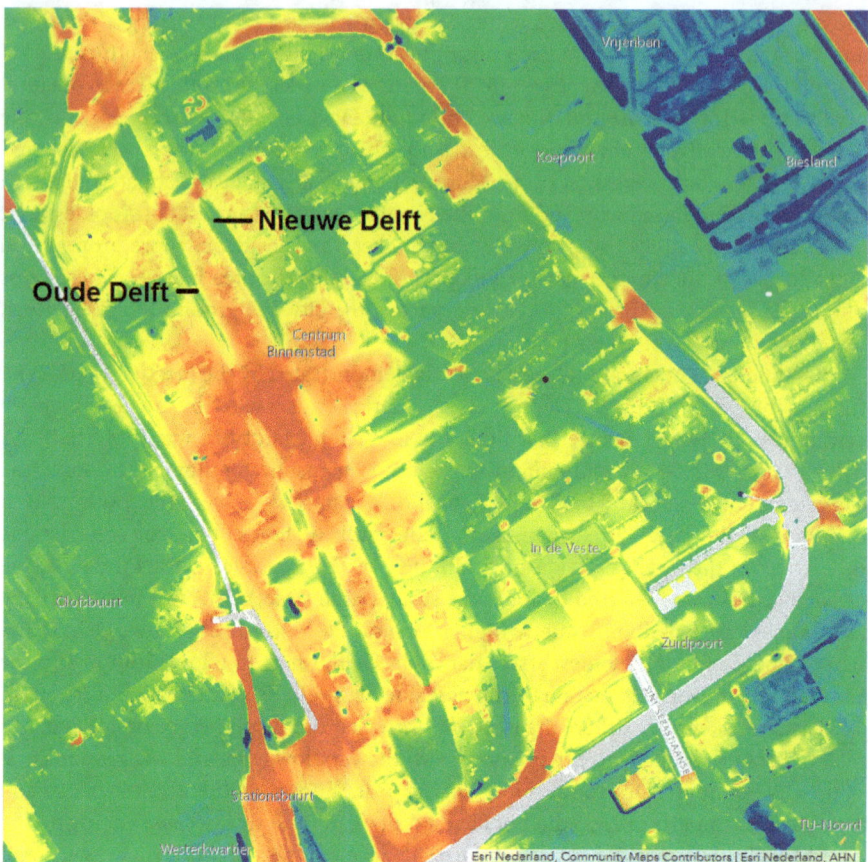

Map 3.2 Current ground level in Delft.

centre in Holland, far outstripping competitors such as Haarlem and Gouda. In the second half of that century production reached its peak. In 1571, for example, no less than 1.1 million hectolitres of beer were brewed in Delft.[30] In 1600, when the industry had already experienced some decline, Delft had eighty-two breweries. Of these, no less than twenty-four were situated on Oude Delft and Noordeinde, and forty-three on Koornmarkt, Voorstraat and Kolk.[31]

The striking presence of breweries along the most prestigious canals partly had to do with the size and location of the plots along these canals. In Delft, brewing was almost always done in premises at the back of the brewer's house. This combination of living and working demanded, certainly for the large-scale beer production practised in Delft, plots of considerable size, situated by clean water, with good accessibility by water for the supply of raw materials (grain, hops) and fuel (peat), and for transport of the end product. The two main canals of Oude Delft and Nieuwe Delft fulfilled these location requirements.[32]

But of course, location requirements are not the only explanation for the fact that for centuries, brewers were able to appropriate space along Delft's most prestigious canals. Of great importance were also the resources at their disposal. In Delft, wealthy brewers belonged to the urban elites and in time they even acquired a dominant position in the city government.[33] This gave them considerable influence on urban policies regarding the location of industries. They used this influence to keep other industries as much as possible away from the main canals and to concentrate these in the eastern half of the city. In doing so, concern about the quality of the water in the main canals, which was used for brewing beer, undoubtedly played a part in this, but also the preservation of the status and prestige of Oude Delft and Nieuwe Delft, for these remained the most desirable residential locations for Delft's elites. The attraction of these main canals was so strong that even after the great city fire of 1536, which reduced almost the entire west side of the city to ashes, the residences of the wealthy elites once again sprang up along the main canals of Oude Delft and Nieuwe Delft, and the brewers among them carried on their business as usual in outbuildings in the backyard.

The dominant presence of breweries along the main canals in the western part of the city only came to an end with the decline of Delft's brewing industry from the end of the sixteenth century. As a result, the main canals changed over time from a busy production area to a quiet and distinguished residential area, housing well-to-do people living of their interest and members of the liberal professions. The quality of this area was monitored by by-laws and industrial activities were no longer tolerated there. At the end of the eighteenth century, for example, it was forbidden to establish brandy distilleries on Oude Delft, Hippolytusbuurt, Voorstraat and Markt, because of the danger of fire and because of the nuisance that the supply of grain and peat would cause in the peaceful canals.[34]

Despite the city's precarious financial situation at the end of the eighteenth century, the well-to-do elites, including, of course, city councillors, managed to persuade the urban government to make costly investments in the quality of their home environment along the prominent canals. Public buildings were refurbished, quay walls repaired, street lighting installed and the pavement maintained by the city.[35] In contrast, the voices of those with fewer economic, cultural and social resources and therefore less access to the city government were not heard. The poorest among them had to content themselves with a residential environment that had been badly deteriorated during the economic downturn and was hardly improved at all, since the scarce financial resources deployed on the main canals were no longer available for improving the situation elsewhere in the city.

The areas that in 1268, 1347 and 1355 were granted the same rights as those granted to the inhabitants of the oldest core in 1246 can be considered city extensions. The eastern side of the city was part of the extension of 1355 and was undoubtedly sparsely built up and thinly populated at the time. So vast was this city extension that until well into the nineteenth century, the area offered sufficient space to accommodate the population of Delft. Because of the space available, it is not surprising that the city government allocated this area to industries (other than the brewing industry) that could better not be located in the more densely populated western half of the city because of noise, stench, pollution and other nuisances.[36] But the trend was set and was confirmed and strengthened by the policies of governments and institutions, and the location decisions of private entrepreneurs. They had resources at their disposal and used them to exert power and thus organize urban space according to their wishes.

In the oldest surviving collection of by-laws (*keurboek*), which dates from the beginning of the fifteenth century, but obviously also contains by-laws from older dates, it was already stipulated that (cloth) dyeing could only be done in the eastern part of the city. And that also applied to the – very polluting – tanneries.[37] In a *keurboek* from the second half of the fifteenth century, the city government decreed that cattle could only be slaughtered at three locations in the city. Two of these were in the eastern half of the city and the third at the city moat in the extreme north-west corner of the city.[38] And the Delft cattle markets, which were traditionally held on Markt square and from the fourteenth century onwards also on the west side of Oude Delft in the western part of the city, were from the middle of the sixteenth century moved to the east side of Verwersdijk in the eastern half of the city. After that they were moved several times more, but the eastern part of the city always became the location.[39] And while the oldest surviving by-laws on brothels only stipulated that no fire or light was allowed to be kept on at night, around 1500 it was decreed that 'all women, who openly sit for money and receive men; or who want to keep similar places [brothels, C.L.]', were henceforth only allowed to do so in Donkerstraat, Hopstraat and Harmenkokslaan, all located in the eastern periphery of the city. There, 'and nowhere else', was added for the sake of clarity.[40] It will not come as a surprise now that the *stille petten*, the city garbage dump, was located in the south-east quadrant of the city. During the severe plague epidemic of 1557, the bedstraw from the houses of plague-stricken inhabitants of Delft had to be taken there to be burnt.[41] Towards the end of the sixteenth century, the Plague Hospice (Pesthuis) was established on Verwersdijk, also in the eastern part of the city, and in 1664, this district became the location of the newly established house of correction, which accommodated more than 100 inmates.[42]

When the traditionally flourishing brewing industry came under pressure towards the end of the sixteenth century and the Delft urban government attempted to stimulate the textile industry, it tried to attract migrants from the Southern Low Countries. They were offered free rights of entry and a starting subsidy. Housing was provided by building a textile workers' quarter in the south-east of the city. The streets laid out on the site of the former St. Ursula convent bore the appropriate names of Brugschestraat, Yperstraat, Rijsselstraat and Doornickstraat.[43] The location of this housing project in the eastern half of the city confirmed the low status of this part of the city and the contrast with the western half, where on vacant convent grounds building plots were also available. More than half a century later, when economic growth increased the size of the population and pressure on the housing market, a second planned residential area arose in the north-east of the city, with three new streets and also intended to house workers in the textile industry.[44] This new district was in fact built in the immediate vicinity of the Kruithuis located in the eastern half of the city (!), where the States of Holland had stored some 80,000 pounds of gunpowder.[45] On 12 October 1654, things went terribly wrong. With what became known as the 'Delffsche Donderslagh' the powder house exploded. It is said that the blast could be heard as far away as Texel, more than 100 kilometres north of Delft. Be that as it may, 200 houses in the area of the disaster site were completely wiped out and of hundreds of others the walls were damaged and the roofs blown off. Hundreds of people in the north-eastern part of the city must have found an untimely death. Among them were undoubtedly many residents of the new housing estate, which had been completed less than a decade before.

The potters traditionally lived and worked in the poor south-east of the city. They produced the same glazed red earthenware products as their colleagues in other cities. From the middle of the sixteenth century, Flemish potters also settled in Holland.[46] They mastered the Italian technique of colourfully painted earthenware or majolica. In Holland, it was known as *plateel*. From Haarlem, the technique also became known in Delft, where the number of *plateel* factories expanded rapidly from three in 1600 to eight in 1620. The great expansion took place when in the 1640s the import of Chinese porcelain was disrupted and the Delft potters started to apply themselves very successfully to the production of earthenware which in shape and colour was very similar to the Chinese porcelain introduced to Holland by the VOC in the first half of the century. In the 1660s, the city counted twenty-six potteries, producing millions of pieces of delftware. Research has shown that the seventeenth-century delftware industry was located almost exclusively in the south-eastern part of Delft.[47] This finding is in line with what has been argued earlier: the character of the eastern half of the city as a location for industries and activities that were deemed a nuisance, and as a place to house the working classes, was continuously reinforced by the policies of the local government and institutions and by the location decisions of private entrepreneurs.

The foregoing shows that from the earliest history of the city, those in Delft with many resources were able to appropriate the most attractive residential and business environment and to secure its desired quality. This applies to the sons of noble lords from the surrounding countryside, well-to-do brewers and, after the decline of the brewing industry, well-to-do people living off their interests and members of the liberal professions. They did not only have financial means at their disposal (economic capital) but also contacts (social capital) that enabled them to influence the urban policy and the policy of important urban institutions. Sometimes, as councillors and regents, they even directly shaped that policy. And if their social network did not include city councillors, the possession of the right social skills (cultural capital) ensured that their wishes were heard by those who mattered in city politics. Throughout all those centuries, the elites thus had resources at their disposal that enabled them to impose their will upon society and cause an effect they desired, a typical example of what Allen calls 'instrumental power' and also a typical example of power in the manifestations of domination, coercion and authority.

Of course, in the field of housing, not only those with many resources competed for the most attractive locations. Social classes with fewer resources or a less suitable combination of resources also did so, but their options were more limited. For those who had to make do with virtually no resources, the least attractive locations remained in dwellings in the inner courtyards of Delft and on the city outskirts, especially in the low lying and polluted eastern part of the city. Although there was no lack of compassion for their plight, the condition of the working classes, including many poor people, did not prompt any action in the areas of housing and the living environment until well into the nineteenth century.

The question that now needs to be answered is whether similar processes of resource-based power and appropriation played a role in residential differentiation at the macro-level in the other cities and whether the physical-geographical environment also influenced socio-spatial patterns there.

The short answer to the latter question is: yes. In an area where the quality of living coincided to a large extent with the distance to groundwater, the level of elevation was an important factor in the distinction between attractive and less attractive locations. This is particularly clear in The Hague, where the first houses were built on the higher ground of an old sandbank (*strandwal*), with extensive peatlands to the north and south.[48] As Map 3.3 clearly shows, the previously established spatial distribution of inhabitants according to socio-economic position and the elevation of the ground level coincide to a large extent. The well-to-do generally lived on high ground (on the sand) and close to the court, and those with less or much less financial means generally lived on low ground (on the peatlands).[49] And it was also there, along an access road on the low grounds south-east of the city, that the leper house was located in the Middle Ages. Because of the danger of infection and also because of the biblical designation of lepers as unclean, lepers in Holland (and elsewhere) were assigned a place outside the community.[50]

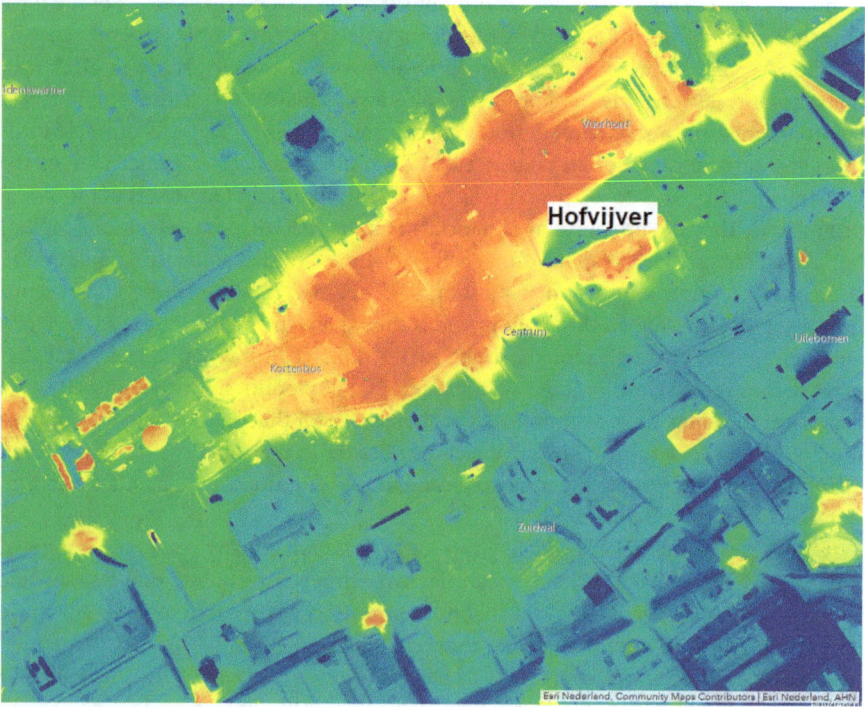

Map 3.3 Current ground level in The Hague.

In Alkmaar, there was a clear difference between the relatively high sandy soils in the west of the city and the low-lying eastern part of the city, which was built on reclaimed land in lake Voormeer. The main church (Grote Kerk), in the west of the city, even stands on a high sand dune. As the current elevation map clearly shows, this is still the highest point in the city centre (Map 3.4).[51] Not coincidentally, it is also the place where the oldest settlement developed. In addition to the area around the Grote Kerk, another urban core developed around the middle of the thirteenth century just west of Mient, and Langestraat started to function as a connection between both cores.[52] As the settlement grew, the higher grounds (and raised grounds) became the residential domain of the wealthy elites in Alkmaar as well. The band of expensive housing identified in Chapter 2, which stretched from the Grote Kerk in the west of the city, via Langestraat to Mient and then in a northerly direction to the Weigh house (Waag), can therefore easily be recognized in the current elevation map. Large parts of the less prestigious and low lying east side of the city were given an industrial function during the various city extensions.[53] This confirmed and perpetuated the status of the western half of the city and more specifically of the residential environment along the affluent streets and canals.

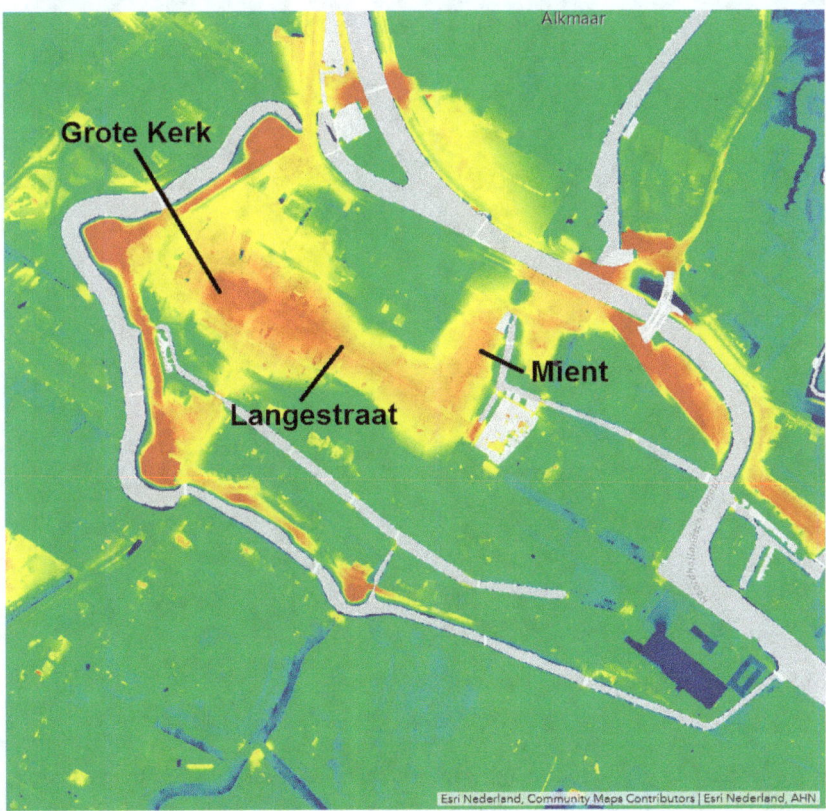

Map 3.4 Current ground level in Alkmaar.

While the differences in the level of elevation within The Hague and Alkmaar were partly based on the natural condition of the terrain, the image on the elevation maps presented here is of course also influenced by human activities.[54] It is precisely the oldest parts of the cities that have been raised most frequently, thus making the contrast with the newer parts of the cities even greater than it might have been on the basis of natural conditions alone. This was already apparent in the discussion of the situation in Delft and is clearly also the case in Leiden. Map 3.5 shows the current elevation map of Leiden. The man-made hill where the Burght was built in the first half of the twelfth century, stands out clearly from the surroundings. The physical environment was of some importance here because in this swampy area the ground level of the 'island' between the two river arms had risen by accretion in the course of time. It was and still is therefore known as Hoogland (High land). The high level of the equally prosperous Breestraat was mainly the work of human hands. In the twelfth century, this dyke along the south bank of the Rhine was raised significantly.[55] This created a situation in Leiden that was the basis for a longstanding pattern of macro-differentiation and residential appropriation by wealthy Leiden citizens.

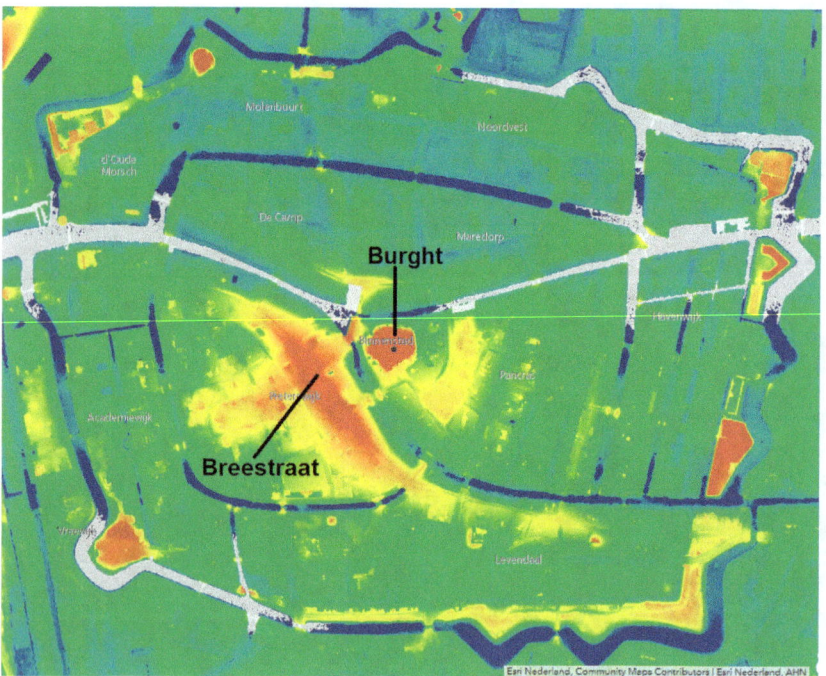

Map 3.5 Current ground level in Leiden.

At the beginning of the fourteenth century, there were already a number of stone houses on Breestraat, an unmistakable sign of wealth. The status of Breestraat was further enhanced when the town hall was built there in the first half of the fourteenth century. Right behind it, on the banks of the Rhine, stood the Wanthuis, where the

Leiden cloth, source of the fortune of part of the urban upper class, was inspected and traded. And on the west side of Breestraat, on the higher grounds near the Pieterskerk, in the Middle Ages was the count's court (grafelijk hof), a fortified house like those owned by the counts of Holland in other cities.[56] Polluting industries were preferably moved to the outskirts of the city, the residence of those of limited means. This pattern is very clear in the plans for urban extension drawn up from the end of the sixteenth century onwards.[57] In a report written by City Secretary Jan van Hout in 1591, it was suggested that serious polluters like the tanneries should be moved to the northern part of the city, where other polluting industries could then also be concentrated. It was also in this northern periphery, on the grounds of the former Nazareth monastery and leper house, that the city developed a housing project of sixty-three back-to-back weaver houses in the 1590s. Due to the very narrow allotment, the large number of residents and the poor hygienic conditions, this soon became a notorious slum known as the *Mierennest* (Ants' Nest).[58]

In later urban extensions, the northern periphery again became the preferred location for highly polluting industries and housing for the poorest sections of the Leiden population.[59] The low status of the city outskirts is clearly demonstrated in the plans that were made for further densification of these already densely built-up parts of the city, which, according to the city government, would not detract from the appearance of the (inner) city.[60] One of the intended aims was to protect the inner city from poor housing and to prevent the demolition of substantial houses there, and their replacement with cheap accommodation in *poortjens*.[61] In this way, those with ample economic, cultural and social resources secured the quality of their residential environment in the city centre and kept polluting industries and the less well-off inhabitants of Leiden at a distance.

Edam, as the name suggests, is one of the dam towns in the peatlands of Holland. Of course, the dam only came into being when the surrounding area – the Zeevang – was protected from the encroaching seawater by a ring dyke in the second half of the thirteenth century.[62] In the preceding period, the land in the Zeevang had been reclaimed and made suitable for habitation and agricultural activities. In that peat area, which had not yet been dyked in, a small settlement had come into being along the west bank of the river Ye, at the location of the later Edam, probably around 1200. The choice of this particular location – far from the mouth of the river Ye – is not easy to reconstruct, but possibly the ground level was slightly higher than in the surrounding area, and the Lake Purmer was nearby.

The inhabitants must have fed themselves with a combination of livestock farming, arable farming and fishing on the inland waters. They lived on a mound (present Lingerzijde) which also housed a small church, a predecessor of the Onze Lieve Vrouwekapel (now Speeltoren). The oldest core of Edam can therefore be found in the western part of the city, that is in the area of the current Lingerzijde, Spui and Bult.[63] In 1357 Edam was granted city rights and permission to dig a harbour that would create an open connection between Lake Purmer and the Zuiderzee at the Oorgat. This harbour – Voorhaven – was dug along a previously constructed ring dyke and the excavated soil was used to construct a dyke on the south side of this harbour as well. The ground level was also raised along the later Grote Kerkstraat, and it was in this northern direction that the still small settlement in the second half of the fourteenth century mainly expanded. Only in the fifteenth century did the built-up area advance in an easterly direction along Voorhaven.

In those years, the main urban structure of Edam consisted of the oldest core of the settlement around the Onze Lieve Vrouwenkapel and Spui, and the offshoots to the north and east. The oldest core had been greatly raised in the course of time and, of course, the dyke streets to the north and east were also considerably above ground level.[64] As the current elevation map clearly shows (Map 3.6), this is still the case after many hundreds of years. Obviously, these high-lying parts of the city were the most attractive for habitation. In addition, the properties in this part of the city had direct access to water, which made them extremely suitable for trading purposes.

And indeed, from time immemorial, Spui in particular, situated on the old harbour basin, was the favourite haunt of Edam's prosperous merchant class.[65] The less well-off and the poor had to make do with the lower-lying and less easily accessible locations at the edges of the built-up area. As a result, the urban periphery took on a completely different character than the higher-lying parts in the city centre.[66] After Edam at the beginning of the sixteenth century was granted the right to build city walls and gates, especially the eastern outlying area along the Oorgat (see Map 2.2 in Chapter 2) developed into a refuge for the poorest people (citizens and non-citizens) who lived there in shabby shelters.[67] In 1569, the average tax assessment in the *schotgeld* tax in the outlying area east of the city was 61 per cent below the city average. The assessment of the *100^e penning* from the same year shows that outside the other city gates too, concentrations of poor people had come into being.[68] Their location at the edges of and outside the city was the spatial expression

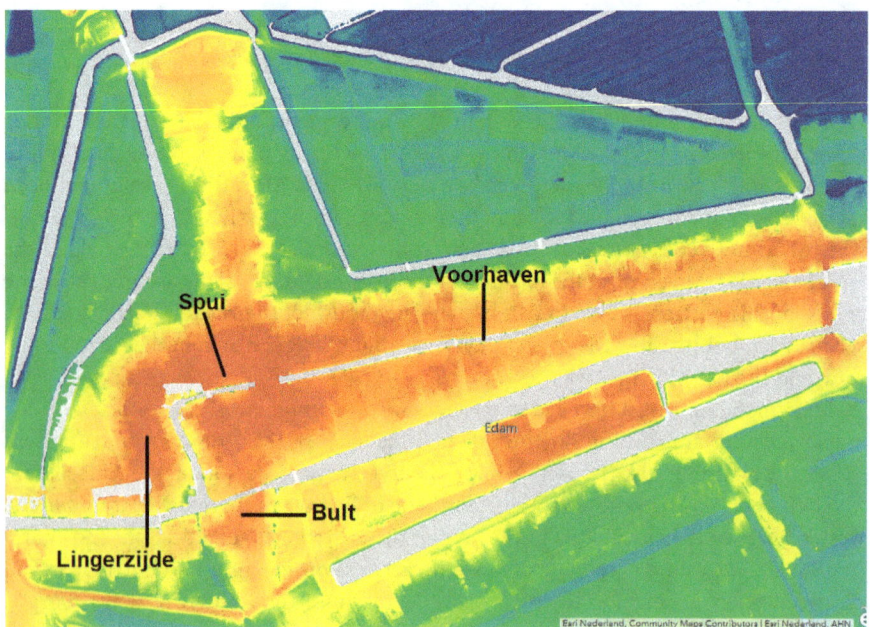

Map 3.6 Current ground level in Edam.

of their marginal position in society. This marginality is also evidenced by the fact that they were simply chased away by the urban militia when the authorities felt that the nuisance caused by this group was becoming too great.[69]

Once this pattern of macro-differentiation was established, zoning by the urban government and location decisions by private individuals reinforced and perpetuated the contrast. Sometimes these location decisions were based on neutral considerations. In the western part of the city, on Schepenmakersdijk and Lingerzijde, many shipyards were established in the Middle Ages, but these locations were not ideal.[70] In order to reach the Zuiderzee, ships had to be towed through the entire city and pass numerous bridges. When, in the course of the sixteenth century, ships and shipyards became larger, relocation to Tuindijk outside the eastern city gates was an obvious choice.[71] And the proximity of the sea and the prevailing wind direction also made the eastern outskirts the obvious location for salt works and, in the seventeenth century, for (whale oil) try-houses.[72] But the establishment of tanneries and the public dump in the southern periphery near the Gevangenpoort confirmed and reinforced the low status of the urban periphery and its inhabitants.[73] Nor was it a coincidence that in 1598 the city council decided to use the city gate in the south-eastern periphery (Zuidoosterpoort) as a house of correction for those who, for whatever reason, were considered a nuisance or threat to society. They were described as 'rebels, unruly ones and wantonly lazy vagabonds'.[74]

That the increasing concentration of poor people in the eastern periphery was no coincidence, but the result of a deliberate policy of the authorities, was clearly demonstrated at the end of the sixteenth century. In connection with the war between the princely and Spanish armies, Diederick Sonoy, appointed governor of the Noorderkwartier (part of Holland north of the IJ-waterway) by William of Orange, insisted on a free field of fire and therefore the demolition of the buildings outside the city gates. Edam complied with this request by demolishing houses on the west and north side of the city, but the much larger number of houses outside the eastern city gates remained untouched. And this despite the fact that the military threat was at its greatest there. This choice by the city authorities not only indicates a lack of affinity with the fate of the residents of this area in the event of a military attack but the selective demolition was also used to solve the 'pauper problem' on the western edge of the city and to concentrate the poor in the outlying area east of the city.[75] The unequal distribution of economic, cultural and social resources, and the exercise of power in the forms of domination and coercion, are very much in evidence here.

Amsterdam lies in a peat bog that was reclaimed in the course of the eleventh and twelfth centuries, but because of flooding at the Amstel estuary, the territory of the later city was not an attractive location for habitation and agriculture.[76] This changed in the last quarter of the twelfth century when drastic changes took place in the geography of the area. A series of storm tides, of which the Allerheiligen flood of 1170 probably had the most influence, gave the Almere near Wieringen an open connection to the Wadden Sea and North Sea, and the IJ, until then a small peat river, became a large inlet that connected to what had formerly been the Almere and now became the Zuiderzee (present IJsselmeer). These hydraulic changes improved the drainage in the Amstel estuary area, making habitation possible and also attractive. The latter especially so because from the Amstel estuary shipping connections became possible with the IJssel cities on the east flank of the Zuiderzee, with more distant areas via the Wadden Sea and North Sea, and with an extensive hinterland that could be reached via inland waterways.

The oldest residential nuclei that arose in Amsterdam at that time were probably washed away by new storm tides in the first decades of the thirteenth century, but around 1225 new residential nuclei arose on the west side of the river Amstel (present Nieuwendijk). People profited from the presence of a river bank that was used as a base on which (individual) mounds were erected. Jayasena speaks of a ribbon of mounds.[77] In the course of time, the number of mounds and the size of the mounds increased, eventually creating an unbroken dyke with houses. On the other side of the river Amstel, things went very differently. There, around 1250, an elongated dyke consisting of sods of clay and peat was constructed in a single large-scale operation. Unlike on the west side, the plots here were placed directly in line, and the boundaries drawn at that time still form the basic structure of the allotment along Warmoesstraat today. In the third quarter of the thirteenth century, the two dykes were connected by a dam in the river Amstel and Amsterdam acquired an urban structure that is still clearly recognizable today.

If we ignore the extensive elevations of the nineteenth and twentieth centuries on the IJ-front and in the eastern part of the city, the high-lying river dykes of Warmoesstraat and Nieuwendijk, and Dam square as connecting link, stand out clearly against the surrounding urban ground level (Map 3.7). And it is no coincidence that until the first half of the seventeenth century, these streets were also the favoured residential domain for those who could afford to live and work there. The relatively high location in the low-lying and wet peat area certainly played a role, but also the favourable location in the vicinity of Amsterdam's inner harbour (Damrak) and outer harbour in the IJ. Especially Warmoesstraat was and remained for a long time Amsterdam's most prestigious street and home to a considerable number of wealthy merchants and political rulers.[78]

IJsselstijn and Rutte point out that in the Middle Ages, conscious separation of functions hardly occurred in Dutch cities.[79] This seems to be true for medieval Amsterdam as well, but nevertheless a remarkable change in the occupational composition of Warmoesstraat's residents can be observed. In the fourteenth century the street still had at least one tanner, and in the fifteenth century at least one blacksmith and several coopers. By the sixteenth century, these trades, which caused nuisance and fire hazard, had disappeared from the street, and more generally, craftsmen were supplanted by merchants. They had more resources at their disposal and used them to appropriate the prestigious Warmoesstraat.[80] And while the status of the residential environment on Warmoesstraat rose, elsewhere it fell correspondingly.[81] The industry that produced the most stench and pollution was tanning, and it is no coincidence that in the sixteenth century this industry was concentrated at the far eastern edge of the city, where the less well-off part of the Amsterdam population found shelter and where people with resources to prevent its presence were absent.[82] Other nuisance and

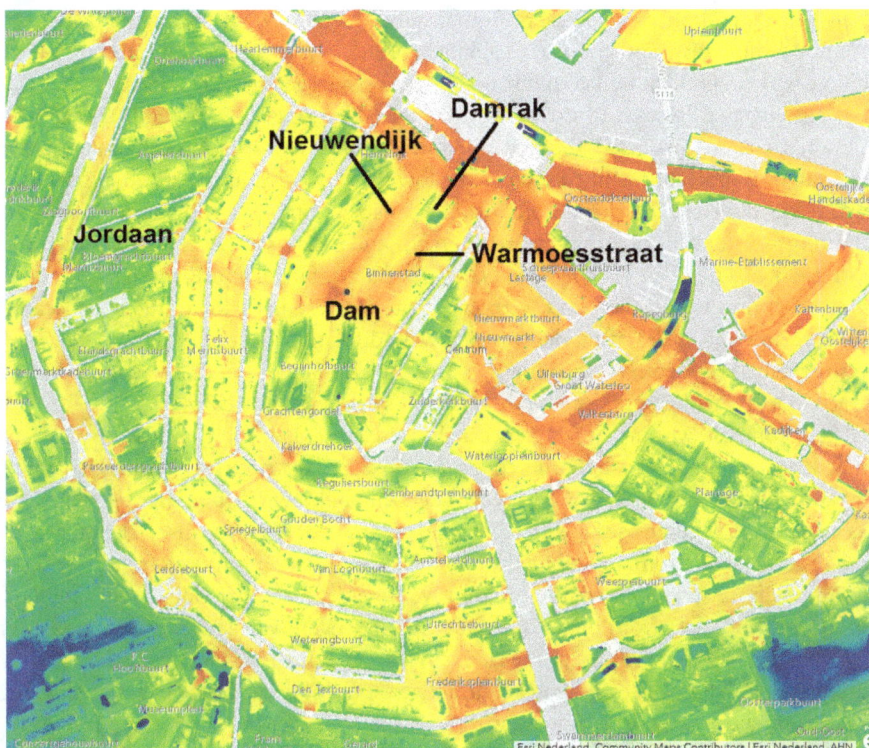

Map 3.7 Current ground level in Amsterdam.

stench-producing industries were to be found at the extreme southern edge of the city, also far from the more prestigious locations around the inner harbour of Damrak.[83]

From the end of the sixteenth century, the substantial increase in the population and the need for industrial areas and port facilities, as well as the limited territory within the city walls, necessitated a series of city extensions. In this period of spatial expansion, the urban periphery remained the residential domain of those with few economic, cultural and social resources and new luxury streets and later new luxury neighbourhoods were designed and built for those who did have ample resources at their disposal. The first initiatives in this direction took place during the so-called First Extension of the years 1585-6. From the existing gates Sint Antoniespoort, Regulierspoort and Haarlemmerpoort three relatively spacious streets were constructed in the extension area: Sint Antoniesbreestraat, Reguliersbreestraat and Haarlemmer(bree)straat. These streets were intended for residential use by wealthy people who could not or would not find suitable housing in the busy inner city.[84] The quality of the living environment along the new streets was guarded by the provision that trades that caused nuisance were not allowed to settle there.[85] Nevertheless, Haarlemmer(bree)straat and Reguliersbreestraat soon lost their appeal to the well-to-do, as nearby Singel, the former city moat, also became available for prestigious housing. Large houses arose there, some on double lots, whose residents benefitted from spacious views and good accessibility by water. The latter was not unimportant at a time when merchant houses often also served as storage for trade goods.

Building for the well-to-do on a wide canal like Singel set a trend. During the Third Extension (1610–13), the idea of luxurious houses on spacious canals and in the vicinity of important facilities such as the town hall, New Church, and the Exchange was realized on a much larger scale with the construction of the ring of canals. Within the ring of canals, it was mainly Herengracht and Keizersgracht that were intended as residential areas for the wealthy. The outer canals, Singel and Prinsengracht, both directly connected to the outer harbour of the IJ, were used for traffic and became the location of a series of markets, which were difficult to reconcile with a quiet and distinguished residential environment.[86] This brought Singel and Prinsengracht within reach of those with fewer resources than Amsterdam's wealthy elites.

The contrast within the ring of canals was expressed, for example, in the fact that Prinsengracht, which bordered on the Jordaan district, was initially spanned by wooden bridges and also had a wooden embankment, while Herengracht and Keizersgracht were provided with stone bridges and stone quay walls.[87] The quality of the residential environment along the two main canals was monitored from the outset by imposing restrictions on the building volume. These restrictions were intended to prevent the plots from being overbuilt, possibly even with less attractive housing, which would leave no room for the large city gardens that the city government had in mind and which were considered an attractive aspect of living along Herengracht and Keizersgracht. And indeed, houses with a spacious view of the canal and a tree-lined quay at the front, and a view of beautiful city gardens at the back, were hardly to be found in the old city centre.

As far as the prevention of nuisance-causing activities was concerned, the restrictions that had already been formulated for well-to-do streets in the First Extension were followed: businesses where hammer and anvil were used were not allowed. This opened the door to a range of other industries, but the city government was reluctant to impose restrictions on potential buyers out of well-understood financial self-interest. The fact that crafts and industries virtually disappeared from Herengracht and Keizersgracht in the somewhat longer term was therefore mainly a result of the agency of the (prospective) residents. They used their economic, cultural and social capital to bring the quality of their residential environment up to the desired level and keep it there. Sometimes they did this by buying a commercial building, having it demolished and replacing it with a house that fitted in with the prestigious surroundings. Sometimes they also did this by collectively urging the city council to enforce laws and regulations. In 1618, for example, residents of blocks of houses between Herengracht and Keizersgracht asked for a ban on soap-making and other 'unneighbourly and dangerous trades'.[88] In terms of the exercise of power, this is a typical example of what Arendt calls 'act in concert' and Allen 'associational power'. During the Fourth Extension of 1662–3, the city council formulated strict rules from the outset, which were intended to protect the prestigious residential canals from all industrial activities that would lead to noise, stench and water pollution, or that would disfigure the beautiful row of façades with deviating buildings. But even then, some people found loopholes in the regulations, and again it was the residents of the adjoining houses themselves who collectively sounded the alarm to the city authorities.[89]

The appropriation of a luxury residential area by wealthy Amsterdam residents, who used their material and immaterial resources to optimize the quality of their residential environment, was not without consequences for residents elsewhere in the city and in the area immediately outside the city walls. After all, the noisy, incendiary, smelly, polluting and health-impairing activities had to find a place somewhere, and that place was not on Herengracht or Keizersgracht. In fact, during the course of the seventeenth century, the requirements for establishing industries in the old city centre also tightened.[90] The result was increasing pressure on the urban periphery, and that was where the crowded Jordaan was located. This neighbourhood was part of the Third Extension and was specifically intended to accommodate industries that were not allowed elsewhere. The financial and organizational problems that the city government faced during the Third Extension are reflected in its level of elevation and street pattern. In the Jordaan the building lots were only raised to a limited extent. Even a modern elevation map (Map 3.7) still shows a significant contrast in ground level between the ring of canals and the Jordaan district. The low ground level also explains why the countless people living in cellars in the Jordaan were regularly plagued by flooding of their homes. The street pattern reveals that during the Third Extension in the area of the later Jordaan, there had been no expropriation of the building land and redevelopment of the entire area either. In fact, the existing pattern of pre-urban paths and ditches was simply adapted to the new urban environment.

Although differentiation existed within the Jordaan between relatively affluent canals such as Rozengracht and Bloemgracht on the one hand, and the poorer northern and southern periphery on the other, no restrictions were placed on crafts and industrial activities of any kind throughout the district. The urban authorities intervened only when different activities were incompatible and the economic functioning of industries was compromised.[91] Nuisance, fire hazard, heavy pollution and danger to the health of the Jordaan residents were not grounds for intervention. A similar lack of attention to the residential environment also existed for the area immediately outside the city walls, as well as for peripheral areas that were developed during the Fourth Extension in the second half of the seventeenth century.

The very substantial city extensions of Amsterdam do not alter the fact that at the macro-level that is the focus of this section, there was also some continuity with the past since the urban periphery was and remained a zone of nuisance-causing or downright dangerous activities. With each city extension this zone of negative externalities shifted to the new periphery, and each time, this new periphery was also the residential area of city dwellers who, due to a lack of economic, cultural and social resources, were unable to settle elsewhere or to persuade the urban authorities to do something about the situation. In a later chapter, however, we shall see that they were not completely invisible and silenced. Those in Holland's cities with few resources were also able to appropriate urban space, if only temporarily.

3.2.2. Residential appropriation of urban space: Meso-level

However prominent the socio-spatial differences between city districts sometimes were, the residential patterns in Holland's cities showed greater variation than just at the macro-level. At the macro-level of urban districts, those with ample resources and the willingness to use them were able to appropriate the most attractive locations, but at the same time, residential mixing at the level of streets occurred throughout the period under study. In the foregoing, we observed that different social classes almost always and everywhere lived around the corner from each other, with the well-to-do elites living along the main streets and canals, the middle classes and part of the working classes in side streets and back streets and along main canals and streets in the less well-to-do parts of the city, and the poor among the working classes in the urban periphery (*intra muros* and *extra muros*) and also in the inner courtyards in the more centrally located parts of the city.[92] The fact that this form of differentiation at the level of streets survived in a world in which – as we shall see – those with resources and the associated potential for exercising power had a clear preference for a socially homogeneous residential environment suggests that meso-differentiation was rooted in permanent structures. And indeed, differentiation at the level of streets was linked to two of the basic elements of the urban landscape in the cities of Holland: street plan and closed blocks of houses.[93]

During the early stages of urban development, these closed blocks were usually not consciously planned and developed.[94] They came about in phases along the linear structures of the street plan, which in Holland's cities was shaped to a considerable extent by the requirements of the physical-geographical environment and water management. As soon as this network of streets and canals reached a certain size, differentiation took place and a hierarchy emerged within the network.[95] In the following, it will become clear that the status of the houses along streets and canals depended to a substantial degree on the hierarchical position of those streets and canals within the network. For this study, it is important to note that this hierarchical ordering of the street network contributed to shaping the residential patterns within the city. After all, while the well-to-do were able to appropriate prestigious residences along the major streets and canals, and retailers occupied the attractive locations for their businesses along thoroughfares and market squares, others had to make do with accommodation in less prominent parts of the street plan.[96]

Analytically, a distinction can be made between primary, secondary and tertiary structures within the street network.[97] The primary structure consists of the 'carriers' of the network, that is the most important connecting and access routes for the city as a whole. These were usually the streets and canals along which the earliest houses were built. The secondary structure is formed by the most important connecting and access routes at the level of city districts and neighbourhoods. As a rule, they open up a series of blocks and are usually linked to the primary structure. The tertiary structure generally provides access to no more than one or two blocks. In the first case, it involves alleys and blind alleys providing access to walled-in houses in inner courtyards; in the second case, it involves a lane that separates two blocks of houses. The tertiary structure often provides access to blocks located between secondary streets, but sometimes it also connects to the primary structure. The hierarchy within the street network is also expressed in the built-up environment. On the primary structure, the streets are generally the broadest, the plots the largest and the buildings the highest. The tertiary structure consists of narrow to very narrow streets, with small plots and buildings of limited height. The secondary structure falls between these extremes in terms of street width, plot size and building height.[98]

Block formation took place from the primary structure. Four processes played a role in this: the joining together of houses along the primary streets and canals to form a street front; the longitudinal division of the existing and generally large plots; the separation of rear yards; and the filling in of the inner courtyard. During the earliest phases of town formation, houses still bore a close resemblance to those in the surrounding countryside.[99] As far as can be ascertained from archaeological excavations, these were often detached buildings on relatively large plots of land. In line with the reclamation structure, in Holland these plots were narrow and deep, with the short side oriented towards the primary structure. In the course of time, the houses on the plots joined together to form a closed front along the primary structure. By that time, the wider plots had often already been split and brick was used on a modest scale in the foundations and possibly also in the lower part of the façade. For Sarfatij, in the Netherlands this use of brick marks the transition from a pre-urban and semi-agricultural settlement to a truly urban one.[100] Continuing population growth and increasing pressure on the existing housing stock led to a further reduction in scale, not only through the longitudinal division of plots (*smaldelen*) but also by splitting off the rear yards on the still deep plots. These now independent rear yards could be built up with commercial buildings, storage spaces or houses, but, of course, they needed their own access in the form of a rear street, which in turn was connected to the primary infrastructure by a side street.[101] In this way the block, a continuous series of plots accessed by four streets, came about.[102] This does not mean, however, that all faces of the block were always entirely built up. Along the primary structure they usually were, but in the side streets and rear streets, depending on the pressure on the existing housing stock, this could still take a considerable time. If that pressure was great and the faces of the block were fully built up, then additional construction could took place in the inner courtyard, accessed by the tertiary structure of alleys and blind alleys.[103]

The processes of block formation described earlier can be well substantiated and illustrated using the cases of Delft, Amsterdam and Edam.[104] The oldest city map of Delft, for instance, offers some clues to the course of block formation. It concerns a painting of what remained of the city shortly after the devastating city fire of 1536. For a long time, it was assumed that this painting was a seventeenth-century copy of a lost original, but it has now been established that the painting is indeed the original.[105] The painting shows that about two-thirds of the city was reduced to ashes by the fire. What interests us here is the remaining third. Due to its large size, the painting gives a good impression of this. It is true that the houses are depicted slightly larger than is in accordance with the scale of the map, and therefore fewer houses are shown per street than were actually there, but this disadvantage has the advantage that the houses could be depicted in considerable

Map 3.8 Delft: Oosteinde and adjacent houses, 1536 (north right).

detail. And where it could be verified, it appears that the unknown painter did this true to life. [106]

Because of the fact that of the primary structure, important routes that span the entire city, Oude Delft and Nieuwe Delft were completely destroyed except for a few houses, we will focus our attention on the third main axis: Oosteinde. It was located in the south-east corner of the city, which was spared by the fire. Oosteinde itself indeed shows a continuous building pattern, but this is not true for all streets that connect Oosteinde with the city wall in the east and the water of Brabantse Turfmarkt (not shown) in the west (Map 3.8). And along the city wall, which can be considered a back street, building is even more scarce. The explanation for these 'unfinished' blocks is, of course, the low population pressure in Delft, which in 1355 reached a size that would prove sufficient for five centuries. What is particularly important here is the observation that the houses in the 1355 extension area confirm the scenario of block formation outlined earlier. In this part of Delft, too, the development of blocks of houses had started from the primary structure and the street network was clearly hierarchical.

The city fire did not result in a large-scale redevelopment of the burnt western part of the city. The owners built new houses on their now empty plots that were in keeping with the function and status of their former accommodations, and that status was closely linked to the location of the plots on the primary, secondary or tertiary structure of canals, streets and alleys. The socio-spatial structure of the city before the fire was thus reproduced and would remain virtually unchanged for centuries.

In Amsterdam, the process of block formation was very similar. The oldest houses were found on the river dykes on both sides of the river Amstel: the primary structure of Warmoesstraat and Nieuwendijk. From the second half of the fourteenth century, the low-lying and marshy grounds between the river dykes and the ramparts were raised and made accessible from the river dykes by means of lanes and side streets (secondary structure).[107] This was also the period when many of the originally very large plots were split both lengthwise and breadthwise.[108] In accordance with the model of block formation, before 1400 Oudezijds Voorburgwal, at that time a back street and part of the secondary structure, did not have a continuous row of houses. The population pressure was apparently still too low for this. In these years densification and infilling in the inner courtyards of already closed blocks of houses also rarely or never occurred.[109]

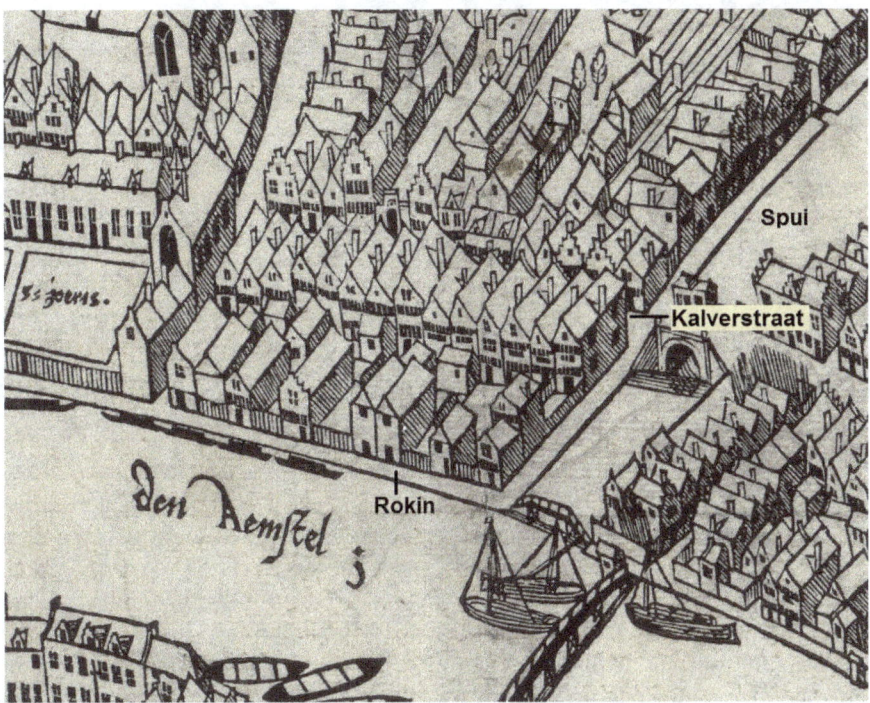

Map 3.9 Amsterdam: block formation on Kalverstraat, 1544 (north right).

Around the middle of the sixteenth century, the process of block formation at the south end of Kalverstraat was still in full swing. Map 3.9, a section of the map by Cornelis Anthonisz. from 1544, shows that in the block south of Spui (left on the map), the primary axis of Kalverstraat has already been completely built up. Some of the once-deep plots have now been split and are independently accessible from the secondary axis (present Rokin) along the Amstel. This process has not yet taken place for other plots, where the rear grounds extend to a fence on Rokin. Note that in accordance with what has been argued earlier, the houses on the primary axis of Kalverstraat in those years were considerably higher and more prestigious than those on the secondary axis along the river Amstel.[110]

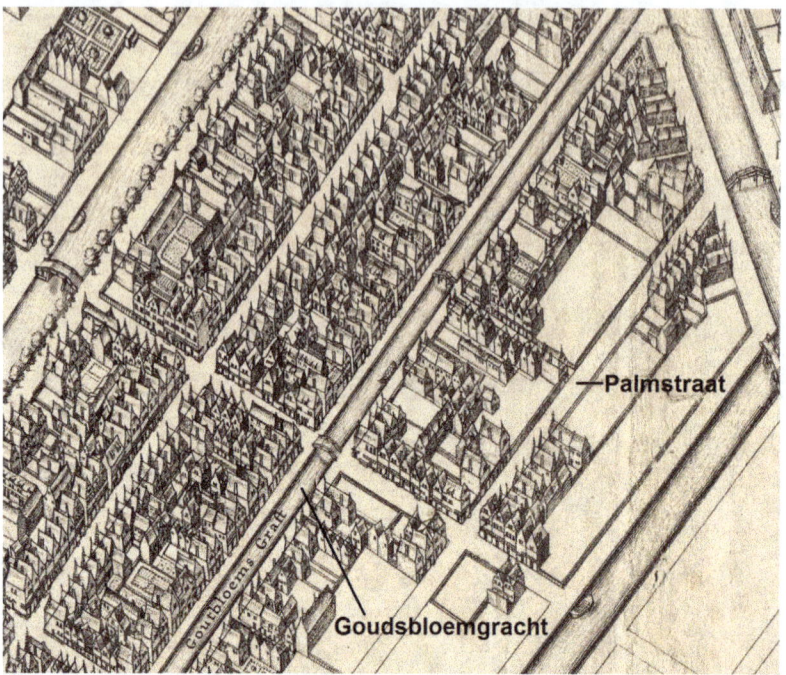

Map 3.10 Amsterdam: block formation in the Jordaan district, 1625 (north below).

The process of block formation described here was not specific to the medieval and sixteenth-century city. The principles described earlier also applied to the large urban extensions of the seventeenth century: houses were generally built first along the main axes, and the blocks were then formed in a process of concatenation and densification. This can be clearly seen on the map by Balthasar Florisz. from 1625, in the period when the Jordaan was under construction (Map 3.10). In the northernmost part of the Jordaan, houses could be found along the main axis of Goudsbloemgracht (present Willemsstraat) and along the cross-streets that provide the north-south connection within the Jordaan. But the houses are not yet contiguous, and along the backstreet (Palmstraat) many of the lots are still undeveloped. After that time, the blocks were closed on four sides and the inner courtyards were also built up and opened up by a tertiary structure of alleys and blind alleys. From those years until well into the nineteenth century, this part of the city was notorious for its high densities, dramatic housing conditions and dire poverty among its inhabitants.

As the smallest of the cities studied here, Edam forms an interesting contrast to Delft (medium sized) and Amsterdam (large). Due to the small size of the city's population and its spacious territory within the city moats, block formation had only taken place to a very limited extent in pre-modern Edam. Closed blocks of houses were mainly found in Edam's old core area: the surroundings of the Onze Lieve Vrouwekapel, Spui and Dam. In the early sixteenth century, houses in the alleys and lanes of this area also became the refuge of the less well-off and the poor who, under the threat of enemy attacks, had left the unsafe east side of the city, close to the Zuiderzee.[111]

Map 3.11 Edam: map by Jacob van Deventer, *c.* 1560.

For a long time, Voorhaven (primary structure), which was developed from this core area, consisted of two rows of houses with partly undeveloped backyards. This situation is clearly depicted on the city map by Jacob van Deventer from around 1560 (Map 3.11).[112] From the sixteenth century onwards the plots were increasingly subdivided and on the former backyards mainly small houses appeared for journeymen and domestic servants.[113] Later larger houses were also built on Achterhaven (south side) and Nieuwehaven (north side), but the map by Blaeu and De Wit, which presents the

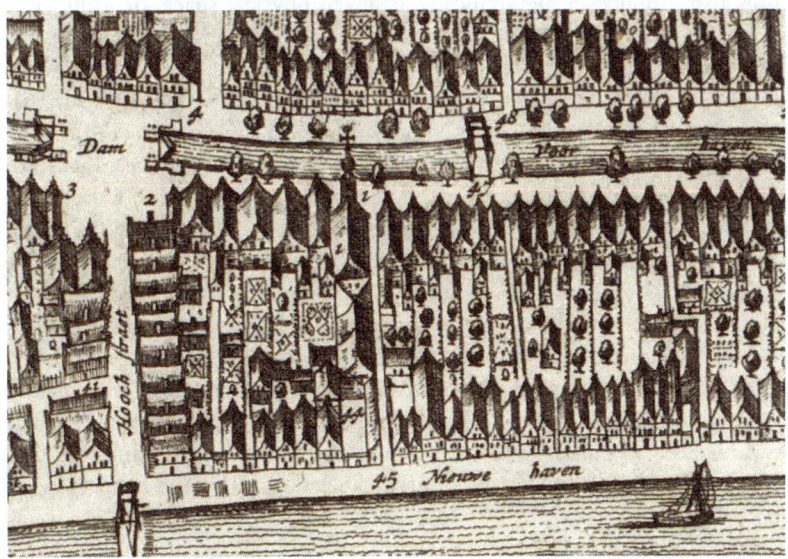

Map 3.12 Edam: blocks of houses between Voorhaven and Nieuwehaven, *c.* 1665.

situation around 1665, still shows a considerable difference in size and status between houses along the main canal of Voorhaven and those along the other canals, especially in the blocks between Voorhaven and Nieuwehaven (Map 3.12); a difference that is still noticeable today.[114]

This section has argued that the emergence and striking continuity of residential differentiation at the meso-level of streets (around-the-corner differentiation) was indeed rooted in two of the enduring elements of the urban landscape: street plan and closed blocks of houses. However, it is important to re-emphasize that these enduring elements of the urban landscape, as well as the permanent characteristics of the physical-geographical environment, do not sufficiently explain the residential patterns at the meso- and macro-level. Indeed, it has been argued in the previous section that these acquired significance only in the broader societal context of the cities in Holland. Bearing this in mind it is now possible to summarize the aforementioned as well as point out the striking fragmentation of private landownership and its effect on the continuity of the patterns of residential appropriation of urban space in Holland.

3.2.3. Establishment and continuity of patterns of urban residential appropriation in pre-modern Holland: Explanations

In explaining the establishment and continuity of the patterns of residential appropriation in the pre-modern cities of Holland the following factors seem to have been of particular importance. A first and fundamental factor is that as argued at length in Chapter 1, society in those cities was characterized by a high degree of *inequality*. In terms of Bourdieu's model of society, the patterns of residential appropriation in Holland's cities were the result of the unequal distribution of economic, cultural and social capital in the field of housing. According to him, a hierarchical society by definition also produces a hierarchically arranged physical space, or in his own words: 'there is no space, in a hierarchical society, that is not hierarchized . . .'.[115] The fact that the residential patterns that have been reconstructed from the sixteenth century onwards have their roots in the period of the city formation, suggests that from early on in their existence, these cities had a social hierarchy based on the unequal distribution of resources. This assumption is supported by the fact that from the thirteenth century onwards the records mention among others bailiffs, aldermen and burgomasters, that is, people who occupied a special position within the urban community and who were able to exercise power partly because of this.[116] The presence of furriers, in Dordrecht at least from the thirteenth century and in Amsterdam at least from the fourteenth, also points to the existence of social differences and the desire of the well-to-do to express their status in luxury garments. The contrast established by archaeological research between the relatively expensive glass and pewter eating and drinking utensils of the well-to-do and the cheap eating and drinking utensils of earthenware and wood used by city dwellers of lesser means is also an indication that social inequality was characteristic of urban societies in Holland from the very beginning.[117]

The *property market* played an important role in 'translating' the position of individuals and groups in social space into their location in physical space. Contrary to Vance's assumption, in Holland location and property characteristics already influenced the economic value of real estate in the Middle Ages. The cities in Holland were not unique in this. For medieval Gloucester, Casson and Casson found that around 1455 and even around 1100, rental values reflected location and property characteristics, as is still the case today in the real estate market.[118] The invisible hand of the real estate market not only played an important role in the distribution of social classes across urban space, but it also ensured that governments, institutions and private individuals rarely, if ever, had to use force. Precisely because of its invisibility, the price mechanism created the impression that the existing residential patterns were a natural given. This apparent self-evidence promoted their acceptance and concealed the fact that they were the result of unequal power relations in the appropriation of urban space.

Although there was no rigorous spatial segregation of social classes at the macro-level of city districts and neighbourhoods, the cities in Holland did show a broad distinction between the parts of the city where the houses of the well-to-do upper classes were located along a number of streets and/or canals, and the urban periphery where the (lower) middle classes and working classes were overrepresented. This broad distinction at the macro-level is related here to the *physical-geographic environment* of the cities. In short, in the low-lying land, the higher and drier locations were the most attractive. This is where the first inhabitants settled, and as the population of cities grew in size, those with the most resources and the best mix of resources used them to appropriate these attractive locations. City dwellers with fewer resources were at a disadvantage in the urban arena and ended up in the less attractive, often lower-lying and peripheral locations. The area's physical and geographical characteristics also explain the lack of a compact elite quarter that Sjoberg considers typical of all pre-industrial cities. In Holland, intersected by natural and man-made waterways, many of these higher grounds had a linear structure in the forms of river banks, dykes and embankments.

In the early period of city formation, the development of the street network also gave the initial impetus to *block formation*. With its distinction between houses along main streets, side streets and back streets, and on inner courtyards, this inevitably generated a mixture of social classes. Along the primary structure, streets were spacious and plots were wide and deep. The primary structure was therefore eminently suitable for the construction of prestigious dwellings for those with sufficient financial resources. Because the allotment of the secondary and tertiary structures was a derivative of the original plots on the primary structure, the plots there had a less favourable location within the street network from the outset, were smaller in size and the houses were often of lower quality. This difference was reflected in the price that had to be paid for housing along the secondary and tertiary structures. And so these houses came within reach of the other city dwellers. They were distributed over the secondary and tertiary structures by the invisible hand of the real estate market in proportion to their financial means.

In combination, the physical-geographical environment of the cities, the process of block formation and the resource-based opportunities for appropriating space on the housing market shaped the residential structure of the cities in Holland as early as the medieval period. The fact that this structure was so enduring is due, among other things, to the *petrification* of these patterns and the *fragmentation of private land ownership*. The petrification of residential patterns is a concrete example of path dependency.[119] Once the differences in the physical-geographical environment and location within the street network had been materialized into buildings, there was an almost inevitable tendency for the existing spatial patterns to become continuous. Even for those with ample economic, cultural and social resources, it was almost impossible to radically change the existing spatial structures. This required demolition of the existing buildings and redevelopment of the area to be built on. Due to the fragmentation of land ownership, this was not only costly and time-consuming, but also the refusal of one or a few land owners to sell their properties could cause the whole project to fail. In this respect, the situation in Holland was very different from the one in London, for example, where the king, nobility and institutions such as Trinity College owned vast and contiguous pieces of land, which they could relatively easily redevelop after the leasehold tenure had expired, if this would improve the exploitation yield.[120] And in early seventeenth-century Paris, it was only because an extensive and vacant tract of land was held by a single owner, in this case, the French crown, that the prestigious Place Royale (current Place des Vosges) could be developed.[121] Conversely, the virtual absence of nobility and noble land ownership in the Holland cities, the absence of a monarch in the long period from the end of the sixteenth to the beginning of the nineteenth century, and the absence of institutions with extensive and contiguous land holdings within the cities, undoubtedly contributed to the permanency of the residential structure in the cities of Holland.

Within the broad context in which the residential appropriation of urban space took shape, the *policies* of urban governments played an important role in both the establishment and continuity of residential patterns. In the case of city extensions, urban authorities exerted an important influence on the social composition of the population in the new developments by establishing the layout of the extension area, by laying down rules on the nature and size of the buildings, and by allocating industrial activities. Even within the existing built-up area, urban governments had an impact on the distribution of social classes across urban space. Regulations on the location of industrial activities, cattle markets, brothels and houses of correction, and policies that accepted or opposed the densification of the existing built-up area, affected the quality of housing and the living environment, and through the price mechanism, the social composition of the residents.

In general, the policies of urban governments matched and reinforced existing residential patterns. The unequal access to the authorities for different social classes also played a part in this as those with ample and the right combination of resources benefitted not only from their economic capital but also from their cultural and social capital. This enabled them to bring their wishes regarding their residential environment to the attention of the authorities and to induce them to adopt policies that monitored and, where possible, improved the quality of that residential environment. The extent to which the remaining urban dwellers were able to bring their wishes and concerns to the attention of the urban authorities varied with the size and composition of the economic, cultural and social capital they were able to deploy. This selective access to the authorities reinforced the existing distribution of externalities and social classes across urban space, thus promoting continuity.

3.3. Urban elites and the desire for a socially homogeneous and exclusive residential environment

It has been established earlier that in Holland, residential differentiation at the macro-level of city districts and the meso-level of streets was not a post-medieval phenomenon, but had already come into being in the period of city formation and had not changed in principle in the following centuries. However, in socio-spatial terms, not everything remained the same. For the cities studied here, none excepted, the reconstruction of residential patterns in the period before the 1832 land register has revealed that within the quasi-unchangeable residential structures there was an interesting development in the location patterns of the elites.[122] In a nutshell, the residential patterns of this social class show a tendency towards clustering and an increasing preference for living in a socially homogenous and distinguished residential environment. With the exception of Amsterdam, this trend has not resulted in any radical changes to the residential landscape anywhere. But in Amsterdam, it did.

Earlier in this chapter, the seventeenth-century city extensions that not only made Amsterdam much larger but also changed the centuries-old residential patterns, were discussed at length. The old situation can be clearly seen in Map 3.13, which shows residential differentiation in 1562.[123] In those years the well-to-do economic and political elites of Amsterdam mainly lived along the linear structures of the old river dykes on both sides of the river Amstel and, in particular, along Warmoesstraat. Those who had the least resources could be found in the urban periphery, but also in alleys and blind alleys in the more centrally located parts of the city. The contrast with the situation after the major city extensions is clear from Map 3.14, which gives a picture of the residential patterns in the first half of the eighteenth century. In addition to rental values for 1733, the map also includes the residences of the 250 people with the highest fiscal incomes in 1742. The residences of the richest quarter of this top 250 are represented by a red square and the other three quarters by a black square. It is evident that by then the old city centre had lost its appeal to the wealthy elites. They were no longer to be found along Warmoesstraat, but in the ring of canals, with a marked concentration of the very richest in the southern part of Herengracht, also known as the *Gouden Bocht* (Golden Bend).

The relocation of wealthy elites to a more luxurious and exclusive residential environment is a phenomenon that we also know for London and Paris. In medieval London, there were two centres: the economic centre of the (walled) City, and to the west of the City the centre of administration and justice around Whitehall in Westminster, connected to the City by the Strand.[124] From the end of the sixteenth

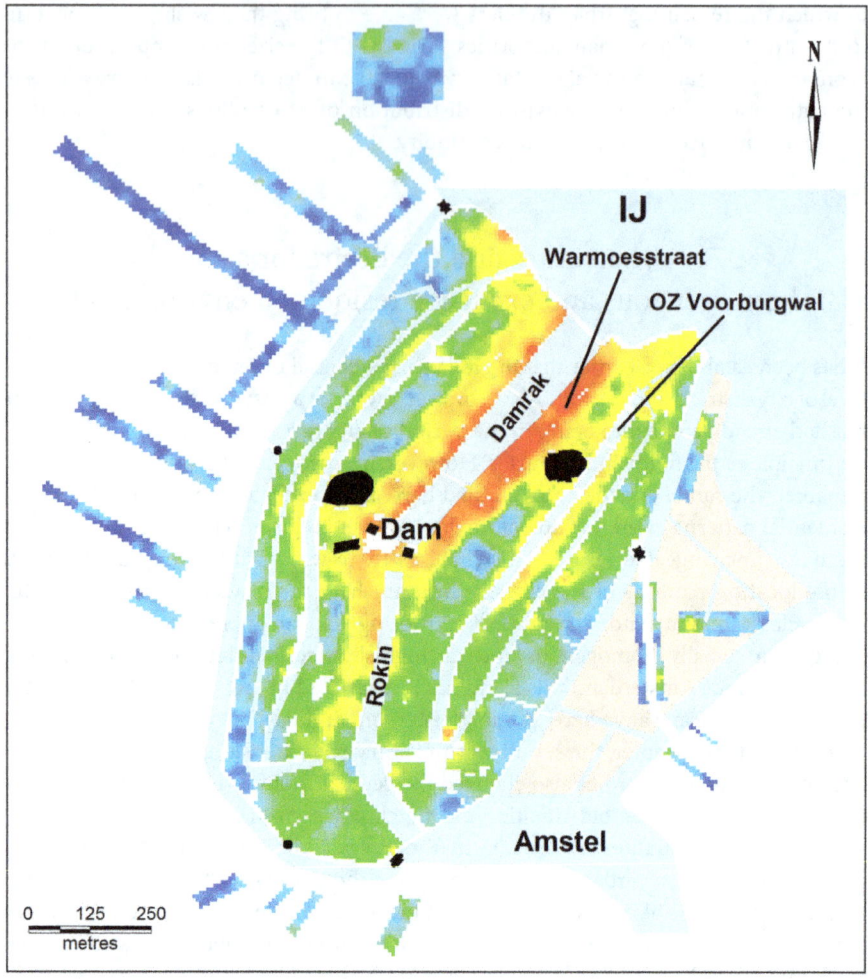

Map 3.13 Residential differentiation in Amsterdam, 1562.

century, there was already a westward migration of wealthy people from the City, which gained momentum in the seventeenth century. The push factor was the increasing pressure on space in the City and the accompanying nuisance and pollution. Pull factors for Westminster included the proximity and status of royal palaces and parks, the availability of large plots of land for the construction of aristocratic residences, and the supply of attractive housing along streets and squares in the building projects of aristocratic landowners. Later, at the end of the seventeenth century, a similar development took place in Paris, when the Parisian aristocracy left the eastern part of the city and moved to the west side of Paris, in the direction of Versailles.[125]

In Amsterdam, the distance that separated the busy old centre from the quiet and prestigious residential environment of the ring of canals was much shorter than the distance between the old centres and the new elite neighbourhoods in London and

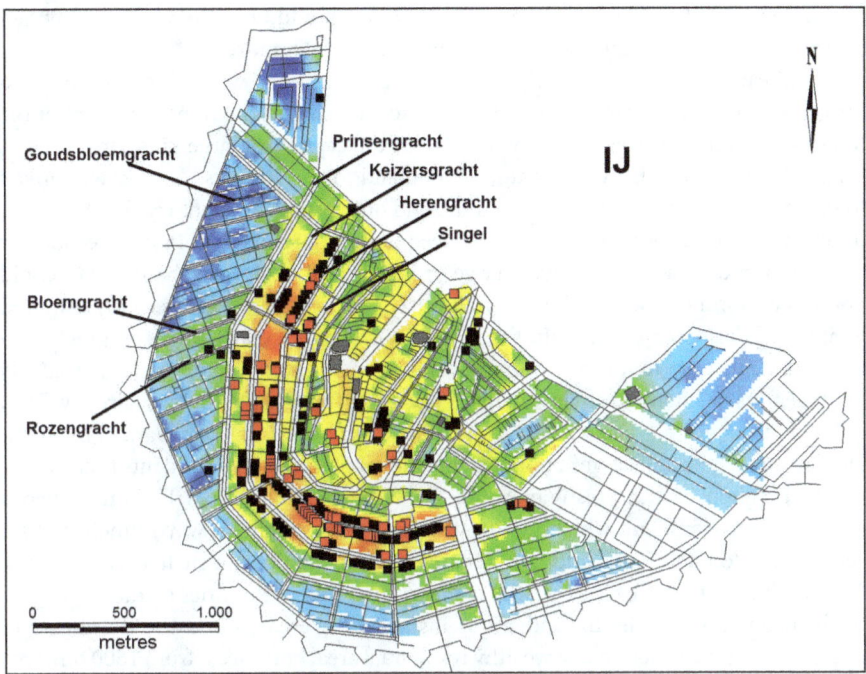

Map 3.14 Residential differentiation in Amsterdam, 1733–42.

Paris. This was of course due to the difference in scale between Amsterdam and early-modern metropolises such as London and Paris, but it also had to do with the social and economic structure of society. Unlike in London and Paris, the well-to-do and non-noble elites in Amsterdam were generally actively involved in commodity trade and other economic activities, which required the proximity of the city centre with important institutions such as the stock exchange, exchange bank and weighing house, and notary offices specialized in drawing up contracts relating to trade and shipping. The ring of canals was ideally situated for this purpose, as it folded around the old city centre, making it relatively close and easily accessible.[126]

The proximity of the city centre was important, since the narrow streets, sharp corners and many bridges in the centre made it difficult to reach by carriage. Moreover, because of the dangers for pedestrians and other street users, the damage they caused to streets and bridges, and possibly also because of a certain aversion to what in the bourgeois Dutch Republic was seen as pretentious noble display, carriages were banned for a long time or their use was severely restricted. The alternative was the slow and not very prestigious coach sleigh.[127] In London, with a built-up area of 920 hectares at the end of the seventeenth century a city of a different scale than Amsterdam (470 hectares), distance and accessibility were less of a problem for those who could afford it, due to the services of Hackney coaches. Their statutory number grew with the size of London's population and urban area. In 1654 there was still a maximum of 300 carriages, but this number increased via 400, 700 and 800 in 1662, 1694 and 1715 respectively, to 1,000 Hackney coaches in 1771.[128] In addition, the very wealthy had private coaches in use, and these also numbered several hundreds.[129]

The creation of predominantly affluent neighbourhoods was, of course, reserved for cities where there was sufficient demand for housing in the upper segment of the housing market. This was certainly the case in the capitals of large kingdoms such as England and France. In Amsterdam, the demand for prestigious housing was linked to the rapid economic expansion from the end of the sixteenth century. The booming development of international trade played an important role in this economic expansion and created a relatively large group of well-to-do merchants, who could not find accommodation in the inner city that matched their often recently acquired wealth and desire for status.[130] In the ring of canals, particularly on Herengracht and Keizersgracht, they found a prestigious and, from a social point of view, relatively homogenous residential environment. Earlier in this chapter it has already been pointed out that the exclusive character of the main canals was safeguarded by urban by-laws and by the collective actions (associational power) of the residents themselves.

The preference for a prestigious and – as far as possible – socially homogeneous residential environment, which manifested itself in a prominent way in metropolises such as London and Paris, and in a dynamic commercial centre such as Amsterdam, was not limited to these cities, on the contrary. In all six of the cities studied here, this preference is discernible. In Leiden, for instance, the area around the Burght never completely lost its function as a wealthy residential area, but at least from 1500 onwards the centre of gravity shifted first to the southern part of Breestraat and then, from the middle of the sixteenth century, to the northern part of Breestraat and to Rapenburg.

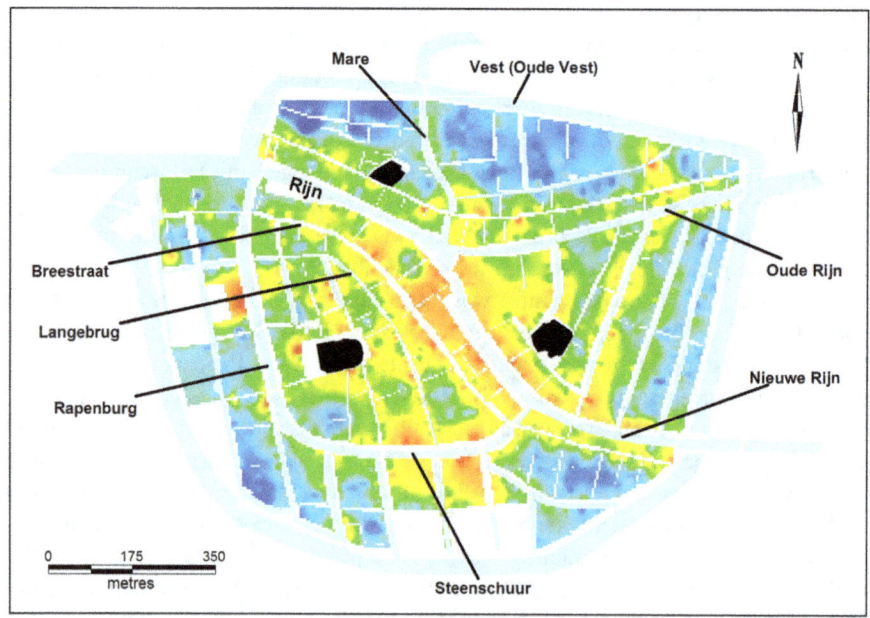

Map 3.15 Residential differentiation in Leiden, 1561.

Map 3.15, which shows the patterns of residential appropriation in 1561, shows a phase in that development. At the time, Rapenburg was not yet popular with the elites of Leiden, but in the course of the seventeenth and eighteenth centuries it became increasingly important as an elite environment, a development that was reflected in the eighteenth century in the fairly radical restructuring of the area west of Rapenburg. The poor little quarters that had traditionally been found there in the urban periphery were largely demolished to make way for the gardens of the canal residents and the extension of the Hortus Botanicus. The result of all this can be clearly seen on the map of around 1830 presented in the previous chapter (Map 2.7). Due to the demolition of cheap housing in the western periphery, Rapenburg and its surroundings had become more socially homogenous than it had been and was now the favourite residential domain of the Leiden elites.

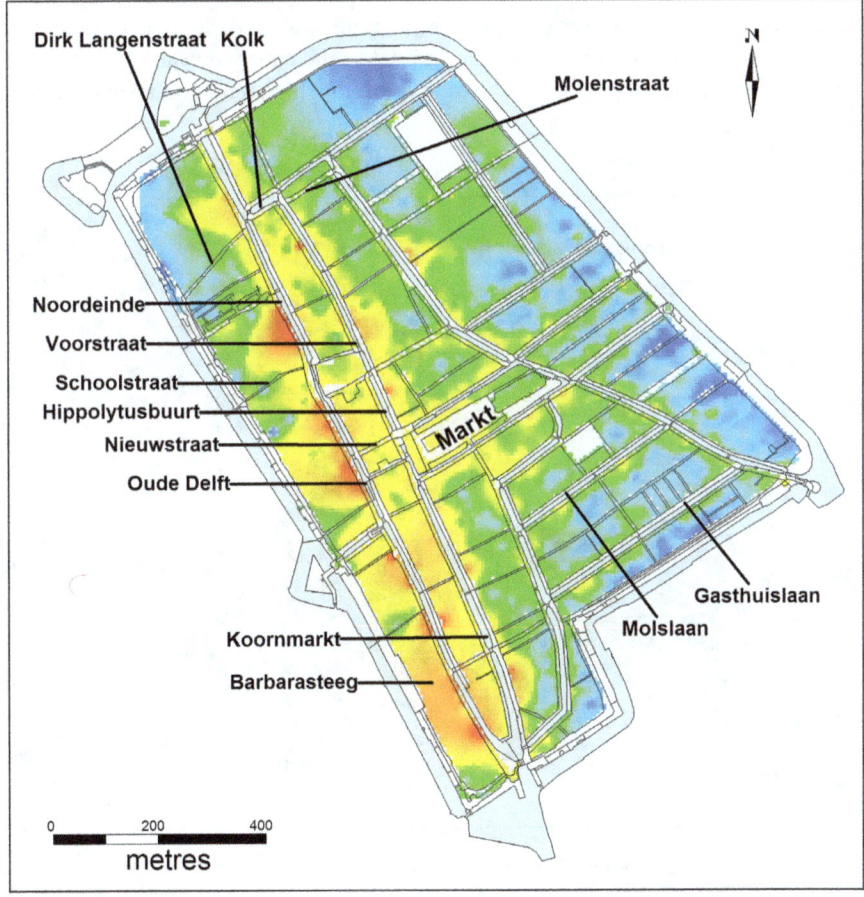

Map 3.16 Residential differentiation in Delft, *c.* 1730.

With the decline of the brewing industry, something similar happened in Delft from the beginning of the seventeenth century. The changes were especially great on Oude Delft. There, former industrial buildings in the backyards were demolished and replaced by spacious gardens, and where the opportunity arose, several adjacent premises were replaced by a single large and prestigious residence. On the map of the situation around 1730 (Map 3.16), the result of these changes is already clearly discernible, and a century later the central part of Oude Delft in particular had an almost homogeneous affluent character (see Map 2.5 in Chapter 2). The quality of this residential environment was protected by by-laws and – as noted before – enhanced by the use of public funds for maintenance and improvement of the environment.

As early as the fourteenth century, the counts of Holland had been using their resources to ensure that the green area around their court – the Haagse Bos – retained its green character. This green character and the proximity of the count's court formed the basis for the development of a pleasant and affluent residential environment in the north-east quadrant of the city from the sixteenth century onwards. In 1561 the beginnings of this development were already visible, but high rental values and wealthy

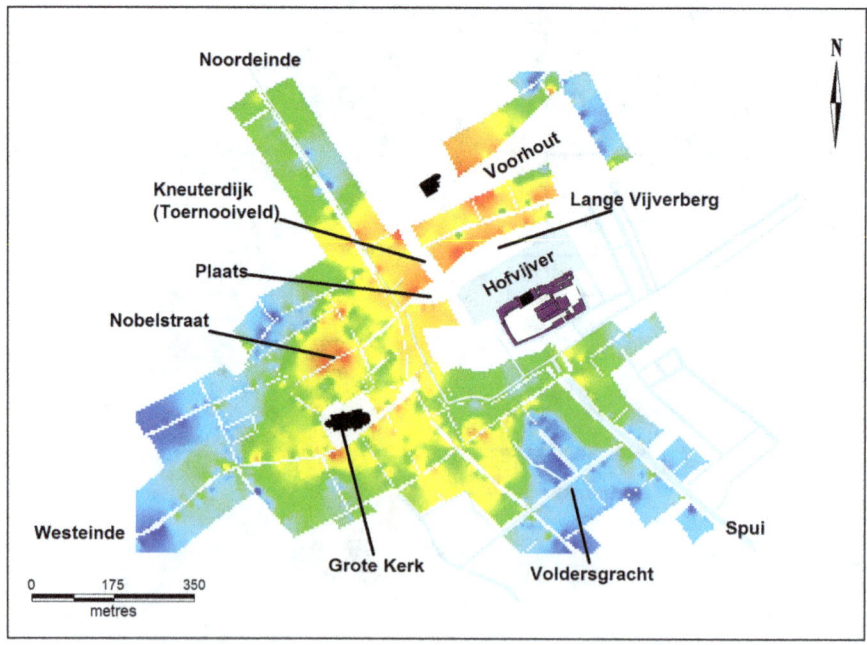

Map 3.17 Residential differentiation in The Hague, 1561.

residents could then also be found along Nobelstraat and around the Grote Kerk (Map 3.17). From the end of the century onwards, the Hofbuurt (Court district) increasingly became the residence of the wealthy elites of The Hague. The map of around 1830 shows the end result of this development: Nobelstraat and the area around the Grote Kerk had lost their appeal and the most well-to-do residents could then only be found in the Hofbuurt (see Chapter 2, Map 2.9).

In Alkmaar, too, there was an increasing clustering of wealthy residents in a specific part of the city, in this case, the western half of the city. In 1561 the residential patterns showed the previously described linear structure of Langestraat as a connection between the old cores around the Grote Kerk of Alkmaar and the area around Mient, as well as an offshoot of Mient in eastern direction along Luttik Oudorp (Map 3.18). Oude Gracht functioned at that time as part of the fortifications and was therefore unattractive as a residence for the city's wealthy inhabitants; an observation that is consistent with Sjoberg's view that elites avoided the city's outskirts because of its insecurity during sieges and shelling. When during the last quarter of the sixteenth century the city was expanded on the south side, this moat was transformed into a residential canal with houses on both sides, a development that corresponds to that of Singel in Amsterdam during the same period. And like Singel, Oude Gracht became an attractive place to live for those with sufficient financial resources because of its width and the unobstructed view over the water, and because of the availability of large building lots.[131]

Map 3.19 shows the increased popularity of Oude Gracht among wealthy elites around 1630. In the longer term, this popularity led to the striking clustering of houses with high rents and wealthy residents along Oude Gracht that we know from the first half of the nineteenth century, and to the enhancement of the status of the western half of the city in general (see Map 2.3 in Chapter 2).

In Edam, the smallest of the cities studied here, there was also a desire among the elites for a pleasant and preferably homogeneous residential environment. Because of the small size of the city, it was a phenomenon of limited scope there. While Spui, Dam and Voorhaven retained their prominent position within the residential landscape, in the second half of the sixteenth century we see an interest among the elites for a residential environment with a rural feel. This was realized in 1583 with the construction of Baanstraat, just south of Dam and in the vicinity of a fancy garden area that had been laid out along the city side of the moat (Map 3.20). This preference for a quiet and green residential environment was also present in the eighteenth and early nineteenth centuries. Many burgomasters and other dignitaries left the busy environment of Spui and Dam to settle on spacious plots on the south-western edge of the city (see Map 2.2 in Chapter 2). In those years, the risk of war at the city outskirts was apparently considered low.

90 Power and Urban Space in Pre-Modern Holland

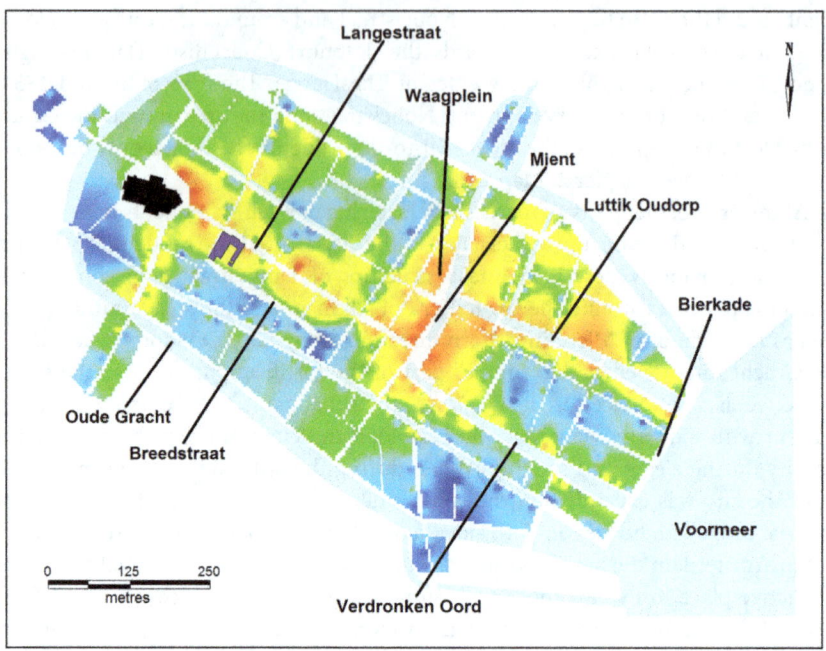

Map 3.18 Residential differentiation in Alkmaar, 1561.

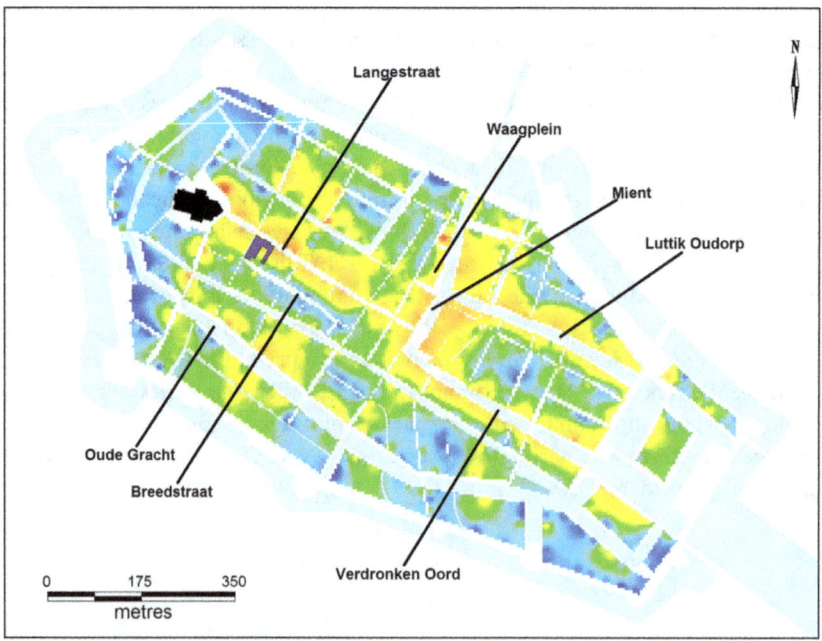

Map 3.19 Residential differentiation in Alkmaar, *c.* 1630.

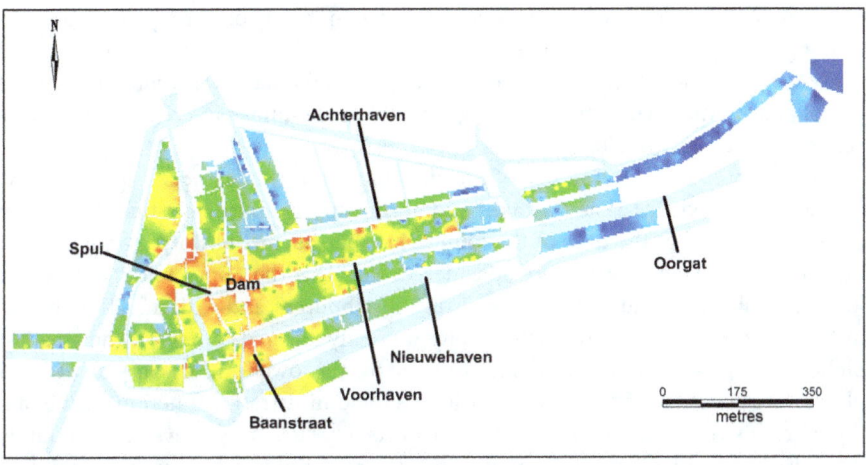

Map 3.20 Residential differentiation in Edam, *c.* 1630.

Considering the foregoing, it can be concluded that in each of the cities studied here, the elites showed an increasing preference for a homogeneous wealthy and prestigious residential environment. The scale on which this preference could be realized depended, of course, on the volume of demand for this type of locations. In Amsterdam, this preference materialized in the development of the ring of canals and in the small city of Edam it concerned only a few streets. It is also clear that the opportunities to create a pleasant and (relatively) homogeneous residential environment mainly presented themselves at times when new neighbourhoods were developed within or outside the former city boundaries, and when economic decline and a fall in the number of inhabitants offered the opportunity to buy up nearby cheap dwellings and replace them with gardens or buildings that the elites considered more in line with the desired quality of their residential environment. In all these cases, the elites appropriated parts of urban space through the use of resources and adapted these to their wishes and preferences. According to Bourdieu, this preference for a socially homogeneous residential environment is an important objective of the struggle in the field of housing. That this social homogeneity of the residential environment was indeed important for well-to-do contemporaries is very clear from the case of Friedrichstadt in what is now northern Germany.

Friedrichstadt (Frederikstad), founded in 1621, is interesting for several reasons. It is important that the city's charter of foundation has been preserved and that it contains information about the desired social and spatial structure of the city. No less important is the fact that the foundation of the city was the initiative of a group of Dutch Remonstrants who, after the National Synod of 1618 in Dordrecht, were looking for a place where they could freely practice their faith.[132] They managed to gain the support of Friedrich III, Duke of Schleswig-Holstein and Oldenburg, who hoped that the foundation of this new city would contribute to the realization of his economic, political and military ambitions. The Friedrichstadt foundation charter and the spatial structure of the city that was built reflect the views on society of a group of people who held a prominent position in Holland before their exodus to Schleswig-Holstein and who can be considered representative of the upper middle classes and elites in the cities of Holland.[133] And finally, the physical-geographical conditions in Friedrichstadt were very similar to those in Holland.

In the city to be built, the size of the plots (and thus the financial capacity of the residents) formed the basis for taxes and administrative participation. Six sizes of plots were offered at the time of the foundation, but Burm and Borger argue that in practice, four social classes were considered: the elite, the upper middle class, the lower middle class and a group consisting of labourers and artisans. The charter of foundation shows that the latter group was only allowed to live on the smallest plots, and in practice it was also made difficult for the lower middle class to settle on plots which, because of their size, gave access to administrative functions. All in all, therefore, a strongly hierarchical structure of society such as we have come to know it for the cities of Holland. In spatial terms, the social hierarchy was expressed in a clear segregation of social classes. The largest plots and wealthiest residents were to be found on the south side of the city, close to the harbour and from south to north the size of the plots and the socio-economic status of the residents decreased. The segregation of the working classes was further reinforced by placing the smallest plots on the other side of a canal (Middenburgwal) in an area that was regularly flooded due to its low level of elevation.[134]

In Friedrichstadt, prominent expatriates from Holland created what they saw as the ideal city and society. This ideal society was characterized by a hierarchical structure and restriction of administrative participation to the higher social classes. From a spatial point of view, the classes were strictly segregated and, by being located in the northernmost part of the city, the working classes were placed at a distance from the rest of society and, moreover, were assigned the least attractive locations. The similarities with the situation in Holland are striking, but in Friedrichstadt the spatial segregation of social classes was much more strict. This was possible there because in Schleswig-Holstein, virgin land was available and the urban planners were not restricted in realizing their ideal city and society by existing spatial patterns and urban planning traditions.

The 'solution' found in Friedrichstadt to the phenomenon of residential differentiation at the meso-level of streets is revealing. In the southern part of the city, the largest plots were planned to stretch across the full depth of the blocks of houses. There was therefore no question of back streets inhabited by social classes with considerably fewer financial resources. And the side streets in Friedrichstadt had no independent housing.[135] The mixture at the level of blocks (around-the-corner differentiation), which was so characteristic for the cities in Holland, was absent in Friedrichstadt, which was designed according to the views and wishes of wealthy Dutch expatriates. And this was probably not by chance, because it is precisely this mixture of residents with different socio-economic positions within the same block of houses that seems to have been a problem for the wealthy elites in Holland.[136] This can be deduced from their spatial behaviour and increasing preference for an exclusive residential environment, and it also appears from the remarks of, for example, Leiden's

City Secretary Jan van Hout. His proposal to divide Leiden into 176 *gebuurten* (small districts), around 1600 ran aground on the fact that in that case families living on main streets and canals would be united in the same *gebuurte* with poor families living in backstreets.[137] And that was something that 'de rijcke' (the rich) did not want and were also able to prevent successfully; a clear expression of associational power: power to achieve something together with others.

It is not far-fetched to see the preference of the well-to-do for a socially homogenous residential environment as an expression of increasing economic inequality within society and changing relationships between social classes. With regard to the first point, recent research has indeed established that in the period from about 1500, when source material becomes available, until 1800, economic inequality in Holland substantially increased.[138] This quantitative research can be supplemented with some observations that Van Ravesteyn made long ago about the relations between social classes in Amsterdam from the beginning of the sixteenth century. In his research, he made a distinction between a wealthy bourgeoisie of merchants and entrepreneurs and a petty bourgeoisie of artisans and craftsmen.[139] Both within and between these groups, differences in social status in the first half of the sixteenth century were relatively small. This is evident, for example, from the fact that within the same family there were merchants and well-to-do owners of soap works as well as carpenters, bakers and shopkeepers. And marriages between craftsmen and daughters of merchants, or between merchants and daughters of craftsmen, were not uncommon. For example, the daughters of the shipmaster Pieter Ysbrandtsz. Hem in the early sixteenth century married a merchant in woollen cloth, a rope maker and a carpenter. And the sister of the merchant Simons Jansz. Vinck married a baker.[140] From the end of the sixteenth century, things changed rapidly. Such socially mixed marriages were then much less common, and if they occurred, they were usually a sign of social decline of the merchant or entrepreneurial family.

The growing distance between social classes and the elites' desire to separate themselves from those they considered inferior also found expression in the homes of the wealthy upper classes. In the course of the seventeenth and eighteenth centuries, the desire for privacy and a growing sense of class sharpened the boundaries between family members and household staff. Domestic servants no longer lived on the same floor as the family members, but were housed in the attic or the basement. In the houses of the most well-off, a double infrastructure of entrances, staircases and corridors was sometimes put in place in order to restrict contact between the well-to-do family members and domestic servants to a necessary minimum.[141] A similar urge to social distancing was expressed in the rebuilding of the Amsterdam theatre around 1770, which created separate exits for the various social classes. It led a certain 'Jacob Toneelliefhebber' (Jacob theatre-lover) to congratulate the Amsterdam elites on the fact that they were now also separated from 'the lesser sort of your fellow spectators' when they left the theatre.[142]

All in all, it will be clear that the sixteenth century in the cities of Holland was rather a period in which the existing differences between social classes intensified than a fundamental break with the medieval past.[143] Nevertheless, the increase in economic inequality and the growing social distance between elites and higher middle classes on the one hand and lower middle classes and working classes on the other hand had, as was argued earlier, spatial consequences.[144] In line with Bourdieu's argument, in pre-modern Holland too, those with ample resources kept negative externalities and fellow citizens they regarded as 'the other' at a distance as much as possible.[145] The limits to residential segregation were set by the meso-differentiation at the level of streets and, of course, also by pre-modern transport technology, which prevented the well-off from living far outside the cities and commuting regularly to the city for work, administrative functions and to maintain their social network. In this context, Amsterdam's ring of canals was for the elites the best that could be achieved: separated from the busy and socially mixed inner city with its indispensable facilities, but not on the edge of the city because one would then have to cross working-class districts like the Jordaan to reach the inner city.

It was only with the expansion of the network of railways and tramways in the second half of the nineteenth century that a suburban existence really became a feasible option. Until then, wealthy citizens in Holland often owned a country house in addition to a prestigious house in the city. As early as the sixteenth century, city residents had so-called *herenkamers* (rooms) on farmsteads that they had acquired. In this way, they combined investments in agricultural land ownership with the opportunity to leave the city every now and then to enjoy the pleasures of country life.[146] From the end of the sixteenth century, the number of country houses in Holland increased spectacularly. This popularity was of course related to the love of the country life, but also to the growing wealth at this time of economic expansion, the desire to invest part of that wealth safely and profitably in landed property, and possibly also to the example of the numerous villas in the Italian Veneto, which people had become aware of directly, through trade or Grand Tours, or indirectly, through treatises of architects like Andrea Palladio. But of great importance was especially the ample supply of land. With the transition to Protestantism, the land holdings of Catholic nobles, monasteries and churches were expropriated and put on the market. Moreover, in the first half of the seventeenth century, numerous lakes were drained in Holland and these 'new' lands also became available.

Initially, country houses in the immediate vicinity of the cities were the most popular, but as the infrastructure of roads and waterways improved, more distant regions came within reach.[147] There is no reliable data on the number of country houses in the seventeenth century, but for 1742 a tax record shows that no fewer than 600 well-to-do households in Amsterdam owned a country house.[148] Together with the country houses owned by wealthy people from other cities in Holland, we are talking about considerable numbers. The majority of these country houses were only occupied for part of the year. Only the very richest could afford to retire completely to their country houses. Of course, they also owned the most beautiful estates, for instance along the river Vecht. After his travels along the Vecht in 1667 and 1669, Cosimo III de' Medici praised the many 'palazzati di buona proporzione e simmetria con giardinetto contiguo' he had seen there.[149]

3.4. Residential appropriation and the continuity of power relations in the cities of Holland

In the following chapters, it will become clear that the appropriation of urban space was not limited to housing, but for now it is important to conclude by noting that the residential structures reconstructed in this chapter and the previous one should not exclusively be seen as the physical manifestation of the unequal distribution of resources and the power based on them in the field of housing and in society as a whole. They were, of course, but they were also more. In Bourdieu's brief study of the appropriation of space, he states: 'Appropriated space is one of the sites where power is asserted and wielded, and no doubt under the most invisible form, that of symbolic violence as unperceived violence.'[150] The patterns of residential differentiation in the cities of Holland, through their physical expression in the tangible wood and bricks of houses, created the impression among all social classes that they resulted from the natural order of things; that they were self-evident and not open to discussion.[151] Thus, appropriated space concealed the fact that it was the expression of unequal power relations in a hierarchical society and, partly because of this, the existing power relations were accepted more easily, which contributed to their continuity.[152]

Continuity was also promoted by path dependency, in which process the material and immaterial expressions of power relations from the past (partly) shape the power relations at a later point in time.[153] Thus, living in a poor neighbourhood or street and the stigma attached to it made it virtually impossible for residents to accumulate sufficient economic, social and cultural capital to escape poverty and deprivation. Appealing to the social network of neighbours, for example, was of little use, since they too generally lacked the necessary financial resources, useful contacts and knowledge and skills. And the stigma of a deprived neighbourhood or street made it almost impossible to gain access to people and institutions outside the neighbourhood or street who did have sufficient and relevant resources. Residents of well-to-do neighbourhoods and streets were not confronted with these problems, on the contrary. The resources that they and their neighbours had at their disposal, as well as the status of their residential environment, contributed to their economic, cultural and social capital. This is what Bourdieu refers to when he states that a poor neighbourhood functions as a ghetto that depresses and stigmatizes its residents, while a well-to-do neighbourhood functions as a club that allows its members to share in the economic, cultural and social capital that the members collectively possess.[154] The physical residential landscape in the cities of Holland thus not only reflected the hierarchically ordered social space, but it was also an independent force in the acceptance and continuity of that social space and its unequal power relations.

4

Power, theatrical violence and ephemeral appropriation of urban space

4.1. Violence and the appropriation of space in the urban arena

The previous chapters have shown that in the field of housing, the different social classes appropriated different parts of urban space. Which parts they were able to appropriate depended on the resources they had at their disposal. The most attractive locations, that is, those with many positive and few negative externalities, were appropriated by the elites and upper middle classes; the least attractive locations by those with the fewest resources and, consequently, the least choice when it came to searching for somewhere to live. The residential patterns that resulted from this form of appropriation proved to be extremely enduring and, partly as a result, almost self-evident. However, the power relations between social classes were also expressed in much less permanent forms of appropriation. This ephemeral appropriation of urban space could take many forms, ranging from the peaceful 'occupation' of bridges by street traders to the violent clearing of streets, canals and squares by armed civic militias.[1]

This chapter focuses on the explicitly violent ways in which sections of the elites, middle classes and working classes in the urban arena demonstrated and reproduced their power through the appropriation of space. Violence is thus seen here as a non-verbal communicative act, which, as will become clear, had a ritual character and also exhibited theatrical features.[2] More specifically, we will discuss public physical punishment imposed by the urban authorities and maintenance of public order by civic militias as public demonstrations and confirmations of existing power relations, and riots and revolts by middle classes and working classes as contestations of these power relations and expressions of discontent.[3] During the long period until around 1800, these expressions of ritual and theatrical violence did not fundamentally change in character, but, as we shall see, after that time, the maintenance of public order was no longer primarily a task of the urban middle classes, and the execution of punishments also took on a different character.

Because of the subject matter of this chapter, it is good to be explicit about what is meant by violence here. In his study on government violence, Van Reenen defines violence as 'that human action, which is aimed at affecting the physical integrity of persons or groups and which has the purpose of limiting the behavioural alternatives of persons or groups'.[4] This definition and the emphasis on limiting behavioural alternatives fit in perfectly with criminal justice and law enforcement, both of which were part of the urban authority system. But also for riots and revolts it can be argued that limiting the behavioural alternatives of the 'opponent' was an essential part of the action. In the vast majority of cases, urban riots and revolts in Holland had a clear cause and thus also the intention to influence the behaviour of persons, groups or institutions in a direction desired by the rioters. What is missing from Van Reenen's definition in the context of this study is the possibility that the violent acts are not (exclusively) aimed at persons or groups, but also at objects. The violent assault on objects can also have the purpose of limiting the behavioural alternatives of persons and groups.[5]

The use of force is a clear manifestation of power in the forms of domination and coercion, but it is worth emphasizing that there can be an effect even without direct physical violence. The latter, as was argued in the introduction, is a condition for being able to speak of power. Van Reenen mentions fear as an important psychological effect of violence. According to him, fear of death or pain, or fear for the well-being of others increases the effect of violence and makes the mere threat of violence work as a means of power.[6] This aspect of violence plays a part in the public punishment by the city authorities of persons who violated the law, which is the focus of the next section.

4.2. Execution of public punishments

Foucault opens the first chapter of his *Discipline and Punish. The Birth of the Prison* with the famous passage about the execution of Robert François Damiens in front of the Paris town hall on the Place de Grève in March 1757. Damiens had made a failed attempt on the life of the French king Louis XV with a knife in January of that year. At the public execution, red-hot pliers were used to remove flesh from his body, and boiling and caustic fluids were poured into the wounds and over the right hand, which had held the knife. Then his body was quartered by horses and the remains were burned.[7] The seriousness of the crime, an attack on the king, may explain the accumulation of physical punishments, but also elsewhere in Europe, perpetrators of very serious (violent) crimes in this period were sentenced by courts to a gruesome end on the scaffold, watched by an often large crowd of spectators.

Holland was no exception in this respect. In 1746, for instance, a woman who had murdered her creditor and the maid of this person and had thrown the maid's body in pieces into several Amsterdam canals was broken 'from below' on the wheel (*geradbraakt*), but before she died, her throat was cut open. Then the executioner decapitated her and placed her head on a stake. Finally, her right hand and both lower legs were cut off and laid on top of the lifeless body. Like Damiens' execution, this one was also carried out on a scaffold in public space and under great public interest.[8] This is not the place to go into detail about the many variations on the death penalty and the heavy impact on the bodies of the condemned. It suffices to glance at Figure 4.1, which

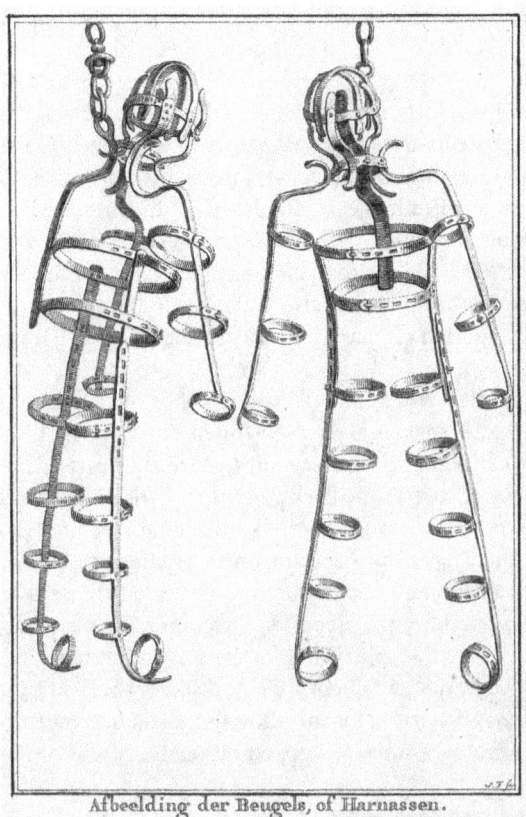

Afbeelding der Beugels, of Harnassen.

Figure 4.1 Harness for corpses of persons broken on the wheel, 1764.

shows the harnesses that were necessary to hold together the lifeless bodies of persons broken on the wheel when they were exhibited on a gallows hill or gallows field.

In the case described earlier, the nature of the crime – a double murder – was very serious, but even for less serious offences punishment often took place in public on a scaffold. Thus, those who, according to the chief prosecutor, had deserved the death penalty, but who were not sentenced to death by the aldermen, were, as it were, symbolically executed.[9] They had to stand under the gallows with a noose around their neck or kneel by a heap of sand while the executioner's sword was swung over their heads. This was usually followed by a number of 'lighter' punishments such as flogging and/or branding. Flogging, as Faber's research shows, was the most common punishment on the scaffold in Amsterdam.[10] The British traveller William Montague attended a public flogging in Amsterdam in 1695 and described the proceedings as follows. The condemned man was

> stripped to the Waist, his Hands tied, and drawn up tight with a Cord to a Post, then the Hangman took up a good handful of large Birch . . . from a great Bundle

which lay close by, and slash'd him as fast as he could, backward and forwards, then took up a fresh handful, and so on for six or seven Minutes.[11]

In total, this probably amounted to some forty to sixty blows with the bundle of birch twigs. When a weapon was involved in the offence, it was sometimes attached to the pole above the condemned man's head. Such was the case, for instance, with Henry Lambert, who at the end of 1783 in a coffee house in The Hague had committed an assault with pistol shots on François Bernard de Chapelle. In March 1784 he was publicly punished on the scaffold in The Hague 'with the noose around the neck under the gallows and with the pistol above his head'. He was also sentenced to fifteen years of confinement in a house of correction and to eternal banishment after his release from the *Tuchthuis*.[12]

If the sense of justice of the aldermen was not sufficiently satisfied after flogging, then branding followed. In the Middle Ages, branding was often done on the face, cheek or forehead, but from the middle of the sixteenth century, at least in Amsterdam, branding was done on less visible places such as the back and the shoulder. The brand was not only a painful punishment but also served as a mark indicating that a person had a 'criminal record'. This was then taken into account in the sentencing if that person was arrested later.[13] Serious facial mutilations, such as cutting off the ears or nose and cutting out the eyes, disappeared from the repertoire of corporal punishment in Holland in the course of the seventeenth century, but locally this trend may have started earlier. In Haarlem, for instance, mutilating corporal punishment was a rarity from the 1530s onwards.[14] In Amsterdam, judicial records show that in the seventeenth and eighteenth centuries thumbs were occasionally chopped off or the cheeks of the condemned were cut.[15]

And finally, lawbreakers could also be sentenced to *tepronkstelling* (the pillory), public display on the scaffold, whereby a text board in front of the chest, an object used for the offence or an object symbolizing the offence would make it clear to the public what the person on the scaffold had done wrong. Figure 4.2 shows the 1805 sentencing of the bigamist Jan Hendrik Richter on a scaffold at the Amsterdam town hall with a plaque bearing the text 'Twee Wyvery' (bigamy).[16] Sometimes the bigamist was also sentenced to hold two spindles, which symbolized a typically female activity at the time such as spinning and thus also the two women.[17]

Foucault refers to public punishment and physical violence against convicts with the term 'supplice': 'a differentiated production of pain, an organized ritual for the marking of victims and the expression of the power that punishes; not the expression of a legal system driven to exasperation and, forgetting its principles, losing all restraint. In the "excesses" of torture, a whole economy of power is invested'.[18] This is also an adequate characterization of the criminal justice system in the cities of Holland. Public punishments were indeed structured and ceremonial in character and like elsewhere in Europe they functioned as a warning to the population not to violate the law and by extension the existing social order.

It is not surprising that the execution of death sentences in particular was surrounded by much ceremony. Through the work of eighteenth-century historian Jan Wagenaar, we are well informed about the course of events in Amsterdam. He indeed

Figure 4.2 The public display of a bigamist in Amsterdam, 1805.

stresses that the execution of death sentences in Amsterdam had a *zeer plechtiglyk* (very solemn) character.[19] The procedure within the walls of the town hall is less relevant here, but it was there that the convicted were informed of the verdict the day before the execution, and the scaffold was already erected that same day. The next morning (usually Saturday) the condemned were officially declared *kinderen des doods* (children of death). Soldiers were assembled in and near the town hall and in Wagenaar's time the city gates were closed to prevent the influx of people from outside the city.[20] At about nine o'clock the bailiff, burgomasters and aldermen arrived at the town hall. They were dressed in a black *Regters-tabbaard*, before Wagenaar's time known as the *bloedmantel* (blood tabard) and with a long velvet band decorated with the coat of arms of Amsterdam, formerly known as the *bloedband*, over the left shoulder. Their arrival was accompanied by trumpet and drum and the soldiers presented rifles. The bell of the town hall was now rung and the *Roede van Justitie* (Rod of Justice) was put out of the window (see Figure 4.2). Then followed the execution of those sentenced to death, often followed by the branding and flogging of those convicted of lesser offences. After receiving their punishment, the latter had to kneel down on the scaffold in front of the bailiff and aldermen and thank them for the leniency of the verdict.[21] When the execution of the sentence was over, the *Roede van Justitie* was brought in and the burgomasters, bailiff and aldermen left the town hall accompanied by a servant of the bailiff who held the Rod of Justice over the bailiff's head. And so ended the ceremony on Dam square.

From the foregoing it will have become clear that the execution of a sentence was a highly orchestrated ceremony, aimed at maximum effect with the convicts themselves and with the public that had gathered in large numbers.[22] On the scaffold, the convicts were expected to show remorse for the crimes they had committed. Such repentance was in keeping with Christian tradition, but it was also a sign of acceptance of the existing social order and recognition of the power of the authorities to decide on life and death.[23] The violent punishments were thus more than just setting a deterrent example, or, as Terpstra puts it: 'Executions were never simply about eliminating a criminal. They were theatrical lessons in public retribution and social order, and like any staged presentation, the drama had to be didactic, cathartic, and compensatory.'[24] This also explains why the authorities involved were not at all keen on convicts who did not wish to fulfil their allotted role in the ceremony. Gillis Nicaes, for instance, in 1653 after flogging and branding did not kneel humbly before the bailiff and aldermen, but exclaimed that he would certainly not behave better in the future, but would misbehave a hundred times more. Contempt of the law and the judiciary, and being a bad example for the public got him an extra flogging. In 1803, Hendrik Jansen resisted decapitation so fiercely that the executioner considered it impossible for it to take place. In order to avoid loss of respect for the judiciary among the convicts and the public, it was decided on the spot to change the sentence to death by hanging. After this was announced, the new sentence was immediately carried out.[25]

The public execution of scaffold punishment is an expression of the appropriation of urban space by the authorities and a powerful demonstration of their power and position in society. This message was addressed to the entire urban society, but especially to the working classes. After all, it was mainly members of the working classes who were subjected to public corporal punishment or met their end on the scaffold. This is evidenced by the fact that the occupations recorded in Amsterdam criminal records were almost always those of the working classes or lower middle classes. The predominance of convicts at the base of the social pyramid is obviously related to the numerical preponderance of this class in society as a whole, but that is not the only explanation. Many of the scaffold punishments, especially flogging and branding, were imposed for relatively minor offences such as theft. It should come as no surprise that in the cities of Holland, with their extreme and visible income inequalities and dire poverty among a significant proportion of the population, it was precisely the low-income groups that were tempted to supplement their meagre income with occasional or more frequent thefts.[26] The severe and public punishment of these minor offences thus functioned in fact as a means of counteracting the undesirable side effects of inequality within society.

A particularly vulnerable group, in both urban and rural areas, were those without a fixed abode. Not only did they lack the social capital – the network of relevant contacts – that could support them in times of lack of income, but they were also seen by governments as a threat to the social order. Anyone without a permanent residence 'had a bad name in advance', according to Egmond.[27] In legal practice, this implied that they could be arrested more quickly on suspicion, were interrogated under torture more often, were imprisoned, had to make do without legal aid and, due to a lack of money or possessions, could hardly ever be sentenced to pay a fine.[28] A trip to the scaffold was then almost inevitable.

In contrast, it was highly unusual to see someone from the upper middle classes or elites being punished on the scaffold. In the long period from 1650 to 1750, Spierenburg found only one case in the Amsterdam judicial archives of a public execution of a member of the *regenten* elite. This was Theodorus van der Perre, who was guilty of large-scale fraud and embezzlement of funds. Moreover, he had been repeatedly warned by his peers, but in vain, to cease his evil practices. In January 1670 he was beheaded, a more honourable and quicker form of execution than hanging or strangulation.[29] The fact that members of the upper middle classes and elites were rarely punished at the scaffold has to do with the widespread use of composing: buying off punishment by a financial settlement (the composition).[30] In many cities, the control of the settlement of crimes was so poor that it was not difficult for people with sufficient financial resources to escape prosecution and scaffold punishment. The Court of Holland, the highest court in the province, had a better reputation for controlling settlements and combating corruption, but even there, composing was an accepted practice and even serious crimes such as assault and manslaughter could be bought off by those with sufficient economic, cultural and social capital.[31] At the end of his study of criminal justice in pre-modern Amsterdam, Faber also concludes that money, knowledge and power made it possible to prevent 'criminal mischief'.[32] Scaffold punishments can certainly be considered part of this criminal mischief.

The virtual absence of the elites at the scaffold, other than in the role of directors of the ceremony, reinforced the character of the public execution of sentences as a demonstration to the urban community of the power of the elites and the self-evident nature of the existing social order, in which some, with the law on their side, could dispose of the bodies and lives of others. The effect of the carefully staged punishments obviously depended on the frequency with which the population was confronted with them. In a large city like Amsterdam, from the middle of the seventeenth century until the first decade of the nineteenth century, an average of 2.2 *justitiedagen* (days of the execution of sentences) were organized per year, during which on average twelve to thirteen convicts per justice day were subjected to public scaffold punishment.[33] With such numbers, it is clear that the residents could witness a large number of public scaffold punishments during their lifetime. Since all indications are that these ceremonies were very well attended, large numbers of inhabitants will have played a role as spectators in this violent and ceremonial appropriation of urban space by the authorities and expression of power in the forms of domination, coercion and implicit threat.

Unfortunately, no comparable information is available for the other cities in Holland, but the number of convicts there was undoubtedly smaller than in Amsterdam, which, from the sixteenth century onwards, had by far the largest population of all cities in Holland. This does not mean, however, that the message of the public execution of punishments was missed in the smaller cities and in the countryside. Besides the actual execution on the scaffold, this message was also conveyed by the practice of exhibiting a considerable number of the corpses of executed lawbreakers on gallows fields just outside the city.[34] These gallows fields were present in all cities and also in the countryside and could not easily be overlooked. They were placed in such a way that they warned approaching strangers that the law was being enforced with a heavy hand. But also the inhabitants themselves were reminded by the nearby gallows fields of the power of the authorities and the way in which this power was effected in the execution of law.[35]

And finally, descriptions and images of scaffold punishments were included in pamphlets and printed matter describing the lives of notorious criminals, including their end on the scaffold. The morality of punishment after sin was also often portrayed in a very realistic manner on cheap penny prints, some of which were especially aimed at children.[36] The latter also applies to Figure 4.3, a moralist penny print from the third quarter of the eighteenth century, depicting a series of scaffold punishments and admonitions set to rhyme.

All in all, it will now be clear that it was virtually impossible to miss the message of power conveyed by the public execution of sentences. As such, this form of legal practice contributed to the continuity of the existing power relations, not only by forcing their acceptance through the threat of violent punishment but also because the ritualistic and theatrical character of the punishments and the central role of the authorities in them made the existing power relations seem self-evident and not liable to change.

All this does not alter the fact that in the course of time there were changes in the way in which the message of power was implemented in the criminal justice system, and in the opinions on the desirability and effectiveness of scaffold punishments. In *Discipline and Punish*, Foucault contrasts the violent execution of Damiens in 1757 with the regulations for a Parisian juvenile prison drafted by Léon Faucher eighty years later, and he concludes: 'By the end of the eighteenth and the beginning of the nineteenth century, the gloomy festival of punishment was dying out, though here and there it flickered momentarily into life.'[37] According to Foucault, scaffold punishments were replaced by the disciplinary system of the prison, and he relates this change, among other things, to the transition from monarchical authority to popular sovereignty during the French Revolution. The essence of the new penal system was that 'it leaves the domain of more or less everyday perception and enters that of abstract consciousness; its effectiveness is seen as resulting from its inevitability, not from its visible intensity; it is the certainty of being punished and not the horrifying spectacle of public punishment that must discourage crime'.[38]

Dutch historians, legal historians and historical sociologists have been critical of this presentation of events. They point out, for instance, that the Netherlands was not a monarchy in the early modern period and that it was only during the French period that the transition from a republic to a monarchy took place.[39] In addition, they emphasize that the system of imprisonment did not follow public scaffold punishment, but that both forms of punishment existed side by side for centuries. For Holland, they point to the existence of houses of correction from the end of the sixteenth century and the ideas of Coornhert, discussed earlier.[40] Much more than Foucault, therefore, they emphasize the importance of gradual developments over the long term. According to Spierenburg and Franke, two developments are central to this long-term development: the process of state formation and the growing instinctive aversion to physical violence among the elites and higher middle classes.

Thus, they argue that violent public punishments arose in a period when the still weak governments tried to prevent people from taking justice into their own hands

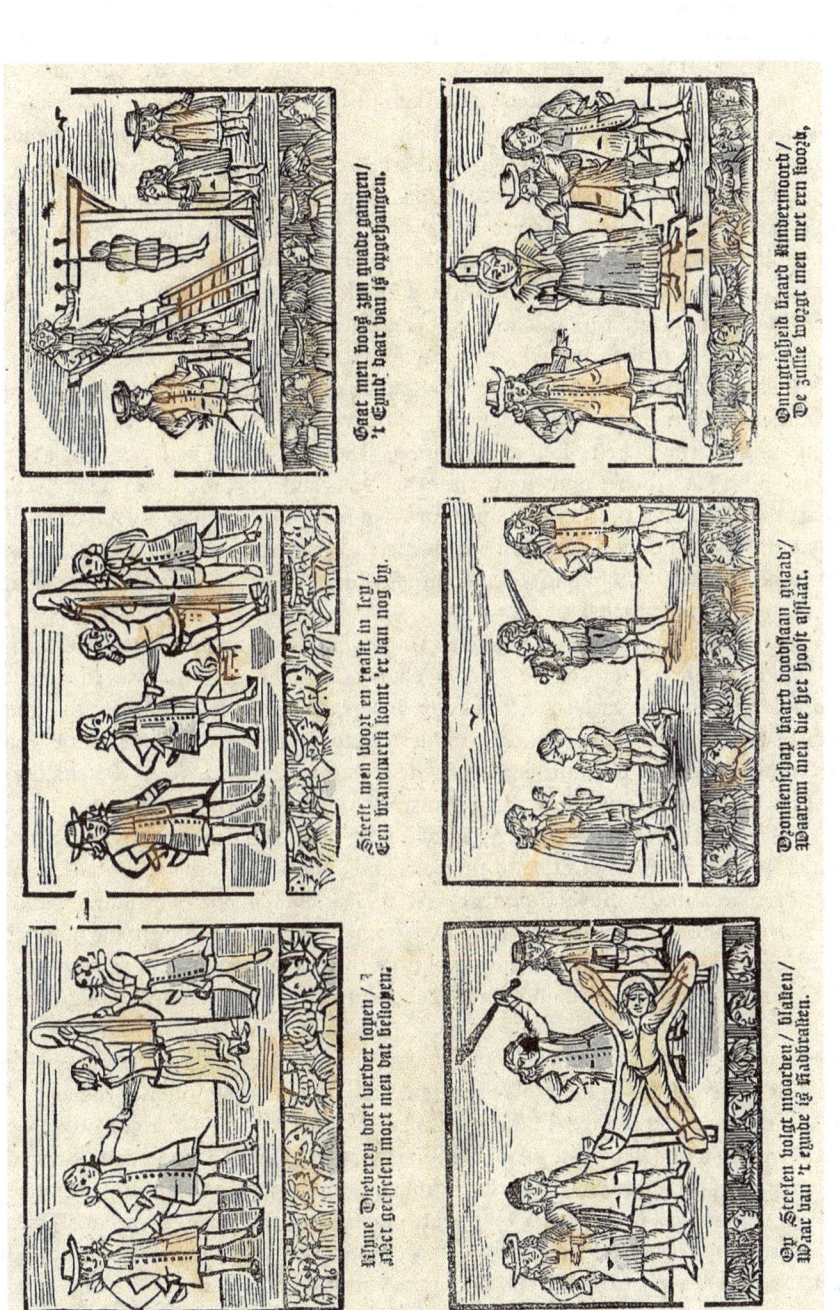

Figure 4.3 Penny print depicting scaffold punishments, third quarter of the eighteenth century.

and to control blood feuds by replacing violent acts of revenge by individuals and kinship groups with government revenge.[41] In order to be accepted by the population, government revenge could not be less visible and less violent than the revenge of individuals and kinship groups. The early modern states, including the Dutch Republic, were generally more stable than those in the preceding period, but the state apparatus was still small and the government's grip on society limited. Under these circumstances, violent public punishments remained important instruments of control. Only with the gradual development of the more stable nation-states in the nineteenth century would the need for public executions as a sign of state power eventually have disappeared.

In addition, both authors emphasize the growing aversion among elites and higher middle classes to the violent nature and visibility of public physical punishments. According to them, this development also had a long history and they place it in the framework of the civilizing process described by Elias, in which state formation once again plays an important role as a driving force.[42] In Elias's theory, state formation not only enables more refined behaviour by pacifying society, but the differentiation of social functions that is linked to state formation also strengthens the interdependence of people and in the longer term it changes their personality structure in the direction of increasing control of behaviour and emotions.[43] Spierenburg in particular explicitly links up with Elias's theory and emphasizes that this civilizing process was expressed, among other things, in the fact that some forms of behaviour, such as the infliction of bodily harm, were no longer seen as acceptable and that many things that once took place without restraint in public space eventually took place exclusively indoors or in some other enclosed space.[44]

Nevertheless, there are some problems with this postulated connection between criminal justice, increasing aversion among elites and upper middle classes to violent and public punishment, and state formation. Evans, for example, points out that the contrast between the instability of early modern states and the stability of states in the nineteenth and twentieth centuries is overstated, and that no evidence is presented to show that the growing objections to violent scaffold punishment from the end of the eighteenth century were in fact the result of a long process of 'conscience formation' in which people became sensitive to the pain and suffering of others.[45] In addition, Müller's research into crime and punishment in Haarlem, cited earlier, shows that at least from the fifteenth century onwards, there was a continuous decline in the number of death sentences carried out, to a low level from the mid-sixteenth century onwards, while the process of state formation in Holland during this period hardly progressed at all.[46]

Because Elias based his theory mainly on the developments in France, state formation plays a central role in his argument, but an increasing interdependence of people and the related changes in their personality structure can of course also be the result of other factors than state formation. In the case of Holland, one might think of a high degree of urbanization and/or the dominance of the market economy, but these too seem to have had no influence on the criminal justice system in Haarlem. This is clearly shown by the large fluctuations in the number of corporal punishments carried out. These rose sharply from the end of the fifteenth century to around the middle of the sixteenth century, declined sharply in the second half of the sixteenth century, and rose sharply again in the first decades of the seventeenth century. It also appears that the trend in death sentences carried out in the cities of Haarlem, Leiden and Gouda took a very different course.[47]

Of course, more research into the criminal justice system in the cities of Holland is necessary for firm conclusions, but for the time being the developments in Holland do not seem to support the view that changes in the criminal justice system can be explained with reference to Elias's theory on state formation and a long-term trend towards more aversion to the infliction of bodily harm. These findings are in line with Geltner's broad inventory of the use of corporal punishment. He concludes that in the long period from antiquity to the present time there was no gradual decline in corporal punishment, but that the degree to which corporal punishment was used in the execution of justice varied according to time and place.[48] In addition, his study shows that the use of corporal punishment has provoked debate almost always and everywhere.[49]

What remains, however, is the observation that from the last decades of the eighteenth century there was a wider criticism in Holland of the system of violent public punishments. Holland was not alone in this. In many European countries, a similar criticism was heard in the eighteenth and early nineteenth centuries.[50] This suggests a common background, in which case the eighteenth-century Enlightenment is the most likely candidate. In his very comprehensive study of capital punishment in Germany, Evans indeed points to the influence of the secularization associated with the Enlightenment, which undermined the Christian belief in divine judgement and a better life after death. For secularized circles, death now became a definitive end, prompting them to criticize a punishment now seen as truly irreparable.[51] Punishments less definitive than the death penalty are not discussed by Evans, but Shoemaker does so in his study of London in the period 1700–1820. He reports the presence 'among late eighteenth-century enlightened opinion of distaste for corporal punishment and a desire to seek the reformation of the offender instead'.[52] In addition, there was a growing concern in London about public order during the execution of the sentences, and a sharp decline in public interest in public scaffold punishments, and the pillory in particular.[53]

Although the connection with Enlightenment thinking is obvious, again more research is needed to determine exactly how the Enlightenment influenced thinking about public scaffold punishments in the cities of Holland. What is clear is that criticism of these scaffold punishments strongly increased in the first half of the nineteenth century and that aspects of Enlightenment thinking played a role in this. Thus, Franke points out that criticism increased because it functioned as a sign of civilization and was also used in the political struggle between the conservative regent aristocracy and liberal citizens. In addition, he emphasizes that the nineteenth-century belief in social progress was also reflected in the confidence that an improved police force, new investigative methods, prison sentences and the 'moral elevation' of the working classes would lead to a decrease in crime. Violent public punishments would then no longer be necessary.[54]

However, the increasing aversion to public and violent punishment did not lead to its swift abolition. The Batavian era did see an end to the practice of exhibiting the bodies of executed lawbreakers on gallows fields but other than that, not much changed initially.[55] Public corporal punishment and the public execution of death sentences remained part of the criminal justice system even though their usefulness and desirability were fiercely contested by opponents.[56] The proponents pointed out the deterrent function of scaffold punishments and some said that people sentenced to imprisonment had 'burst into laughter' after hearing the verdict.[57] The discussion around the draft code of 1827 shows that the majority in the House of Representatives was still in favour of maintaining the existing punishments. In 1848 this was no longer the case, but then the bill to abolish flogging and branding was rejected by a conservative majority in the Senate. And although pardons were increasingly being granted, it would take until 1854 before the public display of lawbreakers, flogging and branding finally were abolished. Death sentences were still carried out in public, however.[58]

The aversion to physical violence prevented part of the elites and middle classes from attending the public execution of sentences, but the number of witnesses remained high and so did the effectiveness of these ceremonial displays of power in the forms of domination, coercion and implicit threat. Around 1840, some 8,000 to 10,000 people are said to have attended public punishments in Amsterdam, and, according to a picture and commentary in the *Leydsche Courant*, the execution of the death sentence on Adrianus Blom in 1856 in Leiden also attracted a large crowd. As in previous centuries, in Leiden, a theatrical effect was sought, in this case by 'the impressive appearance of the scaffold, dressed in mourning cloth'.[59] This had contributed to the fact that according to the reporter, 'this event seems to have made a serious impression on those present'. The new views on public corporal punishment and executions are well expressed in the last sentence of the article, in which the wish is expressed that the city never has to see 'such a spectacle' within its walls again.[60] That wish came true because in Leiden, Blom was indeed the last person to be executed. From the 1850s until the official abolition of capital punishment in 1870, death sentences were still pronounced in the Netherlands, but only in a few cases were they actually carried out.[61]

The conclusion must be that also in the first half of the nineteenth century, public punishment ceremonies functioned as a violent and theatrical form of appropriation of urban space by the authorities. And they still acted as a public demonstration of the power of the political-administrative elites and acceptance of that power by the convicts, as well as a warning to the population not to violate the law and the existing social order.

4.3. Presence of middle-class militias

In the exercise of power, the political-administrative elite in the cities depended on the passive and active support of the middle classes. Chapter 1 has already sketched a picture of the complex web of alliances and interdependencies between elites and middle classes, in which the presence of the large working classes and the fear they instilled was an important factor that brought middle classes and elites together. In short, the alliance between these two classes involved an exchange of livelihood security and political subordination. The middle classes accepted and supported a regime that gave them no direct influence over the local administration and also imposed heavy taxes in exchange for protection against economic competition from non-citizens from inside and outside the city and for welfare arrangements that were intended to ensure that they and their children would not become part of the working classes in the event of economic misfortune or the premature death of the parents.

The foundations of this alliance and the unequal power relations on which it was based were laid in the late Middle Ages. Holland in these years was a relatively peripheral area in economic terms with few large cities and although guilds were not unknown there, they lacked the economic importance and self-confidence of those in the Southern Low Countries.[62] Unlike in the South, they were therefore unable to exert any lasting influence on the administration of the cities. Not coincidentally, it was only in Dordrecht, in the Middle Ages the largest and most important city in Holland, that the guilds did have political influence. In the other cities, a small elite ruled the roost and the middle classes were politically silenced.

The absence of direct political influence in all cities except Dordrecht does not imply that the guilds as an institution were invisible in urban space, on the contrary. In the period before the transition to Protestantism, they were prominently present at processions. Around the middle of the sixteenth century, the great procession on Corpus Christi in Amsterdam was even opened by the guilds, each with its own banner and statues of saints.[63] During the processions, the *schuttersgilden* (militia-guilds) formed a conspicuous group with their uniform dress, armour, weaponry and the often exuberantly decorated headgear or *kaproenen*.[64] In Holland, these militia-guilds originated in the fourteenth century and their most important military task was *der stede wake*, guarding the city gates and ramparts. In addition, it was established early on that the militiamen had to support the city government in case of unrest within the city.[65] From the establishment of the militia-guilds, the militiamen were required to be citizens and also to pay for the weapons and clothing themselves. The first condition excluded strangers and the second condition limited admission to militia-guilds (and later civic militias) to citizens who had some means. The large working classes were excluded from participation because of the latter condition alone.[66]

In medieval cities, the existence of militia-guilds did not remain unnoticed and their presence can be understood as a form of ephemeral appropriation of urban space by (part of) the citizenry. This is because the militiamen marched through the city and fulfilled their defensive tasks in strikingly colourful and identical clothing bearing the city arms or sign of the militia-guild (Figure 4.4).[67] In describing the clothing of the militiamen, Carasso-Kok even speaks of 'bright, aggressive colours'.[68] Moreover, the militiamen were armed and also trained in the use of weapons. The appropriation of urban space by the militia-guilds may have had a reassuring effect on the city's population since the militia would defend the city in case of enemy attacks, but on the other hand, these armed middle classes undoubtedly also posed a certain threat to the administrative elites and working classes. This is evident from the fact that in the fifteenth and sixteenth centuries, magistrates strengthened their grip on the militia-guilds. In this way, they tried to prevent the militiamen from turning against the city government.

Figure 4.4 A subdivision (*rot*) of the Amsterdam militia-guild of the Kloveniers, 1534.

In the cities of Holland, the Protestantization of the government in the second half of the sixteenth century put an end to the tradition of religious processions and from that time onwards, large parades became the exclusive privilege of the militias. At these parades and at other times as well, about which more later, a display of armed force formed a fixed ingredient of their presence in urban space. The years of the Dutch Revolt were an important time for the militia-guilds. Because of the war situation and their indispensable role in the defence of the city, the middle-class militia-guilds managed to gain substantial political influence in a number of cities.[69] This short-lived period in which the militiamen, as representatives of the urban middle classes, elected the city council (*vroedschap*) and were consulted on political matters came to an end in 1581 when the States of Holland prohibited militias from being consulted. Not surprisingly, the later protest movements of the middle classes often referred to this exceptional period of middle-class influence on urban politics and recognition of the middle classes as the cornerstone of the urban community. In the shorter term, however, a reorganization of the urban defence took place and the militia-guilds were absorbed into a new civic guard, the *schutterij* (civic militia).[70]

Unlike the former militia-guilds, the new civic militias had a military and hierarchical organizational structure with chief officers such as colonels, captains, lieutenants and ensigns, non-commissioned officers such as sergeants, corporals and *rotmeesters* (squad-masters) and, of course, the men, recruited from the citizenry.[71] It is in line with this 'militarization' of the organization, that the reforms of the army under Prince Maurice also influenced the militias and that military specialists trained the militias in drill.[72] All in all, this increased the militiamen's military resources and thus also the threat that these armed middle classes posed. Therefore, it was very important for city governments to have a grip on the militias. That is why there were often close ties between city governments and the chief officers of the militias. Sometimes, the highest position in the militia, the colonelcy, was held by a burgomaster, but even when this was not the case, people from the circles of the city magistrate were dominant among the chief officers. The fear of city governments that this armed force within the city would turn against them was not unjustified because, as we will see, the loyalty of the militias, just like that of the earlier militia-guilds, was not a matter of course.

Under the new constellation, the militia still had the task of maintaining public order and defending the city against attacks from outside but they also played a role in ceremonial matters such as receptions of important statesmen, and they took part in military campaigns outside the city to defend the Dutch Republic. In the context of the appropriation of urban space by the middle-class militias, the *optrek* or yearly review played an important role. The exact form could vary from city to city, but the proceedings in Leiden give a good impression of an *optrek*.[73] As in other cities, the *optrek* took place during the annual fair, a time when many people were present in the city. In Leiden the Doelen building (drill hall) functioned as a meeting place on the day of the *optrek*. There, the militiamen were inspected by the officers and some members of the city government to see if everyone's uniform and weaponry were in order. Subsequently, the militia-regiments marched through the city in full regalia. Map 4.1 shows the route followed in 1646.[74]

From the Doelenterrein on the Stadssingel, the militiamen marched in 'goede crijchsordre' (in military order) through Doelensteeg to Rapenburg and followed it in a northerly direction to Breestraat. The important Breestraat with its town hall was walked through completely and via Hogewoerd and Watersteeg the militias reached the

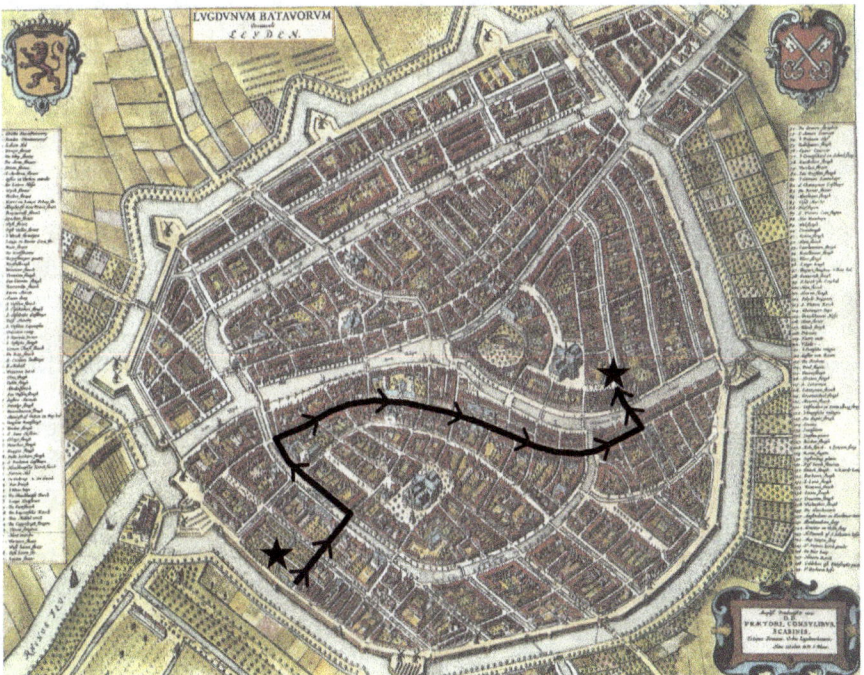

Map 4.1 Route of the Leiden militia during the 1646 *optrek* (north top left).

Gansoord Bridge where they received a medal of honour on behalf of the city.[75] Along the entire route, the inhabitants had to remove dirt, rubbish and obstacles, and even the annual market stalls in Breestraat had to make way temporarily for the appropriation of urban space by the militia during the *optrek*. Their route along prominent streets and canals did not remain unnoticed anyway, as the militiamen apparently fired their weapons during the *optrek*. The latter can be deduced from the ban on shooting with live ammunition and thus using only loose powder.[76]

In a considerably larger city such as Amsterdam, the *optrek* took several days because of the large number of militia-regiments, and Dam square functioned as the end point of the *optrek* (Figure 4.5).[77] But in all cities, large and small, the *optrek* was used by the ruling elites as a way to enhance the reputation of the city and thus the prestige of themselves. The parades therefore contributed to the symbolic capital of this social class. But that was not their only function. Among part of the bystanders and militiamen, the *optrek* undoubtedly aroused feelings of local patriotism which could strengthen the bond between government and governed. So, the *optrek* of militias also played a part in the complex web of alliances and as such, it was an expression of power in the form of seduction.[78] And finally, the image of the armed and military-style militia that marched through the city and gave some demonstrations of its fighting abilities was used to convince the population of the power of the established order and the support it had from the middle classes. Not surprisingly, urban authorities had the working classes in mind. This is clear from the fact that in the second half of the seventeenth century, when the parades had fallen into disuse in some cities, riots and the threat of riots gave rise to pleas for the reinstatement of the *optrek*.[79] The deterrent function of these parades is an expression of power in the form of an implicit threat and this function is also clearly evident in Figure 4.5.[80]

The appropriation of urban space by the middle-class militias, however, was not limited to the *optrek*. The most important regular task of the militia was the night watch: securing the city against attacks from outside and maintaining the peace and safety within the city at night.[81] In order to protect the city against attacks, the guarding of the city gates was a prerequisite, but this task was usually embedded in a ritual that also promoted the visibility of the militia within the city. The militiamen had to report to the town hall before the start of the night watch and after the roll call had been taken they marched from the town hall through the city to the guardhouses that were placed at the various city gates and at strategic locations within the city. Especially in the larger cities, this led to many movements of the armed militia through urban space.

The militia was also responsible for locking the city gates and transferring the keys to the town hall, where they were kept for the night. In the morning, the militiamen collected the keys there and opened the gates, after which they marched from the various guardhouses to the town hall and their presence was again checked during roll call. During the night the militiamen kept watch and from the main guardhouse in the town hall regular rounds were made to the other guardhouses to see if the militiamen were doing their job properly. The fact that this was not always the case, does not alter the fact that the control of the city keys, the opening and closing of the gates and the daily marches from the city hall to the guardhouses and back, were demonstrations of

Figure 4.5 *Optrek* of five regiments of the Amsterdam civic militia, 1683 (detail).

the position of the middle-class militia within the urban community and of the alliance between middle classes and ruling elites.

With the exception of militiamen who fired their guns in a state of drunkenness or sheer boredom when the night watch had come to an end, the resources of the middle-class militiamen, that is weapons and their proficiency in using them, usually remained unused.[82] This changed, however, when there were riots in which the working classes threatened to attack the public order and also the property of the middle classes and urban elites. The involvement of the working classes in riots and revolts will be discussed in more detail in the next section. Here, we are mainly interested in the reaction of the civic militias in times of insurrection. These were moments when they actively used their resources and, by order of city governments, more or less violently appropriated urban space and tried to undo the appropriation by their rioting fellow townsmen and townswomen.

In order to be able to act effectively in case of unrest, a system of *loopplaatsen* was set up. These were strategically important places in the city that had to be immediately occupied by the militia in case of emergency. It is fortunate that from around 1675 for Leiden some maps have been preserved that show the division of the city for the eight militia-regiments and the location of the *loopplaatsen*.[83] Map 4.2 confirms the central position of the town hall on Breestraat as the seat of the magistrate and also shows the government's fear that during an uprising this very place might be attacked by the rioters because no fewer than three regiments had their first *loopplaats* near the town hall. The map also shows that bridges played a strategically important role in the water-rich cities of Holland. Of the sixty-four *loopplaatsen* in Leiden, eight for each of the eight regiments, forty involved a bridge.[84] By occupying these bridges, the militia was able to prevent movement through the city during riots and isolate groups of rioters from each other. It will not be a coincidence that especially the poor districts in the urban periphery could be virtually cut off from the more centrally located parts of Leiden.[85] In his previously cited *Harlemias* (1648), Schrevelius confirms that hindering the mobility of the rioters as much as possible was a tactic used by the militia. According to Schrevelius, when the fire bell was rung in Haarlem, 'the militias immediately take up arms, each in his own district, occupy the roads, stop the furious people, and with a regiment of citizens keep the town hall'.[86]

Studies by Dekker not only show that there were considerably more riots and revolts in Holland than was long thought but also that the militia acted selectively during these disturbances.[87] The latter is very clear from the course of events during the previously mentioned Aansprekersoproer in Amsterdam in 1696 (see Chapter 1). From the detailed report of the revolt by the Amsterdam broker and contemporary Joris Craffurd, we know that the militia did not initially make any move to intervene. Indeed, there were indications that part of the citizenry had little affinity with urban politics and, according to Craffurd, the loyalty of the militia to the city government was also in doubt.[88]

The turning point came with the plundering of the De Pinto-house on Sint Antoniesbreestraat, whose Jewish inhabitants had nothing to do with the new by-law on burials. The two or three regiments present on the nearby Nieuwmarkt (*loopplaats*)

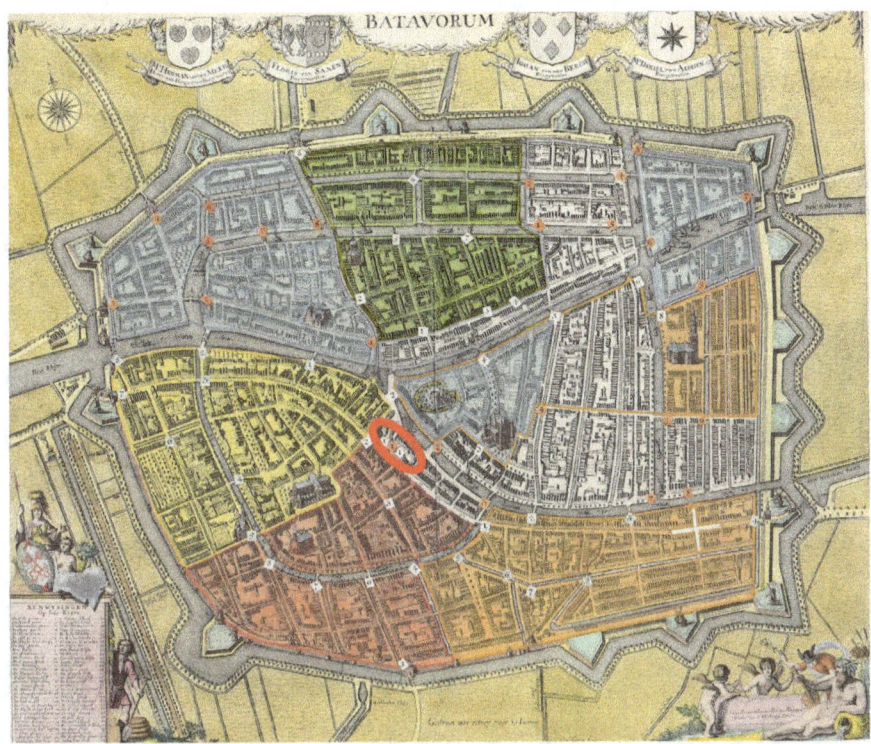

Map 4.2 The eight districts of Leiden and the (numbered) location of *loopplaatsen*, c. 1675 (the location of the town hall is circled).

went to this house to restore order, but when they saw that it was purely a matter of looting and not a protest against the by-law, they realized, according to Craffurd, that the looting might also affect their own houses. The militiamen then forced their way into De Pinto's house and slaughtered the looters so that the house 'was splattered with blood from top to bottom. It flowed down the stairs and on the floor like water . . . .'[89] The middle-class militia had now clearly chosen the side of the ruling elites and the city government announced in a decree that 'to maintain peace and quiet' violence would henceforth be met with violence.[90]

Other segments of the middle classes now also joined the militia and the municipal government. For example, the captains (*overlieden*) of the extensive peat bearers' guild offered 'to punctually obey the orders of the gentlemen of the magistrate . . .' and they guaranteed the reliability of their guild members.[91] They were then armed with pikes and ordered to stand guard at the town hall and on Dam square. In addition, all those who had a horse were called upon to form a cavalry and soon this cavalry, which was to grow to about 300 men, rode 'with bare swords' through all streets and along the ramparts. It caused 'great terror and fear among the common people'.[92] At the same time the militia-regiments in full armour marched through the city which 'caused the common people to be very wary and everyone was overcome by fright . . .'.[93]

By force and also by the threat of force, the middle classes re-appropriated urban space and the alliance between middle classes and elites was confirmed and strengthened. As a reward for their loyalty, the city authorities offered the militiamen food, drink and tobacco, and all citizens who had been under arms received a commemorative medal with an inscription expressing the alliance of the city government and the citizenry against the (mutinous) working classes: 'The Government of Amsterdam / honours Its Citizens with this Medal / as a reward for Their Traditional Virtue / and Encountered Loyalty'.[94] The print commemorating the presentation of the commemorative medal to the *manhafte schuttery van Amsterdam* (brave militia of Amsterdam) also celebrated the alliance between the elites and the middle classes, referring to the rebellious classes as 'the rapacious mob, eager for citizen's loot' (Figure 4.6).[95]

The fact that the alliance between middle classes and elites was not always tight has already been demonstrated by the fact that at the time of the Aanspreekersoproer, the middle-class militia did not immediately and unconditionally side with the city government and the latter doubted the loyalty of the militia. It seems that the middle

Figure 4.6 Commemorative print of the Aansprekersoproer in Amsterdam, 1696.

classes only mobilized when they were confronted with the possibility that their houses might be plundered as well. Craffurd himself also believed this to be a possibility. In his notes on the revolt he writes that without heavy intervention of the militia 'the whole city would have been flooded with general plunder'.[96]

The ambivalent attitude of the middle classes was not specific to the seventeenth century and to the early stages of the Amsterdam Aansprekersoproer. The passivity of the Haarlem militia-guilds was striking, for example, when in 1422 enraged artisans allegedly killed thirty-six members of the city council, without the militia intervening to restore public order and prevent bloodshed.[97] This radical aloofness from an attack on the city government was not common, but it is certain that the interests of government and citizenry did not always coincide. Especially during tax revolts, the militias regularly chose not to act when the working classes proceeded to plunder the houses of the hated tax-farmers. After all, they themselves also suffered from the taxes.[98] In 1748, for instance, when riots broke out in several cities, the militia in Haarlem declared unambiguously 'that they do not want to put themselves in any danger or risk for any tax farmer'. And in Leiden, the militiamen who stood guard at night decided 'that they would not intervene on behalf of the tax farmers or stand in front of their houses, much less save them from further mischief'.[99] In all these cases, therefore, the militias did not make use of their resources – weapons and skill in their use – and, out of a deliberate self-interest, allowed the working classes to appropriate urban space. The alliance between ruling elites and middle classes was then temporarily broken to make way for an alliance between militiamen and the rebellious working classes. That this alliance was also felt by the working classes is evident from the bitterness of the looters when during the tax revolts of 1748 the Amsterdam militiamen fired on them, for they had heard militiamen say that they would not allow themselves to be used to protect the tax-farmer's houses from looters.[100]

The militias played a more active role in the political revolts of 1653, 1672 and 1747. These revolts arose against the background of international crises that caused fear and uncertainty and affected the prestige and legitimacy of the ruling elites.[101] In 1653 the war with England destabilized the internal political situation, in 1672 the combined attack of the English fleet and the armies of Louis XIV did so, and in 1747 another French invasion had the same effect. In the activism of the militias in these years, two things came together: protests of the urban middle classes against the local ruling elites and Orangist sympathies. Boone and Prak refer to the protests against the local administrative elites as the 'Little Tradition'. They see it as an addition to what Blockmans had earlier called the 'Great Tradition' of urban revolts against overlords.[102] Typical for revolts in the Little Tradition is the call for political representation by the middle classes. To support their demands they often referred to old privileges and to periods when the middle classes actually had some political influence, such as during the Dutch Revolt.[103]

In their pursuit of more political influence, the militias usually sought support from the family of Orange in their capacity of stadtholders. Especially in The Hague, the Orange-mindedness of the civic militia was great. In 1653 it was noted that if it had been up to the militia, the young William III – then still a child – would have been proclaimed 'sovereign or imperator'.[104] In Enkhuizen in the same year there was a revolt that had an unmistakably Orangist character and in which the government of the city was in fact taken over by the militia. With the help of the working classes, first armed with sticks and later with muskets, the militia occupied the city gates and ramparts and, with cannon shots, kept the soldiers, who had been sent from The Hague to the riotous Enkhuizen, at bay.[105] Until eleven companies of soldiers put an end to the revolt, the alliance between the elites and the middle classes was broken and the middle classes, supported by the working classes, appropriated urban space.

The call for more political influence and a more prominent position for the Orange-stadtholders had little lasting effect in 1653, but that was different in 1672. Partly under pressure of the disastrous military developments, revolts broke out in many cities against the magistrate in office. The militias played a major role in these revolts as well. Because of their degree of organization and their possession of weapons they were ideally suited to act as spokesmen for the urban middle classes and as leaders of the revolts. In The Hague, the involvement of the militias in the 1672 revolt took an unusually violent turn when militiamen executed the Grand Pensionary Johan de Witt and his brother Cornelis de Witt and delivered their bodies to an angry crowd.[106] Generally speaking, the militia acted violently in popular uprisings, but physical violence against the elites was rare. However, they did not hesitate to march in full armour to town halls and, once there, to shout slogans against the city administrators. In 1672, this demonstration of their power through the appropriation of urban space took place in cities like Purmerend, Alkmaar, Haarlem, Leiden and also in The Hague.[107]

The revolts of 1748 resembled those of 1672 in many ways. Just as in 1748, military invasions, political crisis and dissatisfied middle classes brought an end to a stadtholderless era and again the militias played an important role in the changes. As before, the middle classes demanded the resignation of the magistrate and more political influence, frequently referring to old privileges or previous situations. All these issues are reflected in the 1748 uprising in Leiden.[108] After the temporary suspension of the collection of the farmed taxes had put an end to the revolt, the militia of Leiden presented its programme of political demands, which was adopted by hundreds of militiamen during a meeting in the Schuttersdoelen (drill hall). At the same time, a kind of executive committee of ten spokesmen was elected that publicly challenged the position of members of the city council and exercised actual power in the city for weeks. Regularly, militiamen marched through the streets of Leiden to demonstrate who was in charge in the city.[109] This appropriation of public space by the middle-class militia came to an end when, at the request of some *regenten*, a thousand soldiers entered the city and occupied strategic objects such as the town hall, the city gates and the ammunition depot. All gatherings were forbidden, soldiers patrolled the streets day and night and the old order was restored.

Apart from the disappointing outcome of the revolt for Leiden's middle classes, it will be clear from the aforementioned that the alliance between middle classes and elites in the cities of Holland was not unconditional, that the middle classes had their own interests and political ambitions and that the militias, through their possession of weapons and their degree of organization, could at various times present themselves as representatives of the middle classes and did not hesitate to enter into (temporary)

Figure 4.7 Marching militiamen in The Hague, c. 1750.

alliances with the working classes. The ephemeral appropriation of urban space by the middle classes in those years of civil unrest was based to a large extent on the resources available to the militias and the threat of power in the forms of domination and coercion (see also Figure 4.7).

While order had been restored in Leiden and other cities, the underlying problem, the call for citizen participation in the municipal administration, had not been solved. The immediate effect of the revolts was to strengthen the position of the stadtholder. William IV now became stadtholder of all provinces and the stadtholdership was declared hereditary in both the male and female line. More than before, the stadtholders now had influence on the policies of the Dutch Republic, and in the extensive patronage system that was established, they played a pivotal role.[110] However, the restoration of stadtholder power, which was largely due to protests by urban middle classes, did not lead to the reforms desired by those middle classes and sowed the seeds of anti-Orangist sentiment among this section of society.

For the family of Orange, the strengthening of the stadtholder status may have satisfied their princely ambitions, but it also made them vulnerable to criticism in times when the Dutch Republic found itself in dire straits. This was the case in the 1780s when the Republic clashed with England in the Fourth Anglo-Dutch War (1780–4). The deplorable state of the navy then became clear to everyone and the Republic had to watch powerlessly as the English blocked trade and shipping and captured Asian trading posts. The frustration about the country's lack of resilience joined in with a current within society that since the first half of the century had been pointing towards economic and moral decline and that wanted to turn the tide by founding societies, organizing competitions, publishing periodicals and many other activities. These new journals, the 'spectatorial writings', tirelessly propagated 'the message of virtuous, tolerant, productive and socially engaged citizenship' and attributed a central place in society to the middle classes.[111] Partly due to the demonstrated incapacity in the war against England, the discontent among part of the middle classes acquired a political dimension that manifested itself in fierce criticism by these Patriots, as they called themselves, of the stadtholder, nobility and urban *regenten*, who were held responsible for the situation in which the country had found itself.

But it did not stop at words. Because of the war, the idea that a free people should also be able to defend itself by force of arms gained great appeal. In 1781, Joan Derk van der Capellen tot den Pol, in his anonymous and fiercely anti-Orangist pamphlet 'Aan het Volk van Nederland' (To the People of the Netherlands), gave historical underpinning to this idea and also propagated it forcefully. At the end of his pamphlet, Van der Capellen repeats the central message and writes in plain language: 'Arm yourselves all'.[112] The existing militias would have been a suitable instrument for this ideal of civilian armament, were it not for the fact that in the course of the eighteenth century, these hardly functioned at all in many cities and where they did, the grip of the ruling elites on the militias was considerable.[113] For this reason, *exercitiegenootschappen* (armed drill clubs) and *vrijkorpsen* (volunteer corps) emerged that defended Patriot ideals not only against the conservative urban *regenten*, but also against the Orangists, who were especially well represented among the working classes. And although the working classes were certainly not absent among the Patriots, the *exercitiegenootschappen* and *vrijkorpsen* were mainly a matter of the middle classes.[114] This is evident from the fact that the armed citizens had to bear the costs of uniforms and armaments themselves. In the 1780s, demonstrations around town halls, parades, shooting practices, violent conflicts with Orangists and other armed displays of power were used by the middle-class *exercitiegenootschappen* and *vrijkorpsen* to appropriate urban space (Figure 4.8).[115]

The Patriot period (1780-7) was the last expression of what Boone and Prak call the Little Tradition: revolts of middle classes against the political elites with the important demand of political influence of the middle classes on urban policy and thus recognition of their position in society. As such, these revolts never seriously threatened the continuity of the existing power relations and the hierarchical ordering of society. The aim was to strengthen the position of the middle classes within the existing social order and not to change that social order.[116]

The Patriot Revolution came to an end in 1787, because the *exercitiegenootschappen* and *vrijkorpsen* were no match for the 25,000 Prussian troops that came to the aid of the stadtholder and his Prussian wife (and sister of the Prussian king). Many Patriots fled abroad to escape purges and violence, and many only returned when, with the help of French troops, the old regime was overthrown and in January 1795 the Batavian Republic was proclaimed.[117] That same month, the stadtholder and his retinue went into exile in England.

It was in keeping with the Batavian revolution of 1795 that the idea of civic militias was revived and also that these militias were no longer strictly local but national in character. For this study it is important to note that the militias during the Batavian Republic and thereafter due to their compulsory nature had a social composition

Figure 4.8 *Exercitiegenootschap* (drill club) De Palmboom in Rotterdam, 1785.

that was very different from the militias of the *ancien régime* and therefore they can no longer be regarded as the armed forces of the middle classes who appropriated urban space by demonstrating their (potential) power based on the possession of weapons and proficiency in the handling of them. The militias continued to exist until the beginning of the twentieth century, but in the course of time, despite many reforms and attempts at restoration, they lost importance.[118] There was no place for them in the nascent national state. More and more, their tasks were taken over by a bureaucratic and centrally managed government apparatus, including the army and police.[119] This development ties in with the process of bureaucratization described by Weber a long time ago. The collegial administration by local stakeholders that was typical for the relatively independent cities of the *ancien régime* evolved under the influence of political, economic and social changes towards a fully fledged national bureaucracy.[120] According to Weber, these extensive bureaucracies were marked by a hierarchical structure, internal specialization of functions, selection of staff on the basis of professional qualities and the professional exercise of functions.[121] With the latter we have to think of what Weber describes as 'the dominance of a spirit of formalistic impersonality: "*Sine ira et studio*", without hatred or passion'.[122] Quite different from the performance of duties by armed middle classes such as the local militias.

4.4. Working-class riots and revolts

Other than with urban authorities and middle-class militias, *exercitiegenootschappen* and *vrijkorpsen*, the exercise of power and the violent appropriation of urban space by the working classes did not take place within existing institutional structures. Nevertheless, the working classes were also able to temporarily exercise power and appropriate urban space through the use of resources. The most important resources the working classes had at their disposal were their numerical size and physical presence in the cities.[123] These resources featured prominently in the popular uprisings that are the focus of this section. For the urban middle classes and elites, these riots and revolts were as much evidence of the impulsiveness, irrationality and capriciousness of those commonly referred to as *het gemeen* or *het grauw*.[124] These alleged characteristics of the working classes gave the riots for contemporaries and later generations the character of occasional outbursts of violence, prompted by rapacity or driven by individuals or groups who wanted to use the riots to realize their own goals. In wartime, for example, some people liked to see behind the riots the hand of foreign spies who tried to undermine the position of the Dutch Republic by creating domestic unrest.[125]

That the riots and revolts expressed a programme of the working classes and that many of the actions had a ritual and theatrical character was almost inconceivable to contemporaries because it conflicted with their conception of *het gemeen*. In this section, the programmatic and ritual character of riots and revolts is presented as an ephemeral but structured form of appropriation of urban space and a demonstration of the power of a social class that played only a marginal role in the fields of housing and politics. The emphasis will be on food riots and tax riots because in Holland the working classes played an important part in them.

The idea that pre-modern riots were more than occasional and unstructured outbursts of violence owes much to Thompson's influential article on the moral economy of the English crowd in the eighteenth century. In this article, Thompson focuses on food riots and, based on extensive research, concludes that these should not be regarded as a phenomenon driven solely by economic factors such as high food prices and unemployment. In opposition to this 'spasmodic view', Thompson argues that the food riot 'was a highly-complex form of direct popular action, disciplined and with clear objectives' and rooted in 'a consistent traditional view of social norms and obligations, of the proper economic functions of several parties within the community, which, taken together, can be said to constitute the moral economy of the poor'.[126] Within this moral economy, for example, it was not acceptable for merchants to export grain in times of food shortage and also the government was expected to take measures to prevent merchants and others from profiting from scarcity and to maintain food prices at an acceptable level.[127] Food riots were the means used by the working classes to remind the government of its (attributed) responsibility and to punish merchants and shopkeepers when they, in the opinion of the rioters, implemented unacceptable price increases. In this context, it is also fitting that food riots often had a remarkably disciplined nature and were typified by restraint rather than disorder. Thus, even in times of famine, the stocks of merchants and shopkeepers who charged unjust prices were sometimes destroyed and not taken away by the rioters for their own use. Another option was to force the seller to accept a lower price by the threat of violence. In this *taxation populaire*, to use a term from Rudé's work, the rioters sometimes also urged the authorities to enforce the lower price.[128]

Food riots also occurred in the cities of Holland. For the years 1600–1795 Dekker counted some thirty of them and for the first half of the nineteenth century food riots have been documented in the years 1816, 1817 and 1845.[129] It is striking that the repertoire of actions noted by Thompson, punishment of immoral retailers and enforcement of 'correct' prices, was also used in Holland. Punishment occurred, for example, in Haarlem in 1693, when a crowd threw a dairy merchant's butter on the ground and poured milk into the street. A riot in Alkmaar in 1741 also involved the destruction of a butter supply and eggs were smashed.[130] More often, food riots were about forcing lower prices from grocers, from farmers selling their products on city markets, and from bakers and vegetable sellers. The reason was almost always the suspicion that the sellers were holding back supplies or had made price agreements among themselves. If the sellers did not comply with the demand to sell the food at a lower price, this could be a reason for destroying the trade stocks or for what in our times is sometimes euphemistically referred to as 'proletarian shopping'.

Undoubtedly, not all suspicions were justified and merchants and retailers were also punished unjustly by having their stock destroyed or being forced to sell at too low prices. But that the accusations were not an ad hoc pretext for bargain shopping is shown, for example, by the course of events in the city of Schoonhoven in 1699. The grocers in that city were accused of price fixing. This accusation could of course have major consequences, but after the burgomasters had an investigation carried out in the neighbouring cities, and it turned out that the prices there were quite similar, there were no riots or revolts.[131] For us, the question of whether the accusations of price fixing were always justified is less important. What matters is that in Holland, too, there was a certain consensus among the working classes in the cities about what was acceptable and what was not, and just as in England and elsewhere, riots were used as a means of making it clear to the merchants and retailers involved and to the entire urban community that the moral economy had been violated.

In his much-quoted article, Thompson concentrates on food riots, but it will come as no surprise that the moral universe of the working classes encompassed more than just food prices. Judging by the frequency of their occurrence, in Holland taxes were more of a cause for revolt than market prices.[132] These tax revolts mainly involved opposition to indirect taxes on basic necessities since increasing excise on products such as food and peat directly affected the purchasing power of the population and this was obviously felt most by those with few and very few financial resources. Although taxes were imposed by the government, the rioters directed their actions mainly against those who were responsible for their collection: tax-farmers and tax-collectors. This was the case, for instance, in the Pachtersoproer revolt in Haarlem in June 1748. The houses of seven tax-farmers were looted and because the militia refused to protect the property of tax-farmers, the looters met with little resistance. In the same month, houses of tax-farmers and tax-collectors were plundered in The Hague, Leiden and Amsterdam. As a reaction to these riots, the States of Holland decided on 25 June to abolish the farmed taxes.[133] Since increasing taxes did not always lead to riots and revolts, it seems that there was also a certain consensus among the working classes about the level of tax burden that was still acceptable under the given circumstances.

That the riots and revolts were also an expression of a feeling among the working classes that the government was failing is evident from the interesting phenomenon that the participants sometimes temporarily and symbolically took the place of the ruling elites. In 1747, for instance, rioters stormed the Amsterdam town hall shouting: 'The gentlemen treat us like canaille and then we will play for burgomasters and we will take care of things.'[134] Some even managed to get into the town hall, opened the windows facing Dam square, showed the crowd the cushions on which the members of the magistrate leaned when proclaiming by-laws and, as a substitute for the Rod of Justice, stuck a broom out of the window. And in his chronicle of the 1748 Pachtersoproer in Amsterdam, Abraham Chaim Braatbard wrote that the plunderers first formed a court from their midst, consisting of burgomasters, aldermen, a judge, secretaries, scribes and officers. 'And thus', says Braatbard, 'they judged the case and then they started plundering.'[135] So when the authorities failed, the rioters symbolically took the place of the authorities to do justice after all. Dekker argues that this happened partly in the expectation that the city government would continue the policy of the rioters (which, of course, was almost never the case).[136]

The unspoken consensus also existed when the honour of the working classes was at stake. This became very clear during the Aansprekersoproer of 1696 in Amsterdam. A number of issues were mixed up in that revolt, but above all, the city government's plan to establish a municipal funeral service aroused great indignation among the working classes. The plan implied that everyone would be obliged to make use of the municipal *Aansprekers* (undertakers), but the poor were exempt from this obligation. They could also have the body of the deceased carried by neighbours or others if they had obtained an *Acte voor de Armen*, a certificate stating that someone was poor, from the city secretary.[137] This deed also exempted them from the burial tax that was part of the new construction. The exception for the poor appears to have been a true attempt by the city government to take into account the limited financial resources of a significant part of the population, but it also demonstrates the ruling elites' limited knowledge of what was going on among the working classes. For many of them, a funeral now became a public demonstration of financial insolvency and this prospect aroused great aversion. This aversion was considerably strengthened by the rumour that from now on the poor would be brought to their final resting place in a simple coffin bearing Amsterdam's coat of arms.[138]

In the riot that followed, the residence of burgomaster Boreel, who was held responsible for the plans, was targeted. To begin with, all the windows of this house on Herengracht were smashed. The smashing of windows was a fixed ritual in this kind of action and it was not without meaning. The façade of houses was an important outward sign of social status, and the theatrical defacement of the façade in Holland and elsewhere in Europe symbolically affected the prestige of the residents.[139] Then the front door was forced with a lamppost and the rioters forced their way into the house. There the interior was thoroughly destroyed and the contents were thrown out into the street and into the water of Herengracht. Although at first glance these and similar acts of looting the homes of tax-farmers and food sellers appear to be uncontrolled expressions of popular fury, their ritual character is revealed by the fact that there were indeed rules to which the rioters adhered. For example, household furniture and other items were damaged or destroyed, but violence was almost never used against people. It is illustrative that the firearms which the rioters captured from militiamen and soldiers, or which they found in the armouries of the plundered houses, were never used in confrontations with the authorities. These weapons were disabled or thrown into the water.[140] Apart from accidents during the looting, the casualties during riots and revolts were therefore almost all victims of the violent attempts of the authorities to suppress the insurrections.[141]

Finally, the ritual and organized nature of looting is also evident from the fact that looters destroyed the household goods they found and did not take them as booty (Figure 4.9).[142] During the looting of the house of burgomaster Boreel, for instance, a servant who tried to bring a valuable mirror to safety was mistaken for a looter and reprimanded by other looters: theft was not what this was all about! And when the servant did not smash the mirror himself, the one who had addressed him smashed it to pieces with the hilt of his knife. The plundering of Boreel's house and the houses of tax-farmers and others was meant as a warning and punishment and not as a licence

Figure 4.9 Plundering of the house and storehouses of tax-farmer A.M. van Arssen on Singel in Amsterdam, 1748.

for theft. During the 1748 tax revolts, the rioters had even set up a court that would punish looters as thieves if they took anything from the houses to be looted.[143]

The previous section has shown that looting sometimes did end in theft. In the case of the looting of the De Pinto residence, there was no evident relationship with the cause of the Aansprekersoproer and moreover, the looters took valuables. More than a ritualized warning and punishment, this seems to have been an expression of what Rudé calls the 'levelling instinct', the latently present awareness that the inequality in society was unjust and the pursuit of a 'rough sort of social justice' in the forms of theft and destruction of property belonging to the affluent classes.[144] It is worth emphasizing that in addition to this more or less ideologically motivated behaviour, uprisings, riots and lootings also had (and have) their own dynamics, as a result of which existing notions of what is and what is not acceptable lose influence, the usual restraint disappears and things can get seriously out of hand.[145] Whatever the background may have been, the looters of the De Pinto residence crossed the line of theft, which, as we have seen, was sufficient cause for the militia to intervene in a bloody fashion.

From the foregoing, we may conclude that because of their programmatic and ritual character, the popular riots in Holland's cities can be regarded as communicative acts and expressions of power in the forms of domination, coercion and implicit threat. The working classes temporarily appropriated urban space and used it to demonstrate their power and their views on the behaviour and responsibilities of individuals, social groups and political elites. Urban space was not a neutral backdrop to this, but a factor that actively affected the possibilities of mobilizing supporters and the effectiveness with which the message of the rioters could be propagated. In his 'Cities and insurrections', Hobsbawn mentions four spatial characteristics that make a city an ideal place for riots and insurrections.[146] Let us examine to what extent the cities of Holland corresponded to these ideal conditions for rioters.

The first spatial factor influencing riots and public disorder is the size and population density of cities. Relatively small distances and high population densities were important in disseminating information, mobilizing supporters and participating in riots and public disorder. Until the end of the period covered by this study, distance and population density were of particular importance because mass media were still unknown and the few newspapers were hardly read by the working classes. Calls to action were sometimes distributed in the form of handwritten notes or printed pamphlets, but in order to reach the masses, more was needed, and for a long time women played an important role in this. Hendrik Toren, an eyewitness to the Costerman riot in Rotterdam in 1690 who later moved to England, writes in his *History of Holland* about the role of women in triggering this riot. According to Toren, they had formed a company and appointed 'one of the most resolute women' as its captain. And, he continues:

> Another impudent of that sex tied a small cask upon her belly and was to serve the company to their drummer. An uncle of me did see that an audacious and very immodest woman ... lifted up her petticoats and tore the forepart out of her

dirty and coloured smock for to be put up a standard which she carried upon her unchaist body.¹⁴⁷

And so they marched on the Rotterdam town hall.

It was by no means unusual for women to play an important role in mobilizing the crowd with improvised drums and banners.¹⁴⁸ Often they were assisted by boys. This was also the case in the Aansprekersoproer (Figure 4.10). Women and boys, according to Craffurd, equipped with improvised drums and banners 'marched with a great deal of noise through many streets and along the ramparts. Their numbers grew tremendously, indeed they took the audacity to march in such form over Dam square and past the town hall'. When they arrived there, so Craffurd heard, they stuck a paper on the façade of the town hall with the text 'This house is to let. Immediately available for occupation.'¹⁴⁹ What is described here is a very effective way of mobilizing the working classes. It is also no coincidence that the group marched along the ramparts – the edges of the city – because, as we have seen, that is where those with the lowest incomes lived. The theatrical aspect of this appropriation of urban space was expressed

Figure 4.10 Riot on Dam square during the Aansprekersoproer in Amsterdam, 1696 (detail).

not only in the drums and banners, but also in the brooms, sticks, scrubs, pit hooks and other items that the rioters carried with them and, of course, in the symbolic letting of the town hall, a clear criticism of the policy of the magistrate and a symbolic expropriation of the building where they performed their function.[150]

The other way in which a riot became known was through word of mouth. Here too, working-class women seem to have played a major role. They often maintained intensive contacts with other women in their neighbourhoods, visited markets and shops, organized neighbourly help and often functioned as the pivot of family networks.[151] A clear illustration of the way in which these neighbourhood contacts functioned relates to the *Damoproer* of 1848, described by Bos. In those years, printed notes had replaced handwritten messages, but the oral transmission of information remained as important as ever. In a short pamphlet written in 1848, an elderly man from Amsterdam reports that he was informed about the riot by his wife, when she came home from shopping and excitedly called out to him: 'Do you know, father, what I heard in the grocery shop? ... Neighbour Grietje heard from neighbour Stijntje that neighbour Pieter has found a printed note on the road ...'.[152] It will be clear that these forms of mobilization and dissemination of information worked best in relatively small cities with high population densities. And the cities of Holland were relatively small and densely populated.

Table 4.1 presents information on the built-up area of eight cities in Holland for the period 1500–2010. In 1500, Haarlem, then the largest of the cities listed, had an area of over 98 hectares, or just under one square kilometre. Alkmaar, the smallest in area in the table, came to no more than 38.9 hectares. The table clearly shows that the surface area of the cities did not increase or hardly increased in the period from after the large urban extensions in the seventeenth century until the mid-nineteenth century.[153] With a built-up area of approximately 470 hectares, Amsterdam was by far the largest city in that period and also the only one among the cities of Holland whose size possibly imposed limitations on the mobilization of the working classes and the dissemination of information about riots and insurrections. It is striking, for instance, that among those arrested after the *Damoproer* of 1848 were no inhabitants of the Oostelijke Eilanden (Eastern Islands). It is conceivable that this eccentrically located

Table 4.1 Built-Up Area in Hectares of Selected Cities in Holland, 1500–2010

	c. 1500	*c.* 1750	*c.* 1850	2010*
Amsterdam	88.4	469.9	474.1	7814.2
Rotterdam	57.4	119.6	127.2	6485.3
The Hague	53.5	180.8	199.6	4498.1
Leiden	94.4	144.2	144.2	1227.6
Haarlem	98.1	132.6	146.4	1775.9
Dordrecht	57.1	66.8	103.8	1719.6
Delft	91.5	91.5	91.5	1065.3
Alkmaar	38.9	56.5	62.5	1473.1

* The built-up area in 2010 excludes green areas such as parks and sports fields within the municipal boundaries. The cities are listed in order of the size of their population in 1850.
Source: Reinout Rutte and Jaap Evert Abrahamse (eds), *Atlas of the Dutch Urban Landscape. A Millennium of Spatial Development* (Bussum: Thoth, 2016) 13, and tables E2, E3 and E6.

working-class neighbourhood, about which more later, had relatively little connection to what was happening elsewhere in the city.[154] A similar situation did not exist in the other cities. They could be traversed on foot from north to south and from east to west in relatively little time. A comparison with the situation in 2010 also shows how small the cities were even after the urban extensions of the seventeenth century.

Table 4.2 provides information on population density in number of inhabitants per hectare for the same cities. Due to the strong population growth, densities increased in all cities between 1500 and 1700, despite the often extensive urban extensions. For the cities listed in the table taken together, population density rose from 130 inhabitants per hectare in 1500 to 355 inhabitants in 1700. A century and a half later, with 369 inhabitants per hectare, it was almost the same, but individual cities developed in very different ways. In Rotterdam and The Hague densities rose sharply, in Amsterdam it remained at the same level and in the other cities population decline led to falling densities. Nevertheless, it is clear that even these low densities were still very significant in comparison to the situation in 2010. Between the reference years 1850 and 2010, the density in the eight cities taken together decreased from 369 inhabitants to ninety-three inhabitants per hectare. All in all, we may conclude that rioters in mobilizing supporters and spreading information about riots benefitted from the high population densities and relatively small distances in the pre-modern cities of Holland.

Hobsbawn also argued that his ideal city for riots and revolts would be better off not having a wide river running through it. He points out that in these cities, the police can easily occupy bridges to limit the mobility of the crowd, and, referring to the situation in London and Paris, he states that 'the two banks of a river look away from each other'.[155] Some of the cities in Holland, such as Dordrecht, Rotterdam and Amsterdam, are situated along very wide waterways, but housing in the period studied here was mainly limited to one bank.[156] Thus, the problem of limited interaction between the urban districts on either side of a wide waterway did not arise here, but it cannot be

Table 4.2 Population Density in Number of Inhabitants per Hectare of Selected Cities in Holland, 1500–2010

	c. 1500	c. 1700*	c. 1850	2010
Amsterdam	128.9	466.1	472.5	98.2
Rotterdam	89.1	376.3	708.1	91.4
The Hague	102.8	110.6	361.8	108.6
Leiden	151.0	464.6	248.9	95.4
Haarlem	124.5	286.6	176.6	84.2
Dordrecht	196.1	299.4	201.4	68.9
Delft	127.9	273.2	201.6	90.8
Alkmaar	107.4	241.6	163.1	63.7

* The population figures for around 1700 mentioned by Rutte and Abrahamse are related here to the built-up area in 1750. Because the cities mentioned had no substantial urban extensions in the first half of the eighteenth century, this has no consequences for the calculation of population densities. Only in The Hague will the population density have been slightly higher around 1700 than is indicated here.
Source: Reinout Rutte and Jaap Evert Abrahamse (eds), *Atlas of the Dutch Urban Landscape. A Millennium of Spatial Development* (Bussum: Thoth, 2016) tables D3 and D6 and Piet Lourens and Jan Lucassen, *Inwonertallen van Nederlandse steden ca.1300-1800* (Amsterdam: NEHA, 1997).

denied that water was omnipresent and all cities had a large number of bridges. In the previous section, it was already noted that the authorities and the militias were well aware of the strategic importance of these bridges and during riots and revolts they indeed attempted to limit the mobility of the rioters and to isolate small groups from each other by occupying bridges. In that respect, the cities in Holland were not ideal from the perspective of rioters, but there is no evidence that the physical infrastructure of canals and (numerous) bridges actually nipped riots in the bud. Thus, the situation in the cities of Holland resembled the one in Venice. For Venice, too, the canals were mentioned as a limiting factor in riots, but just as in Holland, the presence of canals does not seem to have had a great deal of influence on the rise and course of riots and other insurrections.[157]

The third factor influencing riots and revolts, a city-centre-oriented spatial structure, gives us more solid ground. Space Syntax Analysis, a technique developed at the Bartlett School of University College London, makes it possible to determine and graphically represent the accessibility of streets, canals and squares within a street network.[158] When we use this technique to get an impression of the spatial structure of Holland's cities, the most important conclusion is that there was a large variation in the degree of accessibility of the political and economic heart of these cities.

In Map 4.3, Space Syntax Analysis is used to get an impression of the accessibility (to-movement potential) of street segments within the Alkmaar street network in the first half of the nineteenth century.[159] Warm colours indicate a high degree of accessibility and cool colours a low one. A single glance at the map suffices to establish that the area around Waagplein, Mient and Houttil was the most easily accessible

Map 4.3 Alkmaar c. 1830: to-movement potential at a radius of 200 metres. A = town hall, B = Waagplein.

from all parts of the city. We have already established that this was one of the oldest settlement locations in Alkmaar. Moreover, Waagplein was the only square of any size in Alkmaar and therefore suitable as a gathering place for large crowds. In contrast, the more westerly core near the Grote Kerk and the town hall was relatively difficult to reach. Of course, this was partly due to its eccentric location in the western periphery of the city.

Alkmaar was a small city, and the distance to the centre of political power, the town hall at the west end of Langestraat and possibly the residences of the wealthy elites along Langestraat and Oude Gracht, would never have been a limiting factor when it came to the accessibility of these locations to rioting classes. Therefore, it is good to look at some of the larger cities as well, bearing in mind that they were also (very) modest in size compared to metropolises such as London and Paris.

Maps 4.4 and 4.5 show that in Leiden and The Hague, too, the political centre was not located in the most accessible part of the city. In Leiden, the area south-east of the town hall, in the vicinity of Steenschuur, was the most accessible and in The Hague the southern periphery, which we noted in Chapter 2 was inhabited mainly by low-income households. The palaces of The Hague and prestigious houses around the Hofvijver were located in the relatively eccentric north-east quadrant of the city. Both Leiden and The Hague lacked a spatial structure focused on the political centre, but again it must be emphasized that in pre-modern times these cities were also limited in size and the centres of political power were therefore not beyond the reach of the insurgents.

Because after the major urban extensions of the seventeenth century, Amsterdam was by far the largest of Holland's cities in geographical size (see Table 4.1), its spatial

Map 4.4 Leiden *c.* 1830: to-movement potential at a radius of 200 metres. A = town hall.

Map 4.5 The Hague *c.* 1830: to-movement potential at a radius of 200 metres. A = town hall, B = Hofvijver.

structure will have had the greatest effect on the potential for mobilizing rioters and on the effectiveness with which their message could be brought to the attention of the city government and society at large. Map 4.6 shows that according to this criterion, Amsterdam was among the cities that Hobsbawn considered ideal for riots and revolts. Dam square, the political and economic heart of Amsterdam, was also the best accessible location from all parts of the city. This made it relatively easy for rioting crowds to reach Dam square and express their dissatisfaction to the magistrate in the town hall. An additional advantage was that Dam square offered space for large numbers of people and that the ring of canals, the residential domain of the wealthy elites, was close by and within easy reach from Dam square.[160] It should therefore come as no surprise that Dam square played an important role in many riots. Because it was also the place where until the first half of the nineteenth century the execution of scaffold punishments took place, and where the militia-regiments gathered for the yearly *optrek*, Dam square functioned as an arena in which the elites represented by the authorities, the middle-class militias, and the working classes demonstrated their power and their views on society through the appropriation of space.

Finally, Hobsbawn points out that in the ideal city for riots and disorder, 'The pattern of functional specialization and residential segregation ought to be fairly tight.'[161] He contrasts this with more recent cities in which socio-spatial cohesion was less strong because the different parts of the city were separated both physically, socially and

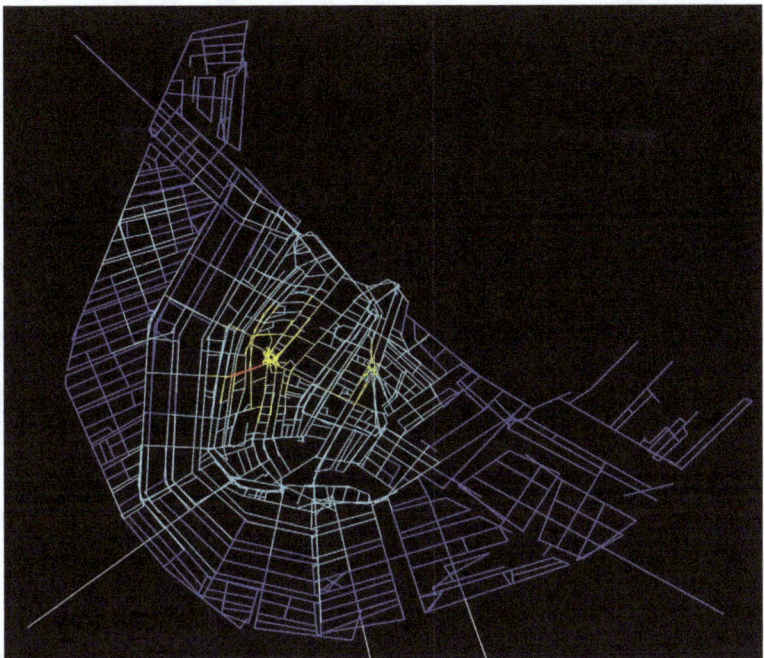

Map 4.6 Amsterdam c. 1830: to-movement potential at a radius of 400 metres.

mentally. In the pre-modern cities of Holland, only Amsterdam was of a size that could affect cohesion. An indication that this was actually the case can be found in research by Bos into the *Damoproer* of 1848. He noted the striking absence of residents of the Jewish quarter and the Oostelijke Eilanden (Eastern Islands) among those arrested. The absence of Jewish inhabitants among those arrested, and, we may assume, their numerical under-representation in the rioting crowd, fits in with the tradition that they did not participate in the major riots in the city. Apparently, the cultural and mental distance to the non-Jewish population of Amsterdam was so great that they did not join the riots and sometimes even helped to suppress them by supporting the militia.[162]

At first glance, it seems strange that the inhabitants of the Oostelijke Eilanden were absent during the Dam riot. Known as *Bijltjes* (little axes), so named after the most important tool of the shipwrights who lived and worked there, they had a solid reputation as rioters and their tools were formidable weapons. Here too, however, a lack of cohesion may have played a role. Bos speaks of possible neighbourhood rivalry and points to the importance of geographical as well as social factors. In the case of the Oostelijke Eilanden, the isolated location of this area in relation to the rest of the city undoubtedly played a role (compare Map 4.6). In fact, the Oostelijke Eilanden were only connected to the city by two bridges over the Nieuwe Vaart canal, and the easternmost of these bridges did not provide direct access to the more centrally located parts of Amsterdam. In combination with the dominance of shipbuilding and intensive contacts through work at the often large shipyards, the spatial isolation of the neighbourhood may have strengthened the mutual ties of the Islanders at the expense of those with the rest of the city.[163] That too shows that urban space was not a neutral and passive backdrop, but a factor with influence on the mindset and actions of individuals and collectives.

Considering the foregoing, it can be concluded that with the possible exception of canals and bridges, the spatial characteristics of the cities of Holland contributed positively to the occurrence and spread of riots and other disturbances. The relatively small size of these cities and their considerable population density was an advantage when it came to mobilizing supporters by means of parades and the dissemination of information. The small size also meant that the targets of the rioters – town halls, food shops, the houses of tax-farmers and magistrates, and other objects – were usually quick and easy to reach. The only city whose size did make distance and accessibility a potential problem was Amsterdam, but that city had a spatial structure strongly oriented towards the city centre.

The spatial characteristics of Holland's cities may have formed a suitable context for riots, but the existing social order was never fundamentally threatened in the long period up to the middle of the nineteenth century. This was, of course, due to the superior strength of the authority apparatus. The rioters were many, but they were up against armed and trained civic militias, and when these proved powerless or unwilling to intervene, against professional soldiers who could be on the spot quickly because of the relatively small distances and excellent infrastructure in Holland. This certainty about the outcome of riots and other insurrections may have contributed to the policy of urban authorities to be reluctant to use force in the early stages of a riot and thus prevent escalation. In his *History of Holland*, Hendrik Toren, cited earlier, reported that in 1690 he had seen with his own eyes that when the 'women's company' reached the Rotterdam city hall during the Costerman riot, the militia allowed the women 'I suppose upon a private order of the magistrates' to pass unhindered and then 'The officiating burgomaster . . . came downstairs with his hat under his arm and he appeared before the women so humble and with such a reverence as if had expected to get audience of a king.' Similar attempts at de-escalation were not uncommon in other cities.[164]

The fact that the popular uprisings did not form a threat to the existing relations within society is not only due to the superior strength of the authority apparatus but also to the character of these riots. In his study of food riots in England in the eighteenth century, Thompson emphasizes that there was a 'notion of legitimation', that is the participants in the riots were motivated by the notion that they were defending traditional rights and customs.[165] The rioters' minds were thus fixed on the past and the aim was to restore the situation as it once was, or as they believed it once had been. In their *The Rebellious Century 1830-1930*, Charles, Louise and Richard Tilly characterize these riots as 'reactive forms of collective action' and they mention food riots and tax riots as typical examples.[166] The existing power relations were hardly ever fundamentally threatened in this type of collective action. Such was the case with the rise of what the authors call 'proactive, demanding forms of collective action', such as strikes and demonstrations. In these, it was not the restoration of old rights and customs that was central, but the offensive pursuit of recognition, a larger share in the available resources and more political influence.[167] In France and Germany, the focus shifted from reactive to proactive collective action after the middle of the nineteenth century, and in Italy this happened at the beginning of the twentieth century, but in each of these countries the Tillys see a connection with the process of state formation, that is to say with the rise of national structures of power, production, distribution and association. Interest groups organized on a national scale and seeking to influence these national structures of power, production and distribution, have increasingly supplanted the old, locally oriented reactive forms of collective action.[168] This does not alter the fact that according to the authors, those traditional reactive forms of collective action still occurred occasionally in the twentieth century.[169]

The developments in Holland are broadly in line with the course of events outlined in *The Rebellious Century*. Until the middle of the nineteenth century, the riots in which the working classes played an important role were predominantly reactive. It is true that throughout the pre-modern period there have been critical accounts of the great social and economic inequalities, but these did not lead to a programme to combat inequality and therefore did not constitute a fundamental threat to the existing distribution of resources and the power relations based on them.[170] This changed with the activities of radical journalists and socialist individuals and groups around the middle of the nineteenth century. Research by Bos informs us about the situation in Amsterdam. The Damoproer of 1848, as his study shows, was the first meeting of these radical *volksvrienden* (friends of the people) with the Amsterdam working classes. The large crowd of people who gathered on Dam square on 24 March of that year responded to an appeal by a few German communists living in the city, who had distributed a thousand printed papers promising that men would be present on Dam square 'who will look after their interests [those of the people present, C.L.], and will thus devise means of improving their fate in the general interest'.[171] According to Bos, this meeting was fraught with misunderstandings and mutual incomprehension. While the German organizers probably thought of a demonstration to incite the city council to do something about the high unemployment and poverty of those years, many of those present seem to have come to Dam square in the expectation that jobs would be given away there. When that turned out not to be the case, a short-lived riot ensued with all the characteristics of the traditional reactive riots that occasionally broke out in the pre-modern cities of Holland.[172] This applies to the theatrical and symbolic looting of houses of authorities in the ring of canals (Map 4.7) and it also applies to the strictly local character of the riot.[173]

With its communist-inspired appeal and traditional action repertoire, the Damoproer set the tone for later expressions of collective action. Contrary to what the sharp distinction between reactive and proactive collective actions suggests, proactive motivations turned out to go hand in hand with a traditional action repertoire. And sometimes the defence of real or perceived old rights and customs gave rise to a more fundamental critique of the existing social relations.[174] The classical popular uprising, with its theatrical and ritualistic violence against the authorities and others who violated

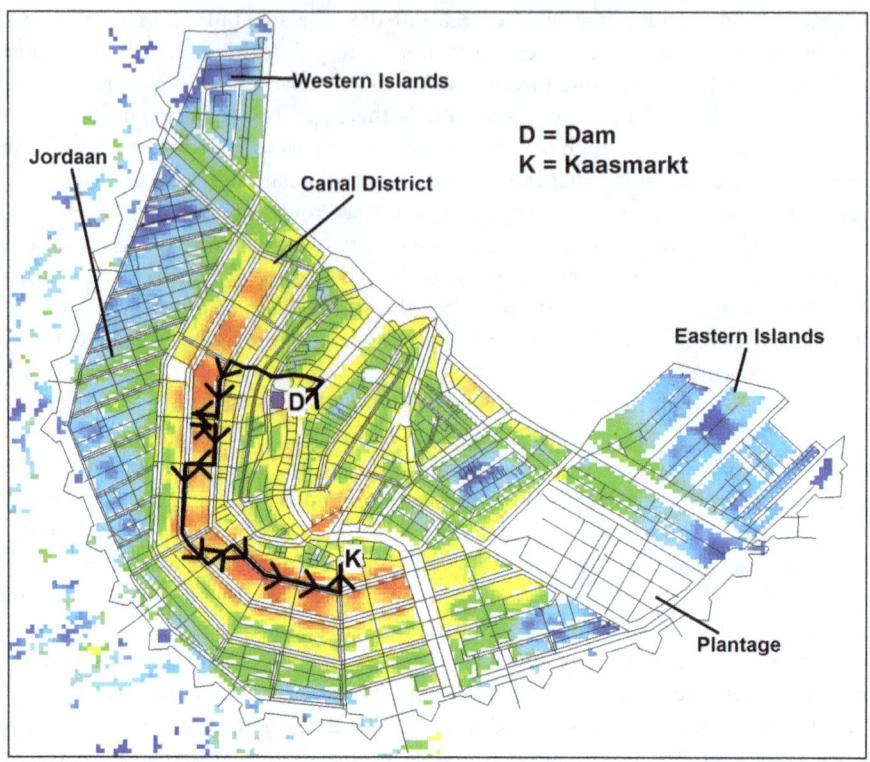

Map 4.7 Spatial distribution of rental values around 1830 and plunder route of the rioters during the Damoproer in Amsterdam, 1848.

the moral economy of the working classes, only really faded into the background at the end of the nineteenth century when a large part of the traditional working classes found work in industry and was transformed into a modern industrial working class. In industrial society, new forms of solidarity and a different repertoire of resistance and protest emerged.[175] In the second half of the nineteenth century, moreover, the cities of Holland grew in size, increasing the distances within the city, and in the largest cities the social classes were increasingly being separated by the development of neighbourhoods with a specific socio-economic profile and by the growing demand for space by offices, stores and industry in the central areas that drove part of the residents out of the once socially-mixed city centres.[176] All this brought an end to the situation in which the working classes lived relatively close to both the wealthy elites and the seat of local government; a spatial structure that Hobsbawn characterizes as 'a standing invitation to riot'.[177]

The old traditions were not completely lost, however. Under the surface, they persisted in old and more recent working-class neighbourhoods, where contacts with other parts of the city were relatively few, authorities were routinely viewed with suspicion, and values and norms did not necessarily correspond to what was common elsewhere in the city.[178]

4.5. Collective violence as a communicative act in urban space

This chapter has shown that physical space in the cities of Holland (also) functioned as an arena in which social classes explicitly demonstrated their power through relatively short-lived but violent appropriation of that space. Both the public physical punishment by urban authorities and the maintenance of public order by middle-class militias, *exercitiegenootschappen* and *vrijkorpsen*, as well as the popular riots and revolts, had a violent character, but they were not unarticulated outbursts of violence. The goal was to limit the behavioural alternatives of persons and groups within society, and to achieve that goal, the violent appropriation of space often had a ritualistic and theatrical character. The expressions of collective violence discussed in this chapter can therefore be regarded as communicative acts within the complex web of alliances that was a distinct feature of urban society in Holland (see Chapter 1). The uncertainty of the changing alliances made it important and perhaps even necessary for the social classes identified in this study to publicly demonstrate their power potential and thereby influence the behaviour of others in a desired direction.

In the cases of violent public punishments and the maintenance of public order by middle-class militia, these violent attempts to influence the behaviour of others were aimed at acceptance and thus continuity of the existing order. This acceptance was achieved not only by forcing acceptance through violence or the threat of violence but also by the more subtle message of order and stability that the alliance between elites and middle classes conveyed in those situations. But even when the middle classes and working classes turned against the elites, the existing power relations were not seriously jeopardized because the riots and revolts were predominantly reactive in character. They were aimed at restoring old rights and customs, and thus these violent forms of appropriating urban space too, promoted the continuity of the power relations in the cities of Holland.

The urban space in which the ritual and theatrical appropriation took place was not a neutral backdrop against which the authorities, militiamen and rioters marked the position of the social class to which they belonged. On the contrary, urban space exerted an independent influence on the behaviour of social classes and the effectiveness of their appropriation of space. For example, the communicative potential of violent actions depended not only on what people did and how they did it but also on where the violence was deployed. The location of the violence was often chosen in such a way that the perpetrators of the violence would benefit from the image and reputation of that location. By placing a scaffold on the square in front of a town hall, the authorities benefitted from the image of the town hall as the seat of the city administration, but at the same time the execution of scaffold punishments, often in the presence of the militia, contributed to the image of power and authority of the built object – the town hall – and of the authorities that ruled there. The image and reputation of the site – the square with the town hall – was in turn an important motivation for rioting middle classes and working classes to raise their voices precisely there and, with more or less violence, bring their wishes to the attention of the authorities and urban society in general. With this appropriation, they temporarily occupied a space dominated by others, in this case, the authorities.[179] The marching of the militias in full armour through working-class neighbourhoods and the plundering of houses in the affluent parts of the city by the working classes are other examples of the temporary appropriation of urban spaces dominated by others. Taken together they show that urban space did indeed (also) function as an arena in which social classes explicitly marked and sometimes fought for their position in society.

5

Discursive appropriation of urban space

5.1. The proximity and yet limited visibility of 'the other'

In this chapter, we will consider the interesting phenomenon that those with sufficient resources had access to a paper and canvas world in which the everyday realities of extreme social inequality, poverty and the proximity of 'the other' were softened and sometimes even ignored or denied. This discursive appropriation of urban space will be presented here as an expression of what Allen refers to as 'smothering'.[1]

In his *Lost Geographies of Power*, Allen takes the phenomenological approach and also concepts of Lefebvre as a starting point for an argument about power in an urban context that he illustrates with examples from spatial practices in the City, London's financial district.[2] Today, the City is indeed dominated by the financial sector. This is where the often very prominent office buildings are found where bankers, stockbrokers, lawyers, financial advisers, accountants and others directly involved in the financial sector spend their working days. But they are not the only ones working there. A whole army of doormen, security guards, cleaners, ICT specialists, maintenance engineers, caterers and many others work there to make the functioning of the financial sector possible. To a large extent these two very different groups share the same physical space, but it is the financial sector that dominates the image of the 'Square Mile', that has appropriated the space and is able to displace 'others'. Of course, this displacement should not be understood as a deliberate policy of physical removal. That would not be possible, for the services of the others cannot be missed. It is more a case of pushing into the background. In this context, Allen speaks of 'smothered spaces': 'social space ... where difference, the traces of others, is effectively smothered by a more dominant presence . . . .'.[3] This is, I will argue below, what in a discursive sense also took place in the pre-modern cities of Holland. The working classes, including many poor, were present and visible in public life, but in texts about the cities and on maps and pictures of these cities they generally occupied a less prominent place. Urban space was coded, to use Lefebvre's and Allen's term, in a way that suggested the presence of only certain groups, thus giving the impression of social homogeneity rather than the diversity and inequality that characterized society in the pre-modern cities of Holland.

In the context of this chapter, that society was, as it were, divided into what one could call 'foreground people' and 'background people', those who are prominently present in texts and images, and those who are not entirely absent, but have been assigned a modest role in the background. This division of roles was not always consciously pursued, but can of course not be seen in isolation from the fact that especially the well-to-do and literate part of the city population had the opportunity to record their views on society or had them recorded on paper and canvas.

The *background people* constituted a significant part of the population. Around the middle of the nineteenth century, no less than about 45–60 per cent of the population in Alkmaar, Dordrecht, Leiden, The Hague, Rotterdam and Amsterdam belonged to the working classes.[4] In the preceding centuries, too, the working classes made up a very substantial part of the urban population. In Amsterdam, around the middle of the eighteenth century, they made up about 50 per cent of the population and in an industrial city like Leiden, 68 per cent of the male heads of household fell into this category in the same period.[5] These are numbers of people that one does not easily overlook in cities. This is all the more true because the working life of many of these men and women took place partly or entirely in the streets. This is true for porters and market vendors, but also for numerous construction workers, errand boys, maidservants and many others, among them street vendors.

To the extent that they did not walk around with their wares, street vendors sought out favourable locations within the urban landscape to display their wares.[6] These favourable locations included busy squares with important public buildings as well as markets and popular shopping streets. In addition, bridges were very popular. This is not surprising, since especially when they were part of busy routes, they functioned as a bottleneck where passers-by could hardly ignore these street vendors and the merchandise they were offering.[7] Their physical presence in public spaces was accentuated by the fact that they usually recommended their merchandise out loud, whether or not in rhyme. For hundreds of years, especially in the big cities, the 'street cry' was a vocal form of appropriating urban space and a reminder of the proximity of the working classes that could not be easily ignored.[8]

Busy squares, streets and bridges were of course also popular locations for beggars. In a rather overstated argument to demonstrate the effectiveness of the Nieuwe Werkhuis (New Workhouse) in Amsterdam (1782), the following was noted about the preceding period: 'A revolting crowd of blind, lame, crippled and others, from the poor community, used to swarm all over the city. They were met, above all, at the sluices or bridges, also along the streets, where they almost fell unbearable on the ears of the pedestrians, by their wailing sound, and by impertinent begging they obstructed the way.'[9]

In the following sections, we will see how the working classes, including the poor among them, despite their prominent presence in the cities, were, as it were, relegated to the background in texts and on maps and pictures by a more dominant discourse, within which – often unconsciously – an image of society was created that corresponded to the preferences and views of society of those who had sufficient resources to purchase or learn about these texts, maps and pictures.

5.2. Power relations and the limited visibility of 'background people': Texts

It has already been pointed out in the first chapter that according to Bourdieu words are not 'innocent' and it is good to recall this here. The written statements about people and places that will be discussed below can indeed be regarded as conscious or unconscious 'deeds' that contributed to the continuity of the existing social relations in the cities of Holland since they were uttered by persons who had ample resources at their disposal and whose words had authority for that reason alone. In line with the concept of smothering introduced earlier, it should be added that the discursive appropriation discussed here, does not only concern who and what was written about but also who and what was not or hardly written about. Indeed, ignoring parts of social and spatial reality can also be part of a discourse and in that case should be considered an expression of power.

Texts in which we may expect (some) attention is paid to the people who populated the cities are city descriptions or chorographies. This genre, which combined geography and history, had its roots in classical antiquity and experienced a new flowering in the humanism of the fifteenth and sixteenth centuries.[10] The *Descrittione di tutti i Paesi Bassi*, published in 1567 by the Antwerp-based Italian merchant and scholar Ludovico Guicciardini, had a great influence on later city descriptions.[11] In this extensive work, the author described the different regions within the Low Countries and a whole series of cities. He paid particular attention to Antwerp, in his time by far the largest city and the most important trading centre in the Low Countries. From the beginning of the seventeenth century, the first chorographies appeared in the then independent Dutch Republic, and it is not surprising that especially the cities in the economically important province of Holland received a lot of attention. Johannes Pontanus and Jan Orlers set the tone with their descriptions of Amsterdam (1611/1614) and Leiden (1614) respectively, but in the course of the century one or more descriptions appeared of all of the larger cities in Holland.[12]

The themes covered in these city descriptions are more or less the same. They are the location of the city, its origin and history, the city's extensions and main public buildings, learned men who were born and/or worked in the city, and the nature and composition of the city government.[13] For us it is important that a number of these city descriptions contain an often extensive topographical section in which the reader is taken on an imaginary walk through the city and is served up all kinds of interesting facts during that 'walk'. The city descriptions were not cheap to buy and the print runs did not exceed a few hundred copies. Therefore, the reading public must be sought among the well-to-do middle classes and urban elites.[14] The authors, too, usually belonged to these circles. This makes the city descriptions very suitable for this research because they offer a view on who and what this literate and well-to-do groups found worth mentioning and reading, and especially who and what they did not find worthwhile.[15]

When reading the city descriptions, it quickly becomes clear that the visibility of the working classes, which were found to make up about half of the population in the cities of Holland, is very limited. This is despite the fact that the city descriptions are generally quite extensive and detailed. If 'the other half' is mentioned at all, it is often more or less in passing or as a necessary context when the author wants to make a specific point. An example of a casual mention is found in the city description of Delft and more specifically in the report of the aforementioned gunpowder disaster of 1654. In that disaster hundreds of people must have died in Delft. The reason why the official death lists mention a much lower number of victims is, according to the topographer and contemporary Van Bleyswijck, because children, strangers and 'Geringe luyden' (the common people) were not included in the lists. Of the adult inhabitants of Delft, strangers and people of little means apparently did not matter enough to register their deaths. In 1654 they were thus effectively excluded from the official record of the disaster, and it is only through Van Bleyswijck's remark that we have caught a glimpse of their existence.[16]

Sometimes the working classes, or part of them, play a necessary supporting role in a broader discourse on the virtues of the urban society in question. This is true, for example, when the descriptions of the city refer to the poor. In such cases, it is not so much about the poor themselves, but rather the authors want to emphasize that people in the city do 'good works', such as supporting the poor. For this reason, many chorographies dwell extensively on the foundation and functioning of institutions for the care of the poor and on the buildings in which they were located. In Orlers's description of Leiden, the entire seventh chapter is about municipal institutions 'tot onderhoudinge der armen gesticht' (for the support of the poor). Referring to the Christian duty of charity, the author states that 'the Gentlemen and Rulers of this City, as well as its Inhabitants and Citizens' ensure that 'the sad, miserable, and from God so highly recommended Poor, Widows, Orphans or Fatherless children, and other infirm persons, are fully supported and provided with all temporal necessities'.[17] And a little later, Orlers concludes that because of all the facilities available in Leiden, there is no poor person there 'or he has and receives help and support in his poverty'.[18]

The message conveyed here by Orlers is that Leiden is a harmonious society where rulers and residents obey the Christian duty of charity and support those in need to the best of their ability. It is no coincidence that he explicitly mentions that the 28 lasts of rye and about 7,000 barrels of peat that the almoners distributed to the poor in 1612 'amounted to a good sum of money'.[19] In the seventh chapter Orlers states that he spoke at length about the poor in order to encourage people to support them and to show posterity how much their ancestors did for the poor so that they too will continue this good work.[20] This reveals a genuine concern for the welfare of the poor, which is often less explicitly expressed in other city descriptions. But Orlers also draws a line and limits the access to poor relief to the 'true' poor.[21] The true poor are those who do not break the harmony of society with uncontrolled begging and ostentatious demonstration of their ailments. For Delft, Van Bleyswijck describes a system whereby the true poor receive a badge (the city arms) from the trustees of the poor relief, which they must wear visibly on their clothing and which entitles them to beg at set hours. This consent was valid for a limited time only and renewal could be refused 'on account of the circumstances of the person or the situation'.[22] Apart from these authorized beggars, no one was allowed to beg in Delft.

The distinction between true and false poor and the deceit by the false poor is widely reported in many city descriptions. In this respect, the authors follow in the footsteps of the previously mentioned Juan Luis Vives and Dirk Volkertsz. Coornhert. Pontanus, a contemporary of Coornhert, uses the description of the Rasphuis (house of correction) in Amsterdam as an occasion for an extensive discourse on the many tricks and deceptions that beggars use to arouse pity and urge the citizenry to give alms. He also reproduces in full the Amsterdam ordinance on begging.[23] In the city description of Delft, too, much attention is paid to the untrue poor and to the house of correction where they are locked up as punishment for their deceit and, in the humanist tradition, led back to a virtuous and industrious life through hard work and discipline.[24] But here, too, the focus on the false poor is no more than a necessary context for the message that the cities in question are powerfully governed and well-ordered societies, where there is no place for beggars and other 'onnutte ledighgangers' (useless idlers).[25] This image is reinforced by including, as in Pontanus' description of Amsterdam, a depiction of the Rasphuis, where in the courtyard two prisoners are grating paint wood and a third is being flogged. All this was done at the foot of a column with a statue of Lady Justice, and from the windows on the first floor, visitors could watch how the *ledighgangers* were dealt with (Figure 5.1).[26]

After the middle of the seventeenth century, city descriptions were published that included extensive topographical sections in which the reader was taken through the city in the form of imaginary walks. With this approach, the authors also aimed at visitors to 'their' city.[27] Whether visitors actually walked through the city with these kinds of books in their hands is not yet a foregone conclusion, but what is certain is that these texts too, are highly selective in the social classes and locations they mention. The intention seems to be to present the city as favourably as possible and to push everything that does not fit into the ideal image of a flourishing city with prestigious houses along beautiful canals and streets into the background.

Figure 5.1 Courtyard of the Rasphuis in Amsterdam, 1614.

Sometimes this is achieved by including only the most important canals and streets. An explicit example of this is the city description by Gysbert de Cretser of The Hague (1711). The title already indicates that it concerns the 'distinguished canals, squares, streets, walks and country roads'.[28] And so the author dwells at length on Voorhout, Kneuterdijk, Vijverberg and Princessegracht, among others. On Voorhout it is an excellent walk on warm days 'under the rustle and the movement of the leaves', carriages drive around especially on Sundays after the sermon in great numbers and behind the rows of lime trees there are 'on both sides very prestigious houses, some of which could be called palaces'.[29] Kneuterdijk, too, is planted with lime trees and has only very prestigious houses that can be called palaces. They were inhabited by the Lord Van Duvenvoorde, Councillor Munter, Lord Van Oyen and other notables. Lange Houtstraat, which according to the author is a spacious and wide street, is also mentioned as being occupied on both sides by large and prestigious houses 'and in which there is not a single house used for trade or industry'.[30] For De Cretser, the absence of economic activities is apparently the criterion that distinguishes the main streets and canals from those with less allure. The lesser streets of The Hague are only mentioned when there are also substantial houses or important public buildings to be found there (see the appendix, Map A.12). The other streets and canals of The Hague are not included in his description of the city and as a result a large part of the city and the majority of the city's inhabitants remain out of the picture: 'smothered places' and 'smothered people' in Allen's terminology. This does not imply that there was a conscious attempt to deny the existence of the less well-off part of the city and society. Rather, De Cretser seems to follow the city description published in 1668 by Jacob van der Does, who in the assignment to the magistrate of The Hague states that he concentrates on the beautiful streets and buildings because they make The Hague stand out from other cities.[31] Nevertheless, the result of this expression of urban pride is that the well-to-do and literate readers are presented with an image of the city that confirms and also reinforces the existing notions of social hierarchy and the marginal position of the working classes.

The relegation of the working classes to the background also took place in descriptions of cities in which at first glance all the streets and canals are reviewed, such as those on Amsterdam by Fokkens (1662), Von Zesen (1664) and Van Domselaer (1665). There, smothering manifests itself in a very unbalanced degree of attention to the various streets, canals and districts of the city. The most prestigious locations are described in detail. On Keizersgracht, for example, which Fokkens considered the most prestigious of all Amsterdam's canals, there are 'the most prestigious and most magnificent houses in the city, and here the richest and most prominent merchants live; no houses of shopkeepers are seen here with open shops, all the houses here are high and neat, as if they had been built by one hand'. This is followed by an extensive report on the rich interiors of the houses that resemble 'palaces of kings', with marble walls and floors, the rooms decorated with precious carpets or gold and silver leather, and furnished with costly paintings and East Indian decorations and so on.[32] Von Zesen speaks of Amsterdam's main canals as 'ein irdisches Paradies' and mentions burgomasters and important merchants living there by name.[33]

The old city centre with its Dam square, Damrak, and important shopping streets also receive ample attention, but the description of the Jordaan district is much shorter and largely confined to a rather matter-of-fact list of the streets and a few attractions, such as the Nieuwe Doolhof (New Maze) on Rozengracht.[34] Some notable economic activities are mentioned, such as the tanneries near Looiersgracht and the large ship's biscuit bakeries on Anjeliersgracht (now Westerstraat), but Fokkens does not tell us anything about the residents or the housing conditions, although the stench of the tanneries would not have escaped anyone. Even the Franse pad (north side of Goudsbloemgracht, now Willemstraat) is mentioned by Fokkens without further comment.[35] This is remarkable since the poverty of the residents and the dramatic housing situation in this part of the Jordaan were already widely known at the time.[36] Von Zesen does make a short remark about the situation at the Franse pad and mentions in passing that there 'meist arme leutlein, in schlechten heusern wohnen', but for the rest he too is extremely sparing with information about poor streets and the least well-off half of the city's population.[37]

More generally, it can be concluded that the working classes are only occasionally and then only in passing mentioned in the topographical descriptions of cities. Van Domselaer is the author of most references. He writes about the Jordaan, for example, that the streets there 'teem and bristle with all kinds of handicraft people'.[38] On Rapenburg, according to this trustee of the Amsterdamse Schouwburg (city theatre), shipwrights, dock-workers and sailors are swarming all over the place, and in Jonkerstraat and Ridderstraat live 'such a gruesome crowd of common sailors, and craftsmen, who earn their living at the shipbuilding yards and at sea, yes, sometimes as many as four families in a house, like in the front houses, back houses, cellars, front rooms and back rooms, that it is unbelievable'.[39] Of all the city descriptions consulted for this study, these are the most concrete references to the existence and living conditions of the working classes, but at the same time, Van Domselaer makes it clear through the degrading terminology he uses that he himself and the reader belong to a very different class. This very explicit form of othering is of course an expression of power differences in society; the power of those who had ample resources to discursively define the other as inferior and to emphasize their own superiority. The city dwellers that Van Domselaer typified in this way will not have read his writings, but for his well-to-do and literate readership, his description of the inhabitants of working-class neighbourhoods confirmed and legitimized the existing social hierarchy, and thus his description of Amsterdam also contributed to the continuation of that hierarchy.[40]

In the course of the eighteenth century and in line with a broader trend in Dutch historiography, city descriptions started to put more emphasis on the use of primary sources to support the argument.[41] However, the use of primary sources does not alter the fact that the characteristic structure and composition of the city descriptions were maintained. This also applies to the more concise editions, aimed at a wider readership or a specific target group such as youth, which appeared from the late eighteenth century onwards and especially in the first half of the nineteenth century.[42]

In terms of content, however, a slight shift in emphasis can be observed. The economic crisis that plagued Holland from the last decades of the eighteenth century until far into the nineteenth century left its mark on the city descriptions. More than before, authors reported on decay in the urban landscape and poverty among the population. Bakker for example, in his *Den opkomst, bloei, verval en tegenwoordigen toestand der stad Delft, in derzelver fabryken en trafyken* (c. 1800), reports that many houses had been demolished, the number of inhabitants had decreased by one third and that half of the population of Delft received some form of assistance. 'Throughout its history', he writes gloomily, 'Delft has never been so sad as it is now'.[43] Van der Vijver too was aware of the difficult economic situation in his city Amsterdam. But unlike Bakker, with his description of the city he tried to increase appreciation of Amsterdam. He opted for a literary form that was popular in the nineteenth century: a report of walks through the city in which the author leads a friend from outside the city, in this case from Brussels, and tells him all sorts of interesting facts while they walk. And just as in the more traditional city descriptions, Van der Vijver's *Wandelingen in en om Amsterdam* (1829) pays ample attention to interesting buildings and the history of the institutions located there.[44]

Van der Vijver's aim to increase appreciation of Amsterdam leads to a very selective view of the city and its inhabitants. The fourteenth walk, for instance, contains an eulogy to Keizersgracht and Herengracht, praising the 'beauty of the shady broad canal and the regularity of the proud and beautiful buildings'. And elsewhere in the city, on Damrak for example, there are 'beautiful houses' and Leidsestraat is a 'broad, beautiful and finely built-up street'.[45] But the dramatic decay and poverty in the Jewish quarter is completely ignored. Of course, there is mention of the hustle and bustle of the streets and the extensive market trade carried on by the Jewish inhabitants. The synagogues and the Moses and Aaron church are also discussed, but the poorest parts of the neighbourhood are simply ignored: 'Having left the church [Moses and Aaron], we walked forward, ignoring *Markensteeg* and *Marken*.'[46] And it was precisely there that large numbers of people lived in abject poverty. Only when the gentlemen walk along the part of Lijnbaansgracht bordering on the Jordaan, do we get an impression of the situation at the poor edge of the city, with dilapidated houses and 'horrible rubbish heaps and rubbish barrels that . . . exhaled a pestilential stench. Also the notorious Franse pad (north side of Goudsbloemgracht, now Willemstraat) was visited and found to be a 'hideous canal' that 'can only evoke a melancholy feeling'.[47] And after an appeal to the city government to do something about the situation, both gentlemen calmly walked on.[48]

What is strikingly absent from the city descriptions is attention to the phenomenon that was common in all the cities under study, that those with the lowest incomes not only lived in the urban periphery but also in the immediate vicinity of the middle classes and the well-to-do elites, namely in the courtyards behind the houses along streets and canals, which were opened up by alleys and blind alleys.[49] In 1662, Fokkens reported only that he passed by 'many small alleys', 'for it would be too sad to mention them all'.[50] And on the basis of De Cretser's description of the city, the reader has no idea that immediately behind the well-to-do streets and canals there were inner courtyards, alleys and streets where the poor of The Hague found a home.[51]

What the well-to-do and literate readers of all these city descriptions were presented with was the clichéd image of a prosperous bourgeois society, under the vigorous and just administration of the ruling elites and with attention to the welfare of the needy, or rather those needy who deserved it. Even as decay and poverty took hold in the early decades of the nineteenth century, the positive image was generally maintained. The existence of the working classes, to which a large part of the inhabitants belonged, was not denied, but they did not play an independent and significant role in the discourse and functioned, as it were, in the background. This makes the city descriptions a discursive form of appropriation of urban space by the literate middle classes and elites. The existing social hierarchy and power relations within society were thereby (often unconsciously) confirmed, legitimized and also continued.

5.3. Power relations and the limited visibility of 'background people': Maps and cityscapes

It is no coincidence that in this section maps and cityscapes are considered together. At first glance, both give the impression of being fairly direct and neutral representations of reality, but there is now an extensive body of academic work that argues, with good reason, that this is not the case. Maps and images have a deeper meaning and can be 'read' to find it out. In the first half of the last century, an important contribution in this direction was made by what is known as the Warburg School.[52] The work of the German-American art historian Erwin Panofsky (1892–1968) was particularly influential. He made a distinction between iconography and iconology. The first is the identification of consciously applied symbols on images, such as a skull, an hourglass and an extinguished candle as symbols of transience. Iconology goes a step further and attempts to reveal the intrinsic meaning of a work of art by, in Panofsky's words, 'ascertaining those underlying principles which reveal the basic attitude of a nation, a period, a class, a religious or philosophical persuasion . . .'.[53] It will be clear that the search for this 'basic attitude' can quickly take on a highly speculative character, with the danger, among other things, that the researcher sees in an image precisely that which he or she has already considered to be the essence of a certain country, period, class or philosophical persuasion.[54] In this section, I want to 'read' and interpret maps and cityscapes, but without the pretension of revealing the 'soul' of the middle classes and elites in the cities of Holland. Like the city descriptions, the images presented below in what they show and especially in what they do not show, are a window into the views of contemporaries on social relations and the ideal urban society. At the same time, however, for those who had the resources to acquire them or become acquainted with them, these images confirmed the existing social relations and thereby contributed to the continuity of these social relations.

Although Holland, and Amsterdam in particular, was the largest producer of cartographic material in Europe in the seventeenth century, the city map genre did not originate there. The genre experienced its early flowering in the sixteenth century in Italy, Germany and the Southern Low Countries. One of the highlights of that era is undoubtedly the bird's-eye view map of Venice by Jacopo de Barbari from 1500. Some two decades later, in 1521, a similar map was made of Augsburg.[55] The knowledge needed to make such complex maps became known in Holland from the Southern Low Countries. Both Cornelis Anthonisz., maker of the painted bird's-eye view (1538) and woodcut (1544) of Amsterdam, and Jacob van Deventer, maker of the extensive series of city maps commissioned by the Spanish king, were born in the Northern Low Countries but studied in Leuven. At the time, Leuven was the most important scientific centre in the field of geography and cartography in North-western Europe, and it is not too bold to assume that they learned the necessary cartographic techniques there.[56]

During the genre's heyday, large numbers of city maps were produced in Holland. For Amsterdam, the most important production centre, Bakker mentions hundreds of editions, reprints and adaptations, each of hundreds of printed copies of regular maps and profiles, and many dozens of copies of the more precious showpieces.[57] The large print runs of the regular maps are of course related to their relatively modest price. In the first half of the seventeenth century, large city maps composed of six printed sheets varied in price between two and three guilders, and the largest copies of more than fifteen sheets cost between three and five guilders.[58] By way of comparison: in Amsterdam in the 1630s, the summer daily wage of an unskilled construction worker was eighteen pennies (0.9 guilders) and that of self-employed carpenters and bricklayers thirty pennies (1.5 guilders). In smaller cities, such as Alkmaar, wages for carpenters were some six to eight pennies lower.[59] This implies that the regular maps could find sales among a relatively broad public.

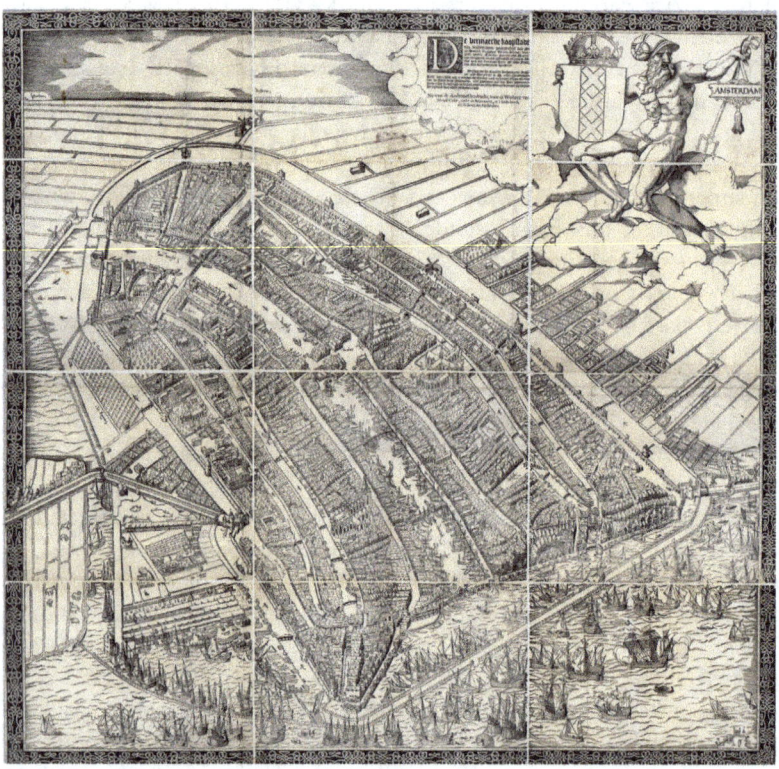

Map 5.1 Bird's-eye view of Amsterdam by Cornelis Anthonisz., 1544 (north below).

Let us now look at some of the city maps that were produced of Holland's cities and pay special attention to what is not depicted there.[60] The obvious place to start is with the iconic bird's-eye view of Amsterdam made by Cornelis Anthonisz. and published in 1544 (Map 5.1). What is only depicted to a limited extent there are, for instance, the hundreds of shabby shelters outside the city gates where those who had insufficient means to rent within the city found shelter.[61] These were wooden structures, as stone houses were not allowed outside the city walls because during sieges the enemy could entrench themselves in stone houses.[62] But also within the city, and especially on the city outskirts, many things are not depicted.[63] We know about the situation there from a report made in 1565 by a committee of inquiry set up by the governess Margaret of Parma in response to complaints from part of the Amsterdam citizenry.[64] Many of the inhabitants of the Achterburgwallen, we read in the report, were so poor that they were unable to shore up the quays and the canal water therefore regularly flowed into their 'cleyne huyskens' (small dwellings).[65] And against the western city wall, 'many and various small houses of old and poor people' were built.[66]

The bird's-eye view shows nothing of the cluttered development on the city's edges. In fact, just like the rest of the city, the outskirts and the outlying area are in good condition (Map 5.2). In *Maps, Knowledge, and Power* Harley writes: 'On many early town plans a map-maker may have unconsciously ignored the alleys and courtyards of the poor in deference of the principal thoroughfares, public buildings and residences

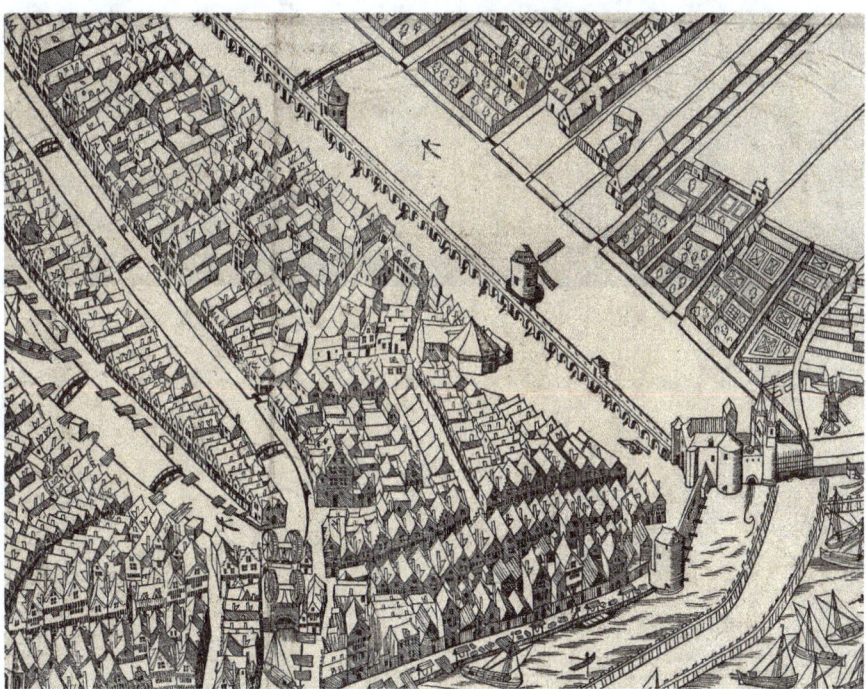

Map 5.2 The western city wall on the bird's-eye view of Amsterdam by Cornelis Anthonisz., 1544 (detail, north below).

of the merchant class in his conscious promotion of civic pride or vaunting commercial success.'[67] That is exactly what happens here. The bird's-eye view map by Anthonisz. is not an attempt to reproduce the city as it appeared to him as faithfully as possible, but it is a message wrapped up in the form of a city map. The message conveyed to the viewer contains several elements. Very prominent, of course, is the presentation of Amsterdam as a centre of trade and shipping. It is no coincidence that the city is depicted from the IJ-side, with numerous ships in the foreground and shipyards on the city's east side (see Map 5.1). Neptune, depicted in large format, and the caption of the map, 'De vermaerde Coopstadt van Amstelredam' (The renowned trading city of Amsterdam), also leave nothing to guess. This deliberately sought to link up with the bird's eye view of Venice, placing Amsterdam, as it were, in the ranks of famous European mercantile cities.

In addition, Amsterdam is presented as a well-ordered, prosperous and Christian society. The two main churches are drawn on a different scale than the surrounding houses and stand out far above them. The monasteries, too, are conspicuously present in the urban landscape, and in the only surviving contemporary coloured copy of the map this is further emphasized by the colours used.[68] This emphasis on an ordered, prosperous and well-governed society naturally explains the emphasis on the main streets on both sides of the river Amstel and the activity on the harbour front and on the roadstead. The poor houses on the edges of the city and against the city walls would be detrimental to this idealized image and have therefore not been included.

At the end of the seventeenth century, Johannes de Ram published a map of Amsterdam printed in four sheets, which also suggests that it is a reasonably faithful representation of the city, but just like on the map by Cornelis Anthonisz. here too, things have been embellished or left out. Map 5.3 shows a detail of the northern part of the Jordaan, with the area around Goudsbloemgracht. Note that Goudsbloemgracht makes a neat impression, with regular houses, few walled-in houses in the inner

Map 5.3 Bird's-eye view of Amsterdam by Johannes de Ram, 1691–3 (detail, north below).

courtyards and even gardens in the back of the houses. The reality was very different, as we have seen in the previous chapters. It is now known that De Ram copied the map image from a map by Nicolaes Visscher from 1662 to 1664, but in these years, and even earlier, Goudsbloemgracht already had a reputation throughout the city for poverty, decay and pollution.[69] This map, too, conveys the message of a prosperous, orderly and well-governed urban society. This is not surprising, since the map is dedicated to Amsterdam's burgomaster Bors van Waveren, whose family coat of arms is also depicted on the map.[70]

The *Kaart Figuratief* (Figurative Map) of Delft from 1678 also presents the viewer with a highly idealized image of reality. This is especially evident when we take a look at the south-east corner of the city for which it was previously established that there, and especially in the streets and alleys close to the city outskirts, a predominantly poor section of the Delft population lived. The poorest lived in 'ramshackle wooden hovels' near the city walls.[71] However, the otherwise very detailed bird's eye view map does not show anything of the poor houses in this part of the city (Map 5.4). The numerous trees in the city and the tilting cranes on the waterfront near the breweries are depicted very accurately on the map, but there is no trace on the map of the houses where poor inhabitants of Delft found shelter. That aspect of urban society has been supplanted in favour of an idealized image of the city; an image that closely matched society as it was desired by the urban elites. This should not surprise us, since it was Dirk Evertsz. van Bleyswijck, the burgomaster of Delft and author of *Beschryvinge der stadt Delft*, who in 1675 took the initiative to make the *Kaart Figuratief*, and several framed copies were hung in Delft's town hall.[72]

Map 5.4 The *Kaart Figuratief* of Delft, 1678 (detail, north left).

Figure 5.2 The outskirts of The Hague, mid-seventeenth century.

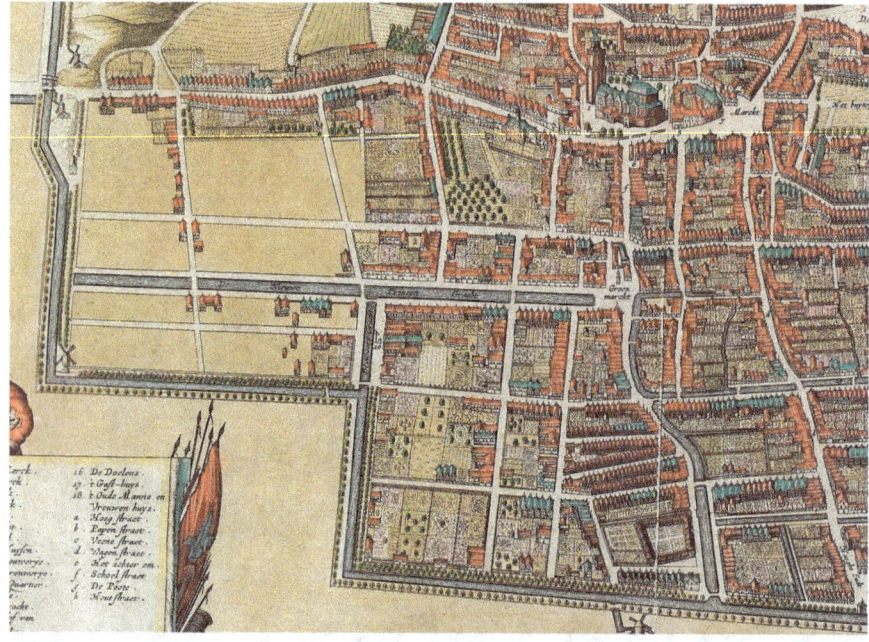

Map 5.5 Map of The Hague, 1657/1698 (detail, north above).

It is significant that almost no pictures have been made of the poor houses on the edges of cities. For this reason alone we can consider ourselves fortunate that around the middle of the seventeenth century an unknown artist made a drawing of the outskirts of The Hague and the tower of the Grote Kerk (Figure 5.2). This image gives us a unique view of the shabby houses that could be found on the city outskirts not only in The Hague but probably in all cities. The precise position of the draughtsman cannot be ascertained, but it seems to have been on the south-western periphery of the city. That part of the city is also depicted on Joan Blaeu's coloured map of 1657, which was included in Frederik de Wit's *Stedenatlas* of 1698 (Map 5.5).[73] A cursory glance at the map is sufficient to establish that this too, is an idealized representation of reality in which the poor frayed edges of the city as depicted in Figure 5.2 are not represented.

In short, the maps made of the cities of Holland were never intended to be as faithful a representation of reality as possible. They presented the viewer with the ideal image of a prosperous and well-ordered society under the wise and powerful rule of the political elites. These maps can therefore be 'read' as an expression of urban pride and 'actively experienced citizenship' among broad layers of the urban middle classes and elites.[74] Things that could distort the positive image of the city were therefore embellished or not included. In practice, this mainly concerned the houses of those who lived in the inner courtyards and on the edges of the city. Their existence was pushed into the background – smothered, as Allen would say – and that makes these pre-modern city maps an expression of the discursive appropriation of urban space by the middle classes and elites. They thus reflected the unequal power relations in Holland's cities and, by suggesting prosperous, orderly and well-governed societies, they also contributed to the obviousness, continuity and possibly even the desirability of the existing power relations.[75]

The conscious or unconscious pushing into the background of people with little economic, cultural and social capital is expressed not only in city descriptions and city maps but also in cityscapes.[76] In the catalogue of an exhibition held in 1977 on seventeenth-century cityscapes in the Northern Low Countries, the cityscape is defined as 'a painting, drawing or print of a prospect of a city or a part of a city, such as can be taken in at a glance from one point of view'.[77] The criterion that the depicted part of the city must be taken in at a single glance excludes city profiles, panoramas and bird's-eye views, but these are often seen as important sources from which the cityscape developed.[78] And although urban buildings had already been depicted in paintings before, 'true' cityscapes, where a view of a city or part of a city is the subject of the depiction, were virtually non-existent before the seventeenth century.[79] Early examples are the prints that were included in the city descriptions of Pontanus and Orlers at the beginning of the seventeenth century, but the heyday of the genre only started after the middle of the century. That is when painters such as Fabritius, Vermeer, Vosmaer, the Berckheyde brothers and Jan van der Heyden also began to work in this genre.[80] The literature explains the relatively sudden interest in cityscapes by a whole range of factors, including the wish to depict striking events such as the fire in the old town hall of Amsterdam (1652) or the gunpowder disaster in Delft (1654), local self-confidence and chauvinism, which also played a role in the publication of city descriptions, and a general public interest in the topography of distant regions as well as their own surroundings.[81] Towards the end of the seventeenth century, the genre lost vitality, but in the second half of the eighteenth century it experienced a new and greatest flowering.[82]

Because they give the impression of being a faithful representation of reality at the time, cityscapes have had a great influence on our perception of the pre-modern cities of Holland. In 1977 Wattenmaker wrote that seventeenth-century cityscape painters 'disclose fascinating glimpses into contemporary life', and the preface to a 2017 publication of a survey of Amsterdam cityscapes speaks of '[depicting] the surroundings in detail and faithfully'.[83] There are a few things to be said against this. The cityscapes are not snapshots of concrete situations in the cities of the seventeenth and eighteenth centuries. As early as 1932, Fritz put it as follows: 'das "Stadtbild" [ist] die künstlerische Interpretation eines Stadtmotivs, die Umformung des gegenständlich Vorhandenen durch die Auffassung des Künstlers'.[84] And indeed, the depiction of buildings is by no means always realistic, as Jan van der Heyden's oeuvre shows. He painted cityscapes composed of buildings that did not actually stand together, sometimes supplemented with fantasy architecture.[85] But even in pictures that make a more topographically reliable impression, buildings were omitted or added for the sake of composition and the architecture of buildings was adjusted. And dated images are not without their problems either, as they can be (partly) based on preliminary studies from many years earlier or copied from older images.[86]

Just as the buildings depicted in cityscapes are not necessarily an accurate representation of historical reality, so too the staffage, the decoration of a picture with people, animals, carriages, street furniture and the like, should not be seen as a truthful representation of a specific moment in time. This is shown, for example, by the fact that the staffage in a preliminary study can differ greatly from those in the final painting, as is the case with Gerrit Berckheyde's depiction of the Grote Markt in Haarlem in the 1670s.[87] There could also be a considerable difference between the subject matter of a painting and that of an etching by the same artist that was derived from it.[88] It is also evident from the not-at-all-uncommon situation that the staffage on a painting was applied by a painter specialized in it. A number of cityscapes by Jan van der Heyden had staffage by Adriaan van de Velde and some of Gerrit Berckheyde's cityscapes are co-signed by Jan van Huchtenburgh, an expert in depicting riders on horseback.[89] This is not to say, however, that the staffage was scattered randomly over the canvases. It usually served to support and emphasize the character and function of the location and buildings depicted.[90]

In fact, the cityscapes create an urban world rather than simply depicting it, and this is precisely what makes them interesting for this study.[91] The message that the seventeenth-century cityscapes convey to the viewer corresponds to that of the previously discussed city descriptions and city maps from the same period. Lawrence writes: 'these pictures reflect the authority of Dutch governmental and civic institutions, the vitality of commerce, and the quality of everyday life, all of which were indications of the country's self-confidence and pride'.[92] A painting of Dam square in Amsterdam by Gerrit Berckheyde (1668) clearly conveys this message (Figure 5.3).

The centrally placed town hall obviously represents the city's secular power, wealth and self-confidence. In the foreground, the weigh house refers to trade, which is the basis of that wealth and power, and in the left foreground there is a group of foreign merchants who, with their exotic clothes and turbans, emphasize the city's role in international trade.[93] The barrels, packs and bales around the weigh house underline the importance of local trade, as do the market women offering their merchandise in the foreground. A large number of men dressed in solemn black with white collars and broad-brimmed black hats are conspicuously present. Referring to a passage in Vondel's *Inwydinge van 't Stadhuis t' Amsterdam*, Stapel identifies them as the city's rulers and civil servants working in the town hall. They reinforce the image of Dam square as the administrative centre of the city.[94]

The way in which the people depicted on Dam square demonstrate the social differences and spatial separation of social classes is striking. Porters and wagoners are grouped around the weigh house, the market women have their own piece of Dam square, the administrators and civil servants stand together in clusters, and the same applies to the foreign merchants. There is no question of mixing. The spotlessly clean surroundings are also striking. The pavement is spotless, there is no rubbish anywhere and the buildings are in perfect condition. Even the porters and other representatives of the working classes are neatly dressed. The whole painting therefore exudes the atmosphere of a prosperous, bourgeois, well-ordered and well-governed society. And Berckheyde is not alone in this. Many of the cityscapes from the seventeenth and eighteenth centuries provide an idealized image of the urban

Figure 5.3 Dam square in Amsterdam by Gerrit Berckheyde, 1668.

landscape and of society in Holland; an image that is closely associated with the views and wishes of the well-to-do middle-class and elite clientele of art lovers.[95] This is also very clearly the case with the painting by Jan ten Compe of Plein (seen from Korte Vijverberg) in the prosperous part of The Hague (Figure 5.4). Both the buildings and the staffage with wealthy people and a carriage in the background exude prosperity, order and peace.

Figure 5.4 Plein in The Hague, 1750.

The preference for an idealized image of the cities does not mean, however, that the well-to-do art lovers of the seventeenth century were not at all interested in images depicting 'the other half' of the population. There was indeed interest, but it was generally limited to market scenes and to pictures of the poor, beggars, vagrants and itinerant artists that were not located in the cities of Holland, but in Rome, where in the seventeenth century Dutch and Flemish painters, the so-called Bamboccianti, devoted themselves to this genre in imitation of Pieter van Laer.[96]

The contrast between image and reality became particularly poignant in the last decades of the eighteenth century and the beginning of the nineteenth century when the cities of Holland were plagued by economic decline and poverty.[97] The cityscapes show no sign of this poverty. In their emphasis on the prosperous bourgeois society, the cityscapes effectively push the presence of the least affluent half of the city's

Figure 5.5 Bricklayer and assistant at work on Oudezijds Achterburgwal in Amsterdam, 1796.

population into the background. Not that the working classes and the poor never feature in the pictures. They do, but if they appear in the paintings, drawings and prints, they do not dominate the scene and it is almost always with a for the more affluent half of the city population reassuring modesty. And so, craftsmen are at work repairing quay walls, porters and hauliers are busy with barrels, packs and bales, street and market vendors are selling their wares, maidservants scrub the front-step and peat carriers ensure that the citizens do not have to suffer from cold in winter (Figure 5.5).

The scene painted by Maria Margaretha la Fargue in 1780 expresses the social relationships in the pre-modern cities of Holland very clearly (Figure 5.6). *In front of the front-step* stands a neatly dressed fishmonger, who in a slightly stooped posture, a sign of humility, is showing a turbot to the lady of the house. She is standing *on the front-step*, dressed in an expensive gown and towering over both the fishmonger and the seated maid servant. The maid has the daughter of the house, dressed in expensive children's clothing, on her lap, but is herself dressed in the subdued colours that were deemed appropriate for her position and place in society. In other words, the picture shows us the world as the wealthy consumers of La Fargue's cityscapes liked to see it: prosperous and hierarchical.

Figure 5.6 A fishmonger selling turbot on Bierkade in The Hague, 1780.

And yes, there are beggars in the streets, but there is no pushiness or harassment of passers-by. They sit modestly on the pavement, hoping for a handout or they ask, hat in hand, for some small change. It is striking that in a number of prints beggars are completely ignored by well-to-do passers-by (Figures 5.7 and 5.8). Here, too, the message is clear: everyone knows his or her place in society and the poor are at the bottom of the social hierarchy.[98]

The idyll of a prosperous bourgeois society could be maintained because the poor parts of the cities were hardly ever depicted. During the genre's first heyday in the second half of the seventeenth century, it is in fact only the painter, draughtsman, engraver, inventor and entrepreneur Jan van der Heyden who gives us a glimpse of the neighbourhoods inhabited by the working classes. These pictures do not belong to his well-known series of cityscapes but were made as promotional material for one of his inventions, a fire engine with improved fire hose.[99] Because these pictures were not commissioned by or for sale to well-to-do townspeople, Van der Heyden did not feel the need to idealize the cityscape. Of course, this does not mean that the images are a photographic representation of the reality of the time, but they do give us an impression of the houses and other buildings in neighbourhoods that traditionally remained out of the picture, such as the area around Elandsgracht and Elandsstraat in Amsterdam's Jordaan district

Figure 5.7 Beggar with children in Kalverstraat near Muntplein in Amsterdam, 1778 (detail).

Figure 5.8 Beggar woman with child at the Gasthuis gate in Amsterdam, 1793.

Figure 5.9 Image of the Elandsgracht/Elandsstraat area in Amsterdam, 1690.

(Figure 5.9). According to the caption, the print shows some fifty houses and tanneries, many constructed of wood that had caught fire during a lightning strike. By deploying seven or eight of his fire engines, Van der Heyden claims, more than half of the buildings could be saved.

There is no eighteenth-century Jan van de Heyden, and we therefore lack pictures of the streets, canals, alleys, slums and neighbourhoods where the less well-off half of the city's population lived. It is typical that Cornelis Pronk, who travelled the whole country to make his hundreds of topographical drawings, never depicted his immediate living environment nor the houses of his family members in or just outside Amsterdam's working-class district the Jordaan.[100] Only the Mennonite church in Bloemstraat was worth portraying in his drawings (Figure 5.10). And with a drawing of the Westertoren by Herman Schouten, on which the corner houses of Prinsengracht-Bloemstraat are just visible, this is the only pre-modern image of Bloemstraat and one of the very few of the Jordaan district. But Pronk's drawing also shows us a rather tidy and polished version of this certainly not wealthy street.

The scarcity of depictions of 'lesser' neighbourhoods, which was the result of pushing a large part of the population and houses in Holland's cities into the background, has to do with a preference for depicting iconic buildings (town halls, churches, orphanages) and well-known locations such as the Grote Markt in Delft and Haarlem, Dam square in Amsterdam and streets and canals in well-to-do neighbourhoods.[101] But that is not the only explanation. The cityscapes, which were

Figure 5.10 The Mennonite church in Bloemstraat in Amsterdam, 1729.

particularly popular in the seventeenth and eighteenth centuries, found a ready market among a well-to-do audience of art lovers and collectors. A harsh confrontation with the shabby houses and extreme poverty in working-class neighbourhoods and in the alleys and inner courtyards of their city was not what these enthusiasts had in mind for their collection. They wanted – and got – pictures of cities, where order, peace and prosperity ruled.[102] This wish fitted in with the classicist preference for taking visible reality as the starting point of a work of art but depicting it in an elevated style.[103] And that is exactly what the cityscapes present us with: an idealized and elevated version of the cities in which there was no room for the raw reality of the living conditions and lives of 'the other half'.[104]

It was only in the course of the nineteenth century that the parts of the cities that were traditionally pushed into the background could count on more interest from artists. At the beginning of the nineteenth century, this interest seems to have been aroused by the decay that was then affecting the cities of Holland. This was the case, for instance, with the artist Gerrit Lamberts, whose drawings of Amsterdam and its surroundings do not present an idealized version of reality. This is clear from Figure 5.11, in which he depicts a wasteland in Amsterdam's Jordaan district that had been cleared of houses, and it is also evident from Figure 5.12, one of the earliest depictions of Goudsbloemgracht, for centuries one of the poorest and most impoverished locations in Amsterdam.

Figure 5.11 Decay and demolition of houses in the Jordaan district, 1816 (detail).

Figure 5.12 Goudsbloemgracht in Amsterdam, 1816.

When, after the middle of the nineteenth century, the cities of Holland came into the grip of economic modernization and increases in scale, artists began to take more notice of the picturesque character of the old working-class neighbourhoods. Foreign artists played a major role in this new appreciation. The title of Henry Havard's illustrated and highly successful travel report speaks volumes: *La Hollande Pittoresque: Voyage aux villes mortes du Zuyderzee* (1874). His fellow countryman Claude Monet and the American James McNeill Whistler also travelled to the Dutch cities and recorded the decay that was now considered picturesque. Havard and Whistler did not limit themselves to the old city centres but also included working-class neighbourhoods in their work. Dutch artists and art connoisseurs did not pay much attention to this at first. In 1890, the painter and art critic Jan Veth wrote in the daily newspaper 'De Amsterdammer': 'Mr Whistler told us already in November, in his characteristic sarcastic tone, that Dutch painters did not know what they were neglecting by not making anything of their wonderful Amsterdam, the city he praised more than Venice. And now, he said, a foreigner had to come and do here what would have been so obvious to do for the Dutch.'[105] Partly because of the appreciation for the work of these foreign artists, the interest in the picturesque beauty of run-down working-class neighbourhoods also grew among Dutch artists and art connoisseurs. Harvard and Whistler thus became the forerunners of artists such as Breitner, Witsen and Wenckebach.[106]

Having an eye for the picturesque aspects of old working-class neighbourhoods should obviously not be seen as a genuine interest in the living conditions and the well-being of the working classes. This interest emerged slowly and hesitantly in the course of the nineteenth century because it presupposed in the well-to-do and literate middle classes and elites a different view of the social order and the awareness that in modern industrial society, extreme poverty and deprivation could and should be ended.

5.4. Smothering and the discursive appropriation of urban space

In this chapter, the texts about and the maps and pictures of the cities of Holland have been interpreted as discursive forms of appropriation. That is, they functioned in a discourse in which those who had the resources to purchase or become acquainted with these texts, maps and cityscapes were presented with an image of urban society that corresponded to their preferences and to their views on the social order. Unlike residential and ephemeral appropriation, this discursive appropriation of urban space was a mental construct, a product of the imagination, but one that was not unrelated to reality in the cities of Holland.

The basic attitude expressed in the texts, maps and pictures discussed here, is one of smothering. Due to the selective view of the city and of fellow townspeople, parts of society have been pushed into the background. This does not imply that the writers, cartographers and artists who produced their work on commission or for the market always made conscious attempts to create a world in which the existence of the 'other half' of the population was denied or marginalized through the manipulation of text and image. Sometimes the alleys, slums and poor dwellings at the city's edges were unconsciously ignored in favour of major streets, public buildings and harbours in a deliberate attempt to express city pride, good governance or commercial success. Sometimes, too, the result was influenced by the classicist preference for representing visible reality in an elevated style. But even in those cases, the result of their efforts on paper and canvas was not 'innocent' and without effect, for the images evoked matched the views and prejudices that guided the thinking and actions of their readers and observers. And in their turn, the texts, maps and cityscapes confirmed and reinforced these views and prejudices. This gave the existing power relations a self-evident character, which in turn supported policies that while attempting to counteract the worst forms of poverty and deprivation through poor relief and private charity, maintained and even sanctioned the extreme degree of inequality within the cities of Holland.

Conclusion

Power relations and appropriation of urban space in pre-modern Holland

There can be no doubt, of course, that harmony and consensus played a role in pre-modern Dutch society (as it did in other societies and other times), but it must be emphasized that studies in this consensual tradition describe only part of social reality. Issues such as contradictions of interest, conflict and power relations remain usually underexposed. The present study focuses on this underexposed flip side of the consensual interpretation of history in an argument about the appropriation of urban space and its effect on the continuity of power relations in the cities of pre-modern Holland. The work of especially Allen on power and Bourdieu's model of society functioned here as a heuristic tool and interpretative framework. Within that framework, access to resources held an important place. Bourdieu aggregates these resources into the three principal species of economic, cultural and social capital. The amount and composition of the capital available to social classes determined to a large extent their ability to exercise the power that enabled them to physically and discursively appropriate (parts of) urban space.

This conclusion will first summarize how the power relations in the pre-modern cities of Holland were expressed in the appropriation of urban space and will then consider the influence of the types of appropriation described here on the acceptance and continuity of these power relations over centuries. It concludes with a brief reflection on the new social dynamics after the mid-nineteenth century in the perspective of Bourdieu's societal model used here.

In an urban context, one of the most fundamental and widespread expressions of the appropriation of space was (and is) to be found in the field of housing. Research into the residential patterns in six cities has shown that these patterns were not only similar for large, medium-sized and small cities but also extremely enduring and relatively insensitive to urban growth and decline. The socio-spatial structures that came into being during the medieval period remained essentially the same until the middle of the nineteenth century: the well-to-do elites lived along the main streets and canals, the middle classes and part of the working classes lived in side streets and back streets as well as along main streets and main canals in the less prosperous parts of the cities, and the poor among the working classes lived in the urban periphery (inside and outside the city walls) and also in the inner courtyards in the more centrally located parts of the cities, which were opened up by alleys and blind alleys.

This residential structure differed in many respects from what Sjoberg and Vance argued. Unlike in Sjoberg's pre-industrial city, the elites in Holland did not live in a compact and homogenous wealthy city centre, but along streets and canals that often cut across large parts of the cities, and those with the least resources lived not only in the urban periphery but also in the immediate vicinity of the middle classes and elites. And contrary to what Vance's model suggests, in Holland the transition from the medieval to the early modern period did not give rise to a fundamentally different – because capitalist – approach to urban real estate and corresponding new residential patterns. As explanations for both the patterns of residential appropriation and their permanency, the very *unequal distribution of resources* and the power relations based upon them have been pointed out, as well as the functioning of a *relatively modern real estate market* in which the price of housing reflected the quality of the object and the externalities of the location. Furthermore, the *physical-geographical environment*, and more specifically the distance to the groundwater in the wet peatlands of Holland, and the process of *block formation* that in combination with the hierarchical structure of the street network led to differentiation between dwellings on main streets, side streets, back streets and inner courtyards played a role, as well as the *'petrification'* of existing residential patterns and the *fragmented private land ownership* that prevented large-scale clearance and redevelopment, and, of course, the *policies of local authorities*, which tended to fit in with existing residential patterns and the housing preferences of the elites, the social class to which the authorities themselves obviously also belonged.

In practice, who ended up where in the city depended on the quantity and composition of the resources available to them and their corresponding position in the field of housing. In this field of housing, the possession of financial resources was particularly important. Those with ample financial resources had the first choice in appropriating an attractive dwelling in an environment with few negative externalities. On the housing market, the other city dwellers took up an entirely different position. The less money they could spend on housing, the fewer options they had and the more often they had to settle for poorer-quality housing in an environment with more negative externalities. The importance of economic capital in the field of housing does not alter the fact that the possession of cultural and social capital could also affect the residential environment of social classes. The elites, who were themselves members of the city councils or who, partly because of their knowledge and social skills (cultural capital), had good contacts in the circles of city administrators (social capital), were usually successful in bringing their interests to the attention of the local authorities and in encouraging them to maintain or improve the quality of their residential environment. Middle classes and especially the working classes were much less successful in this.

Within the field of housing, the power of political elites and the social class associated with them was greatest when city councils had to make decisions about the social status of newly to-be-built neighbourhoods and the location of polluting and nuisance-causing industries during times of population growth and urban extensions. These were moments when they deployed instrumental power in the forms of domination and authority to impose their will upon society and – within the limits of the possible – realized a socio-spatial structure which they believed to be the most appropriate. In the course of time, these decisions acquired a material character in the form of the street network, the buildings and the quality of the residential environment. From that moment on, it was the 'invisible hand' of the housing market that brought about the sorting out of social classes across urban space and that concealed the fact that the residential patterns were not self-evident, but to a considerable extent based on decisions taken by a small group within society and that they reflected the preferences and the view of society of that small elite. In this sense, city dwellers with fewer resources were living in someone else's space.

As economic inequality increased in the pre-modern cities of Holland, the financial power of well-to-do elites and upper middle classes also manifested itself in more or less subtle attempts to appropriate their own socially homogeneous residential environment. According to Bourdieu, that homogeneous, well-to-do environment is an important stake in the struggle in the field of housing. It needs to be stressed, however, that full segregation never came about, because this was prevented by the – previously mentioned – differentiation within blocks of houses, based on the hierarchy of the street network, and the lack of opportunity for large-scale reconstruction of neighbourhoods due to the fragmentation of private land ownership. The absence in Holland of a noble upper class with extensive urban land holdings was a factor of significance here. In this context, the highest possible level of residential segregation was realized in Amsterdam's ring of canals.

While the 'invisible hand' of the housing market coordinated the residential appropriation of urban space in a rather implicit way, city dwellers were also confronted with and participated in relatively short-lived, but explicit and violent forms of appropriation. Specifically, we have looked here at the relatively short-lived appropriation of urban space as expressed in the public execution of scaffold punishments by the urban authorities, the maintenance of public order and the pursuit of political influence by middle classes, and the occasional popular uprisings in the cities of Holland. Violence played a prominent role in these ephemeral forms of appropriation, but they were not unarticulated outbursts of violence, quite the contrary. The violence usually had a ritual and theatrical character and also a clear goal: to limit the behavioural alternatives of others and to demonstrate one's own views and position in society. This made these violent forms of appropriating urban space communicative acts within a complex web of alliances.

Within this web of alliances, all social classes used the resources at their disposal to limit the behavioural alternatives of others. The working classes, which were virtually without resources within the existing social hierarchy, made use of their numerical size and physical presence in the cities. They were particularly agitated when individuals, groups or the authorities violated the unwritten rules of the moral economy, for instance by speculating and forcing up prices in times of scarcity, by imposing heavy taxes or by violating the honour of the working classes, as seems to have been the case in the 1696 revolt in Amsterdam over a new by-law on burials. Through the use of ritual and theatrical violence or the threat of violence, they exercised collective power in the forms of domination, coercion and implicit threats in order to have their grievances heard and to punish demonstratively those who had violated the moral economy. In the looting that usually accompanied the riots and revolts, the working classes often targeted the houses and other possessions of urban magistrates and tax-farmers. Especially when the latter group was being 'punished' by the rioters, the middle-class militias did not always intervene, for the middle classes too suffered from the high tax burden in Holland.

The middle classes, and especially those in possession of formal citizenship and active in militias, *exercitiegenootschappen* and *vrijkorpsen*, could dispose over more economic capital than the working classes and were therefore able to buy uniforms and armour and to train in the use of weapons. They appropriated parts of urban space in a ritualistic and theatrical manner when guarding the city gates and during the daily marches from the town hall to the city gates and back, and they did the same on a much larger scale and more pronounced during the annual review or *optrek*, when they tried to restore public order in the event of popular uprisings, and when they turned against the ruling elites and their monopolization of political power. Until the development of the national state in the nineteenth century and the bureaucratization and professionalization of the authority apparatus that accompanied it, the militias, *exercitiegenootschappen* and *vrijkorpsen*, in all these situations, exercised power in the forms of domination, coercion and implicit threat.

The public execution of scaffold punishments by the authorities can also be regarded as an expression of the appropriation of urban space and of power in the forms of domination, coercion and implicit threat. After all, the public punishments were not only meant to punish lawbreakers but also served as a warning from the ruling elites to the rest of society not to violate the existing order. This attempt to limit the behavioural alternatives of their fellow townspeople was reinforced by the explicit violence and the theatrical and public character of the penal procedure at a location that could accommodate a large number of spectators, and by the ostentatious presence of armed militias or soldiers.

Finally, this study considered a discursive form of appropriation of urban space and the related power to – consciously or unconsciously – push social classes into the background; smothering in Allen's terminology. City descriptions, maps and cityscapes were used to study this phenomenon. These were objects that only those with sufficient financial means could afford and this, of course, colours the content of the texts and pictures. The working classes, which were prominently present in urban space simply because of their numerical size and indispensable economic activities, play a remarkably modest role in the city descriptions and on maps and pictures. Insofar as there are references to the working classes in city descriptions, they often appear in a supporting role, for example when urban poor relief is praised or when, in an argument about powerful rule, the readers are informed about the tricks and deceptions of the 'false' poor who, when they get caught, are locked up in houses of correction and brought to heel with a heavy hand.

The topographical sections in the city descriptions and the numerous maps and cityscapes produced in the course of the seventeenth and eighteenth centuries show a strikingly similar blind spot for the dwellings of the working classes. The shabby dwellings at the edges of the city and the countless dwellings in the inner courtyards remained out of sight for those who read the chorographies and looked at the maps and cityscapes. The working classes and the poor themselves are sometimes depicted in the cityscapes, but there are never many of them, and they show a submissiveness that is reassuring to the audience of well-to-do citizens. In words and pictures, this audience was presented with an idealized image of the city and urban society, in which the presence of the working classes and the raw aspects of poverty and want were pushed into the background.

In the forms of appropriation described here, urban space was not a neutral backdrop, but an integral part of the process of appropriation. In the field of housing, this would include, for instance, the impact of physical-geographical conditions (type of soil and level of elevation) on the patterns of residential appropriation. In the theatrical and violent appropriation of space, the location within the city was of great importance. It is no coincidence that the square or street in front of the town hall often played an important role in these ephemeral forms of appropriation. There, both those who represented authority and those who defied it benefitted from the town hall's aura as the seat of the city government and a symbol of political power. In a very concrete way, the size and physical structure of the city during riots and other insurrections influenced the possibilities of mobilizing people and organizing 'punitive expeditions' to the homes of – mostly wealthy – citizens who had violated the moral economy. From the perspective of the rioters Hobsbawn even characterized the proximity of the working classes to both town halls and the homes of the wealthy political and economic elites, which was also typical of the cities in Holland, as 'a standing invitation to riot'. And because of the highly selective nature of texts and pictures of the cities in Holland, there too urban space was an integral part of the process of appropriation.

It is beyond doubt that the web of alliances that bound social classes together and provided stability has contributed to the fact that the extremely unequal distribution of resources and the power relations based upon them have persisted for hundreds of years without leading to large-scale confrontations between social classes and the disintegration of society. But that is not all there is to say. The functioning of this web of alliances required, after all, a certain degree of acceptance of the existing situation by all social classes, and the appropriation of urban space studied here has in several ways contributed to that acceptance.

With regard to the patterns of residential appropriation, it has been argued that their physical expression in the street network and in the bricks, stone and wood of the built environment gave all social classes the impression that they were self-evident and not open to discussion or change. This suggested that the social hierarchy and the distinction between social classes were also self-evident and of all times, rather than the result of the unequal distribution of economic, cultural and social capital. The concealment of the underlying power relations therefore promoted their acceptance. Yet, the residential structure not only promoted acceptance of the existing power relations but also reproduced them. The reputation of streets and neighbourhoods, for instance, had a major influence on the possibilities for the residents to gather (more) economic, cultural and social capital. As mentioned earlier, Bourdieu refers to poor neighbourhoods as 'ghettos' that stigmatize the residents and keep them imprisoned in poverty, while he characterizes rich neighbourhoods as 'clubs' that allow their members to profit, as it were, from the capital that the neighbourhood residents collectively possess. This reproduction of social positions in turn reinforced the idea that the existing social hierarchy was self-evident.

The ephemeral but violent appropriation of urban space by the authorities, middle classes and working classes contributed in various ways to the acceptance of the existing power relations. The most direct way, of course, was the use of violence or the threat of using violence to force acceptance. This played a role in the public execution of punishments, the suppression of riots and revolts, the daily marches of armed militiamen from the town hall to the city gates and back, and in the annual *optrek* during which the militiamen marched through the city in full regalia and demonstrated their skill at handling weapons at a prominent place, often in front of the town hall.

However, the same activities also promoted acceptance of the existing power relations in more subtle ways. Since they also functioned as a public demonstration of the ties between middle classes and elites, these expressions of (potential) power evoked an image of social stability and an ordered and hierarchical society in which different classes had their own roles to play: the political elites were at the helm and the middle-class militias carried out the policy of the city council. In addition, the presence of the civic militias in the city and the ceremonial *optrek* may have aroused feelings of safety and local pride in parts of the city population, which also subtly promoted acceptance of the existing power relations.

The image of a harmonious and well-ordered hierarchical society was of course undermined when the working classes and middle classes turned against the political and economic elites, but it is worth emphasizing that the existing power relations were seldom called into question in this way. Riotous working classes generally wanted restoration of the moral economy, and until the end of the eighteenth-century insurgent middle classes – often referring to the situation during the Dutch Revolt – demanded political influence, but the existing social hierarchy and power relations were rarely, if ever, questioned or rejected in principle. In that respect, these riots and revolts had the character of what Charles, Louise and Richard Tilly call reactive forms of collective action.

The discursive appropriation of urban space also contributed to the acceptance of the existing power relations, at least among those who could afford the city descriptions, maps and cityscapes or could become acquainted with them within their social network. The creation of an idealized world in which poverty, want and dramatically poor housing conditions for a significant part of the urban population were eliminated or at least pushed into the background, made the problems seem less urgent and facilitated acceptance of the social hierarchy and the unequal distribution of resources. The acceptance of existing social relations was further enhanced by texts and pictures that portrayed beggars as imposters – false poor – and made the poor themselves responsible for their miserable conditions. By their alleged immorality and lack of work ethic, thrift, refinement and virtue, they were said to have brought poverty upon themselves. Thus, the poverty problem had been redefined into an individual and moral problem that did not stand in the way of acceptance of the existing power relations and possibly even sanctioned them.

There is little point in criticizing people who lived centuries ago for their limited interest in the lives and well-being of their fellow townspeople who lived in less and often far less favourable conditions. It is more interesting to find out what factors played a role in the acceptance and continuity of the existing distribution of resources and the power relations based upon it. It has become clear from the foregoing that the forms of appropriation of urban space described in this study contributed to the acceptance and continuity of social reality, but to explain the centuries-long stability of the power relations, this appropriation must be placed in the context of what Bourdieu calls habitus. In the introduction, habitus was described as a mental framework established during childhood through socialization in a specific social environment that shapes the way individuals tend to perceive the world, appreciate it and act within it. Within groups with a similar background, the habitus of individuals shows strong similarities because as an internalization of external social structures, habitus reflects the similar circumstances in which these individuals grew up and were socialized.[1]

The fact that the power relations as expressed in the residential, violent and discursive appropriation of urban space were also accepted in the long term, therefore, had to do with their being in line with the values, opinions and ideologies stored in the habitus of social classes.[2] Bourdieu writes: 'The habitus – embodied history, internalized as a second nature and so forgotten as history – is the active presence of the whole past of which it is the product.'[3] In their turn, those same power relations confirmed the habitus of social classes, reinforced it and carried it forward into the future through the socialization of children. Habitus thus built a bridge between past, present and future and as such functioned as a force that promoted continuity in the long term.[4]

Formulated in this way, it is difficult to see how change could ever occur in the premodern power relations, but change was possible and did occur. In the introduction, it was pointed out that from the second half of the nineteenth century onwards, a fundamentally different power structure emerged, which was supported by different views on the social relations within society. In order to explain the occurrence of these changes, it is useful to make a distinction between the habitus formed by socialization during youth, also referred to as the primary habitus, and the additional habitus formed during later life through education, occupation and experience. The primary habitus is the most enduring and functions as a second nature, but the influence of the additional habitus creates room for change.[5] In one of his later publications, Bourdieu also explicitly pointed to the dynamics of habitus: 'Habitus change constantly in response to new experiences. Dispositions are subject to a kind of permanent revision, but one which is never radical, because it works on the basis of the premises established in the previous state.'[6] Radical changes are therefore possible but will generally not be achieved overnight, and the more the additional habitus is at variance with the primary habitus, the more difficult the changes will be to internalize. The resistance of part of the elites to the abolition of public and violent punishment in the first half of the nineteenth century is a striking example of this.

This is not the place to elaborate on the backgrounds of the changes after the middle of the nineteenth century. In his *Koninkrijk vol sloppen*, Van der Woud does so for changes in housing and public health, and he rightly notes that among elites and middle classes, a different mentality and vision of society was needed, a different habitus in the terminology of this study.[7] And partly as a result of the burgeoning socialism, which presented a different vision of society and also the perspective that change was possible and also necessary, the habitus among the working classes also changed in time. The fact that the centuries-old power relations in the cities of Holland actually began to shift seems, therefore, to have been the result of a complex process in which the slowly changing habitus of social classes, political reforms and modernization of the economy interacted.[8] And in these new and more dynamic times too, the cities of Holland functioned as arenas in which social classes marked and sometimes fought for their position in society through the physical and discursive appropriation of urban space.

Appendix: Patterns of residential differentiation in the cities of Holland, fourteenth-nineteenth centuries

For the six cities selected in this study, this appendix attempts to reconstruct the residential patterns in the long period before the first land register of 1832. The results of this reconstruction are briefly summarized in Chapter 3 and play an important role in explaining the patterns of residential appropriation in the pre-modern cities of Holland.

A.1. Delft

It is no coincidence that in reconstructing the residential patterns in the centuries before the 1832 land register, Delft is the first city to be considered. Of the cities studied here, Delft occupies an intermediate position in terms of population size. This offers the possibility to confront the developments observed there in the following sections with those in the smaller cities (Alkmaar and Edam) and the larger cities (The Hague, Leiden and Amsterdam). Moreover, a lot of preliminary work has already been done for Delft, which also makes it attractive to first reconstruct the residential patterns for this city.

The *redres van de verponding* from the years 1730-3 is a useful starting point. The *verponding*, a tax based on the rental value of houses and land, had been levied since the early years of the Dutch Republic, but in the 1720s, the States of Holland felt the need for a redress or revision. The immediate cause was the rising tensions in Europe and the chronic lack of financial resources available to the Dutch Republic, a small country that had to maintain both an army and a fleet in order to survive.[1] With the revision of the *verponding*, it was hoped to generate more tax revenue and the revision was also used to bring the tax in line with the changed size of the cities. Since the last revision of the verponding a century earlier, many of the small and medium-sized cities in Holland had been hit by population decline and dwindling housing stock, while Amsterdam, Rotterdam, Schiedam and The Hague had grown in size. The latter cities therefore paid too little under the existing tax regime, while the shrinking cities paid too much.[2] After much wrangling, in June 1730 the new tax and the instructions for the commissioners to be appointed were finally accepted.[3]

The *redres van de verponding* is a useful source for this research because all pieces of land and built objects were registered and a realistic estimate was made of their rental value. To this end, the tenants of dwellings had to show their leases and, in the case of owner-occupied dwellings, the persons in charge of drafting the redress estimated the rental value on the basis of comparable dwellings for which leases – and thus market prices – were available. The instruction that 'all houses, small or large, public or other, that receive rent or profit' shall be taxed implies that dwellings that were made available free of charge to the poor, fell outside the terms of the tax.[4] Therefore, they have not been included in this study, nor have dwellings in almshouses (*hofjes*), which were usually not operated at market rents and therefore do not give an adequate indication of the socio-economic status of the residents.

Since no corresponding set of maps was created in addition to the *verponding* lists, the location of some houses can only be approximated.[5] Nevertheless, the result is clear and shows a great resemblance to the situation at the time of the first national land

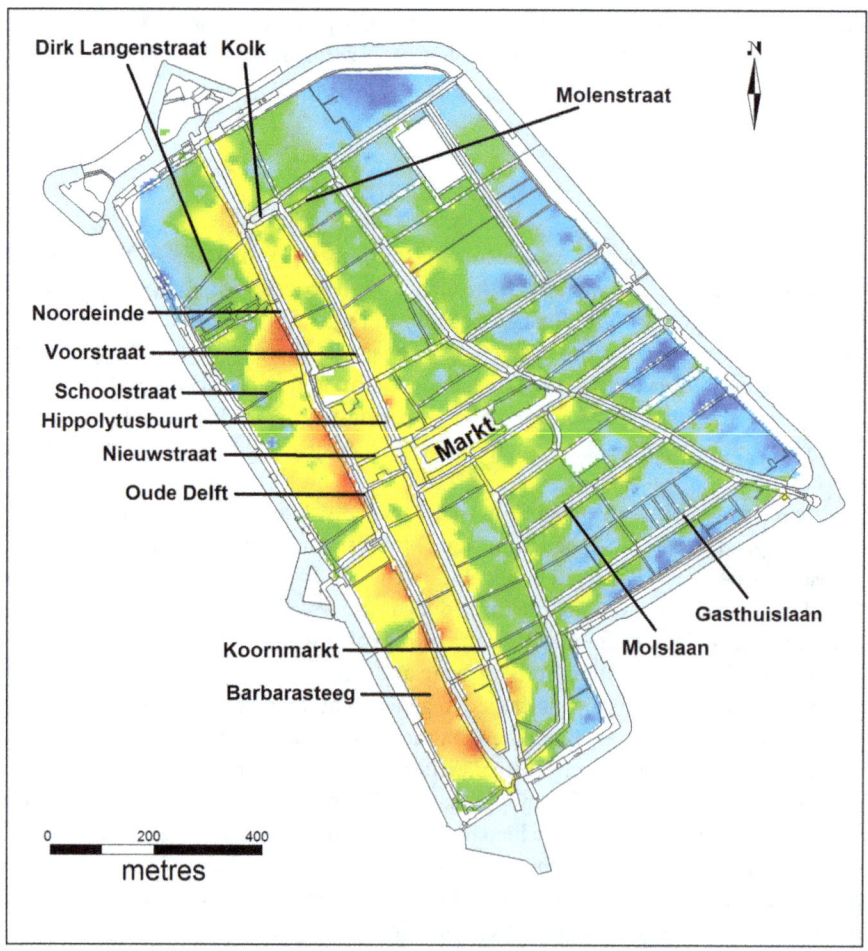

Map A.1 Residential differentiation in Delft within the city walls, *c.* 1730.

register. Around 1730 too, Delft seems to have been divided into a wealthy western half and a much poorer eastern half (Map A.1). And like in the nineteenth century, the two main canals (Noordeinde-Oude Delft and Voorstraat-Koornmarkt) were the favourite residential domain of the well-to-do urban upper classes. But just as in the first half of the nineteenth century, social classes in Delft in the eighteenth century were not 'confined' to their own parts of the city. Map A.1 clearly shows that in the western half of the city rents in side streets and backstreets were considerably lower than along the main canals. And in the eastern half of the city, although rents were generally low, significantly higher rents were paid along the canals which housed people with more financial resources. It is also clear that streets and canals in Delft did not usually have the same level of rents along their entire length. Map A.1 therefore shows a combination of macro-differentiation at the level of city districts and meso-level differentiation between and within streets. This is also clearly visible in Map A.2, where the 10 per cent of dwellings with the highest rental values (red squares) and the 10 per cent with the lowest rental values (blue squares) are plotted. The lowest rental values (4–17 guilders per year) were overwhelmingly found in the eastern half of the city, but they were not entirely absent in the western half. There, they were mainly located in the outermost periphery of the city. Conversely, houses with the highest rental values (140–1250 guilders per year) were mainly found along the two main canals and at the Market Square, but some were also found along the canals in the eastern half of the city.

For housing patterns in seventeenth-century Delft we can make use of the study by Van der Vlis of Delft's indigent households receiving poor relief. Her research into the archives of the Chamber of Charity yielded 1,158 addresses for the mid-seventeenth century of a total of 656 indigent households.[6] The twelve streets with the largest number of entries, accounting for 660 of the 1,158 addresses, were without exception located in the eastern half of the city. It was in the vicinity of these 'poor' streets that a large proportion of the remaining needy households lived. Especially in the south-east corner of the city, in the area between Molslaan and Gasthuislaan (see Map A.1 for the location of streets) a large concentration of poor households was found. This is also the neighbourhood where the lowest rental values were recorded around 1730 and 1832. Nevertheless, Van der Vlis emphasizes that destitute people could be found elsewhere in the city as well. Even in the alleys leading to the fashionable Oude Delft, some seven households were supported by the Chamber of Charity.

The tax register of the *Groot Familiegeld* of 1674, studied by Van der Wiel, is a useful addition to the registers of the Chamber of Charity because it lists for the sixteen districts of Delft the number of well-to-do households, that is those with an assessed wealth of one thousand guilders or more. For the city and the two suburbs, there were 1,269 tax assessments: 1,190 for heads of households and seventy-nine for fortunes managed by stewards.[7] Not surprisingly, the percentage of taxed households in the western half of the city was much higher than in the eastern half. Especially in the area between Barbarasteeg/Breestraat in the south and Schoolstraat in the north, the percentage of wealthy households was very high: 81–98 per cent.[8] Around 1730 and 1832, this was also an area with many high rental values and very few low ones. East of Voorstraat-Koornmarkt, the percentage of wealthy households was considerably

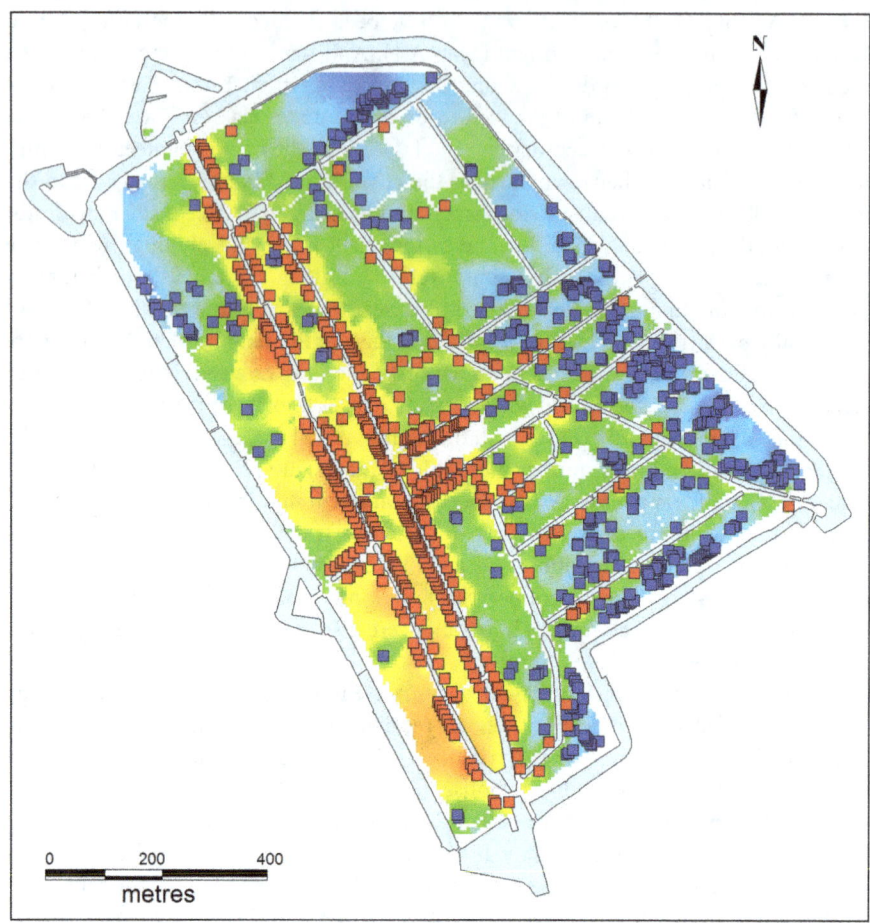

Map A.2 Highest and lowest rental values in Delft within the city walls, c. 1730.

lower: 11–29 per cent.[9] In combination, the alms registers of the Chamber of Charity and the *Groot Familiegeld* confirm the picture sketched earlier for the eighteenth and nineteenth centuries: striking differences between the western and eastern halves of the city, but no strict segregation of rich and poor.

The tax register of the *10ᵉ penning* of 1543, published by Verhoeven, makes it possible to go back in time to the middle of the sixteenth century.[10] That was the time that the central government wanted to reform the tax system and the governess Mary of Hungary asked the States of Holland for permission to impose three new taxes. Of interest to us is the *10ᵉ penning*, a 10 per cent levy on the income from real estate.[11] And although the revision of the tax system was intended, among other things, to put an end to the numerous exemptions that adversely affected revenues under the old tax regime, the *10ᵉ penning* also had exemptions. Thus, monasteries were exempt from payment as well as public buildings and charitable institutions and also all houses with an annual rent of up to two guilders. Nevertheless, in the Delft tax register many of these cheap houses have been recorded without assessment. What is unclear is whether the houses that were destroyed in the great fire of May 1536 were excluded from the registration, or whether they were already rebuilt and subject to taxation. This problem is particularly acute for the western half of the city, which suffered much more from the fire than the eastern half.[12]

Because Verhoeven was able to reconstruct the route taken by the tax-collectors, most of the rental values can also be plotted on a map, although the exact location within the street face of a block of houses cannot be determined.[13] Map A.3 shows the rental value of houses in Delft in 1543 and there is no doubt that the residential structure of Delft as we know it for the period from the seventeenth to the first half of the nineteenth century already existed in the sixteenth century. The two main canals with mainly expensive houses and by implication well-to-do residents, are easily

Map A.3 Residential differentiation and dwellings with weekly rents in Delft, 1543.

recognizable. And just like in later times, the rental values and material wealth of the residents in the eastern half of the city and in the outlying area were considerably lower. The latter is confirmed by the location of the dwellings for which the source mentions that weekly rents were paid (black squares in map A.3). After all, this was the usual payment term for cheap housing for centuries. But the presence of houses with weekly rents in the western half of the city and of more expensive houses in the eastern half show that there was also residential differentiation at the meso-level of streets. The side streets and back streets in the affluent part of the city housed the middle and lower-income classes, and conversely, the canals in the eastern part of the city were home to relatively well-off people. And again, the map demonstrates that especially along long streets and canals, the status of the housing and socio-economic position of the residents could vary considerably. This can be seen very clearly at the south end of Koornmarkt, with low rental values and a series of houses with weekly rents.

To determine whether, as Vance argues, the sixteenth century was a period of transition in which residential structures changed radically, it is important to know whether the residential patterns mapped out earlier originated in the sixteenth century or are of an earlier date. Many sources are not available to us for answering this question, but it is fortunate that the registers of the *Kerkgeld* for the parish of the Oude Kerk from the beginning of the fifteenth century (1410) have been preserved. The source was analysed by De Boer in 1979 and the following is based on his findings.[14] For a correct interpretation of the source it is good to know that the parish of the Oude Kerk comprised the western part of the city and that in this parish lived about two-thirds of the population of Delft. It is possible that the poorest were exempt from the levy, but the registers also mention small alleys, which argues for the completeness of the source. In any case, the *Kerkgeld* register gives an indication of the prosperity of a considerable part of the Delft population for an early period and is therefore of interest to us.

Of the 713 registered households, 247 (34.6 per cent) paid the minimum assessment of two pennies and some fourteen (2.0 per cent) paid the maximum assessment of thirty-two pennies.[15] It is a pity that the assessments for the parish of the Nieuwe Kerk are missing, but nevertheless it is possible to make some tentative statements about the difference between the western and eastern halves of the city. From the register it becomes clear that already at the beginning of the fifteenth century the highest assessments were collected on the two main canals. Especially on Oude Delft near the Oude Kerk, and also on the Kolk (then Houtmarkt) the assessments were very high. They were followed by those on Koornmarkt and Hippolytusbuurt (then Hoogstraat), the eastern of the two main canals. These high assessments contrast with the low to very low assessments paid in the streets immediately east of the main canals: in Molenstraat and Nieuwstraat.[16] But the eastern part of the city was certainly not uniformly poor. A comparison of the names in the registers of the *Kerkgeld* with the lists of aldermen from the years 1400 to 1415 shows that a considerable number of them lived in the parish of the Nieuwe Kerk, although we do not know exactly where.[17]

Around-the-corner differentiation is clearly evident in the parish of the Oude Kerk. The high assessments on the main canals, where many of the burgomasters and aldermen lived, contrast sharply with the low to very low assessments in Dirk

Langenstraat (then Langensteeg) and Schoolstraat (then Schoolsteeg), both located between Oude Delft and the city moat. This form of meso-differentiation also makes it plausible that the occurrence of a few low assessments in a series of high assessments on, for instance, Oude Delft, does indeed point, as De Boer argues, to the presence of poor people in dwellings in backyards and in nameless alleys.[18]

The analysis of the *Kerkgeld* registers suggests that the residential patterns reconstructed on the basis of the land register from the 1830s go back to the very substantial city extension of 1355, when Delft acquired the size and spatial structure that it would retain until well into the nineteenth century. This means that we have traced a spatial continuity of four to five centuries and it has also been demonstrated that in the case of Delft, the transition from medieval to early modern times was not also expressed in fundamental changes in the residential patterns within the city. However, within the margins of this almost unchanging residential structure, subtle shifts took place that should not be missed in the analysis and that can best be described as an attempt to create a quiet and distinguished residential environment by and for the elites of Delft. The decline of the Delft brewing industry, for centuries an important pillar of the local economy and the wealth of the elites, played a major role in this.

Until the last quarter of the sixteenth century, the wealthy brewers lived on the western main canals and conducted their business in outbuildings at the rear. The latter situation came to an end with the decline of Delft's brewing industry. This began at the end of the 1580s and, after a brief period of recovery in the first decade of the seventeenth century, took on dramatic proportions from around 1610 onwards. In 1645, only twenty-five breweries were still operating, a number that declined further to fifteen in 1667.[19] The decline had major consequences for the residential environment along the main canals, where only a few remained of the dozens of breweries that had once been located there. The changes were especially great along Oude Delft, where almost all breweries disappeared. Whereas Oude Delft had previously been dominated by the busy activity of beer production, the supply of grain and peat and the removal of many thousands of barrels of beer, it could now be turned into a quiet and distinguished canal.[20] This was not least because the new large-scale earthenware industry did not settle there, but in the poor south-east quadrant of the city. And the capital of the brewer families found its way, among other things, to the Dutch East India Company (VOC) and the major land reclamations that took place in the first half of the seventeenth century.[21]

In time, Delft's political elite no longer consisted of brewers and retired brewers, but of regents, often with academic titles.[22] In the eighteenth century, these regents and also the directors of the VOC and high officials lived almost without exception along Oude Delft. There, and also along Nieuwe Delft (Voorstraat-Hippolytusbuurt-Wijnhaven-Koornmarkt), many houses were modernized in the first half of the century and, if the opportunity arose, enlarged by merging them with one or more neighbouring plots. And many of the industrial buildings in the backyards were demolished and made way for gardens.[23] The quality of this quiet and affluent residential environment was protected by by-laws and urban resources were used for a general upgrading of the built environment and infrastructure in this part of the city. After the middle of the eighteenth century, we also see that the location preferences of the wealthy earthenware manufacturers started to change. According to Wijsenbeek-Olthuis, before 1750 they all lived near their factories in the eastern half of the city, but by the end of the century not a single one did.[24] They had moved to the much more fashionable western half of the city.

Is this combination of socio-spatial continuity and the desire among elites for an exclusive and well-to-do residential environment specific to Delft, or does it also hold true for other cities? And does the size of the cities play a role in this? To be able to answer these questions, we will first focus on two smaller cities in Holland: Edam and Alkmaar.

A.2. The small cities of Edam and Alkmaar

Edam was the smallest of the cities included in this study. In 1830, the city had about 4,000 inhabitants, in 1732 the number was in the same order of magnitude, in 1622 some 5,500 inhabitants were counted, and in 1563 the figure was about 3,750 inhabitants.[25] In Chapter 2 we have already established that at the time of the 1832 land register, the highest rental values and therefore also the wealthiest inhabitants were to be found along the waterways that cut through the city from west to east: Spui, Dam and Voorhaven. At the east end of Voorhaven, rental values were considerably lower, but the lowest rents and poorest inhabitants were predominantly to be found in the urban periphery and just outside the former city gates. Especially, the area outside the eastern city gate (Oosterpoort), along the waterway that connected Voorhaven to the Zuiderzee, housed many poor people.

The *redres van de verponding* of 1630, similar to the previously used *redres* of 1730, enables us to test whether the pattern of residential differentiation, as reconstructed on the basis of the land register, also existed two centuries earlier. The *redres* differs from the land register in a positive way, because it lists rooms, front houses, back houses and other units within the same property separately, so that a more realistic picture of the rent paid by individual households is obtained. The disadvantage is that for Edam, the exact location of houses is often not known, and also the route of the tax-collectors who compiled the register often remains unclear. Map A.4, therefore, provides a rough indication of the distribution of rental values across urban space.[26] However, this caveat does not alter the fact that the global picture matches that of two centuries later.

Around 1630, as in later centuries, the surroundings of Spui, Dam and Voorhaven was the preferred residential area of Edam's wealthy inhabitants. And again, the prosperity of the inhabitants especially in the northern and eastern periphery was much lower than in the more centrally located parts of the city and on Baanstraat in the southern periphery. Moreover, just like in the first half of the nineteenth century, the inhabitants of the area outside the eastern city gate belonged to the poorest segment of the population. In addition to these patterns at the macro-level, around 1630 there was also residential differentiation in Edam at the meso-level of streets. It is abundantly clear that rental values varied along Voorhaven, Achterhaven and Nieuwehaven

Appendix

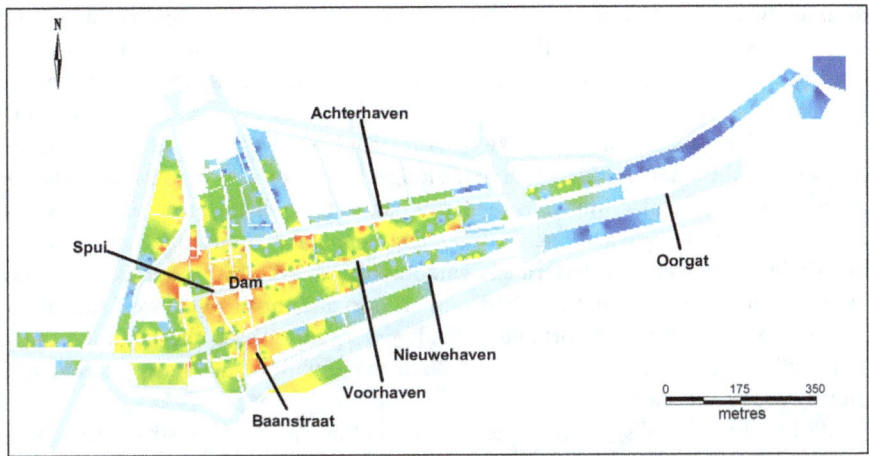

Map A.4 Residential differentiation in Edam, c. 1630.

in particular. However, because the tax collector did not always indicate when he included side streets and alleys in his route, meso-differentiation at the level of blocks (around-the-corner differentiation) is not clearly discernible in Map A.4. Nevertheless, the descriptions in the tax register show that 120 out of the 1,022 registered properties were composite properties, such as house and back house. In the case of the 1630 *redres*, these seem to refer mainly to small, more or less independent dwellings in the backyard and not to a backroom within the main building.

The arrival of the Duke of Alva in the Low Countries and the introduction under Philip II of a fixed tax system caused many problems at the time, but has provided historians and other researchers with the records of a levy on movable and immovable property from 1569.[27] For us, the levy on immovable property is important. It was a tax of 1 per cent on the assessed value of houses in Edam (and the other cities in Holland). The usefulness of this 100^e *penning* tax for the reconstruction of residential patterns lies mainly in the fact that unlike the taxes on real estate introduced earlier by the governess Mary of Hungary, no exemptions were granted. Therefore, all habitable dwellings were registered in the tax roll and indications such as *huijs, huijsken, camerken* and *woninckgen* give an impression of the status and size of these dwellings.[28] Unfortunately, also with this source it is not possible to establish a one-to-one match with an exact location on the map, and we must also take into account that the value of houses occupied by owners is assessed considerably lower than the value of houses rented out.

While the area enclosed by the city wall erected in the first half of the sixteenth century is the same as in 1630, in 1569 Edam had considerably fewer houses.[29] The maps by Jacob van Deventer and Taems Sijmonsz., both from the 1560s, clearly show this, as does the register of the 100^e *penning* tax (Map A.5).[30] But the overall picture of the distribution of social classes across urban space does not look very different from later times. In 1569, too, the elites in Edam were mainly found along the water of Spui, Dam and Voorhaven. The previously observed phenomenon that wealth on Voorhaven declined when approaching the eastern city gate is here especially noticeable on the south side of Voorhaven. On the north side, during the first half of the sixteenth century, some wealthy timber merchants had established themselves near the city gates, and they also set up their timber yards there.[31] Outside the eastern city gate, and especially along the Oorgat and Luckeside, the population was poor. To a lesser extent, this was also the case along Tuindijk. In the longer term, a process of social degradation seems to have taken place there. In 1630, this part of the outlying area was already less distinct from the Oorgat and Luckeside, and in the first half of the nineteenth century, the whole area outside the eastern city gate was almost uniformly poor. Poor in 1569 were also the inhabitants outside the Noorderpoort and those on the west side of the city, outside the Middelierpoort and Volendammerpoort. This continued the pattern from within the city walls, because households in cheap dwellings were found mainly on the edges of the city.

Within the city walls, macro-differentiation at the level of city districts was not as pronounced as in the case of, for instance, Delft, but the aforementioned makes clear that in 1569 a distinction can nevertheless be made between the central part of the city, that is the area around Spui, Dam and Voorhaven, and the urban periphery. This distinction does not imply that social classes lived segregated from each other, because just as in the days of the *redres* (c. 1630) and the 1832 land register, there was also meso-differentiation at the level of streets. The most pronounced, and also clearly visible on the map, was the contrast between the houses on the north side of Voorhaven and those on the south side of Achterhaven.

Due to the virtual absence of street names in the source, it is not possible to distinguish between houses on main streets and in side streets or alleys, but there are indications that around-the-corner differentiation did exist in 1569. For example, owners of corner houses built small dwellings that could be rented out with an independent entrance on the side street or alley. In sixteenth-century Edam, where

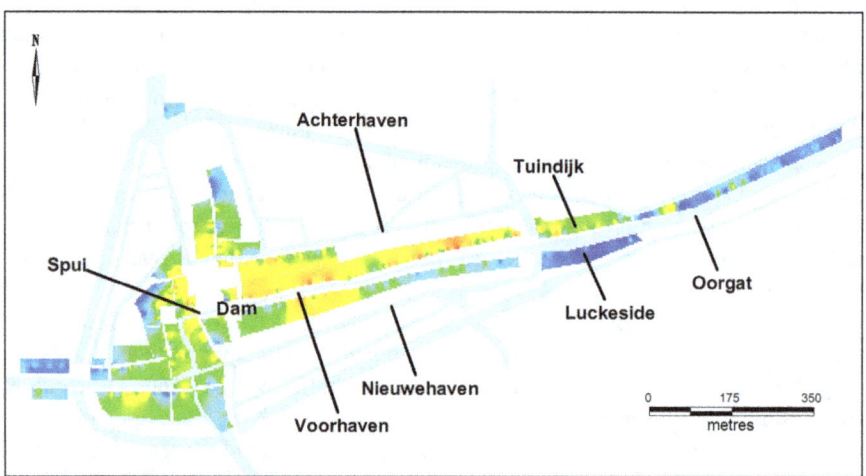

Map A.5 Residential differentiation in Edam, 1569.

even along the main streets and canals many houses were built of wood, these small houses will also have been built of wood. From the beginning of the sixteenth century, however, the term *camer* also appears in the sources, and they are also mentioned in the 1569 tax register. These were often stone-built one-room dwellings, built again behind the main house and accessible via a side street or alley.[32]

The predominant image of Edam in this (and later) period is therefore that of a city with a relatively uncomplicated residential structure, but one that is consistent with what has already been observed for other cities and later periods. At the level of the city as a whole, Edam also had an overrepresentation of poor and underprivileged people in the periphery and outside the city walls. But they were not absent elsewhere in the city, for while high-rent houses and well-to-do residents were to be found mainly along Spui, Dam and Voorhaven, residential accommodation for the middle classes and working classes could also be found in back streets, side streets and alleys close by. Can that pattern be observed in earlier periods as well?

To answer that question, in most cities we have to resort to occasional references or educated guesses. This is not the case in Edam. Here, researchers have at their disposal the records of the *schotgeld* tax. The *schotgeld* originated from a medieval tax that the residents of Holland owed to the count. In Holland, only fragmentary material of this tax has survived, but for Edam, records are available for a number of years between 1462 and 1569.[33] The *pachtboeken* contain information on the possessions of the inhabitants of Edam (and the villages in the Zeevang-area that fell under the city's jurisdiction) and the *schotboeken* contain the amount of the assessment based on the information in the *pachtboeken*. Although street names are missing from this source too, Boschma-Aarnoudse succeeded in bringing together the entries in the *schotgeld* registers into nine districts. Districts are of course not the most appropriate unit for studying residential patterns, but due to the small population size and low building density of Edam in these early years, these districts often coincide with streets. Thus, districts 4 and 5 contain information on the property and wealth of the residents on the north side of Voorhaven, districts 7 and 8 on the residents on the south side, and district 3 on the residents of Grote Kerkstraat. The area outside the eastern city gates (district 6) was mentioned separately in the source.

All this offers the possibility of following the patterns of residential differentiation back in time, as far as 1462. But let us start with the *schotgeld* of 1569, which can be compared to the data from the *100^e penning* tax. Map A.6 shows for each district the average assessment compared to the average assessment for the city as a whole. In the districts coloured red, the assessment was above the city average, in the districts coloured grey around the city average, and in the districts coloured blue below the city average. The resulting picture is very similar to Map A.5, which shows the estimated rental value of houses in Edam. The highest positive deviations from the city average were found in the westernmost parts of Voorhaven. There the inhabitants were taxed for an average of 8.1 (north side of Voorhaven) and 11.6 (south side of Voorhaven) *verndel* in the *schotgeld* tax, compared to a city average of 3.8 *verndel* per tax payer.[34] The lowest averages were recorded in the south-eastern part of Voorhaven (2.3 *verndel*) and especially among the residents outside the eastern city gates (1.5 *verndel*). In the western, southern and northern periphery of the city, the assessments were also below

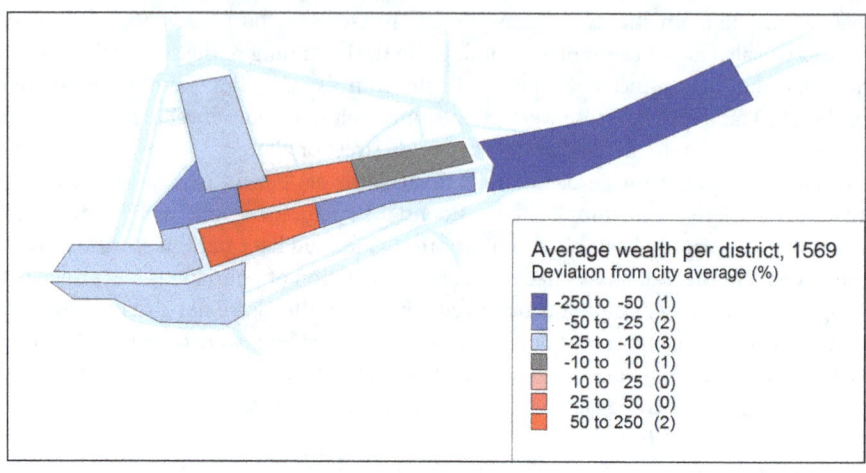

Map A.6 Residential differentiation in Edam based on the *schotgeld* tax, 1569.

the city average, but the difference here was considerably less than in the eastern periphery. This too is in line with the picture that was reconstructed earlier on the basis of the tax register of the *100ᵉ penning* tax. The similarity between both sources from 1569 gives confidence in the usefulness of the *schotgeld* tax for mapping the residential patterns in the preceding period.

Maps A.7 and A.8 show the situation in 1514 and 1462 respectively.[35] The most important conclusion we may draw on the basis of the three maps is that the socio-spatial differentiation between 1462 and 1569 did not change significantly. Also around the middle of the fifteenth century, rich Edammers lived in houses along Spui, Dam and (the western part of) Voorhaven, and the least well-off could be found in the eastern part of the city and the adjoining outlying area. This points to a continuity of almost four centuries (1462–1832), and it is not unlikely that this pattern already existed before 1462 and continued for some time after 1832. But the three maps also show a clear development. In the period 1462–1569, the contrast between the districts became more pronounced. In 1462, three of the nine districts still showed an average assessment around the city average, but this number decreased via two districts in 1514 to one district in 1569. At the same time, the extremes gained in importance. In 1462, the tax rate in the south-western part of Voorhaven was exactly 50 per cent above the city average, but by 1514 that percentage had risen to +79 per cent and in 1569 to +205 per cent. In the latter year, the tax in the north-western part of Voorhaven was also considerably above the city average (+113 per cent). And while in 1462 and 1514 three districts had an average assessment below the city average, in 1569 there were six. That is also the only year of the three survey years in which a district scored more than 50 per cent below the city average. It was – not unexpectedly – the eastern suburbs (–61 per cent).

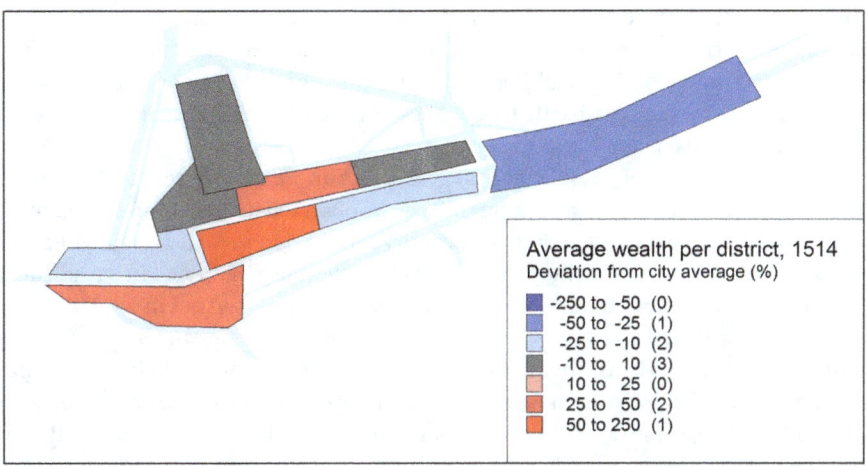

Map A.7 Residential differentiation in Edam based on the *schotgeld* tax, 1514.

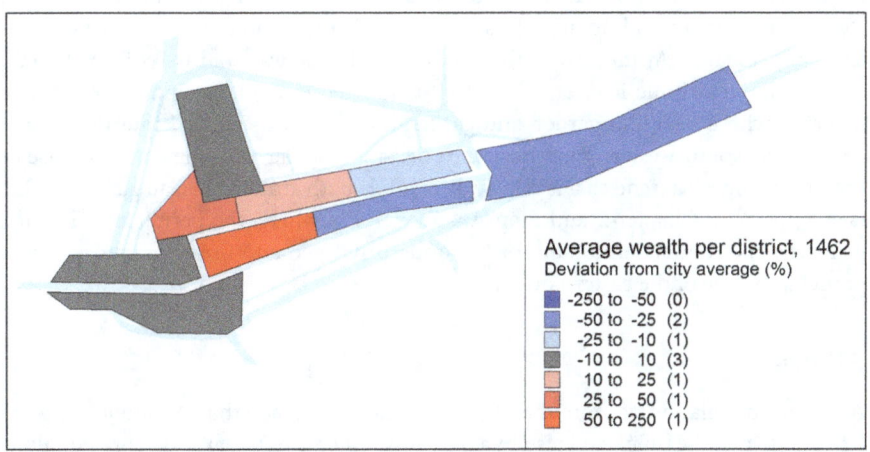

Map A.8 Residential differentiation in Edam based on the *schotgeld* tax, 1462.

More generally, the urban periphery lost wealth and prosperity, and the city's wealth was increasingly concentrated in the western part of Voorhaven. Thus, the percentage of wealthy people on the north side of Voorhaven was 8.0 per cent in 1462 and 19.0 per cent in 1569; on the south side these figures were 12.8 and 23.3 per cent respectively. In the same years, the percentage of poor people in the eastern suburbs increased from 76.3 to 95.8 per cent of all people in that district who had to contribute to the *schotgeld* tax. More and more the eastern suburbs took on the character of a poor quarter. And although wealthy people were hardly to be found in the eastern suburbs in 1569, less wealthy people were not absent in the well-to-do districts. With 51 and 35 per cent respectively in the north-western and south-western parts of Voorhaven, their presence there was undeniable. Mixing of the highest and the lowest wealth classes was therefore common even there and it is reasonable to assume that the less wealthy found accommodation in small houses behind the more prestigious ones along the main canals. It is even possible that along the west end of Voorhaven different types of houses had found a place.[36]

While the patterns of residential differentiation in Edam did not fundamentally change over many centuries, a striking shift can be observed in the housing preferences of the elites. The popularity of Spui, Dam and Voorhaven in particular, among Edam's wealthy elites, does not alter the fact that the elites were also interested in a residential location with a more rural feel. This was found in Baanstraat, laid out in 1583, a stone's throw from Dam and Spui, and close to the elegant gardens along the Singel. When a house commissioned by the burgomaster Sijmon Garbrantsz. was sold in 1617, it was no coincidence that the garden was extensively praised, but the house itself also had a distinguished appearance, with marble floors and beautiful paintings on the ceiling of the main room.[37] And the predilection for a more rural environment continued. In the eighteenth century, many burgomasters and other dignitaries left the area around Dam and Spui to settle on the south-western edge of the city. Around 1700, for example, two existing houses on Lingerzijde were combined to form a residence for the burgomaster, VOC administrator and notary Claes Harmensz. Bost, a scion of a wealthy family of timber merchants. At the end of the century the house was sold to William Pont, a very wealthy maritime insurer, who had it converted into a large and representative mansion with a beautiful garden and garden house with Louis XVI interior.[38] Some parts of the south-western periphery thus became popular with the elites because of their rural appeal; a trend that is clearly discernible both around 1630 and around 1830 (see Map 2.2 in Chapter 2 and Map A.4 above). Elsewhere, the periphery remained primarily the residential domain of the underprivileged and the poor, and this was particularly true of the eastern outlying area.

Alkmaar

Alkmaar's population of more than 9,400 around 1830 made the city about twice the size of Edam at the time. And also in a more distant past Alkmaar was more populous than Edam. Around 1730 the city had about 12,500 inhabitants and a century earlier about a thousand more. In 1561 the population was estimated at almost 8,000 and in 1514 at over 4,000.[39] How were these people distributed across urban space?

In Chapter 2, it became clear that the well-to-do inhabitants of Alkmaar around 1830 found a home along Langestraat, Oude Gracht, in the vicinity of Mient/Waagplein and along the north side of Luttik Oudorp. Households with few of very few financial resources were overrepresented at the edges of the city, in the outlying area and especially in the south-east quadrant of Alkmaar. But the middle classes and working classes not only lived in the urban periphery, but often literally around the corner from the well-to-do, in side streets and backstreets.

The 'Historisch Kadaster Alkmaar', a project by Willem van den Berg, makes it possible to reconstruct the residential history of Alkmaar in the period before the 1832 land register. Map A.9 presents the situation around 1730, based on the aforementioned

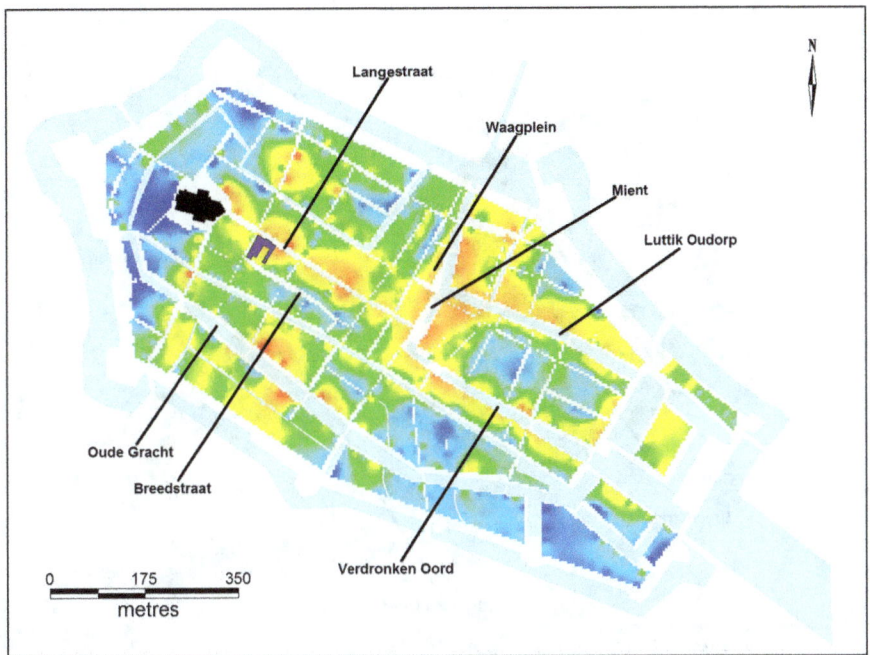

Map A.9 Residential differentiation in Alkmaar within the city walls, c. 1730.

redres van de verponding.[40] The map clearly shows that the pattern of residential differentiation around 1730 was not fundamentally different from that at the time of 1832 land register. Social classes in 1730 occupied roughly the same streets and parts of the city as they did around 1830, and the patterns of meso-differentiation between and within streets were also similar. And so the wealth of the residents in a back street like Breedstraat was again considerably lower than along the nearby Langestraat. And also in the area between Luttik Oudorp and Verdronken Oord the rental values, and by implication the socio-economic position of the residents, were much lower than along the two canals. Finally, the interpolation map shows that there was also differentiation within streets. Especially towards the urban periphery, rental values and the wealth of the residents decreased.

But besides all the continuity, the interpolation maps based on rental data in the 1832 land register and the *redres van de verponding* also show some differences. It is striking that the rental values at Verdronken Oord and thus the wealth of the residents were considerably higher around 1730 than a century later. More generally, the western half of the city seems to have gained in status at the expense of the area east of Mient in the decades following 1730. A clear manifestation of this trend is that in the first half of the nineteenth century, Alkmaar's wealthy elites mainly lived along Langestraat and the western part of Oude Gracht (compare Chapter 2, Map 2.3).

Map A.10, where the patterns of residential differentiation have been mapped for around 1630, is very similar to the interpolation map for 1730. But at the same time, the image reinforces the impression that the western half of the city became more

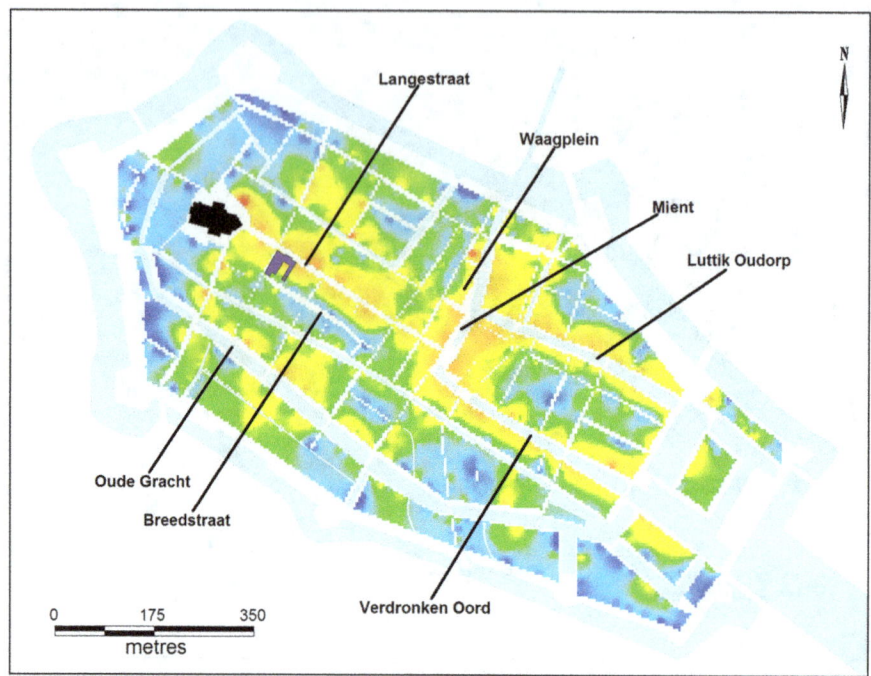

Map A.10 Residential differentiation in Alkmaar within the city walls, c. 1630.

important over time. Indeed, around 1630 Oude Gracht and its surroundings had less of the character of an elite neighbourhood than in 1730 and much less than in 1830. A glance at Map A.11, which shows the rental values from the 1561 *10ᵉ penning* tax, leaves no doubt that Oude Gracht only became a wealthy residential area after that time.[41] In 1561, Oude Gracht was still part of Alkmaar's fortified moat and defences and therefore unattractive as a residence for the city's wealthy residents, a finding that concurs with Sjoberg's view that elites avoided the city's periphery, which was a dangerous place to live during sieges and hostile attacks.

The turnaround took place in the years 1575–85 when the city was extended on the south side and the moat was transformed into a residential canal with houses on the opposite side as well.[42] In this time of economic and demographic growth, Verdronken Oord will also have acquired a higher status and more wealthy inhabitants, which it lost again between the data points of about 1730 and 1830. But apart from the transformation of Oude Gracht and Verdronken Oord from the end of the sixteenth century onwards, the situation in 1561 already shows all the characteristics of the situation in the centuries that followed. High rental values and wealthy inhabitants were found in Alkmaar mainly along the streets and canals that cut through the city from west to east, and along the axis of Mient and Waagplein that crossed this west to east route at the east end of Langestraat. Even the pattern of meso-differentiation at the level of streets is clearly visible on the map of 1561 and would not change significantly until well into the nineteenth century. Breedstraat and the area between Luttik Oudorp and Verdronken Oord are clear examples of this.[43]

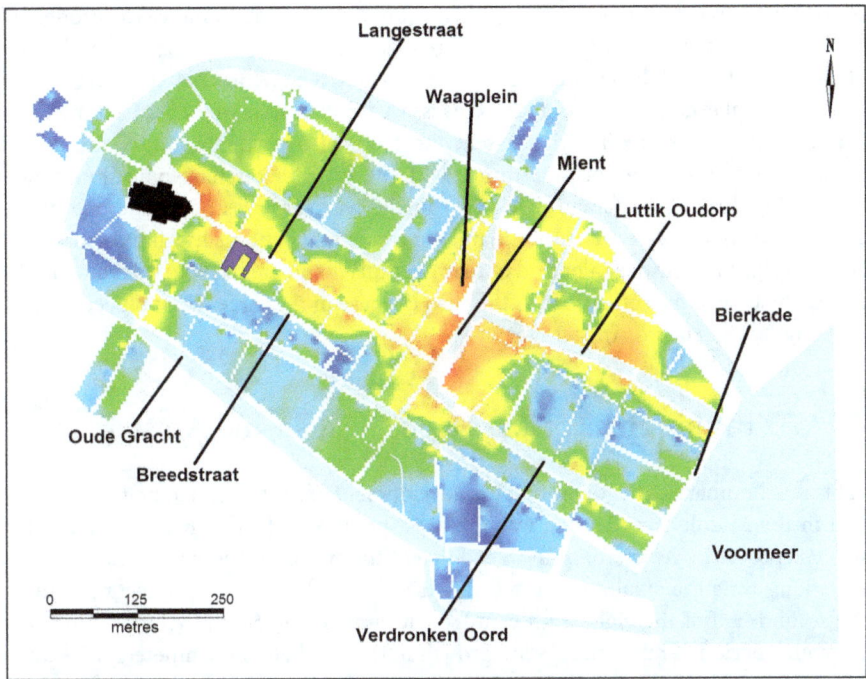

Map A.11 Residential differentiation in Alkmaar inside and outside the city walls, 1561.

For the fifteenth century and earlier, there are to my knowledge no archival sources that allow a detailed reconstruction of the residential patterns in Alkmaar.[44] However, building on the findings for 1561, it is nevertheless possible to say something about the earlier period. The entire eastern half of the city, that is the area east of Mient, was in all likelihood constructed in the second half of the fifteenth century and completed at the beginning of the sixteenth century with the construction of Bierkade, which still forms the eastern boundary of the inner city.[45] The medieval history of Alkmaar therefore largely took place in the area west of Mient.[46] There, around the middle of the thirteenth century, and east of the old settlement around the tuff predecessor of the present Grote Kerk (main church), a new urban core seems to have developed, namely at the present Houttil, a little west of Mient. Both cores contained large stone houses according to the standards of the time. Near the church, for example, stood the so-called 'Hooge Huys', a complex surrounded by a moat, which may have had its origins in a fortified manor belonging to the counts of Holland. Near Houttil, archaeological research has uncovered the foundations of two large brick houses from the mid-thirteenth century. Langestraat functioned as the connection between these two urban cores and was initially less prominent. Only from around 1300 did brick houses appear there too.

At a time when most houses were still built of wood, stone houses indicated the (great) wealth of their inhabitants. In fact, here we see the roots of the pattern that is so clearly visible on the map of 1561 (and those of later centuries): well-to-do urban cores around the Grote Kerk and Mient, and Langestraat as the equally well-to-do connecting axis between both cores. When Alkmaar's population increased strongly in the fourteenth century, city extensions were realized especially to the north and south of Langestraat, which had to provide space for the many newcomers.[47] It is not too bold to assume that even then these areas were less wealthy than the well-to-do axis running through the city centre. To what extent there was also residential differentiation at the level of streets cannot be determined with the available (archaeological) evidence, but renting out *camers* (small dwellings) in the backyard was of course one of the possibilities. In any case, just as in Edam, the residential patterns in Alkmaar have not changed significantly over a period of many centuries and are likely to be rooted in the earliest history of the settlement. Is this also the case in the three much bigger cities of The Hague, Leiden and Amsterdam?

A.3. The big cities of The Hague, Leiden and Amsterdam

Table A.1 summarizes the demographic development of the three major cities. It shows that in the Middle Ages Leiden was the most populous of the three; a position that was taken over by Amsterdam in the course of the sixteenth century. The Hague was for a long time the smallest of the three. It surpassed Leiden in population only in the second half of the eighteenth century and, unlike Leiden and Amsterdam, went through a period of rapid population growth in the first half of the nineteenth century, which, of course, was related to the growing importance of the nation state and its administrative and clerical apparatus.

Table A.1 Population of Amsterdam, Leiden and The Hague, c. 1398–1830

	Amsterdam	Leiden	The Hague
1830	200,784	34,564	56,000
1795	221,000	30,955	38,433
1732	239,866	70,000	33,500
1622	104,932	44,745	15,825
1560	30,000	12,456 (1570)	6,000 (1550)
1514	11,394	14,250	5,500
1477	8,410	11,000 (1497)	6,066
1398	4,400	5,000	1,300

Source: Piet Lourens and Jan Lucassen, *Inwonertallen van Nederlandse steden c. 1300-1800* (Amsterdam: NEHA 1997) and for 1830 J.D. Hoeufft and J.C.R. van Hoorn van Burgh, *Kadastrale uitkomsten van Noord-en Zuid-Holland 1832*. Reissue with an introduction by W.J. van den Berg and Ph. Kint (Dordrecht: Historische Vereniging Holland, 1993).

The Hague

At the time of the 1832 land register, the residential structure of The Hague was characterized by a striking concentration of high rental values, and by implication well-to-do residents, in the area around the Hofvijver and the royal palaces in the northeast quadrant of the city (see Chapter 2, Map 2.9). From this *Hofbuurt* (court district), houses with relatively high rental values fanned out in south-western direction. In the north-western and south-east quadrant of the city, on the other hand, rents were low to very low. This pattern of macro-differentiation was supplemented by meso-differentiation between and within streets. Thus, along main streets and main canals in relatively poor parts of The Hague, residents with some financial resources lived, and in side streets and back streets in well-to-do neighbourhoods, residents with limited and very limited resources. Within streets there was in many cases a declining status gradient towards the urban periphery. The following will attempt to establish when these residential patterns took shape.

For the beginning of the eighteenth century, Stal was able to map the status of a large number of streets and canals in The Hague on the basis of Gysbert de Cretser's city description. He has grouped De Cretser's characterizations of streets into three categories. The most prestigious were the streets lined with palaces and very large houses (red on the map). Then come the streets with substantial houses (orange on the map) and finally streets with the houses of tradesmen and craftsmen (blue on the map). All other streets played no role in De Cretser's scheme. In Map A.12 I have reproduced the streets that Stal put on the map and completed this information with the poor streets and neighbourhoods (blue circles/ellipses) mentioned by him and by Wijsenbeek. The map also shows the boundary of the *Hofbuurt* with a broken black line.[48]

When comparing the map image from Map A.12 with the situation at the time of the national land register (1832), it immediately becomes clear that the distribution of social classes across urban space has not fundamentally changed in the intervening

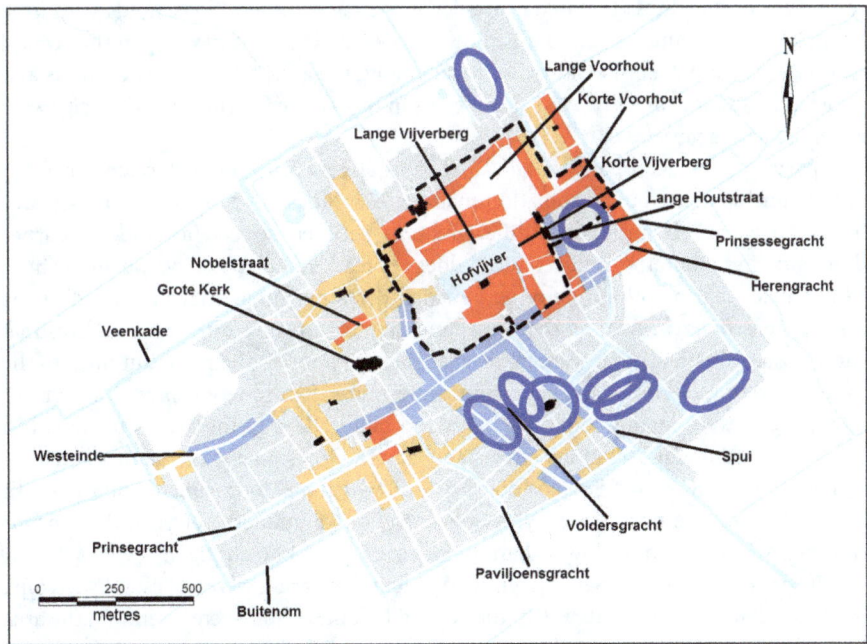

Map A.12 Residential differentiation in The Hague, 1711.

period. Also at the beginning of the eighteenth century, the wealth of The Hague was concentrated in the north-east quadrant and many poor people were to be found in the south-east quadrant. The very substantial houses on Nobelstraat and at the east end of Prinsegracht mentioned by De Cretser can also be found without difficulty on the cadastral map from the second quarter of the nineteenth century. The fact that De Cretser did not consider the houses in the north-western and south-western part of the city worth mentioning makes it plausible that these parts of the city were then already mainly inhabited by the lower middle classes and the working classes.

In addition to this pattern of residential differentiation at the level of city districts, the poor little neighbourhood behind Lange Houtstraat shows that differentiation at the meso-level of streets also occurred at the beginning of the eighteenth century. And the phenomenon was not limited to this neighbourhood. In many places in the city, behind the houses of the well-to-do and the middle classes, there were houses in side streets, back streets, alleys and blind alleys that accommodated those who had few resources and therefore little power in the field of housing.[49]

Taking a considerable step back in time, we arrive at Map A.13. Here the rental values as registered in the *10^e penning* tax of 1561 have been put on a map.[50] In those years The Hague was considerably smaller than at the beginning of the eighteenth century, but the residential structure is nevertheless familiar. For although the area east of Binnenhof and Hofvijver was still undeveloped, it is clear that also in this period the court functioned as the centre of an area with expensive houses and wealthy residents. The prestigious houses on Nobelstraat described by De Cretser in 1711 also have equally prestigious predecessors in 1561. The continuity was not limited to the residences of the elites. The area around Voldersgracht, where households with little financial means found shelter both in the early eighteenth century and in the second quarter of the nineteenth century, was also among the areas with the lowest rents and poorest inhabitants in 1561. And again, rents in the western periphery of the city were generally low to very low.

Apart from the decreasing rental values along streets that extended to the periphery of the built-up area, the interpolation map for 1561 does not provide much evidence for the existence of residential differentiation between streets (around-the-corner differentiation), but the register itself does. Spread across the city, we find about forty entries that mention one or more small dwellings or, as they are called in the tax register, *cameren*. Among them was an entry with twelve *cameren* in Lorrestraat (now Assendelftstraat) that were made available pro bono to the poor, but most of the *cameren* were rented out. In total, there were more than ninety *cameren*, which we may assume were mainly found in alleys and blind alleys giving access to walled-in houses behind the houses along streets and canals. Occasionally, the name of an alley is mentioned, such as Jan Soetenslopje on Spui, which had four *cameren* on the south side and six on the north side. With an average of 4.3 guilders per year, the rent for *cameren* was considerably lower than the city average of 14.6 guilders.

The patterns of residential differentiation identified earlier were not established only in the sixteenth century. Already in the second half of the fourteenth century, the area around the count's court was the most prestigious part of the settlement. Specifically, this concerned the houses on Plaats and Toernooiveld (present Kneuterdijk), both

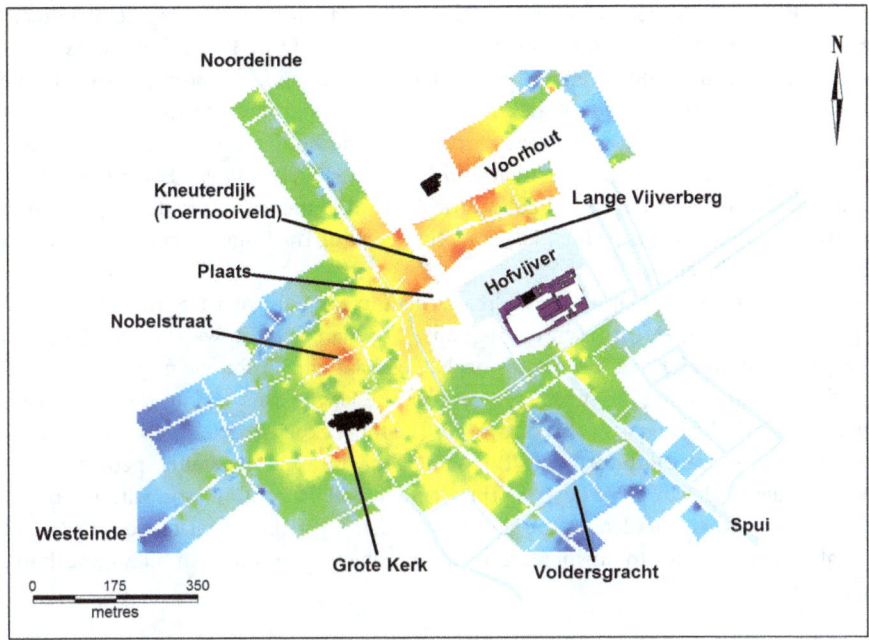

Map A.13 Residential differentiation in The Hague, 1561.

located north-west of the Hofvijver, and also (Lange) Vijverberg to the north of the Hofvijver. But even then, prestigious houses and wealthy inhabitants were also found around the Grote Kerk, which was built in stone around 1370, and along Nobelstraat. Archaeological research has shown the presence of stone houses there, which at that time were a sign of considerable wealth.[51] The less well-off part of the population will have found shelter at the periphery of the settlement and possibly also on the backyards in the rich neighbourhoods. For the fifteenth century, the existence of differentiation at the level of streets is evident because around 1470 there were about 800 houses in The Hague and no less than 200 *cameren* in the backyards.[52] It is also in those years that The Hague morphologically lost its predominantly village-like character. Some 50–60 per cent of the plots then had the dimensions of a city plot. In 1363 this was only 16 per cent and at the beginning of the fourteenth century no more than 3 per cent.[53]

The socio-spatial continuity observed earlier for almost five centuries does not alter the fact that in the long term, there was an increasing concentration of wealthy inhabitants in the *Hofbuurt*. In The Hague, this process started early. From the fourteenth century onwards, measures were taken that show that the counts of Holland considered the Haagse Bos, and also Voorhout – an offshoot of this forest – and (Lange) Vijverberg as their 'backyard'.[54] The green character of this area was therefore maintained and created the conditions for the development of a prosperous and lush residential environment in the sixteenth century. For this to happen, the traffic function of Voorhout, which was the starting and finishing point of the road to Leiden, had to be removed. When this was realized, in 1539 Voorhout could be planted with rows of trees and it got the allure of a distinguished and park-like residential area.[55] But even then there were still some farms to be found.[56] From the end of the sixteenth century, Voorhout underwent a true metamorphosis and increasingly became the exclusive residential domain of the elites. Grand Pensionary Johan van Oldenbarnevelt and Christiaan Huygens senior, secretary to the stadtholder and the council of state, initially rented houses on Spuistraat and Nobelstraat respectively, but around 1610 they moved to Voorhout in the Hofbuurt. And while the Hofbuurt developed into a pleasant and prestigious residential area, other parts of The Hague became less and less attractive for the elites.[57]

The interpolation map based on rental data in the land register from the second quarter of the nineteenth century (Chapter 2, Map 2.9) shows the result of this development. While in 1561 houses on Nobelstraat and in the vicinity of the Grote Kerk were still among the most expensive in The Hague, this was no longer the case when the 1832 land register was drawn up. The most expensive houses were then only to be found in the Hofbuurt. And this same concentration of wealthy people caused the average wealth in other parts of The Hague to fall. In combination with the influx of poor migrants, this led to the decline of what were once well-to-do streets and neighbourhoods and to an increase in the number of dwellings in alleys and blind alleys.[58]

Leiden

Based on the 1832 land register, it was established in Chapter 2 that Leiden lacked a compact and wealthy centre. The elites of Leiden in the second quarter of the nineteenth century were mainly to be found along Breestraat, Rapenburg and to a lesser extent in the area around the Burght (see Chapter 2, Map 2.7). Low rents and poor residents were predominant in the periphery, but there was no such thing as strictly segregated residential areas. In the predominantly poor northern part of the city, we also found relatively well-off inhabitants, and close to the wealthy Rapenburg there were poor streets and neighbourhoods. This mixture already indicates the existence of meso-differentiation and indeed, in Leiden there was the now familiar pattern whereby roughly speaking the well-to-do mainly lived along prominent canals and main streets, middle classes and part of the working classes in side streets and back streets and along main streets and canals in less prosperous neighbourhoods, and the poor among the working classes in walled-in houses in inner courtyards which were opened up by alleys and blind alleys. Just as in The Hague, in the latter case Leiden people often spoke of *poorten* and *poortwoningen*. Can this pattern also be found in the more distant past?

Researchers at Leiden University have combined a number of sources to create an extensive database on the population of Leiden in the years 1748–9.[59] For this study, the rental data from the *verpondingskohier* of 1749 and the registration of poor households in the *provisioneel middel* of 1748 are particularly relevant. It should be possible to map the nearly 10,000 objects on a map one by one, but in the context of this study that would be too much of a burden on the available research time. Therefore, an analysis at the level of the twenty-seven *bonnen* (districts) that were then distinguished within

Leiden has been opted for.⁶⁰ Map A.14 shows the average rental values in the *verponding* tax per *bon* compared to the city average. A comparison with the situation at the time of the first national land register (1832) shows that the residential structure of Leiden remained roughly unchanged in the intervening three-quarters of a century. In 1749 the medieval core of the city was also the area where the most expensive houses and richest residents could be found. In particular, the *bonnen* on either side of the northern part of the Breestraat showed much higher rental values than the city average and a similar situation can be seen on the interpolation map of the cadastral assessments around 1830. There is also similarity in the location of cheap houses in the urban periphery.

The aggregation of information on individual plots into larger units is particularly regrettable in the case of the Noord-Rapenburg *bon*, on the western side of the city. It shows an average rental value of 10 to 25 per cent above the city average, but the situation in the first half of the nineteenth century suggests that this *bon* was divided into a wealthy part along the western quay of Rapenburg and a poor part near the city ramparts.⁶¹ The fact that in *bon* Rapenburg many poor people lived is clearly shown by the 19.5 per cent of poor households.⁶²

The percentages of poor households confirm the information about the average rent per *bon*: low percentages in the central *bonnen* and high to very high percentages in the periphery. Of course, the poor did not live on the prominent canals and main streets, but mainly in *poorten*. There were many of these in Leiden. Around the middle of the eighteenth century more than 10 per cent of all houses was located in a *poort*, which confirms that meso-differentiation at the level of streets was a very common phenomenon in Leiden.⁶³

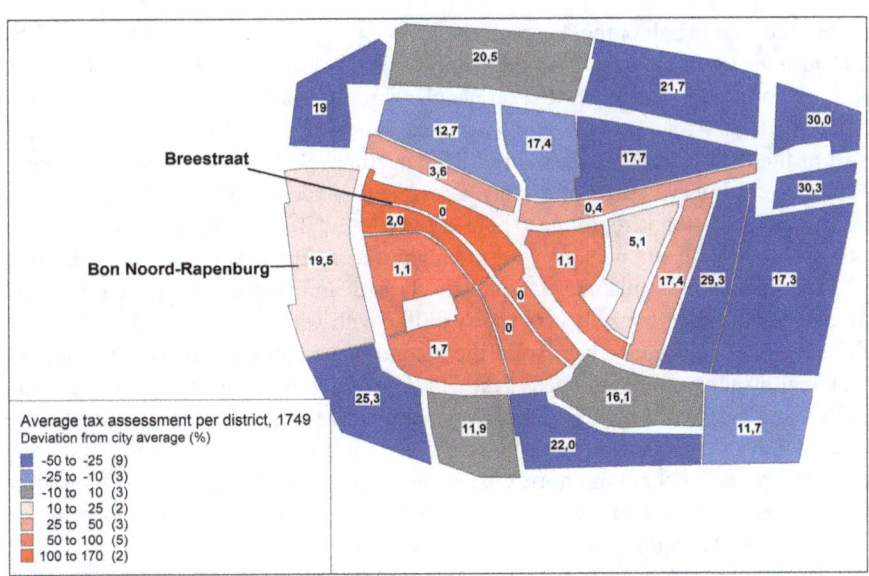

Map A.14 Rental values in the *verponding* tax and percentage of poor households per *bon* in Leiden, 1748–9.

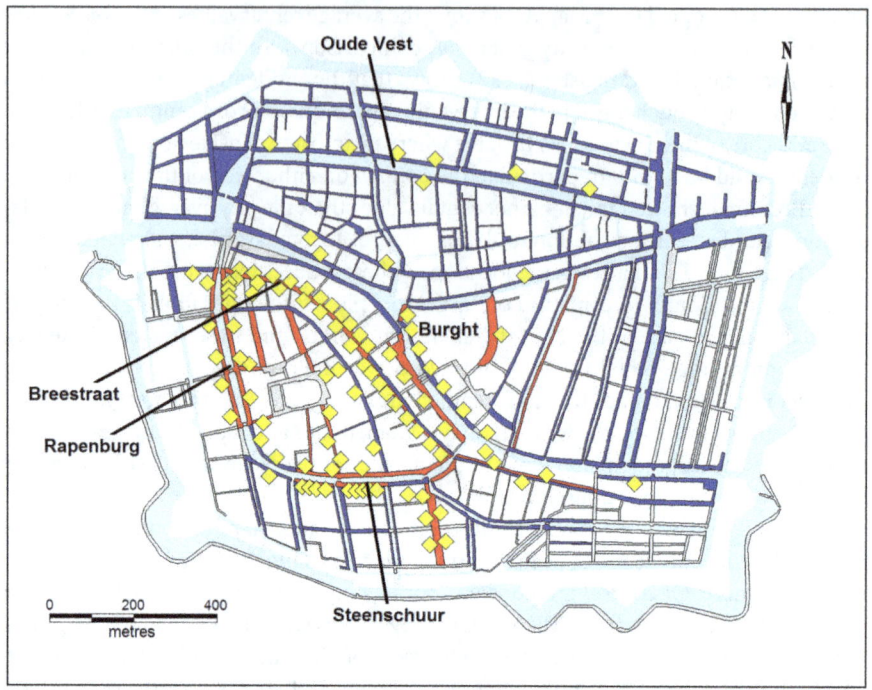

Map A.15 Streets with an average tax above (red) and below (blue) the city average and location of the top-100 most prosperous inhabitants in Leiden, 1674.

For the second half of the seventeenth century, information from the register of the *200ᵉ penning* tax of 1674 can be used to good effect.[64] However, it should be noted that this tax on wealth was only levied on people who were wealthy to the sum of at least 1,000 guilders. In total, 2,016 persons were taxed and thus a relatively small and wealthy part of the Leiden population.[65] For all Leiden streets with at least four assessments, Peltjes determined whether the average assessment was above or below the city average and that information is reproduced here in Map A.15.[66] To this I have added the places of residence of the 100 persons with the highest assessment for whom an indication of their address is available.[67] Despite the lack of information on people with no taxable wealth, the picture is very much in line with what has been observed earlier for the middle of the eighteenth and the second quarter of the nineteenth centuries. The wealthy elites of Leiden lived mainly in the oldest part of the city (Breestraat and the surroundings of the Burght) and also along Rapenburg and Steenschuur. But the distribution of the 100 wealthiest people also shows that they were not completely absent from the much poorer northern periphery. Incidentally – and this will not come as a surprise – there too they lived in the more attractive locations, in this case along the waterfront of Oude Vest.

The latter is in itself an indication of the existence of meso-differentiation. On the presence of *poorten* and dwellings in inner courtyards this property tax obviously gives no information, but that they were there, and even in large numbers, leads no doubt.

Pieter de la Court reported this in his *'t Welvaren van Leiden* (1659), writing that the housing shortage was so great that 'beautiful houses with their yards' has changed into 'dirty, unsound places and hovels; and this so beautiful city has become filled . . . with always lewd, and quarrelsome *poorten*'.[68] This densification in times of housing shortage ties in with Vance's argument about the spatial developments in the 'capitalist' city.

When we continue our research back in time, the register of the 1561 10^e *penning* tax on rental values offers useful information.[69] As Map A.16 shows, by then the city was considerably smaller than after the middle of the seventeenth century, but at the level of city districts the similarity is still striking. Also in the sixteenth century the rich lived mainly along streets and waterways in the old medieval centre of Leiden and the poor in the periphery. A comparison with the interpolation map based on the cadastral data from around 1830 (Chapter 2, Map 2.7) shows that even at the level of streets the similarities are remarkable. The main exceptions are the northern part of Breestraat and Rapenburg, which in 1561 did not yet have the same level of prosperity as in later centuries.

The 1561 interpolation map also shows that residential differentiation at the level of streets was, as in later centuries, a common phenomenon. Rental values in back streets and side streets were considerably lower than those along main streets such as Breestraat and Steenschuur. This implies that there were no homogenously rich or poor districts, even though it is clear that houses with very low rental values formed a small minority in the area between the southern part of Breestraat and Nieuwe Rijn.[70] The very considerable number of *cameren* mentioned in the source also points to

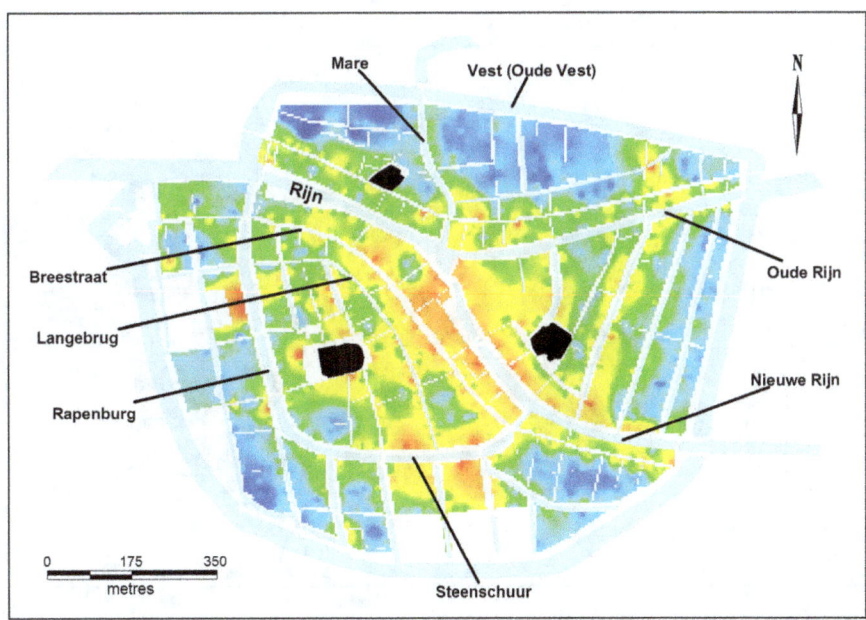

Map A.16 Residential differentiation in Leiden, 1561.

the existence of meso-differentiation. A large number of these *cameren* were made available to poor citizens 'om Godtswille' (free of charge), but many were also rented out. From casual remarks in the source it appears that these were often small dwellings in the backyards of houses and/or in *poorten*.

For the end of the fifteenth century (1498), we have at our disposal the register of a tax on wealth that Posthumus used long ago in his study of Leiden's cloth industry.[71] Unfortunately, only part of the more than 3,000 entries in the tax roll also recorded the street name, so that the analysis must be limited to the level of *bonnen*. Map A.17 shows the average wealth of each *bon* compared to the average for the city as a whole and it also shows the percentage of impecunious heads of household.[72] Despite the much lesser degree of detail, the map image shows a high degree of similarity to the situation in 1561. The southern part of the old medieval city was the most prosperous. Especially *bon* Burgstreng (the area around the still existing Burght of Leiden) was wealthy. The average wealth there was the highest in the city (*c.* 205 per cent above the city average) and no impecunious people were recorded. On the opposite (south) bank of Nieuwe Rijn *bon* Wanthuis was also without people of little means, but the average wealth there was 'only' 51 per cent above the city average. *Bon* Rapenburg, which was still peripheral at the time, had a relatively low average wealth and many poor people, but the poorest *bonnen* were those in the northern periphery, with low to very low average wealth and high percentages of poor people.

The analysis at the level of *bonnen* hides a large variation in the level of wealth within the *bonnen*. Map A.18 therefore maps the coefficients of variation. These make it abundantly clear that especially the *bonnen* in the urban periphery were not uniformly poor, but housed households with very different levels of wealth. It

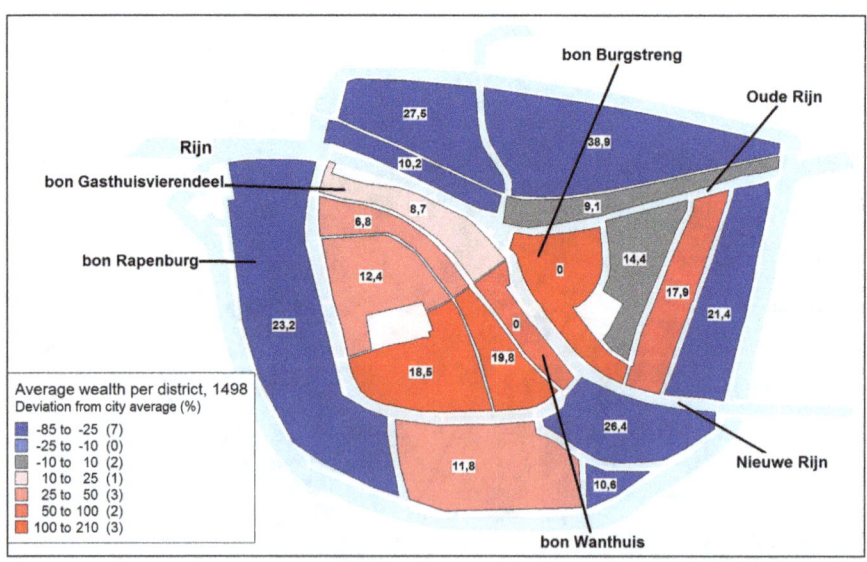

Map A.17 Average wealth and percentage of impecunious households per *bon* in Leiden, 1498.

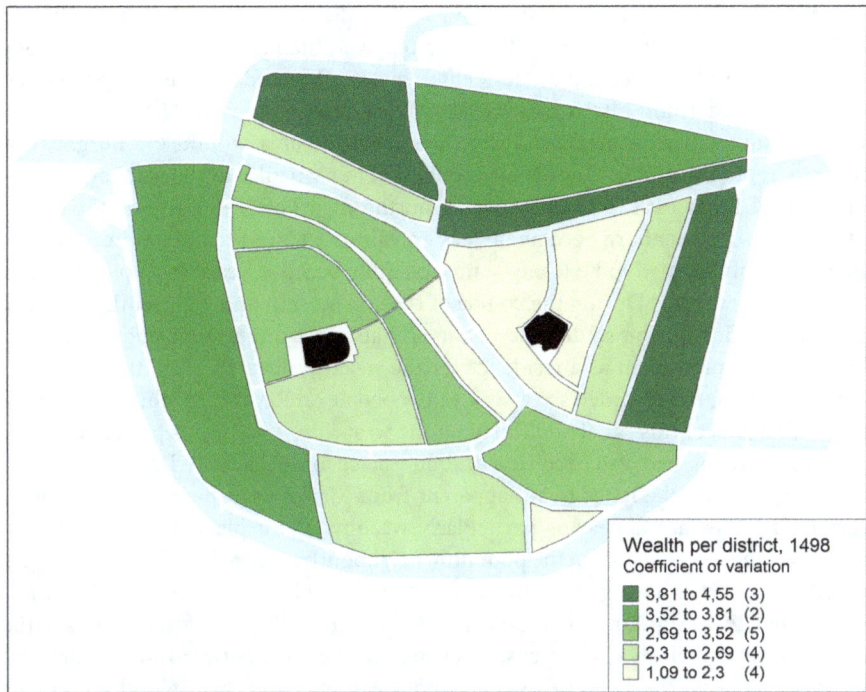

Map A.18 Coefficients of variation of wealth per *bon* in Leiden, 1498.

is obvious to interpret this variety as the result of around-the-corner residential differentiation.[73]

Sources that provide a picture of the residential distribution of the entire population of Leiden in the period before the end of the fifteenth century are unfortunately not available, but research by Bisschops into the Holy Ghost collection from 1438 to 1439 does give an indication.[74] This collection, the proceeds of which were intended to support the poor, was only held among the wealthy part of the Leiden population and had neither an obligatory character nor a fixed footing on which the contribution was based. This makes the results difficult to compare with the findings for 1498, but it is clear that on average the highest contributions were collected in the medieval centre of Leiden.[75]

For an even more distant past, we can only conclude that the earliest residential settlement was located on a dyke that was erected in the twelfth century on the south bank of the river Rhine, the later Breestraat. At the beginning of the fourteenth century, a number of large, stone-built houses testify to the status of this oldest street. Nevertheless, stone houses were also found elsewhere in the still young settlement and Breestraat itself will also have had a socially mixed character. Where the less well-off inhabitants of Leiden lived, to my knowledge, has not (yet) been investigated, but it is more than likely that they were to be found in the area between Breestraat and Langebrug to the west, which was then the city moat and thus the boundary between urban Leiden and the property of the counts of Holland.[76]

The maps show the residential structure of Leiden over the centuries, but just as in The Hague and other cities, within this relatively stable structure, a more subtle shift in the residences of the wealthy elites can be observed. This development can be documented from 1498 onwards. From that year until 1561 (*10ᵉ penning* tax) we see a shift in the residences of the elites from the area around the Burght (*bon* Burgstreng) to the other side of Nieuwe Rijn and in particular to the southern part of Breestraat.[77] From 1561 to about 1600, the northern part of Breestraat and the northeastern part of Rapenburg became increasingly prominent. At the same time, the east side of the city seemed to be losing status, possibly because wealthy people settled in and near Breestraat.[78] During the course of the seventeenth and eighteenth centuries, neighbourhoods on the south side of the city also lost importance and Rapenburg became more prominent as a residence for the wealthy elites. In 1674, the register of the *200ᵉ penning* tax recorded sixty-six wealthy people on Rapenburg: thirty-six people on the east side of this canal and thirty on the west side.[79] So, in this period, the west side of Rapenburg had also become a desirable place for the elites to live.

At first glance, the latter is not apparent from Map A.14, where the west side of Rapenburg does not appear as particularly wealthy. The explanation is that in the analysis at the level of *bonnen*, the poor little neighbourhoods to the west of Rapenburg heavily depress the average rental values in the *verponding* tax. These small districts were razed to the ground in the years 1736-54 to make way for the substantial expansion of the Hortus Botanicus. Elsewhere in the zone between Rapenburg and the city ramparts, cheap houses were demolished, which enabled wealthy residents of Rapenburg to expand their gardens.[80] The end result of this development, which continued after the middle of the eighteenth century, can be seen on the interpolation map of around 1830 (Chapter 2, Map 2.7). Breestraat and both sides of Rapenburg were then unmistakably the residential domain of the wealthiest people in Leiden.

Amsterdam

And finally, the largest city, at least from the first half of the sixteenth century onwards. Before that time Leiden was the largest among the cities studied here. For the situation in the years of the 1832 land register, we have established that Amsterdam in sociospatial terms was roughly divided into three parts: the medieval city centre, where all social classes found a place to live; the ring of canals as a residential domain for the elites and (higher) middle classes; and a periphery where mainly the (lower) middle classes and the working classes lived. Between the ring of canals and the western periphery, Prinsengracht functioned as a transitional zone and Singel was a transitional zone between the ring of canals and the inner city, and just like Prinsengracht, rental values here were generally considerably lower than along the two main canals of Herengracht and Keizersgracht. The houses along the paths and ditches in the outlying area corresponded to the status of the peripheral districts within the city (see Chapter 2, Map 2.11).

The tax register of 1733 gives us a glimpse of the situation in the first half of the eighteenth century. Map A.19 shows the tax assessments based on rental values and this information is supplemented with the location of the residences of the 250 inhabitants

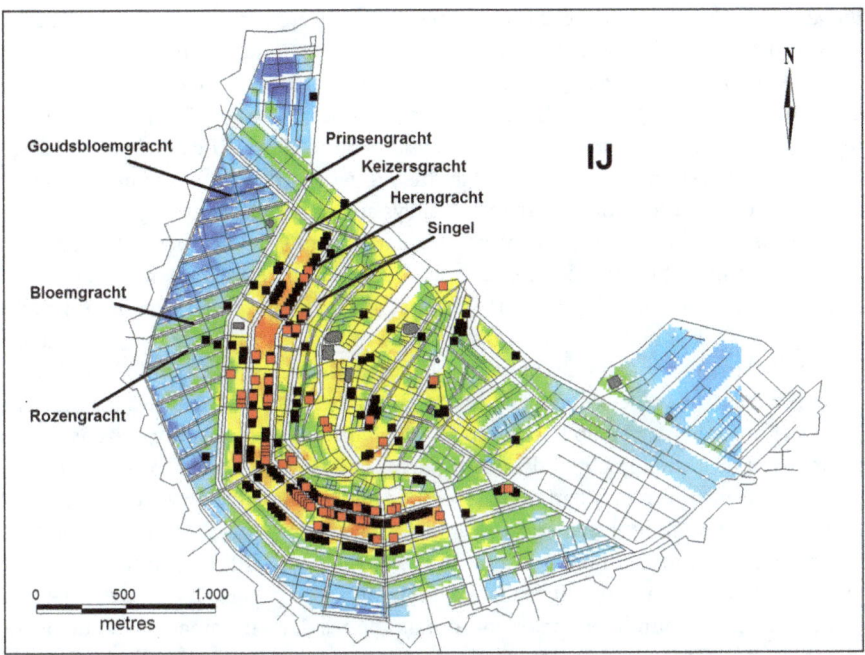

Map A.19 Assessments in the 1733 *verponding* tax and location of the top-250 incomes in 1742 in Amsterdam.

who enjoyed the highest incomes in 1742. The richest quarter of this top 250 is represented by a red square, the other three quarters by a black one.[81] The map clearly demonstrates that when it comes to social differentiation at the level of city districts, the situation in the second quarter of the eighteenth century was virtually identical to that of a century later. In the eighteenth century, too, the three residential domains are immediately recognizable on the map. The residences of the 250 top earners also confirm the exceptional status of the ring of canals as a residential environment for the economic elites, and the concentration of the very richest at the *Gouden Bocht* (Golden Bend) of Herengracht in the southern part of the ring of canals, confirms and reinforces the picture sketched on the basis of the *verponding* assessments. The mixed character of the inner city is also clearly shown on the map.

At the same time, however, the interpolation map also shows meso-differentiation between and within streets. The side streets in the ring of canals were inhabited by households paying significantly lower rents than those along the canals, and in the Jordaan district there was a clear distinction between the rents along Rozengracht and Bloemgracht in particular and those in side streets and back streets. The rents in the Jordaan also clearly show the declining wealth of the inhabitants in the same street as one approaches the city outskirts. Due to the scale of the map and the incomplete number of observations, walled-in housing is not clearly distinguishable, but we do not have to doubt its existence. Especially the Jordaan and the poor part of the Jewish neighbourhood were notorious in this respect. Map A.20 shows a detail of the 1775

Burgerwijk map. This map of the Goudsbloemgracht area shows the outlines of the houses in this poorest part of the Jordaan and within these outlines the number of inhabited units (including inhabited cellars) are indicated by dots. Clearly, there were large numbers of dwellings in the inner courtyards of the blocks, which could only be reached from the streets and canals via alleys and blind alleys. The extent of walled-in housing is also evident from the fact that this *Burgerwijk* district in the northern part of the Jordaan counted no fewer than 232 alleys and blind alleys.

For the seventeenth century, relevant information about the socio-spatial structure of the city is considerably more scarce, but Map A.21 gives an impression of the residential locations of the wealthy elites in 1631. The map is based on the assessment of the *200^e penning* tax, a tax of half a per cent on the wealth of persons who owned 1,000 guilders or more.[82] Among the 250 wealthiest people, whose addresses could only be indicated approximately, the value of the taxed assets varied from 500,000 guilders for the heirs of former burgomaster Jacob Poppen to 55,000 guilders for six wealthy citizens, five of whom lived on Herengracht and Keizersgracht.[83] The ring of canals, of which in that year only the northern part had been developed, indeed already housed a considerable number of the wealthy (black squares) and very wealthy (red squares) inhabitants of Amsterdam. But the old medieval part of the city, whose outline is indicated on the map, also housed many wealthy people. There, it was especially Warmoesstraat and its immediate surroundings that stood out as the residential domain of some of the wealthiest Amsterdammers of their time.

The top 250 was noticeably absent in the Jordaan district and in the urban periphery in general. This shows that already then, these areas were primarily the residential domain of the (lower) middle classes and the working classes (including

Map A.20 Goudsbloemgracht in Amsterdam and surroundings, 1775.

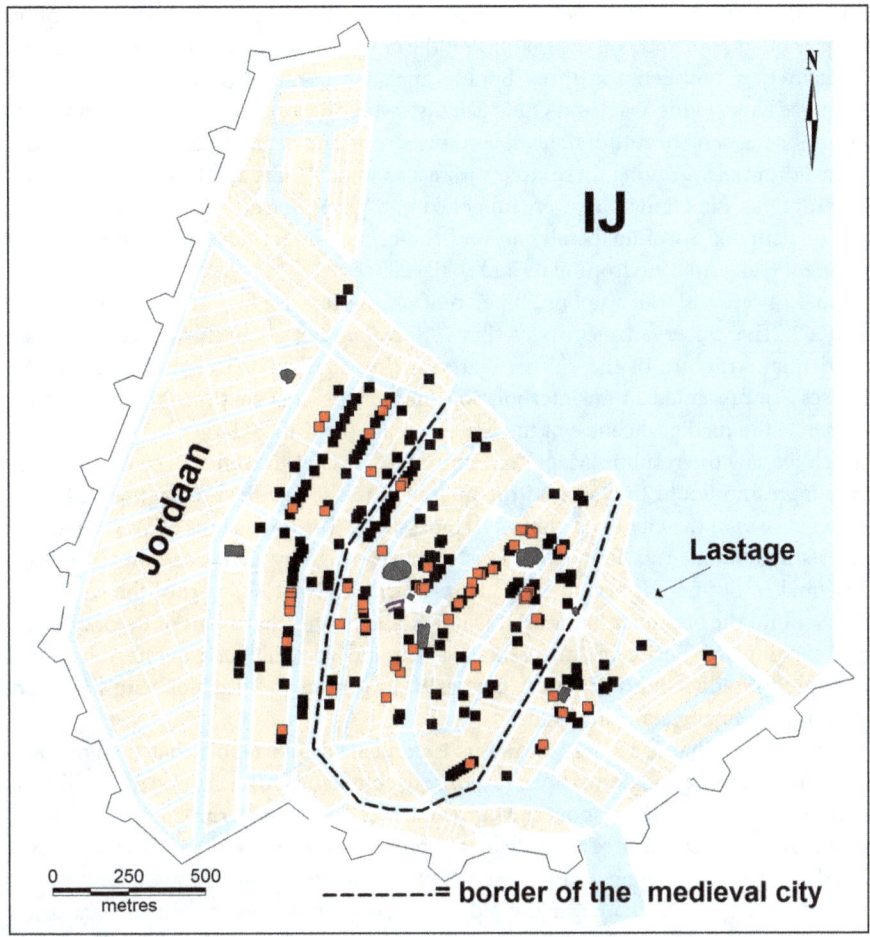

Map A.21 Residences of the wealthiest inhabitants of Amsterdam, 1631.

the poor). Writing about the Jordaan in 1665, Tobias van Domselaer said: 'And all these streets teem and bristle with all kinds of handicraft people.'[84] Van Domselaer notwithstanding, it needs to be stressed that socially the Jordaan was certainly not homogeneous. As in later times, a number of Jordaan canals in particular were not beneath the middle classes. Painters like Rembrandt, Govert Flinck, Karel du Jardin and Jan Lievens, and cartographer Willem Jansz. Blaeu spent at least part of their lives on a Jordaan canal.[85] This also demonstrates that differentiation at the level of streets was not an unknown phenomenon at the time. This is also evidenced by the existence of walled-in houses. On the map of Amsterdam drawn by Balthasar Florisz. van Berckenrode in 1625, walled-in houses are visible particularly in the northern part of the Jordaan, but in the 1647 edition, in parallel with the filling-in of this new neighbourhood, this phenomenon had grown enormously and was no longer limited mainly to the northern part of the Jordaan.[86] In other parts of the city one could also find differentiation at the level of streets. For example, in his 1665 description of the Lastage neighbourhood on the east side of the city, Van Domselaer, cited earlier, makes a distinction between the three broad canals or *burgwallen* (Kloveniersburgwal/ Gelderse kade, Oude Waal and Oude Schans), which according to him were built with 'heerlijke huijsen' (beautiful houses), and the streets and canals that were connected to these *burgwallen*. Among these streets were also Jonkerstraat and Ridderstraat, which, according to Van Domselaer, were inhabited by a 'gruesome crowd of common sailors, and craftsmen'.[87] So, quite literally, around-the-corner differentiation between two very different residential environments and social classes.

In Amsterdam, too, a tax of 10 per cent on the rental value of houses was levied in 1562. The preserved records of this *10^e penning* tax allow us to reconstruct the residential structure of the city in that year. In Map A.22 the rental values of the houses are presented in an interpolation map of the area that has been referred to earlier as the medieval centre of the city. After all, the time of large city extensions, of which we saw the result in Maps A.21 and A.19, was yet to come.[88] The interpolation map leaves no doubt that around the middle of the sixteenth century the well-to-do upper classes of the city lived along Warmoesstraat. The high status of Warmoesstraat and its inhabitants was already demonstrated years ago by Kam and Van der Leeuw-Kistemaker, but here it becomes clear that Warmoesstraat was part of the well-to-do area around the old inner harbour of Damrak and the northern part of Rokin.[89] When approaching the periphery, the rental values and the affluence of the inhabitants decreased rapidly, and outside the city walls, in general, households with limited or very limited financial means lived.[90]

The picture that Map A.22 shows us is confirmed in a report that the governess Margaret of Parma had drawn up in response to complaints from a group of Amsterdam citizens – the Doleanten – about the functioning of the city government. In the context of this report, a committee toured the periphery of the city and found many 'cleyne huyskens' (small dwellings) inhabited by 'scamele luyden' (poor people). On the west side of the city in particular, many old and shabby houses were built up against the city walls, and outside the walls too, we read in the Doleanten's complaint, there were hundreds of small dwellings inhabited by labourers who were unable to pay the high rents within the city.[91] Differentiation at the meso-level of streets is clearly visible along the river Amstel and also along the Voorburgwallen, which run parallel to it. There, the rental values of the houses increased from south to north. Map A.22 also shows around-the-corner differentiation in the area between Warmoesstraat and Oudezijds Voorburgwal, where the houses along the cross-streets and Voorburgwal had much lower rental values than those along Warmoesstraat. The large numbers of dwellings in the inner courtyards (map A.23), which were opened up by alleys and blind alleys, had the lowest rents and, in addition to the outskirts of the city and the outlying area, functioned as a place of residence for the least well-off.

In contrast to Leiden and Edam, no sources from the period before the middle of the sixteenth century have been preserved to allow the residential structure of the city to be mapped. However, the fact that after a pre-urban phase with five spatially separated neighbourhoods on mound-like embankments, in the second half of the thirteenth century the settlement took the form of buildings on contiguous dykes

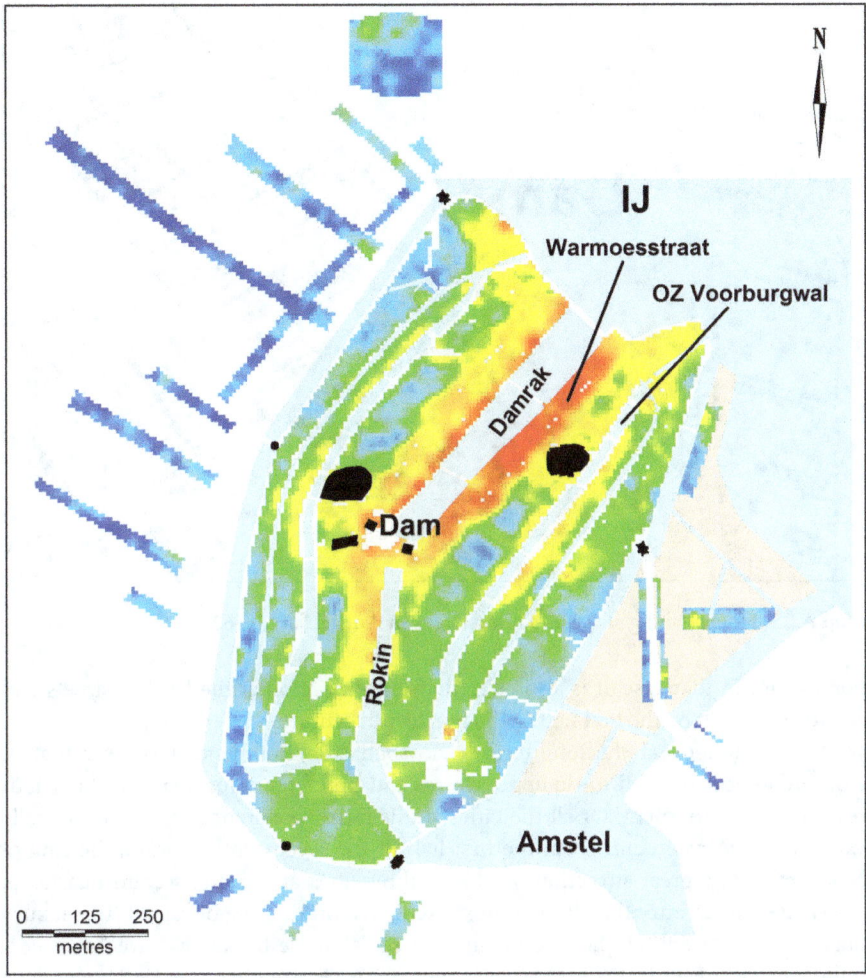

Map A.22 Residential differentiation in Amsterdam, 1562.

along both sides of the river Amstel, suggests that the overall picture sketched for 1562 dates from much earlier.[92] Of course, the city was much smaller then. In the middle of the fourteenth century the Voorburgwallen, earthen walls with a wooden palisade, formed the defensible boundary of the city; half a century later the Achterburgwallen performed this function. Amsterdam did not get its sixteenth-century size and stone city wall until the last quarter of the fifteenth century.[93] But much earlier, from the first half of the fourteenth century, alleys were constructed from the main streets on either side of the river Amstel (Warmoesstraat-Nes on the east side and Nieuwendijk-Kalverstraat on the west side) towards the city outskirts to provide access to the rear yards of the houses and/or to make building on the rear yards possible.[94] It is obvious that even then, the houses in these backyards had a lower status than those along the main streets and also housed a different and less well-off section of the city's

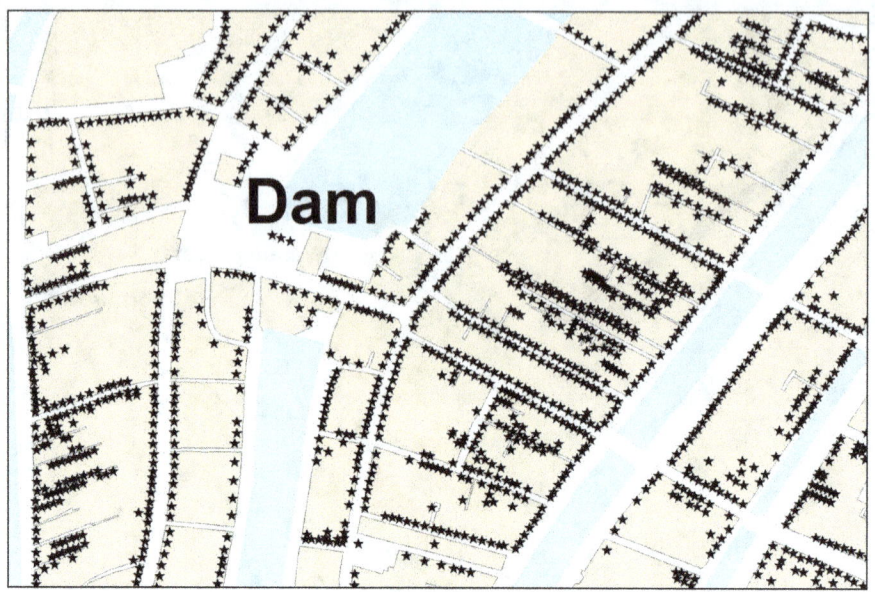

Map A.23 Houses along alleys and blind alleys in Amsterdam, 1562.

population. In that case, it is also clear that differentiation at the level of streets had already occurred by the first half of the fourteenth century.

If we now look at the long-term socio-spatial development, it is clear that in Amsterdam too, the well-to-do upper classes had a preference for their own luxurious residential environment. Of all the cities studied, this preference was most radically expressed in Amsterdam. From the first half of the seventeenth century, the ring of canals exerted a great attraction on the wealthy elites and in the second quarter of the eighteenth century they lived almost exclusively in the ring of canals. This luxury quarter was not entirely homogeneous in a social sense because, as we have seen, middle classes lived in the side streets, and in a back street such as Kerkstraat even poor people were to be found. But the canals themselves, and especially Keizersgracht and Herengracht, were the scene of distinguished peace and quiet, wealth and luxury in a city where a significant part of the population was barely able to survive and also had to contend with miserable housing conditions.

The aim of this appendix was to find out when the residential patterns as reconstructed on the basis of the 1832 land register came into being. The answer to that question is that everything indicates that residential differentiation at the macro-level of city districts and at the meso-level of streets goes back to the medieval period and the early history of the cities in Holland.

Notes

Preface

1   Michiel Wagenaar, *Amsterdam 1876-1914. Economisch herstel, ruimtelijke expansie en de veranderende ordening van het stedelijk grondgebruik* (Amsterdam: Historisch Seminarium, Universiteit van Amsterdam, 1990).

Introduction

1   See the survey of consensus theory and conflict theory in Katy Hayward, 'Conflict and Consensus', in *International Encyclopedia of the Social & Behavioral Sciences*, ed. James D. Wright (Amsterdam: Elsevier, 2015).
2   The term 'polder model' has been in use since the early 1990s and initially referred mainly to the Wassenaar Agreement (1982) between organizations of employees and employers that paved the way for a consultative economy in the Netherlands in which these organizations of employees and employers, as well as the government, formulated economic policy jointly (Henk te Velde, 'Het poldermodel. Een introductie', in *Harmonie in Holland. Het poldermodel van 1500 tot nu*, ed. Dennis Bos, Maurits Ebben and Henk te Velde (Amsterdam: Bert Bakker, 2007), 11–18, and Maarten Prak and Jan Luiten van Zanden, *Nederland en het poldermodel. Sociaal-economische geschiedenis van Nederland, 1000-2000* (Amsterdam: Bert Bakker, 2013), 10–11.
3   This image imposes itself, for example, in Willem Frijhoff and Marijke Spies, *1650. Bevochten eendracht. Nederlandse cultuur in Europese context* (Den Haag: Sdu Uitgevers, 1999), Prak and Van Zanden, *Nederland en het poldermodel*, and in some of the contributions in Justin Colson and Arie van Steensel, eds, *Cities and Solidarities: Urban Communities in Pre-Modern Europe* (Abingdon, Oxon: Routledge, 2017). For a critical discussion of some of the more popular publications on the *polder model*, see Marjolein 't Hart, 'Polderen en ploeteren. Een debat over geschiedenis, continuïteit en Nederlandse identiteit', in *Vroegmoderne geschiedenis in actuele debatten*, ed. Hans Cools and Jasper van de Steen (Leuven: Leuven University Press, 2020) and the introduction in Peter van Dam, Jouke Turpijn and Bram Mellink, eds, *Onbehagen in de polder. Nederland in conflict sinds 1795* (Amsterdam: Amsterdam University Press, 2014).
4   The side note, of course, is that this influence was a favour and not a right. See for instance Judith Pollmann, 'Eendracht maakt macht. Stedelijke cultuuridealen en politieke werkelijkheid in de Republiek', in *Harmonie in Holland. Het poldermodel van 1500 tot nu*, ed. Dennis Bos, Maurits Ebben and Henk te Velde (Amsterdam: Bert Bakker, 2007), 149.

5 To my knowledge, Pahl was the first to characterize cities as arenas (R. E. Pahl, *Whose City? And Further Essays on Urban Society* (Harmondsworth: Penquin Books, 1975), 234–5). This perspective distanced itself from the functionalist legacy of the Chicago School in which cities were seen as an integrated and functional whole rather than as contested spaces. A brief introduction to the concept of appropriation in Jose Antonio Lara-Hernandez, 'General Introduction', in *Temporary Appropriation in Cities: Human Spatialisation in Public Spaces and Community Resilience*, ed. Alessandro Melis, Jose Antonio Lara-Hernandez and James Thompson (Cham: Springer International Publishing, 2020), 2–3.
6 The literature on power is extraordinarily vast. Good introductions are Barry Hindess, *Discourses of Power: From Hobbes to Foucault* (Oxford: Blackwell, 1996) and Mark Haugaard, ed. *Power: A Reader* (Manchester: Manchester University Press, 2002).
7 John Allen, *Lost Geographies of Power* (Oxford: Blackwell, 2003), 96, 105–6. This distinction between resources and power was made earlier by Giddens (Anthony Giddens, *A Contemporary Critique of Historical Materialism* (1981; Stanford: Stanford University Press, 1995), 50, and Idem, *The Constitution of Society. Outline of the Theory of Structuration* (Oxford: Polity Press, 1984), 16).
8 Mark Haugaard, *The Constitution of Power. A Theoretical Analysis of Power, Knowledge and Structure* (Manchester: Manchester University Press, 1997), 2. A brief overview of theories of power in the social and political sciences in Idem, 'Power, Social and Political Theories of', in *Encyclopedia of Violence, Peace, and Conflict*, ed. Lester Kurtz and Jennifer Turpin (San Diego: Academic Press, 1999).
9 Allen, *Lost Geographies of Power*, and see also a brief summary of this study in his 'The Whereabouts of Power: Politics, Government and Space', *Geografiska Annaler, Series B* 86 (2004): 19–32.
10 Allen, *Lost Geographies of Power*, 2.
11 Ted Kilian, 'Public and Private, Power and Space', in *Philosophy and Geography II. The Production of Public Space*, ed. Andrew Light and Jonathan M. Smith (Lanham: Rowman & Littlefield, 1998), 126, where he states that 'power [must] be understood as a relationship rather than a commodity'. Giddens, too, sees power and the use of resources in the context of interaction (Giddens, *The Constitution of Society*, 15–16).
12 Allen, *Lost Geographies of Power*, 5, 128.
13 Kilian, 'Public and Private', 126. On the importance of the context in which power is exercised, see also Haugaard, *Power*, 115.
14 Giddens, *A Contemporary Critique*, 63. A similar conception of the reciprocity of power relations by Foucault (see Hindess, *Discourses of Power*, 102–3).
15 Max Weber, 'Wirtschaft und Gesellschaft', in *Max Weber-Gesamtausgabe digital*, ed. Knut Borchardt, Edith Hanke and Wolfgang Schluchter (Unvollendet, 1919-1920), chapter 1, §16: 'Macht und Herrschaft', and see also Hindess, *Discourses of Power*, 2. This interpretation of power is often referred to as the 'first dimension of power' or the 'first face of power'. See Steven Lukes, *Power. A Radical View* (1974; Basingstoke: Palgrave, 2005), 16–19, and Peter Digeser, 'The Fourth Face of Power', *The Journal of Politics* 54 (1992): 978.
16 Quoted in Mark Haugaard, 'Concerted Power over', *Constellations* 22 (2015): 147, and see also Nancy Bell, 'Power, Alternative Theories of', in *Encyclopedia of Violence, Peace, and Conflict*, ed. Lester Kurtz and Jennifer Turpin (San Diego: Academic Press, 1999), 99.
17 Allen, *Lost Geographies of Power*, 5.

18 Ibid., 2, and see also page 9, where inducement is added to the list. An infinite series of power expressions arise when it is assumed that each type of relationship also has its own expression of power (ibid., 100).
19 Ibid., 121. Unlike Allen, I do not deal in this study with the specifically spatial aspects of the different modalities of power. Within the pre-modern cities, these played a lesser role than in the current globalized world.
20 Loïc J. D. Wacquant, 'Pierre Bourdieu', in *Key Sociological Thinkers*, ed. Rob Stones (Houndmills: MacMillan, 1998), 221.
21 By distinguishing different forms of capital, Bourdieu is echoing the work of Weber, who also objected to the one-sided emphasis on the relations of production by Marxists and argued that social reality is far too complex to see it solely as the result of economic forces (David Swartz, *Culture & Power. The Sociology of Pierre Bourdieu* (Chicago: The University of Chicago Press, 1997), 145–6).
22 Pierre Bourdieu, 'The Forms of Capital', in *Handbook of Theory and Research for the Sociology of Education*, ed. J. Richardson (Westport, CT: Greenwood, 1986) and Wacquant, 'Pierre Bourdieu'. See also John B. Thompson, 'Editor's Introduction', in *Language and Symbolic Power*, ed. Pierre Bourdieu (Cambridge, MA: Harvard University Press, 1991). In this study I will mainly use the term 'resources' and reserve the term 'capital' for the three *principal species* and symbolic capital.
23 Bourdieu, 'The Forms of Capital', 245, and Wacquant, 'Pierre Bourdieu', 221.
24 Bourdieu, 'The Forms of Capital', 252.
25 Ibid.
26 Swartz, *Culture & Power*, 117 where he also quotes the definition of Bourdieu himself. See also Richard Jenkins, *Pierre Bourdieu*, Key Sociologists (London: Routledge, 1992), 84–5.
27 In this context, the development of societies over time can be regarded as a process of differentiation and increase in the number of fields (Thompson, 'Editor's Introduction', 25; Jenkins, *Pierre Bourdieu*, 85, and Wacquant, 'Pierre Bourdieu', 221).
28 Pierre Bourdieu, 'The Social Space and the Genesis of Groups', *Theory and Society* 14 (1985): 724–5, and Wacquant, 'Pierre Bourdieu', 221.
29 Wacquant, 'Pierre Bourdieu', 224.
30 Ibid., 220 defines habitus as 'the system of durable and transposable *dispositions* through which we perceive, judge, and act in the world' (emphasis in original). See also Jenkins, *Pierre Bourdieu*, 74–84, and Swartz, *Culture & Power*, chapter 5. The habitus established during childhood is called the primary habitus. In the conclusion of this study, attention will also be paid to additional habitus.
31 However, Jenkins, *Pierre Bourdieu*, 90 argues that the relationship between field and habitus in Bourdieu's work is 'far from clear'. See also Thompson, 'Editor's Introduction', 12–14.
32 Bourdieu, 'The Social Space', 724. Walzer believes it to be possible to prevent the convergence of social positions in different fields (in Walzer's case 'spheres') and thereby achieve 'complex equality' (Michael Walzer, *Spheres of Justice. A Defense of Pluralism and Equality* (New York: Basic Books, 1983), 19–20). In practice, however, convergence seems to be dominant in both pre-modern and modern times.
33 Thompson, 'Editor's Introduction', 30, and see also Wacquant, 'Pierre Bourdieu', 225.
34 Bourdieu, 'The Social Space', 725.
35 A critique of the all-encompassing influence of power in discourse power theory and in the work of Foucault in Seumas Miller, 'Foucault on Discourse and Power', *Theoria: A Journal of Social and Political Theory* 76 (1990): 115–25.

36　See also Peter Burke, *History and Social Theory* (Cambridge: Polity Press, 2016), 27.
37　Population figures and the degree of urbanization in Holland in A. M. van der Woude, 'Demografische ontwikkeling van de Noordelijke Nederlanden 1500-1800', in *Algemene Geschiedenis der Nederlanden*, vol. 5 (Haarlem: Fibula-Van Dishoeck, 1980), 135, table 11.
38　The development of the urban landscape is discussed in detail in Reinout Rutte and Jaap Evert Abrahamse, eds, *Atlas of the Dutch Urban Landscape. A Millennium of Spatial Development* (Bussum: Thoth, 2016).
39　Amsterdam was one of the few cities in Holland that saw its population increase after the third quarter of the seventeenth century. Figures for Amsterdam in Piet Lourens and Jan Lucassen, *Inwonertallen van Nederlandse steden ca.1300-1800* (Amsterdam: NEHA, 1997); Marco H. D. van Leeuwen and James E. Oeppen, 'Reconstructing the Demographic Regime of Amsterdam 1681-1920', *Economic and Social History in the Netherlands* 5 (1993): 61-102 and Hubert Nusteling, 'De homeostatische bevolkingsreeks voor Amsterdam in 1586-1865 toegelicht en getoetst', *Tijdschrift voor Sociale en Economische Geschiedenis* 15 (2018): 31-65.
40　Jan de Vries, *European Urbanization 1500-1800* (Cambridge, MA: Harvard University Press, 1984), Appendix 1, and P. Bairoch, J. Batou and P. Chèvre, *La population des villes Européennes. Banque de données et analyse sommaire des résultats, 800-1850* (Genève: Droz, 1988), part A. In 1800 Moscow and Vienna also had more inhabitants than Amsterdam and St. Petersburg had about the same number (Peter Clark, *European Cities and Towns 400-2000* (Oxford: Oxford University Press, 2009), 131).
41　H. F. K. van Nierop, *Van ridders tot regenten. De Hollandse adel in de zestiende en de eerste helft van de zeventiende eeuw* (Amsterdam: De Bataafsche Leeuw, 1984), 155, 235-41. In the long run, of course, the Dutch Revolt, the renunciation of the monarch and the establishment of a Republic were not without effect. The absence of a monarchy made it impossible to raise new persons to the peerage and, in combination with high mortality rates and a strong preference for marriages within the own group, this led to the virtual disappearance of Holland's nobility as a social group (ibid., 78-9, 82, 241). Only with the establishment of the Kingdom in the first half of the nineteenth century, the possibility of appointing nobles arose again. At that time, it was mainly the urban regent families from the time of the Republic who were considered for this.
42　Clark, *European Cities and Towns*, 131, and for the presence of the nobility in London at the end of the seventeenth century, see Craig Spence, *London in the 1690s. A Social Atlas* (London: Centre for Metropolitan History, University of London, 2000), 81-8 and especially figures 4.8 and 4.9. As in England and France, the nobility in Spain was also clearly present in the cities (Teofilo F. Ruiz, *Spanish Society, 1400-1600*, A Social History of Europe (Harlow: Longman, 2001), 54-65). In Germany, this was much less the case (Christopher R. Friedrichs, 'German Social Structure', in *Germany. A New Social and Economic History*, ed. Bob Scribner (London: Arnold, 1996), 240).
43　For the regent elite in the first half of the nineteenth century, see F. J. E. van Lennep, *Late regenten* (Haarlem: H. D. Tjeenk Willink, 1962) and for the changing composition of the Amsterdam city council Peter Hofland, *Leden van de Raad. De Amsterdamse gemeenteraad 1814-1941* (Amsterdam: Gemeentearchief Amsterdam; H. J. Duyvisfonds, 1998). The development of exclusive residential villages is described in detail in G. A. Hoekveld, *Baarn. Schets van de ontwikkeling van een villadorp* (Baarn: Bosch & Keuning, n.d.) and see also H. Schmal, 'De trek naar buiten. De opkomst van het forensisme', in *Amsterdam in kaarten. Verandering van*

de stad in vier eeuwen cartografie, ed. W. F. Heinemeijer and M. F. Wagenaar (Ede: Zomer & Keuning, 1987).

44 A similar development took place elsewhere in Europe, for example, in Denmark (Mikkel Thelle, 'Crowding as Appropriation: Voting, Violence and Bodies in a Nineteenth-Century Urban Space', *Distinktion: Journal of Social Theory* 17 (2016): 276-93).

45 See Homme Wedman, 'Socialisme en burgerlijke cultuur in Nederland', in *De stijl van de burger. Over Nederlandse burgerlijke cultuur vanaf de middeleeuwen*, ed. Remieg Aerts and Henk te Velde (Kampen: Kok Agora, 1998), 224-5, and in a more general sense Dennis Bos, *Waarachtige volksvrienden. De vroege socialistische beweging in Amsterdam 1848-1898* (Amsterdam: Bert Bakker, 2001). In Holland large demonstrations for women's suffrage only took place in the first decades of the twentieth century.

46 See for example Josine Blok, 'Hemelse rozen door 't wereldse leven. Sekse en de Nederlandse burgerij in de negentiende eeuw', in *De stijl van de burger. Over Nederlandse burgerlijke cultuur vanaf de middeleeuwen*, ed. Remieg Aerts and Henk te Velde (Kampen: Kok Agora, 1998), 148-9, and Auke van der Woud, *Koninkrijk van sloppen. Achterbuurten en vuil in de negentiende eeuw* (Amsterdam: Bert Bakker, 2010), 167-8.

47 Unlike the class perspective used here, the urban space of pre-modern Amsterdam (and Edo) is studied from a gender perspective in the research project The Freedom of the Streets by Danielle van den Heuvel (https://www.freedomofthestreets.org/).

48 I am aware that attributing behaviours and attitudes to a limited number of classes always overestimates the homogeneity of those classes, but this loss of detail is – I hope – compensated for by a better understanding of some fundamental manifestations of appropriation of urban space in pre-modern Holland.

49 See Jan de Vries and Ad van der Woude, *The First Modern Economy. Success, Failure, and Perseverance of the Dutch Economy, 1500-1815* (Cambridge: Cambridge University Press, 1997), 561-5.

50 For the seventeenth and eighteenth centuries, see ibid., and Derek Phillips, *Well-Being in Amsterdam's Golden Age* (Amsterdam: Amsterdam University Press, 2008), chapter 2. For the nineteenth century, Marco H. D. van Leeuwen, *The Logic of Charity. Amsterdam, 1800-1850* (Houndmills: MacMillan, 2000), 43, table 2.2; Boudien de Vries, *Electoraat en elite. Sociale structuur en sociale mobiliteit in Amsterdam 1850-1895* (Amsterdam: De Bataafsche Leeuw, 1986), 28-31, and Jacques J. Giele and Geert Jan van Oenen, 'Theorie en praktijk van het onderzoek naar de sociale structuur', *Tijdschrift voor Sociale Geschiedenis* 5 (1976): 167-85. A classification based on legal status in H. F. K. van Nierop, 'Popular Participation in Politics in the Dutch Republic', in *Resistance, Representation and Community*, ed. Peter Blickle (Oxford: Clarendon Press, 1997), 277-9, and in Phillips, *Well-Being in Amsterdam's Golden Age*, chapter 1.

Chapter 1

1 Quoted in Van Nierop, 'Popular Participation', 280.
2 Heidi Deneweth, 'Real Property, Speculation and Housing Inequality. Bruges, 1550-1670', in *Inequality and the City in the Low Countries (1200-2020)*, ed. B. Blondé et al. (Turnhout: Brepols, 2020), 265; Bert de Munck, 'Diachrony, Synchrony and

Modernity. How to Contribute to the Debate on Economic Inequality from an Historical Perspective?', ibid., 379–82, and Clé Lesger, *Huur en conjunctuur. De woningmarkt in Amsterdam, 1550-1850* (Amsterdam: Historisch Seminarium van de Universiteit van Amsterdam, 1986).

3 W. J. van den Berg and J. L. van Zanden, 'Vier eeuwen welstandsongelijkheid in Alkmaar, ca 1530-1930', *Tijdschrift voor Sociale Geschiedenis* 19 (1993): 196.

4 Rogier van Kooten, 'Levelling through Space? The Redistributive Capacity of Demographic Decline in Antwerp's Darkest Hour (1584-1586)', in *Inequality and the City in the Low Countries (1200-2020)*, ed. B. Blondé et al. (Turnhout: Brepols, 2020), 235; B. Blondé et al., 'The Low Countries' Paradox. Historical Perspectives on Inequality and the City', ibid., 25, and Deneweth, 'Real Property, Speculation and Housing Inequality', 256. The slight deviation of the Gini's for Delft, Leiden and Amsterdam by Soltow and Van Zanden is probably due to the fact that they included dwellings that were occupied 'for free' with a rental value of 0 in the calculation. See Lee Soltow and Jan Luiten van Zanden, *Income and Wealth Inequality in the Netherlands, 16th-20th Century* (Amsterdam: Het Spinhuis, 1998), 27 and Table 3.1.

5 Blondé et al., 'The Low Countries' Paradox', 25, and Marco H. D. van Leeuwen, *Bijstand in Amsterdam, ca.1800-1850. Armenzorg als beheersings-en overlevingsstrategie* (Zwolle: Waanders; Amsterdam: Gemeentearchief Amsterdam, 1992), 70 and 311. In Edam, where for 1569 both the Gini for rental values and the Gini for wealth (based on the *schotgeld* tax) can be calculated, the difference is also considerable: 0.39 based on rental values and 0.60 based on wealth. For the *schotgeld* tax, see the appendix.

6 *Materiële welvaart in Nederland 2020* (Den Haag: Centraal Bureau voor Statistiek, 2020), 87.

7 The figures are taken from an overview compiled by the World Bank: https://data.worldbank.org/indicator/SI.POV.GINI?name_desc=false&view=map (consulted on 31 January 2022). Another way to put income inequality in pre-modern Dutch cities in a contemporary perspective can be found in De Vries and Van der Woude, *The First Modern Economy*, 569.

8 In the winter of 1816–17, the percentage of Amsterdam residents living below the poverty line rose to approximately 57 per cent (Van Leeuwen, *The Logic of Charity*, 42, 188). It is important to emphasize that support from poor relief institutions was only a supplement to insufficient income from work and (almost) never the only source of income.

9 Jurjen Vis, 'Chirurgijns, aalmoezeniers en weesmeesters. Welzijn, armoede en gezondheidszorg', in *Geschiedenis van Alkmaar*, ed. Diederik Aten et al. (Zwolle: Waanders, 2007), 290.

10 'arme ende behoeftighe persoonen' (Jan Orlers, *Beschrijvinge der stad Leyden. Inhoudende 't begin, den voortgang, ende den wasdom der selver . . . met groote moeijten, uyt verscheyden schriften ende papieren by een vergadert, ende beschreven door I.I. Orlers* (Leiden: Henrick Haestens, Jan Orlers and Jan Maire, 1614), 104).

11 Ingrid van der Vlis, *Leven in armoede. Delftse bedeelden in de zeventiende eeuw* (Amsterdam: Prometheus; Bert Bakker, 2001), 64, table 2, and Gerrit Verhoeven, *De derde stad van Holland. Geschiedenis van Delft tot 1795* (Zwolle: WBooks, 2015), 364 and 91.

12 The poverty line of 200 guilders in De Vries and Van der Woude, *The First Modern Economy*, 564, and the line of 250 guilders in the mid-nineteenth century in Van Leeuwen, *The Logic of Charity*, 41–2.

13 W. F. H. Oldewelt, ed. *Kohier van de Personeele Quotisatie te Amsterdam over het jaar 1742* (Amsterdam: Genootschap Amstelodamum, 1945), part 1, 15. These taxable incomes estimated by tax-collectors are an underestimate of the real income.
14 De Vries and Van der Woude, *The First Modern Economy*, 609–20, and Soltow and Van Zanden, *Income and Wealth Inequality*, 41–5.
15 Van Zanden in *Income and Wealth Inequality*, 38–41. Anne E. C. McCants, 'Goods at Pawn. The Overlapping Worlds of Material Possessions and Family Finance in Early Modern Amsterdam', *Social Science History* 31 (2007): 219 calculates a Gini coefficient of 0.7 to 0.8 for the wealth distribution in Amsterdam in 1742.
16 When no reliable information was available from private documents such as estates and wills, Zandvliet had to rely on tax data. Because the tax data are almost always an underestimate of the actual wealth, the figures in the table are also an underestimate of the actual size of the fortunes (Kees Zandvliet, *De 500 rijksten van de Republiek. Rijkdom, geloof, macht & cultuur* (Zutphen: Walburg Pers, 2018), 17).
17 Ibid., 262–6. In the eighteenth century, members of the Gouda vroedschap left an average of 70,000 guilders, those in Leiden 154,000 guilders and those in Hoorn 208,000 guilders (De Vries and Van der Woude, *The First Modern Economy*, table 11.25).
18 Zandvliet, *De 500 rijksten van de Republiek*, 132 ff. An overview of the large fortunes in Dutch cities on the illustrative map in Kees Zandvliet, *De 250 rijksten van de Gouden Eeuw. Kapitaal, macht, familie en levensstijl* (Amsterdam: Nieuw Amsterdam, 2006), XXIV.
19 Because Foucault gives the concept 'discourse' a different interpretation in different publications and interviews, there is little agreement in the literature about its exact content. Johannes Angermuller, 'Discourse Studies', in *International Encyclopedia of the Social & Behavioral Sciences*, ed. James D. Wright (Amsterdam: Elsevier, 2015), 512 gives the following short description: 'As a socially-situated activity of producing meaning, discourse produces, establishes, and legitimizes knowledge in social groups and communities.' See also Miller, 'Foucault on Discourse and Power', and Charles L. Briggs, 'Anthropology of Discourse', in *International Encyclopedia of the Social & Behavioral Sciences*, ed. James D. Wright (Amsterdam: Elsevier, 2015).
20 Bourdieu, 'The Social Space', 729–30, and Jenkins, *Pierre Bourdieu*, 153–7.
21 The difference is that in the older literature, the division of society into classes or groups was usually accompanied by strongly disqualifying remarks about the working classes. See §1.4 below. A general introduction to social stratifications in early modern Europe in Peter Burke, 'The Language of Orders in Early Modern Europe', in *Social Orders and Social Classes in Europe since 1500: Studies in Social Stratification*, ed. M. L. Bush (London: Longman, 1992).
22 Cited in Catharina Lis and Hugo Soly, *Worthy Efforts: Attitudes to Work and Workers in Pre-Industrial Europe* (Leiden: Brill, 2012), 313. For medieval stratifications, see also Catrien Santing, 'Tegen ledigheid en potverteren. De habitus van de laatmiddeleeuwse stadsburger', in *De stijl van de burger. Over Nederlandse burgerlijke cultuur vanaf de middeleeuwen*, ed. Remieg Aerts and Henk te Velde (Kampen: Kok Agora, 1998).
23 Aristotle's view in Aristotle, *Aristotle's Politics*, trans. Benjamin Jowett (New York: Random House, 1943), book IV, chapter 11.
24 Theodorus Schrevelius, *Harlemias, ofte, om beter te seggen, de eerste stichtinghe der Stadt Haerlem, het toe-nemen en vergrootinge der selfden ... de oeffeninghe van de Inghesetenen, in alle Wetenschap, Kunst ende Gheleertheydt, Neeringhe en Hanteringe, en*

wat dies meer is (Haarlem: Thomas Fonteyn, 1648), books V and VI. See also Marijke Meijer Drees, '"Burgerlijke" zeventiende-eeuwse literatuur', in *Burger*, ed. Joost Kloek and Karin Tilmans (Amsterdam: Amsterdam University Press, 2002), 140–2.
25 Schrevelius, *Harlemias*, 327.
26 Ibid., 395–6.
27 The Aansprekersoproer will be discussed in more detail later in this study.
28 R. M. Dekker, *Oproeren in Holland gezien door tijdgenoten. Ooggetuigenverslagen van oproeren in de provincie Holland ten tijde van de Republiek (1690-1750)* (Assen: Van Gorcum, 1979), 45, and see also Paul Knevel, 'Een kwestie van overleven. De kunst van het samenleven', in *Geschiedenis van Holland*, ed. Thimo de Nijs and Eelco Beukers (Hilversum: Verloren, 2002), 219–20. The social stratifications by Schrevelius and Craffurd are not very different from those made by contemporaries for the German cities (Friedrichs, 'German Social Structure', 245).
29 A third classification, that of Martinus Schoockius from 1652, is in line with the ones by Schrevelius and Craffurd and is discussed in Van Nierop, *Van ridders tot regenten*, 30–1.
30 Een-Amsterdammer, *Amsterdam en de Amsterdammers* (Deventer: A. J. van den Sigtenhorst, 1875), 20–8.
31 In pre-modern times it would have been no different.
32 Een-Amsterdammer, *Amsterdam en de Amsterdammers*, 136.
33 Ibid., 74.
34 The content and boundaries of the term 'middle classes' have been debated extensively, especially in English historiography. See for instance Jonathan Barry and Christopher Brooks, eds, *The Middling Sort of People. Culture, Society and Politics in England, 1550-1800* (Basingstoke: MacMillan, 1994).
35 The overall similarity of the stratifications does not alter the fact that the precise details varied according to time and place and, of course, according to the author's background and social position.
36 The hardiness of thinking in terms of social hierarchies is demonstrated by the fact that, even today, it is difficult to describe social classes in more neutral terms than high, middle and low.
37 J. L. Price, 'De regent', in *Gestalten van de Gouden Eeuw. Een Hollands groepsportret*, ed. H. M. Beliën, A. Th. van Deursen and G. J. van Setten (Amsterdam: Bert Bakker, 1995), 60. An explanation of the terms *regent* and *magistraat* can be found in ibid., 29–30. Here, too, *regenten* are the members of the oligarchies that wielded power in the cities of Holland and used cooptation to restrict access to their own group of established families. The *magistraat* was the daily administration of the city, consisting of burgomasters, bailiffs and aldermen. For more information on the Amsterdam city government, see Maarten Hell, 'De Oude Geuzen en de Opstand. Politiek en lokaal bestuur in tijd van oorlog en expansie 1578-1650', in *Geschiedenis van Amsterdam. Centrum van de Wereld 1578-1650*, ed. Willem Frijhoff and Maarten Prak (Amsterdam: SUN, 2004).
38 Pollmann, 'Eendracht maakt macht', 143.
39 Ibid., 148–9, and A. Th. Van Deursen, *Het kopergeld van de Gouden Eeuw*, vol. III, *Volk en overheid* (Assen: Van Gorcum, 1979), 3–4.
40 This is one of the reasons why almost no archival documents have been preserved of the discussions that formed the basis of the numerous decisions of the city governments. In addition, discussions as such were not seen as an essential contribution to decision making and were rarely minuted. See also H. A. Enno van

Gelder, *De levensbeschouwing van Cornelis Pieterszoon Hooft, Burgemeester van Amsterdam 1547-1626* (1918; Utrecht: HES, 1982), 192.

41 'Alzoo doorgaens der wijven geslacht, als kouder en vochtiger, minder bequaemheid heeft tot zaken, verstand vereisschende, als 't geslacht der mannen, zoo is het mannelick gheslacht genoegzaam aengeboren eenige opperheid over de wijven'. Quoted in Els Kloek, 'De Vrouw', in *Gestalten van de Gouden Eeuw. Een Hollands groepsportret*, ed. H. M. Beliën, A. Th. van Deursen and G. J. van Setten (Amsterdam: Bert Bakker, 1995), 251 and 253 for the view of Cats. See also Van Gelder, *De levensbeschouwing van Cornelis Pieterszoon Hooft*, 148–9.

42 A brief summary of this development in Price, 'De regent', 26–7.

43 '[niet] dat vroeger onaanzienlijken nu boven kwamen drijven, maar dat een aantal reeds welgestelde families nu wat sneller en gemakkelijker het patriciaat binnendrong' (Van Deursen, *Het kopergeld van de Gouden Eeuw*, 5).

44 For example, in Delft in 1418 it was laid down that only persons who possessed a certain level of wealth could be included in the city council (R. Fruin, *Geschiedenis der staatsinstellingen in Nederland tot den val der Republiek*, ed. H. T. Colenbrander (1901; Den Haag: Martinus Nijhoff, 1980, 74)).

45 Examples of corruption and self-enrichment in J. E. Elias, *De vroedschap van Amsterdam 1578-1795* (1903-1905; Amsterdam: N. Israel, 1963), part I, LXI-LXVII, and in Van Deursen, *Het kopergeld van de Gouden Eeuw*, 11–15.

46 '. . . Godt Almachtigh, die naer sijn vaderlijcke goedertierentheyt gewoon is, daer hy een ampt wettelijcken geeft, oock gaven te geven om hetselve ampt bequamelijck uyt te voeren' (quoted in Van Deursen, *Het kopergeld van de Gouden Eeuw*, 9).

47 For the relationship between the *regenten* elite and the citizenry, see Van Nierop, 'Popular Participation', and Erika Kuijpers and Maarten Prak, 'Burger, ingezetene, vreemdeling: burgerschap in Amsterdam in de 17e en 18e eeuw', in *Burger*, ed. Joost Kloek and Karin Tilmans (Amsterdam: Amsterdam University Press, 2002).

48 Van Gelder, *De levensbeschouwing van Cornelis Pieterszoon Hooft*, 143.

49 Paul Knevel, *Burgers in het geweer. De schutterijen in Holland, 1550-1700* (Dordrecht: Historische Vereniging Holland; Hilversum: Verloren, 1994), hfst. 10.

50 Dekker, *Oproeren in Holland*, 51.

51 Indirectly, through petitions, the middle classes exerted some influence on urban policy, but the power asymmetry is reflected in the fact that these petitions are requests to the city government and requests can also be ignored or refused. On petitions as a form of political participation, see Van Nierop, 'Popular Participation', and Maarten Prak, 'Individu, corporatie en samenleving. De retoriek van de Amsterdamse gilden in de 18de eeuw', in *Werelden van verschil. Ambachtsgilden in de Lage Landen*, ed. Catharina Lis and Hugo Soly (Brussel: VUB Press, 1997).

52 Anne E. C. McCants, *Civic Charity in a Golden Age. Orphan Care in Early Modern Amsterdam* (Urbana: University of Illinois Press, 1997), 201–2. In doing so, she is in line with Van Ravesteyn's research from the beginning of the last century (W. Van Ravesteyn Jr, *Onderzoekingen over de economische en sociale ontwikkeling van Amsterdam gedurende de 16de en het eerste kwart der 17de eeuw* (Amsterdam: S. L. van Looy, 1906), 162–6).

53 Quoted in Van Nierop, 'Popular Participation', 290.

54 The spread of unrest was also what was feared during the Aansprekersoproer (Dekker, *Oproeren in Holland*, 82–3).

55 Maarten Prak, 'Velerlei soort van volk. Sociale verhoudingen in Amsterdam in de zeventiende eeuw', *Jaarboek Amstelodamum* 91 (1999): 41–3, and see also Van

Nierop, 'Popular Participation', 286–8, where it becomes clear that municipal by-laws were often created at the request of interested parties and that the text of these by-laws was sometimes copied verbatim from the petitions.

56 See Ian W. Archer, 'Responses to Alien Immigrants in London, c.1400-1650', in *Le Migrazioni in Europa secc. XIII-XVIII*, ed. Simonetta Cavaciocchi (Prato: Le Monnier, 1994) for the triangular relationship between government, resident population and foreigners/migrants in London.

57 Richard Sennett, *Authority* (New York: Vintage Books, 1981), 19 puts the emphasis on strength when talking about authority. According to him authority is an attempt 'to give the conditions of control and influence a meaning by defining an image of strength'.

58 See Chapter 4.

59 The role of the Orange dynasty in this web of alliances is discussed in Chapter 4.

60 With the existence of this web of alliances, the situation in Holland also seems to differ from that in Brabant and Flanders, where the guilds had political power and strong middle classes reproduced social inequality by excluding the working classes. In this context, Blondé et al. speak of the 'Low Countries' Paradox' (Blondé et al., 'The Low Countries' Paradox', 22–3).

61 I use the English version here: Gustave Le Bon, *The Crowd: A Study of the Popular Mind* (1895; London: T. F. Unwin, 1908), 40.

62 'ons oproerige volk, dat zich gemakkelijk overgeeft aan wanordelijkheden' (quoted in R. Künzel, *Beelden en zelfbeelden van middeleeuwse mensen. Historisch-antropologische studies over groepsculturen in de Nederlanden* (Nijmegen: SUN, 1997), 157). Compare also the English term 'mob', which is derived from the Latin 'mobile vulgus': quickly excited, capricious crowd (Robert B. Shoemaker, 'The London "Mob" in the Early Eighteenth Century', in *The Eighteenth-Century Town. A Reader in English Urban History 1688-1820*, ed. Peter Borsay (London: Longman, 1990), 188).

63 Quoted in H. Brugmans, *Geschiedenis van Amsterdam*, vol. 3, *Bloeitijd 1621/1697* (Utrecht: Het Spectrum, 1973), 341.

64 Van Gelder, *De levensbeschouwing van Cornelis Pieterszoon Hooft*, 126–8, and *Memoriën en Adviezen van Cornelis Pietersz. Hooft*. Werken uitgegeven door het Historisch Genootschap, 3e serie, vol. 48 (Utrecht, 1925), 42–3.

65 'opgehits door quaadaardige en qualijk geïntentioneerde, die de gemene rust en welstand benijden en die bij eenig toeval van tweedragt ofte tumult ofte verandering van saacken haar eijgen voordeel zoecken te voldoen' (quoted in Dekker, *Oproeren in Holland*, 45) and ibid., 48 and 88 for the role of women and boys according to Craffurd.

66 A detailed description of the images of the poor and other marginal groups in pre-modern Europe in Bronisław Geremek, *Het Kaïnsteken. Het beeld van armen en vagebonden in de Europese literatuur van de 15e tot de 17e eeuw* (Baarn: Anthos, 1992) and see also Natalie Zemon Davis, 'The Rites of Violence: Religious Riots in Sixteenth-Century France', *Past and Present* 59 (1973): 52.

67 Lis and Soly, *Worthy Efforts*, 452–3, 567–8.

68 Charles Tilly, 'Demographic Origins of the European Proletariat', in *Proletarianization and Family History*, ed. David Levine (Orlando: Academic Press, 1984), table 1.6. These figures are, of course, no more than very rough indications.

69 Stuart Woolf, 'Order, Class and the Urban Poor', in *Social Orders and Social Classes in Europe since 1500: Studies in Social Stratification*, ed. M. L. Bush (London: Longman, 1992), 186 states: 'Poverty was a recurrent economic reality experienced by a large proportion of the labouring classes in all European societies in all periods.' Pot's

detailed research into the poor in Leiden in the second half of the eighteenth and first half of the nineteenth centuries also shows that the poor formed an integral part of the working classes (G. P. M. Pot, *Arm Leiden. Levensstandaard, bedeling en bedeelden, 1750-1854* (Hilversum: Verloren, 1994), 295).

70 Lis and Soly, *Worthy Efforts*, 568. On growing economic inequality in Europe, see Wouter Ryckbosch, 'Economic Inequality and Growth before the Industrial Revolution: The Case of the Low Countries (Fourteenth to Nineteenth Centuries)', *European Review of Economic History* 20 (2015): 1–22; Guido Alfani and Wouter Ryckbosch, 'Growing Apart in Early Modern Europe? A Comparison of Inequality Trends in Italy and the Low Countries,1500–1800', *Explorations in Economic History* 62 (2016): 143–53 and the contributions in B. Blondé et al., eds, *Inequality and the City in the Low Countries (1200-2020)* (Turnhout: Brepols, 2020).

71 Sharon Kettering, *French Society 1589-1715*, A Social History of Europe (Harlow: Longman, 2001), 127, 141.

72 'die arme sijn die lede Christi ende hy is hoer hoefft' (quoted in Anita Boele, *Leden van één lichaam. Denkbeelden over armen, armenzorg en liefdadigheid in de Noordelijke Nederlanden 1300-1650* (Hilversum: Verloren, 2013), 225–6, 235).

73 Ibid., 238. The symbolic character of this act is of course also reflected in the fact that no more than thirteen people were invited from among the large group of poor. In the fifteenth century, this ritual fell into disuse.

74 'wi sijn alle sonen Gods ende der Heyliger Kerken. Ende die ene broeder soude ymmer den anderen in sijnre noot te helpen comen' (quoted in ibid., 240).

75 Ibid., 245.

76 In a Leiden by-law of 1716, substitute bailiffs and constables were ordered to pick up beggars and street singers from bridges and streets (G. P. M. Pot, 'Het beleid ten aanzien van bedelaars, passanten en immigranten te Leiden, 1700-1795', *Leids Jaarboekje* 79 (1987): 87). For the Amsterdam burgomaster C. P. Hooft's contempt for these groups, see Van Gelder, *De levensbeschouwing van Cornelis Pieterszoon Hooft*, 46 and 194–5.

77 Lis and Soly, *Worthy Efforts*, 454 ff. Prints of the 'false poor' such as Figure 1.1 also made these ideas accessible to those who were not familiar with the texts.

78 Vagebonden, dieven, luiaards, rabouwen, legegangers, troggelaers, loey schuymsel, janrap, janhagel, grauw and gepeupel. I thank the late Prof. E. K. Grootes for his contribution to this list and see further Boele, *Leden van één lichaam*, 255–9, and Rudolf Dekker, *Holland in beroering. Oproeren in de 17de en 18de eeuw* (Baarn: Ambo, 1982), 14.

79 On the left in the background are two 'true poor', one of whom is missing a leg. They are on their way to church and pass by the inn. For images of 'false beggars', see also Tom Nichols, 'The Vagabond Image: Depictions of False Beggars in Northern Art of the Sixteenth Century', in *Others and Outcasts in Early Modern Europe. Picturing the Social Margins*, ed. Tom Nichols (Aldershot: Ashgate, 2007).

80 Boele, *Leden van één lichaam*, 151–5.

81 Ibid., 91, 255–7. Similar views can be heard in the Leiden poor report of 1577 by city secretary Jan van Hout (ibid., 259, and see also Pot, 'Het beleid ten aanzien van bedelaars', 84). According to Van Hout, from the marriages of these undeserving poor, children were born who 'sucked the rashness, flabbiness and laziness [from] their parents' breasts' ('de lichtvaerdicheyt, vadsicheyt ende loyheit [uit] haer ouders borsten gezoogen [hebben]'). Quoted in Kees Walle, *Buurthouden. De geschiedenis van burengebruiken en buurtorganisaties in Leiden (14e-19e eeuw)* (Leiden: Ginkgo,

2005), 39. Pontanus included extensive examples of the deceitfulness of beggars in his 1614 description of Amsterdam (Johannes Isacius Pontanus, *Historische beschrijvinghe der seer wijt beroemde coop-stadt Amsterdam: waer inne benevens de eerste beginselen ende opcomsten der stadt, verscheyden privilegien . . . in Nederduyts overgheset door Petrvm Montanvm* (Amsterdam: Jodocus Hondius, 1614), 134–6). The distinction between deserving and undeserving poor was also made in France and elsewhere in Europe (Kettering, *French Society* 128 and John Marriott, 'The Spatiality of the Poor in Eighteenth-Century London', in *The Streets of London; from the Great Fire to the Great Stink*, ed. Tim Hitchcock and Heather Shore (London: Rivers Oram Press, 2003), 128).

82 See for instance the Amsterdam 'Ordonnantie nopende de Bedelaers' (Pontanus, *Historische beschrijvinghe*, 306–9). Only in Delft did the poor-care come to an organization that in practice functioned as a centralized system (Van der Vlis, *Leven in armoede*, 47).

83 Van der Vlis, *Leven in armoede*, 52–3. This was actually true for all cities in Holland. See also Pot, 'Het beleid ten aanzien van bedelaars.' for the increasing hardening of the policy towards beggars in Leiden in the eighteenth century.

84 Van der Vlis, *Leven in armoede*, 254–5.

85 In 1716, in Leiden, access to the *beiaarden* or *baaierden* (shelters for passers-by) was subjected to strict rules and limited to one night (Pot, 'Het beleid ten aanzien van bedelaars').

86 Boele, *Leden van één lichaam*, 91, 259–61.

87 These houses of correction can be regarded a radical form of segregation and the expulsion of people from the community.

88 'Dus snoeijen wy den boom die quaede vruchten geeft, Ja buygen selfs de tack die nu sijn wasdom heeft'.
   Quoted in Boele, *Leden van één lichaam*, 266.

89 '[die] zich bij de minste samenloop van een zeker hoeveelheid volk de gelegenheid ten nutte . . . maken om zich aan de ergste buitensporigheden over te geven'. Quoted in Van Leeuwen, *Bijstand in Amsterdam*, 123, and 124 for the fear of looting.

90 'Alle nasporingen, die men zoo in ons Vaderland als ook in andere landen, en met name in Groot-Brittanje, heeft in het werk gesteld, naar de ware oorzaken der armoede en der misdrijven leveren deze slotsom op: de ledigheid en de ondeugd zijn de ware oorzaken der armoede en der misdrijven.' (quoted in ibid., 41).

91 '. . . de eerste oorzaak van armoede bestaat in den boozen wil der armen' (quoted in ibid).

92 'Zij leven zorgeloos voort, sparen zelden voor den dag van morgen en wanneer zij dan eens zonder verdiensten zijn, vervallen zij onmiddellijk aan de armenkassen.' (quoted in ibid., 42). The poorest part of the urban population was also viewed with suspicion and disdain by the young socialist movement and referred to with the derogatory term *lumpenproletariat*. In the *Communist Manifesto*, Marx and Engels wrote: 'The "dangerous class" [*lumpenproletariat*], the social scum, that passively rotting mass thrown off by the lowest layers of the old society, may, here and there, be swept into the movement by a proletarian revolution; its conditions of life, however, prepare it far more for the part of a bribed tool of reactionary intrigue.' (Karl Marx and Friedrich Engels, *The Communist Manifesto* (1848; London: Pluto Press, 2008, 49)).

93 Van Leeuwen, *The Logic of Charity*, 118–20, and see Pot, *Arm Leiden*, § 3.4.4, where he observes that also in Leiden poor relief was totally insufficient to live on.

94 This was no different in the seventeenth century. From an Amsterdam ordinance on begging of 1613 it becomes clear that relief was exclusively given to 'true' poor: needy sick and old people, and families with young children (Erika Kuijpers and Maarten Prak, 'Gevestigden en buitenstaanders', in *Geschiedenis van Amsterdam. Centrum van de Wereld 1578-1650*, ed. Willem Frijhoff and Maarten Prak (Amsterdam: SUN, 2004), 227–8). In Delft too, these were the groups that were eligible for almsgiving (Van der Vlis, *Leven in armoede*, chapter 3).

95 Van Leeuwen, *The Logic of Charity*, 68, and see also the study by Pot about Leiden which shows that in the years 1750, 1813 and 1854 some 89–97 per cent of those receiving poor relief were born in Leiden itself (Pot, *Arm Leiden*, 262, tables 5.5 and 5.6).

96 C. A. Davids, 'De migratiebeweging in Leiden in de achttiende eeuw', in *Armoede en sociale spanning. Sociaal-historische studies over Leiden in de achttiende eeuw*, ed. H. A. Diederiks, D. J. Noordam and H. D. Tjalsma (Hilversum: Verloren, 1985), 144–6, and for Amsterdam H. A. Diederiks, *Een stad in verval. Amsterdam omstreeks 1800: demografisch, economisch, ruimtelijk* (Amsterdam: Historisch Seminarium van de Universiteit van Amsterdam, 1982), 287. The striking fall in house rents in Amsterdam in the period 1736–55 and again in the French Period also points to vacancy and extensive emigration (Lesger, *Huur en Conjunctuur*, 51 and Chart 2).

97 In these cases, it was recognized that people could fall into poverty through no fault of their own. In the discourse on poverty among the working classes, this awareness was almost entirely absent. *Schaamsarmen* (shamefaced poor, *pauvres honteux, poveri vergognosi*) and their privileges in the provision of poor relief were to be found all over Europe (Woolf, 'Order, Class and the Urban Poor', 191–2).

98 Van Leeuwen, *The Logic of Charity*, 6, 69–70.

99 Pot, *Arm Leiden*, 177–9. In Delft in the seventeenth century the situation was similar to that in Amsterdam (Van der Vlis, *Leven in armoede*, 281–4).

100 Unless violence is also understood to mean the withholding of support in difficult times. There is certainly something to be said for that view.

101 'wiender hulp en dienst de ghemeenschap en societeyt van de Burgerschap niet kan missen, sy konnen malkander niet ontbeeren...'(Schrevelius, *Harlemias*, book VI, 395–6) and see also Gabrielle Dorren, *Eenheid in verscheidenheid. De burgers van Haarlem in de Gouden Eeuw* (Amsterdam: Prometheus; Bert Bakker, 2001), 34–7. Maclot interprets the bird's-eye view of Antwerp by Virgilius Bononiensis (1565) as a visual representation of the *societas populusque Antverpiae* in which all social classes contribute to its health and strength (Petra Maclot, 'A Portrait Unmasked: The Iconology of the Birds'-Eye View of Antwerp by Virgilius Bononiensis (1565) as a Source for Typological Research of Private Buildings in Fifteenth- and Sixteenth-Century Antwerp', in *Portraits of the City. Representing Urban Space in Later Medieval and Early Modern Europe*, ed. Katrien Lichtert, Jan Dumolyn and Maximiliaan P. J. Martens (Turnhout: Brepols, 2014), 47).

102 Quoted in Van Leeuwen, *The Logic of Charity*, 74. Original text: 'den maatschappij niet wel onttrokken worden, zonder aan deze... wezenlijk nadeel te brengen en... te verlammen zo niet te breken' (quoted in Idem, *Bijstand in Amsterdam*, 121).

103 Quoted in Van Leeuwen, *The Logic of Charity*, 75. In Dutch: 'het hoofdmerk eener goede opvoeding moet zijn om ieder in zijn rang en stand tot een goed en nuttig ingezeeten van den staat te maken' (quoted in Idem, *Bijstand in Amsterdam*, 122).

104 Sune Qvotrup Jensen, 'Othering, Identity Formation and Agency', *Qualitative Studies* 2 (2011): 65.

Chapter 2

1. Pierre Bourdieu, 'Social Space and the Genesis of Appropriated Physical Space', *International Journal of Urban and Regional Research* 42 (2018): 108. A German-language version of this article was previously published as 'Physischer, sozialer und angeeigneter physischer Raum', in *Stadt-Räume: Die Zukunft Des Städtischen*, ed. Martin Wentz (Frankfurt am Main: Campus; Suhrkamp, 1991).
2. Bourdieu, 'Social Space and Appropriated Physical Space', 110.
3. Ibid.
4. Ibid., 112. Bourdieu rightly stresses that the home and the residential environment of individuals and groups also have an effect on their mental dispositions and aspirations (ibid., 113).
5. Gideon Sjoberg, *The Pre-Industrial City. Past and Present* (New York: The Free Press, 1960); J. E. Vance Jr., 'Land Assignment in the Pre-Capitalist, Capitalist and Post-Capitalist City', *Economic Geography* 47 (1971): 101–20. See Colin G. Pooley, 'Patterns on the Ground: Urban Form, Residential Structure and the Social Construction of Space', in *The Cambridge Urban History of Britain*, ed. Martin Daunton (Cambridge: Cambridge University Press, 2000), 430–5, for a brief overview of the different perspectives in research on residential structures.
6. Quoted in John P. Radford, 'Testing the Model of the Pre-Industrial City. The Case of Ante-Bellum Charleston, South Carolina', *Transactions of the Institute of British Geographers* 4 (1979): 392. Herbert and Thomas call Sjoberg's study 'a pace setter in this field' (David T. Herbert and Colin J. Thomas, *Cities in Space: City as Place* (London: David Fulton, 1997), 21).
7. Sjoberg, *The Pre-Industrial City*, 11.
8. Ibid., 97–8.
9. Ibid., 99 ff.
10. Ibid., 121–3.
11. Ibid., 99.
12. Ibid., 189 and see also page 100. A graphical representation of Sjoberg's model in Radford, 'Testing the Model', 394, and in Dominique Vanneste, *De pré-industriële Vlaamse stad: een sociaal-economische survey. Interne differentiatie te Gent en te Kortrijk op het einde van de 18e eeuw* (Leuven: Geografisch Instituut Katholieke Universiteit te Leuven, 1987), 24.
13. It is not surprising that a model that claims to provide insight into the residential structure of cities from the earliest urban settlements to industrialization, and that does so regardless of the continent in which those cities were located, can count on a lot of criticism. See for example J. Langton, 'Residential Patterns in Pre-Industrial Cities: Some Case Studies from Seventeenth-Century Britain', *Transactions of the Institute of British Geographers* 65 (1975): 1–27; Peter Burke, 'Some Reflections on the Pre-Industrial City', *Urban History Yearbook* 2 (1975): 13–21; Vanneste, *De pré-industriële Vlaamse stad*, 32–3, and Herbert and Thomas, *Cities in Space*, 21–5.
14. Sjoberg, *The Pre-Industrial City*, 99. As we have seen, also according to Bourdieu, one of the goals in the field of housing is to keep those who are considered 'less' at a distance.
15. Ibid., 109.
16. Ibid., 11.
17. Ibid., 224–33. See also the previously mentioned concept of 'symbolic power' in Bourdieu's work.

18 Vance Jr., 'Land Assignment', and for a good summary of his views, see Langton, 'Residential Patterns in Pre-Industrial Cities', 3–5.
19 Vance Jr., 'Land Assignment', 107.
20 Ibid., 102–3. Although Vance does not use the term, it is obvious that he is thinking of industrial linkages, the situation where one company depends for its production on information and/or products from another company. In a time of limited and costly transport, physical proximity is common.
21 Ibid., 105.
22 Ibid., 106.
23 Ibid., 107.
24 Ibid., 108–9.
25 A short note on terminology. In this study, lanes (*stegen* in Dutch) are narrow streets that separate two blocks of houses, alleys (*gangen*) are very narrow streets that sometimes run through buildings and are then partially covered, and blind alleys (*sloppen*) are dead-end alleys. Alleys and blind alleys open up blocks of houses on the inside; lanes do not. In the sources for Leiden and The Hague especially, alleys and blind alleys are often referred to as *poorten*.
26 Differentiation between streets is also referred to here as 'around-the-corner' differentiation. In this study, meso-level differentiation also includes differentiation within streets.
27 Vance Jr., 'Land Assignment', 110.
28 Ibid.
29 Ibid., 111–13.
30 In fact, Vance's model for the capitalist city is very similar to Burgess's model for Chicago in the 1920s (Ernest W. Burgess, 'The Growth of the City: An Introduction to a Research Project', in *The City*, ed. Robert E. Park, Ernest W. Burgess and Roderick D. MacKenzie (Chicago: University of Chicago Press, 1925)).
31 Langton, 'Residential Patterns in Pre-Industrial Cities', 4.
32 What Bourdieu writes about housing in contemporary France is equally applicable to housing in pre-modern Dutch cities: 'As a material good which (like clothing) is exposed to the general gaze, and is so *on a lasting basis*, this form of property expresses or betrays, in a more decisive way than many other goods, the social being of its owners, the extent of their "means", as we say' (Pierre Bourdieu, *The Social Structures of the Economy* (Cambridge: Polity Press, 2005), 19).
33 On the land registry, see F. Keverling Buisman and E. Muller, *"Kadaster-Gids". Gids voor de raadpleging van hypothecaire en kadastrale archieven uit de 19e en de eerste helft van de 20e eeuw* (Den Haag: Rijksarchiefdienst, 1979); A. D. M. Veldhorst, 'Het Nederlandse vroeg-19e-eeuwse kadaster als bron voor andersoortig onderzoek, een verkenning', *Historisch-Geografisch Tijdschrift* 9 (1991): 8–27; the introduction to J. D. Hoeufft and J. C. R. van Hoorn van Burgh, *Kadastrale uitkomsten van Noord- en Zuid-Holland 1832*. Reissue with an introduction by W. J. van den Berg and Ph. Kint (Dordrecht: Historische Vereniging Holland, 1993) and G. A. M. van Synghel, ed., *Bronnen betreffende de registratie van onroerend goed in de negentiende en twintigste eeuw*, Broncommentaren, vol. 3 (Den Haag: Instituut voor Nederlandse Geschiedenis, 1997). An introduction to the digital version of the 1832 land register in Hans Mol, 'Het Napoleontisch kadaster van Holland in GIS: belang en perspectieven', *Holland* 52 (2020): 20–8.
34 W. J. van den Berg and Ph. Kint, 'Inleiding', in *Kadastrale uitkomsten van Noord- en Zuid-Holland 1832*, ed. J. D. Hoeufft and J. C. R. van Hoorn van Burgh (Dordrecht: Historische Vereniging Holland, 1993), 9.

35 For other cadastral records, see Veldhorst, 'Het Nederlandse vroeg-19e-eeuwse kadaster'.
36 For houses, a quarter of the estimated rental value could be deducted for maintenance when determining the taxable yield. The rental value was therefore 4/3 times the taxable yield. In the case of built-up areas, the taxable income of the building's subsoil could also be deducted, but this was negligible in cities (Van den Berg and Kint, 'Inleiding', 18–19).
37 The map shows the borders of the province of Holland in 1648.
38 Delft is the exception here, because by 1355 this city had already reached a size that would prove sufficient to accommodate the population until the middle of the nineteenth century (see Chapter 3).
39 By way of comparison: the built-up area of London at the end of the seventeenth century was 920 hectares, or 740 hectares if all areas without a residential function (parks, markets, cemeteries, squares, etc.) are excluded (Spence, *London in the 1690s*, 41 and figure 3.1). The figure of 920 hectares is most closely comparable to the surface areas of the cities listed in the table.
40 For Amsterdam and Leiden I was allowed to make use of the digital files produced by the Fryske Akademie in the context of HisGis. I am also very grateful to the Amsterdams Universiteitsfonds, whose substantial financial contribution to this research project provided HisGis the means to also digitize the *OAT* and *Minuutplans* of The Hague. The data for Delft are supplied by George Buzing, those for Edam by Reinout Klaarenbeek and for Alkmaar use was made of a map provided by the Archeologische Dienst van Alkmaar and data files produced by Willem van den Berg. I am much obliged to all these people and institutions.
41 It must be emphasized, however, that the nature of the cadastral registration does not allow the rental values of dwellings within the same property to be taken into account. Assuming that it was mainly the less well-off who occupied part of a house, this implies that the differences in rental values – and the socio-economic status of the inhabitants derived from these – are even greater than the data in the land register would suggest.
42 Hoeufft and Van Hoorn van Burgh, *Kadastrale uitkomsten*, section Noord-Holland, Appendix C.
43 See C. Boschma-Aarnoudse, D. M. Bunskoeke and J. Sparreboom, *Vestingwerken van Edam* (Edam: Vereniging Oud Edam, 1998), in particular chapter IV.
44 Of course, only the rental values of residential properties are included in the analysis.
45 The interpolation maps are based on the range of rental values recorded in the cities under study. As the average and median rents per city differ considerably, the colours in the various cities therefore reflect very different nominal rents. The advantage of this procedure is that it allows for visual comparison of the residential patterns in different cities.
46 See for this map Kees Hulskemper, ed., *500 Jaar Edamse cartografie. Plattegronden, landmeters en kaarttekenaars sinds 1540 (met een genealogische bijdrage van Jan Doets)* (Edam: Vereniging Oud Edam, 1993), 25, and also the collection of images (*Beeldbank*) at the website of the Waterlands Archief. The map by Frederik de Wit is an updated version of Joan Blaeu's map from the mid-seventeenth century.
47 On the inset map, the large plot between Voorhaven and Achterhaven is the location of a spinning factory.
48 Hoeufft and Van Hoorn van Burgh, *Kadastrale uitkomsten*, section Noord-Holland, Appendix C.

49 The quartile boundaries were determined by using the distribution of all rental values of occupied properties, excluding almshouses (*hofjes*) and other dwellings that were not let out at market prices. Subsequently, the block faces were allocated to one of the quartiles on the basis of their average rental value. A more detailed account of the procedure can be found in W. J. van den Berg, Marco H. D. van Leeuwen and Clé Lesger, 'Residentiële segregatie in Hollandse steden. Theorie, methodologie en empirische bevindingen voor Alkmaar en Amsterdam, 16e-19e eeuw', *Tijdschrift voor Sociale Geschiedenis* 24 (1998): 402–36.
50 The ample supply of housing due to the population decline in the previous period played an important role in this.
51 Hoeufft and Van Hoorn van Burgh, *Kadastrale uitkomsten*, section Zuid-Holland, Appendix C.
52 For residential patterns in Delft, see also Clé Lesger, Marco H. D. van Leeuwen and George Buzing, 'Residentiële segregatie in Delft. Een verkenning van ruimtelijke patronen in 1832', in *Tijd en ruimte. Nieuwe toepassingen van GIS in de alfawetenschappen*, ed. Onno Boonstra and Anton Schuurman (Utrecht: Matrijs, 2009).
53 Hoeufft and Van Hoorn van Burgh, *Kadastrale uitkomsten*, section Zuid-Holland, Appendix C.
54 Outside the city walls of Leiden, there were few residential buildings in this period.
55 See for the traditional manufactories in Leiden's textile production and also for the transition to mechanized industry A. J. Backer, *Leidse wevers onder gaslicht. Schering en inslag van Zaalberg dekens onder gaslicht (1850-1915)* (Leiden: N. V. Koninklijke Nederlandse Fabriek van Wollen Dekens, 1952).
56 Hoeufft and Van Hoorn van Burgh, *Kadastrale uitkomsten*, section Zuid-Holland, Appendix C. These figures include the population and houses in Scheveningen, where there were just under 700 houses. In contrast to the other cities in Holland, The Hague did not have city rights until the beginning of the nineteenth century and was not surrounded by defenses either.
57 In the *OAT* of the The Hague land register, there are several hundreds of objects with descriptions such as 'house, building and yard' ('huis, gebouw en erf'). The estimated rental value of these objects is usually very substantial and higher than that of objects described as 'house and yard'. Since it is not clear what 'building' stands for, these objects are not included in the interpolation map. If they are included, however, the pattern hardly differs from that shown in Map 2.9. These relatively expensive properties were mainly located in districts that stood out anyway due to their high rental values.
58 See for the *Logement van Amsterdam* on Plein in The Hague Geert Medema, *Achter de façade van de Hollandse stad. Het stedelijk bouwbedrijf in de achttiende eeuw* (Nijmegen: Vantilt, 2011), 262–3.
59 For this canon foundry, see Thera Wijsenbeek, 'Economisch Leven', in *Den Haag. Geschiedenis van de stad*, vol. 2, *De tijd van de Republiek*, ed. Th. Wijsenbeek (Zwolle: Waanders, 2005), 60–2.
60 Hoeufft and Van Hoorn van Burgh, *Kadastrale uitkomsten*, section Noord-Holland, Appendix C.
61 For residential patterns in Amsterdam, see also Clé Lesger, Marco H. D. van Leeuwen and Bart Vissers, 'Residentiële segregatie in vroeg-moderne steden. Amsterdam in de eerste helft van de negentiende eeuw', *Tijdschrift voor Sociale en Economische Geschiedenis* 10 (2013): 102–32.
62 The churches and synagogues in Amsterdam are marked with a black square.

63 A striking example of this phenomenon were the houses in Kerkstraat, a back street in the wealthy southern part of the ring of canals.
64 This applies not only to the cities studied here but also, for example, to Haarlem (Dorren, *Eenheid in verscheidenheid*, 72) and Rotterdam (Hans Bonke, *De kleyne mast van de Hollandse coopsteden. Stadsontwikkeling in Rotterdam 1572-1795* (Amsterdam: Historisch Seminarium van de Universiteit van Amsterdam, 1996), 135–6).
65 A summary of studies for European cities in Clé Lesger and Marco H. D. van Leeuwen, 'Residential Segregation from the Sixteenth to the Nineteenth Century. Evidence from the Netherlands', *Journal of Interdisciplinary History* XLII (2012): 335–9. For a similar situation in Ghent and Kortrijk, see Vanneste, *De pré-industriële Vlaamse stad*, 28. For Antwerp, the situation is less clear-cut, but in 1834 there too, most of the poor neighbourhoods were to be found in the periphery (P. Vandermeersch, B. Blondé and R. Marynissen, 'Typologie sociale du parc de logements à Anvers basée sur la Cadastre de 1834', in *Nouvelles approches concernant la culture de l'habitat / New Approaches to Living Patterns*, ed. R. Baetens and B. Blondé (Turnhout: Brepols, 1991), picture 3). Yet this zonal pattern was not ubiquitous. In Cahors and Romans, the elites lived relatively scattered throughout the city, and elites in Bologna and Naples did not build their palaces exclusively in the centre either (Paul White, *The West European City. A Social Geography* (London: Longman, 1984), 6).
66 The field of housing thus functioned as a *force field* that imposed specific rules on all who entered it, for even those with the least resources had to accept (implicitly) that in the field of housing money determined where and how someone lived (Wacquant, 'Pierre Bourdieu', 221).
67 R. J. Johnston, *City and Society. An Outline for Urban Geography* (London: Hutchinson, 1984), 164. For externalities, see also David Harvey, *Social Justice and the City* (Baltimore: John Hopkins University Press, 1973), 57–60.
68 Bourdieu, 'Social Space and Appropriated Physical Space', 110 (emphasis in original).

Chapter 3

1 L. Mumford, *The City in History. Its Origins, Its Transformations, and Its Prospects* (1961; London: Penguin Books, 1966), 356 and see also 354.
2 Ibid., 396. A similar argument in Robert E. Dickinson, *The West European City. A Geographical Interpretation* (1951; London: Routledge & Kegan Paul, 1962), 301 and 417.
3 G. A. Hoekveld, 'Over de voorspelbaarheid van ruimtelijke patronen: areale modellen van de Noordwest-Europese Stad, 1300-heden', *Historisch-Geografisch Tijdschrift* 8 (1990): 6–8. A different view in Donald J. Olsen, *The City as a Work of Art: London, Paris, Vienna* (New Haven: Yale University Press, 1986), 132–3.
4 'De middeleeuwse stad kende alleen een ordening naar de produktie van goederen – de gildekwartieren –, verder woonde eenieder rond plekken van gemeenschappelijk belang, kerken, stadshuizen en markten. In de renaissance ontstond een scheiding tussen stadsdelen waar geregeerd wordt, dat wil zeggen de controle over de economische activiteiten wordt uitgeoefend, en delen waar geproduceerd wordt.' (L. A. de Klerk, '"Verscheydentheydt behaecht". Enige hoofdstukken uit de geschiedenis

van het publieke domein', in *De openbare ruimte van de stad*, ed. G. van der Plas (Amsterdam: Genootschap Amstelodamum; Stadsuitgeverij, 1991), 16). In the previous chapter, we have already seen that Sjoberg also holds the view that guild members were spatially clustered in guild quarters or along specific streets.

5   Christopher R. Friedrichs, *The Early Modern City 1450-1750* (London: Longman, 1995), 10.
6   For the transition debate, see for example Paul Sweezy et al., eds, *The Transition from Feudalism to Capitalism* (London: NLB, 1976).
7   'de eigenwaan der humanisten' (R. van Uytven, 'Sociaal-economische evoluties in de Nederlanden voor de revoluties (14e-16e eeuw)', *Bijdragen en Mededelingen betreffende de Geschiedenis der Nederlanden* 87 (1972): 61).
8   See also Wim Boerefijn, 'De totstandkoming van de stedelijke vorm', in *Stadswording in de Nederlanden. Op zoek naar overzicht*, ed. Reinout Rutte and Hildo van Engen (Hilversum: Verloren, 2008), 142.
9   This similarity is not surprising, since the presence of the court made The Hague most similar to the pre-industrial cities that Sjoberg had in mind.
10 Research by Berry shows that in late medieval London too, the urban fringe was not a socially homogenous area (Charlotte Berry, *The Margins of Late Medieval London, 1430-1541* (London: University of London Press, 2022), 8–16).
11 For the landscape and the large peat reclamations in Holland, see H. van der Linden, 'Het platteland in het noordwesten met nadruk op de occupatie circa 1000-1300', in *Algemene Geschiedenis der Nederlanden*, vol. 2, ed. Dirk P. Blok et.al. (Haarlem: Fibula-Van Dishoeck, 1982); J. C. Besteman and A. J. Guiran, 'De middeleeuwse bewoningsgeschiedenis van Noord-Holland boven het IJ en de ontginning van de veengebieden. Opgravingen in Assendelft in perspectief', in *Rotterdam Papers V, A Contribution to Prehistoric, Roman and Medieval Archeology*, ed. M. C. van Trierum and H. E. Henkes (Rotterdam, 1986); Arie van der Schoor, *Het ontstaan van de middeleeuwse stad Rotterdam. Nederzettingsgeschiedenis in het Maas-Merwedegebied van ca. 400-1400* (Canaletto, 1992); H. Schoorl, 'Het Hollandse kustgebied tussen Helinium en Vlie vanaf de Romeinse tijd tot 1421', in *Holland en het water in de middeleeuwen*, ed. J. J. M. Beenakker et al. (Hilversum: Verloren, 1997) and P. C. M. Hoppenbrouwers, 'Van Waterland tot stedenland. De Hollandse economie c. 975-c. 1570', in *Geschiedenis van Holland tot 1572*, ed. Thimo de Nijs and Eelco Beukers (Hilversum: Verloren, 2002), 103–18. A more recent study on the earliest history of Holland is Henk Looijesteijn et al., eds, 'Het ontstaan van het graafschap Holland', *Holland* 50 (2018).
12 The explanation of the Great Reclamation must be sought in a combination of factors. The long period of drought in the tenth century probably played an important role. In an ecologically vulnerable and relatively densely populated area like the dune strip, the drought led to dehydration of fields, sand-drift and the formation of dunes. This put pressure on agricultural production. It is very likely that in Holland, as elsewhere in Western Europe, in these same years the population grew in numbers. In combination, drought and population growth led to relative overpopulation. At the same time, however, the vast peat bogs became more accessible due to the drought and consequently the possibilities for reclaiming these wastelands increased (Besteman and Guiran, 'De middeleeuwse bewoningsgeschiedenis', 185 and 192, and D. E. H. de Boer, '"Op weg naar volwassenheid". De ontwikkeling van produktie en consumptie in de Hollandse en Zeeuwse steden in de dertiende eeuw', in *De Hollandse stad in de dertiende eeuw*, ed. J. M. Baart et al. (Zutphen: Walburg Pers, 1988), 32).

13 Jaap Evert Abrahamse et al., 'Water System and Urban Form in Holland. A Survey in Maps: 1575, 1680, 1900 and 2015', *OverHolland* 21 (2021): 49, and see also Rutte and Abrahamse, eds, *Atlas of the Dutch Urban Landscape*, Part II, 2.
14 A similar dynamic in Hoorn (Clé Lesger, *Hoorn als stedelijk knooppunt. Stedensystemen tijdens de late middeleeuwen en vroegmoderne tijd* (Dordrecht: Historische Vereniging Holland; Hilversum: Verloren, 1990), 23–4).
15 In general, the settlements on the high ground behind the dunes and along the rivers already showed signs of urban development in the twelfth century, while those in the peat areas only did so in the thirteenth century, or even later (Hans Renes, 'De stad in het Landschap', in *Stadswording in de Nederlanden. Op zoek naar overzicht*, ed. Reinout Rutte and Hildo van Engen (Hilversum: Verloren, 2008), 23, 27). Of course, many more factors played a role in the process of city formation than the ones mentioned here. See for this Reinout Rutte, *Stedenpolitiek en stadsplanning in de Lage Landen (12de-13de eeuw)* (Zutphen: Walburg Pers, 2002) and also Reinout Rutte and G. A. Hoekveld, 'Stadswording en machtspolitiek. Vergelijkend onderzoek met een modelmatige benadering', *Historisch-Geografisch Tijdschrift* 21 (2003): 77–92.
16 On the earliest history of Delft, see J. C. Visser, 'Het Delftse stadsplan', in *Delftse Studiën. Een bundel historische opstellen over de stad Delft geschreven voor Dr. E. H. Ter Kuile naar aanleiding van zijn afscheid als hoogleraar in de geschiedenis van de Bouwkunst*, ed. Rudolf Meischke and Jacobus C. Visser (Assen: Van Gorcum, 1967); J. J. Raue, *De stad Delft: vorming en ruimtelijke ontwikkeling in de late middeleeuwen. Interpretatie van 25 Jaar binnenstadsonderzoek* (Delft: Delftse Universitaire Pers, 1982), chapter 1; Verhoeven, *De derde stad*, chapter 1, and Stef van der Gaag, *Historische atlas van Delft. Stad van ambacht en techniek* (Nijmegen: Vantilt, 2015), chapters 1–5.
17 The word 'Delf' refers to a dug watercourse.
18 Nieuwe Delft lies some hundred metres east of Oude Delft. This was the distance for which it had been established in the peat reclamations that the water level could be controlled (Han Meyer, 'Het bouwblok als microkosmos van de stad', in *Atlas van het Hollandse bouwblok*, ed. Susanne Komossa et al. (Bussum: Thoth, 2002), 253.
19 Raue, *De stad Delft*, 185, and Verhoeven, *De derde stad*, 23–4.
20 Verhoeven, *De derde stad*, 25–6.
21 Ibid., 32–5, and see also Table 2.1 in the previous chapter.
22 D. Wijbenga, *Delft. Een verhaal van de stad en haar bewoners*, vol. I, *Van de vroegste tijd tot het jaar 1572* (Rijswijk: Elmar, 1984), 73.
23 P. C. J. van der Krogt, *Geschiedenis en verklaring van de straatnamen in Delft* (Den Haag: Kruseman, 1985), 147–8, 196.
24 Ibid., 79–80.
25 A *vlouw* or *vluwe* is a net for catching water birds (ibid., 198). For Donkerstraat see Rob Rentenaar, 'De oudste stedelijke toponymie in het graafschap Holland', in *De Hollandse stad in de dertiende eeuw*, ed. Erich H. P. Cordfunke, Frederik W. N. Hugenholtz, and Klaes Sierksma (Zutphen: Walburg Pers, 1988), 72.
26 Van der Gaag, *Historische atlas Delft*, 20.
27 The colour sequence is from orange (highest values) through green to blue (lowest values). This one and the following elevation maps are taken from 'Actueel Hoogtebestand Nederland', map layer 'AHN2 maaiveld, dynamic layout' (https://www.ahn.nl/).
28 Verhoeven, *De derde stad*, 39–41.

29 For the brewing industry in Holland, see Richard Yntema, 'The Brewing Industry in Holland, 1300-1800: A Study in Industrial Development' (PhD thesis, University of Chicago, 1992); Richard Yntema, 'Een kapitale nering. De brouwindustrie in Holland tussen 1500 en 1800', in *Bier! Geschiedenis van een volksdrank*, ed. R. E. Kistemaker and V. T. van Vilsteren (Amsterdam: De Bataafsche Leeuw, 1994) and Richard W. Unger, *A History of Brewing in Holland 900-1900: Economy, Technology and the State* (Leiden: Brill, 2001). For the Delft brewery Verhoeven, *De derde stad*, 47–9, 97–101, 163–5 and 283–6.
30 Verhoeven, *De derde stad*, 164.
31 Ibid., 285 and see the map in Van der Gaag, *Historische atlas Delft*, 22.
32 The by-laws therefore show great concern for the quality of the water in Oude Delft, Nieuwe Delft and the western city moat, which was indispensable for the breweries (J. A. Fruin, 'Het oudste der tot dusver bekende keurboeken van Delft', *Nieuwe bijdragen voor rechtsgeleerdheid en wetgeving*, nieuwe reeks 8 (1882): 348–50; J. Soutendam, 'Het oudste keurboek van Delft', *Nieuwe bijdragen voor rechtsgeleerdheid en wetgeving*, nieuwe reeks 2/3 (1876): 418–32, and idem, *Keuren en ordonnantiën der stad Delft van den aanvang der XVIe eeuw tot het jaar 1536* (Delft: J. H. Molenbroek, 1870), 99–116).
33 Verhoeven, *De derde stad*, 197–202. Material prosperity was an important criterion for admission to the city government (ibid., 134).
34 Thera Wijsenbeek-Olthuis, *Achter de gevels van delft. Bezit en bestaan van rijk en arm in een periode van achteruitgang (1700-1800)* (Hilversum: Verloren, 1987), 66.
35 Ibid., 156–7. In 1773 it was also decided to build a new corn exchange on Haverbrug-bridge near Oude Delft, in order to prevent vacancy and decline of the Oude Delft area. Despite the city's precarious financial situation, this apparently outweighed the fact that cheaper and equally suitable sites were available elsewhere in the city (Medema, *Achter de façade van de Hollandse stad*, 26).
36 Due to the prevailing westerly winds, the concentration of polluting industries in the eastern part of the city was particularly attractive.
37 Fruin, 'Het oudste der tot dusver bekende keurboeken', 347. For the dating of these by-laws and also the ones published by Soutendam, see ibid., 277–90. At the time of the 1832 land register, the tanneries were still located on the east side of the city (see Chapter 2).
38 A fourth site lay outside the western city gate at Buitenwatersloot (Soutendam, 'Het oudste keurboek van Delft, 532).
39 Except for a few years around 1580, when the churchyard around the Nieuwe Kerk temporarily functioned as a cattle market (Wijbenga, *Delft*, vol. I, 57).
40 'Ende allen vrouwen, die openbaerlijke omme gelt sitten ende gesellen toelaeten; ofte die gelijcke plaetsen willen houden, sullen woonen Indie dronckenstege, hopsteege ende hermen cockelaens laen ende nerghens elders'. (Soutendam, *Keuren en ordonnantiën der stad Delft*, 90). The other decrees on prostitution in Fruin, 'Het oudste der tot dusver bekende keurboeken', 302 and Soutendam, 'Het oudste keurboek van Delft', 483. See also E. C. van der Borch tot Verwolde-Swemle, 'Wonen in Delft', in *De stad Delft. Cultuur en maatschappij, tot 1572*, ed. I. V. T. Spaander and R. A. van Leeuw (Delft: Delft Stedelijk Museum 'Het Prinsenhof', 1979). For the allocation of specific locations to prostitutes in Italian cities, see Fabrizio Nevola, *Street Life in Renaissance Italy* (New Haven: Yale University Press, 2020), 120–6.
41 Wijbenga, *Delft*, vol. I, 146.

42 Reinier Boitet, *Beschryving der stadt Delft, behelzende een zeer naaukeurige en uitvoerige verhandeling van deszelfs eerste oorsprong, benaming, bevolking ... en regeeringsvorm* (Delft: Reinier Boitet, 1729), 456 and 492-5.
43 D. Wijbenga, *Delft. Een verhaal van de stad en haar bewoners*, vol. II, *Van 1572 tot het jaar 1700* (Rijswijk: Elmar, 1986), 112 and Verhoeven, *De derde stad*, 290.
44 Van der Krogt, *Straatnamen in Delft*, XIX-XX; Bas van der Wulp, 'Het stadsbeeld van Delft tijdens het leven van Vermeer: Delft in Hollands verband', in *De Hollandse samenleving in de tijd van Vermeer*, ed. Donald Haks and Marie Christine van der Sman (Zwolle: Waanders, 1996), 42, and Verhoeven, *De derde stad*, 343.
45 This largely underground gunpowder storage was of relatively recent date (1637), but gunpowder had already been stored in the north-east corner of the city since 1589. For the gunpowder disaster, see Verhoeven, *De derde stad*, 342-9.
46 Surveys of the history of the delftware industry in Wijsenbeek-Olthuis, *Achter de gevels van Delft*, 66-71; Verhoeven, *De derde stad*, 357-63, and Van der Gaag, *Historische atlas Delft*, 30-1.
47 See the illustrative map in Van der Gaag, *Historische atlas Delft*, 30.
48 Arie de Klerk, *Bouwen aan de hofstad. De geschiedenis van het bouwtoezicht in Den Haag 1250-1900, in sociaal en cultureel perspectief* (Delft: Delft University Press, 1998), 9.
49 That there was more variation within this broad dichotomy has already been noted and will be given more attention in the next section. The contrast is also nicely illustrated in H. Schmal, *Den Haag of 's-Gravenhage? De 19de-eeuwse gordel, een zone gemodelleerd door zand en veen* (Utrecht: Matrijs, 1995).
50 Daan van Leeuwen, 'Lepra en de bouw van leprosaria. Ziekte en segregatie in middeleeuws Holland', *Holland* 51 (2019).
51 Peter Bitter, 'Nederzetting op het zand. Landschappelijk dynamiek en menselijke bewoning', in *Geschiedenis van Alkmaar*, ed. Diederik Aten et al. (Zwolle: Waanders, 2007), 17-21.
52 See the appendix.
53 Peter Bitter, 'Ommuurd, volgebouwd en uitgelegd. Ruimtelijke ontwikkeling van de middeleeuwse stad', in *Geschiedenis van Alkmaar*, ed. Diederik Aten, Jan Drewes, Joop Kila and Harry de Raad (Zwolle: Waanders, 2007), 71-7, and Peter Bitter and Willem van den Berg, 'Historische gegevens over huizen en bedrijven, hun eigenaren en bewoners', in *Afval van gorters, brouwers en een hospitaal. Archeologisch onderzoek van het Wortelsteegplein*, ed. S. Ostkamp et al., *Rapporten over de Alkmaarse monumentenzorg en archeologie*, 6 (Alkmaar: Gemeente Alkmaar, 1998).
54 In Alkmaar, too, new building sites were considerably raised (Bitter, 'Nederzetting op het zand', 16, and Idem, 'Ommuurd, volgebouwd en uitgelegd', 68).
55 Ed van der Vlist, 'De stedelijke ruimte en haar bewoners', in *Leiden. De geschiedenis van een Hollandse stad*, vol. 1, *Leiden tot 1574*, ed. J. W. Marsilje (Leiden: Stichting Geschiedschrijving Leiden, 2002), 16 and 22. The early history of Leiden also in Edwin D. Orsel, 'Hausbau in Leiden', in *Hausbau in Holland. Baugeschichte und Stadtentwicklung*, ed. Gabri van Tussenbroek, *Jahrbuch für Hausforschung* (Marburg: Jonas Verlag, 2010).
56 Van der Vlist, 'De stedelijke ruimte', 26-7, 51-5.
57 But already in 1581, tanneries could be found in the northern and – to a lesser extent – eastern periphery of the city (Roos van Oosten and Sanne Muurling, 'Smelly Business. De clustering en concentratie van vieze en stinkende beroepen in Leiden in 1581', *Holland* 51 (2019): picture 4).

58 E. Taverne, *In 't land van belofte: in de nieue stadt. Ideaal en werkelijkheid van de stadsuitleg in de Republiek 1580-1680* (Maarssen: Gary Schwartz, 1978), 185. The use of the term 'Mierennest' (Ants' Nest) is also significant. Metaphors borrowed from the animal world were often used to define poor neighbourhoods as the domain of 'the other' (Alan Mayne, 'Representing the Slum', *Urban History Yearbook* 17 (1990): 75).
59 Taverne, *In 't land van belofte*, 186 ff.; R. C. J. van Maanen, 'Stadsbeeld en ruimtelijke ordening', in *Leiden. De geschiedenis van een Hollandse stad*, vol. 2, *1574-1795*, ed. S. Groenveld (Leiden: Stichting Geschiedschrijving Leiden, 2003), 25–7, 31, and see also Medema, *Achter de façade van de Hollandse stad*, 221–3.
60 Taverne, *In 't land van belofte*, 205, 209.
61 Ibid., 194–5, 212, 215–16. The city government was well aware of the poor situation in the *poorten* (alleys and blind alleys) and the associated public health problems. In a by-law issued in 1656 to oppose further densification in the inner city of Leiden, it was stated that the inhabitants of the *poorten* 'are hardly able to see the air, since they live in stuffy dwellings, all this causing a noticeable defacement of the city and also the unhealthiness of the occupants' ('nauwelijcx de lucht konnen sien, immers seer bedompt zijn woonende, streckende alle tselve tot merckelijcke ontcieringhe deser Stede en oock dickmael geen kleyne occasie ende oorsaecke gevende tot de ongesontheyt vande Inwoonders vande selve'). Quoted in ibid., 222.
62 In the following I have mainly used C. Boschma-Aarnoudse, *Tot verbeteringe van de neeringe deser stede. Edam en de Zeevang in de late middeleeuwen en de 16de eeuw* (Hilversum: Verloren, 2003), chapters 1 and 2; Idem, *Edam, behouden stad. Houten en stenen huizen 1500-1800* (Utrecht: Matrijs, 2007), chapter 1, and Ben Speet, *Edam. Duizend jaar geschiedenis van een stad* (Zwolle: Waanders 2007), chapter 1.
63 An illustrative map in Boschma-Aarnoudse, *Edam, behouden stad*, 18.
64 Ibid., 18–21.
65 Ibid., 20.
66 For example, it was not by coincidence that around 1400 the Gasthuis van de Heilige Geest (Hospital of the Holy Spirit) was built on Nieuwehaven, close to what was then the eastern city boundary. This part of the city also housed the poorhouse (ibid., 43).
67 Ibid., 31, and Boschma-Aarnoudse, *Tot verbeteringe van de neeringe*, 329.
68 The *schotgeld* tax and 100^e *penning* tax are discussed in detail in the appendix.
69 Boschma-Aarnoudse, *Edam, behouden stad*, 31.
70 The history of Lingerzijde and Schepenmakersdijk since the middle of the sixteenth century is covered in Boschma-Aarnoudse, *Het Westeinde van Edam. Armoede en welvaren van een stadsbuurt. Een onderzoek naar wonen en werken aan de Lingerzijde en Schepenmakersdijk sinds 1560* (Edam: Hoogheemraadschap van Uitwaterende Sluizen, 1994).
71 Boschma-Aarnoudse, *Tot verbeteringe van de neeringe*, 233, 281–3.
72 Space requirements were also responsible for the status of the north-eastern part of Voorhaven rising over time. In the second half of the sixteenth century, well-to-do timber merchants settled there, setting up their timber yards along the water of Voorhaven (ibid., 283–5).
73 Boschma-Aarnoudse, *Edam, behouden stad*, 248.
74 'rebellen, onstuirijgen ende moetwilligen luije rabbouwen' (Speet, *Edam*, 296 and 202).

75 Boschma-Aarnoudse, *Tot verbeteringe van de neeringe*, 356-7.
76 The following is mainly based on Jerzy Gawronski, 'Ontstaan uit een storm. De vroegste geschiedenis van Amsterdam archeologisch en landschappelijk belicht', *Jaarboek Amstelodamum* 109 (2017): 54-91 and Ranjith Jayasena, 'Amsterdam 1200-1300, stadswording aan de monding van de Amstel', Ibid., 113-49.
77 Jayasena, 'Amsterdam 1200-1300', 121.
78 R. E. van der Leeuw-Kistemaker, *Wonen en werken in de Warmoesstraat van de 14de tot het midden van de 16de eeuw* (Amsterdam: Historisch Seminarium van de Universiteit van Amsterdam, 1974), 95-6. Nieuwendijk lost part of its attraction after the construction of a quay on the west side of the river Amstel (Op 't Water / Damrak) in the first half of the sixteenth century.
79 Marcel IJsselstijn and Reinout Rutte, 'Meer dan honderdtwintig steden en ruim veertig mislukkingen. Vijfhonderd jaar stadswording in Nederland (elfde-vijftiende eeuw)', *Amstelodamum* 109 (2017): 37.
80 Van der Leeuw-Kistemaker, *Wonen en werken in de Warmoesstraat*, 7, 88-91. Those who could hold their own were the soap-boilers, but that is not surprising since they were often members of the city council themselves (ibid., 53).
81 Earlier, around 1413, the city council had already banned brothels to the urban periphery and the area outside Regulierspoort. Everywhere else it was forbidden to keep brothels (Maarten Hell, *De Amsterdamse herberg 1450-1800. Geestrijk centrum van het openbare leven* (Nijmegen: Vantilt, 2017), 39).
82 A. Margaretha van Gelder, *Amsterdamsche straatnamen geschiedkundig verklaard* (Amsterdam: P. N. van Kampen & Zoon, 1913), 82.
83 Gabri van Tussenbroek, 'Geografie van arm en rijk. Het kohier van de tiende penning van Amsterdam (1562) in GIS', *Tijdschrift voor Historische Geografie* 3 (2018): 251 and 252 for a map showing the location of fullers in 1562.
84 See also Van Tussenbroek, 'Voor de grote uitleg. Stedelijke transformatie en huisbouw in Amsterdam, 1452-1578', *Stadsgeschiedenis* 10 (2015): 1-23.
85 J. C. Breen, 'De verordeningen op het bouwen te Amsterdam vóór de negentiende eeuw', *Jaarboek Amstelodamum* 6 (1908): 127-8, and S. A. C. Dudok van Heel, 'Regent Families and Urban Development in Amsterdam', in *Rome - Amsterdam. Two Growing Cities in Seventeenth-Century Europe*, ed. Peter van Kessel and Elisja Schulte (Amsterdam: Amsterdam University Press, 1997), 127-8.
86 Clé Lesger, *Shopping Spaces and the Urban Landscape in Early Modern Amsterdam, 1550-1850* (Amsterdam: Amsterdam University Press, 2020), figure 3.9, and Jaap Evert Abrahamse, *Metropolis in the Making. A Planning History of Amsterdam in the Dutch Golden Age* (Turnhout: Brepols, 2019), 349-51. For the following, see especially ibid., chapter 4.
87 Dudok van Heel, 'Regent Families and Urban Development', 132-3, and Abrahamse, *Metropolis in the Making*, 85.
88 'unbuyrlycke and periculose trades' (Abrahamse, *Metropolis in the Making*, 288). See ibid., 290-4 for the purchase of industrial premises on the residential canals and their replacement with residential houses.
89 Ibid., 294-7. Similar actions by neighbours in Leiden are mentioned in Walle, *Buurthouden*, 121-2.
90 Abrahamse, *Metropolis in the Making*, 310-12.
91 Ibid., 298-9.
92 Herengracht and Keizersgracht in Amsterdam were the exception, as walled-in houses were prohibited from the outset and the area was therefore inhabited by the

(very) well-to-do on the canals themselves and the middle classes in the side streets between these residential canals and in a small number of back streets.
93 The third basic element, the individual house, is included here when discussing blocks of houses.
94 However, this was the case in cities such as Elburg and Naarden, which were built by order of a lord (Reinout Rutte, Ko Visser and Wim Boerefijn, 'Stadsaanleg in de late middeleeuwen. Over bouwpercelen, straten en standaardmaten in Elburg en enige andere steden', *Bulletin KNOB* 102 (2003): 122–37).
95 Gerhard Curdes, 'Spatial Organization of Towns at the Level of the Smallest Urban Unit: Plots and Buildings', in *Urban Landscape Dynamics. A Multi-Level Innovation Process*, ed. Armando Montanari, Gerhard Curdes and Leslie Forsyth (Aldershot: Avebury, 1993), 285–6.
96 M. L. Craane, 'Spatial Patterns. The Late-Medieval and Early-Modern Economy of the Bailiwick of 's-Hertogenbosch from an Interregional, Regional and Local Spatial Perspective' (PhD thesis, Tilburg University, 2013), 151–63 speaks in this context of a 'topological layer', based on accessibility within the street network. A topological analysis of the location patterns of the retail business in Amsterdam in Lesger, *Shopping Spaces*. See also Rogier van Kooten, 'Antwerpen 1584. Oorlog en ongelijkheid in de stedelijke ruimte' (PhD thesis, Universiteit Antwerpen, 2020), chapter 6.
97 I follow here the analysis in *Patroon: lineaire, hiërarchische structuren en (gesloten) bouwblokken. Bouwprincipes historische stad* (Rotterdam: FlexusAWC, 2008). I thank Marcel van Winsen for making this study available to me. A similar approach is also taken in Rudolph Meischke, 'Städtischer Parzellenzuschnitt und Wohnhaustypen nach 1400', in *Hausbau in den Niederlanden, Jahrbuch für Hausforschung*, ed. G. Ulrich Großmann, Fred Kaspar, Klaus Freckmann, and Ulrich Klein (Marburg: Jonas Verlag, 1990). Following Hillier, Froy uses a dichotomy into a 'foreground network' and a 'background network' (Francesca Froy, 'Understanding the Spatial Organisation of Economic Activities in Early 19th Century Antwerp' *Journal of Space Syntax* 6 (2016): 226).
98 For Antwerp Maclot drew up a typology of houses based on the Bononiensis bird's-eye view from 1565, but unfortunately without relating the house types to locations within the city (Maclot, 'A Portrait Unmasked', 36–8).
99 For the following, see H. Sarfatij, 'Dutch Towns in the Formative Period (Ad 1000-1400). The Archaeology of Settlement and Building', in *Medieval Archaeology in the Netherlands. Studies Presented to H. H. van Regteren Altena*, ed. J. C. Besteman, J. M. Bos and H. A. Heidinga (Assen: Van Gorcum, 1990); Meischke, 'Städtischer Parzellenzuschnitt'; Meyer, 'Het bouwblok als microkosmos'; Boerefijn, 'De totstandkoming van de stedelijke vorm' and *Patroon: lineaire, hiërarchische structuren*. Long ago, Peteri also dealt with these issues. See for instance W. B. Peteri, *Overheidsbemoeiingen met de stedebouw tot aan de vrede van Münster* (Alkmaar: W. B., 1913), 141–4 and 197.
100 Sarfatij, 'Dutch Towns', 189.
101 Ibid., 191; Meyer, 'Het bouwblok als microkosmos', 252, and *Patroon: lineaire, hiërarchische structuren*.
102 The definition of block is taken from Meyer, 'Het bouwblok als microkosmos', 251. The whole process is graphically represented in Edwin D. Orsel, 'Zijn er nog "veel" middeleeuwse huizen in Leiden?', in *Dwars door de stad. Archeologische en bouwhistorische ontdekkingen in Leiden*, ed. Chrystel R. Brandenburgh (Leiden:

Primavera Pers; Dienst Bouwen en Wonen, 2007), 116–17, and in Orsel, 'Hausbau in Leiden', 246–7.

103 It is interesting to note that in a city like Enkhuizen, which was hit by a dramatic population decline from the second quarter of the seventeenth century, the process of 'block decay' went in exactly the opposite direction. First the houses on the secondary and tertiary structure disappeared and only when the demand for housing continued to decline did empty plots appear along the primary structure (Ronald Stenvert, 'Enkhuizen: Morphologie einer schrumpfenden vormodernen Stadt', in *Hausbau in Holland. Baugeschichte und Stadtentwicklung*, ed. Gabri van Tussenbroek, *Jahrbuch für Hausforschung* (Marburg: Jonas Verlag, 2010), 228–30, 239). For the demographic development of Enkhuizen, see R. T. H. Willemsen, *Enkhuizen tijdens de Republiek. Een economisch-historisch onderzoek naar stad en samenleving van de 16e tot de 19e eeuw* (Hilversum: Verloren, 1988), chapter 4.

104 IJsselstijn and Rutte observe similar processes for cities in all parts of the Netherlands (IJsselstijn and Rutte, 'Meer dan honderdtwintig steden', 37–8).

105 Wim Weve, *Huizen in Delft in de 16de en 17de eeuw* (Zwolle: WBooks, 2013), 17–19, and Verhoeven, *De derde stad*, 187–9.

106 See for example Weve, *Huizen in Delft*, 19, 29, 34 and 43. I thank Museum Prinsenhof Delft for making a scan of this map available to me.

107 Jayasena, 'Amsterdam 1200-1300', 140–1, and Jan Baart, 'De ontstaansgeschiedenis van Amsterdam', in *Van stadskern tot stadsgewest. Stedebouwkundige geschiedenis van Amsterdam*, ed. Michiel Jonker, Leo Noordegraaf and Michiel Wagenaar (Amsterdam: Verloren, 1984), 22, 25.

108 The undivided plots between Nieuwezijds Voorburgwal and Nieuwezijds Achterburgwal (present-day Spuistraat) on the 1832 cadastral map still remind us of the old situation. See also Van Tussenbroek, 'Geografie van arm en rijk', 250.

109 T. ten Cate, 'De topografie van de "Oude Zijde" van Amsterdam in de 14e eeuw. Onderzoekingen naar de bruikbaarheid en de waarde van het middeleeuwse oorkondenmateriaal als bron voor topografisch onderzoek' (MA dissertation, Universiteit van Amsterdam, 1989), 82, 97.

110 A single building on the quay along the river Amstel has no entrance and apparently functions as the back part of the house on Kalverstraat. The first traces of infilling are also visible.

111 Boschma-Aarnoudse, *Tot verbeteringe van de neeringe*, 205.

112 The manuscript map by Taems Sijmonsz. from 1567 confirms this situation (see the illustrations in Boschma-Aarnoudse, *Edam, behouden stad*, 318–19, and Speet, *Edam*, 286). The map by Van Deventer has been made accessible via Biblioteca Digital Hispánica (Biblioteca Nacional de España).

113 Boschma-Aarnoudse, *Edam, behouden stad*, 24.

114 The map by Joan Blaeu was published in 1698 by Frederik de Wit (see https://www.kb.nl/themas/atlassen/stedenatlas-de-wit). Based on her long experience with the urban development and architectural history of Edam, Boschma-Aarnoudse argues that the number of houses, the number of floors per house, the gardens and the outbuildings are depicted reliably on Blaeu's map (ibid., 257).

115 Bourdieu, 'Social Space and Appropriated Physical Space', 107.

116 C. van de Kieft, 'Perspectief van de Hollandse stad', in *De Hollandse stad in de dertiende eeuw*, ed. E. H. P. Cordfunke, F. W. N Hugenholtz and K. Sierksma (Zutphen: Walburg Pers, 1988), 116.

117 Baart, 'De materiële stadskultuur', 96 and 106.

118 Catherine Casson and Mark Casson, 'Location, Location, Location? Analysing Property Rents in Medieval Gloucester', *Economic History Review* 69 (2016): 593-4.
119 Within these fossilized structures, however, changes were possible, according to research into the situation in Bruges by Heidi Deneweth, Ward Leloup and Mathijs Speecke as reported in 'Een versteende ruimte? De impact van stedelijke veranderingsprocessen op de sociale geografie van Brugge, 1380-1670', *Stadsgeschiedenis* 13 (2018): 19-40.
120 John Summerson, *Georgian London* (London: Barrie & Jenkins, 1988), 22-7 and chapters 7, 12 and 14; Donald J. Olsen, *The Growth of Victorian London* (London: Batsford, 1976), chapter 4, and see also Michiel Wagenaar, *Stedebouw en burgerlijke vrijheid. De constrasterende carrières van zes Europese hoofdsteden* (Bussum: Thoth, 1998), 114-18.
121 Hilary Ballon, *The Paris of Henri IV. Architecture and Urbanism* (New York: The Architectural History Foundation; Cambridge, MA: The MIT Press, 1991), chapter 2.
122 See the appendix for a detailed report on this trend.
123 This map and the following ones are also included in the appendix, which also discusses the sources on which these maps are based. For this particular map of Amsterdam, I was allowed to use a dataset created by my colleague Gabri van Tussenbroek. For this I am grateful to him.
124 Emrys Jones, 'London in the Early Seventeenth Century: An Ecological Appraoch', *The London Journal* 6 (1980): 128-33, and D. J. Keene, 'Suburban Growth', in *The English Medieval Town. A Reader in English Urban History*, ed. Richard Holt and Gervase Rosser (London: Longman, 1990), 117. For the social topography of London in the late seventeenth century, see also Spence, *London in the 1690s*, Chapter 4 and especially Figure 4.4 and 106-12.
125 Natacha Coquery, 'Shopping Streets in Eighteenth-Century Paris. A Landscape Shaped by Historical, Economic and Social Forces', in *The Landscape of Consumption. Shopping Streets and Cultures in Western Europe, 1600-1900*, ed. Jan Hein Furnée and Clé Lesger (Houndmills: Palgrave Macmillan, 2014), 64.
126 The proximity to the city centre also ensured that the wealthy residents of the ring of canals did not have to cross working-class neighbourhoods on their way to the city centre. In London, some of the poorest neighbourhoods of the city were located around the fleet immediately west of the City and therefore in the direction of Westminster (Jones, 'London in the Early Seventeenth Century', 132).
127 Bob Pierik, 'Urban Life on the Move. Gender and Mobility in Early Modern Amsterdam' (PhD thesis, Universiteit van Amsterdam, 2022), 188-99.
128 Mark Jenner, 'Circulation and Disorder. London Streets and Hackney Coaches, *c.* 1640-*c.* 1740', in *The Streets of London; from the Great Fire to the Great Stink*, ed. Tim Hitchcock and Heather Shore (London: Rivers Oram Press, 2003), 41, and Spence, *London in the 1690s*, 34-6.
129 Spence, *London in the 1690s*, 36. The reconstruction of the City after the Great Fire of 1666 also made London more suitable for vehicular traffic than the essentially medieval street pattern of the centre of Amsterdam.
130 For the economic dynamics in Amsterdam in the decades around 1600, see Oscar Gelderblom, 'From Antwerp to Amsterdam. The Contribution of Merchants from the Southern Netherlands to the Commercial Expansion of Amsterdam (*c.* 1540-1609)', *Review (Fernand Braudel Center)* 26 (2003): 247-82; Clé Lesger, *The Rise of the Amsterdam Market and Information Exchange; Merchants, Commercial Expansion*

and *Change in the Spatial Economy of the Low Countries, c. 1550-1630* (Aldershot: Ashgate, 2006) and idem, 'De wereld als horizon. De economie tussen 1578 en 1650', in *Geschiedenis van Amsterdam. Centrum van de wereld 1578-1650*, ed. Willem Frijhoff and Maarten Prak (Amsterdam: SUN, 2004).

131 But unlike in Amsterdam, Oude Gracht in Alkmaar did not lose its appeal as a result of the development of even more attractive locations, as was the case with Singel in Amsterdam when Herengracht and Keizersgracht were developed.

132 Paul Burm and Guus J. Borger, 'De stichting van Friedrichstadt in 1621. Sociale segregatie in een geplande nederzetting', *Bulletin KNOB* 102 (2003): 170–85.

133 Burm and Borger have found no evidence that the social and spatial design of Friedrichstadt can be traced back to the religious views of these Arminians (ibid., 184).

134 Ibid., 179, 182.

135 See ibid., image 5.

136 In the trading settlements in Asia, the VOC pursued a policy of residential segregation based on ethnicity, but the reality was much more complex (R. van Oers, *Dutch Town Planning Overseas During VOC and WIC Rule (1600-1800)* (Zutphen: Walburg Pers, 2000), 94–6, 131). Remco Raben, 'Colonial Shorthand and Historical Knowledge: Segregation and Localisation in a Dutch Colonial Society', *Journal of Modern European History* 18 (2020): 179 describes colonial Batavia (present-day Jakarta in Indonesia) as 'a society of different and overlapping socio-cultural spheres and as circles of trust rather than of bounded ethnic communities'.

137 'de achterhuysen die gemeenlicken in achterstraten uytgaen ende meest bij de schamele bewoont werden mitte voorhuysen gebuyrschappe zouden moeten houden' (cited in Walle, *Buurthouden*, 53 and 64). A similar development occurred in The Hague, where from the second half of the seventeenth century, elites no longer participated in communal neighbourhood festivities (Thera Wijsenbeek, 'Schutters, gilden en buurten', in *Den Haag. Geschiedenis van de stad*, vol. 2, *De tijd van de Republiek*, ed. Th. Wijsenbeek (Zwolle: Waanders, 2005), 176) and in Haarlem, where wealthy people were able, in return for payment, to evade the obligation to attend the funerals of (less affluent) neighbourhood residents (Dorren, *Eenheid in verscheidenheid*, 78).

138 Alfani and Ryckbosch, 'Growing Apart in Early Modern Europe?', 145–6 and in particular figure 2. The authors used rental values for Alkmaar, Delft, Amsterdam, Hoorn, Rotterdam and Dordrecht. For the growing inequality in Holland and elsewhere, see also Ryckbosch, 'Economic Inequality and Growth' and the contributions in Blondé et al., eds, *Inequality and the City*. Growing economic inequality in Amsterdam in Clé Lesger, 'Economic Growth, Social Differentiation and the Reshaping of the Urban Landscape in Amsterdam During Its Golden Age', in *The English Urban Renaissance Revisited*, ed. John Hinks and Catherine Armstrong (Cambridge Scholars, 2018), 192–7.

139 Van Ravesteyn Jr, *Onderzoekingen*, 273 ff.

140 Van Gelder, *De levensbeschouwing van C. P. Hooft*, 22–3.

141 Joop de Jong, *Een deftig bestaan. Het dagelijks leven van regenten in de 17de en 18de eeuw* (Utrecht: Kosmos, 1987), 156.

142 'van het mindere zoort uwer medeaanschouwers' (cited in Medema, *Achter de façade van de Hollandse stad*, 286).

143 This development had a parallel in the growing cultural distance of literate middle classes and elites from popular culture in Europe since the sixteenth century (Peter

Burke, *Popular Culture in Early Modern Europe* (London: Temple Smith, 1979), 270–81).
144 See also Friedrichs, *The Early Modern City 1450-1750*, 10.
145 Bourdieu, 'Social Space and Appropriated Physical Space', 110.
146 The following is based on Gerdy Verschuur-Stuip and Hans Renes, 'Hollandse buitenplaatsenlandschappen. Buitenplaatsen en hun relatie met het landschap (1609-1672)', in *Buitenplaatsen in de Gouden Eeuw: de rijkdom van het buitenleven in de Republiek*, ed. Y. Kuiper, B. Olde Meierink and E. Storms-Smeets (Hilversum: Verloren, 2015); Rob van der Laarse, 'Amsterdam en Oranje: de politieke cultuur van kasteel en buitenplaats in Hollands Gouden Eeuw', ibid; René W.Chr. Dessing, *De Amsterdamse buitenplaatsen. Een vergeten stadsgeschiedenis* (Utrecht: Matrijs, 2015) and C. Boschma-Aarnoudse, *Buitenplaatsen in de Purmer. Investeren en buiten leven in een Noord-Hollandse polder* (Stichting Uitgeverij Noord-Holland, 2016).
147 See Jan de Vries, *Barges and Capitalism. Passenger Transportation in the Dutch Economy, 1632-1839* (Utrecht: HES publishers, 1981), map 2.2 for the network of canals in 1665. In France in the eighteenth century, a *maison de campagne* also became popular with wealthy shopkeepers, master craftsmen, merchants and other members of the middle classes (D. Garrioch, *Neighbourhood and Community in Paris 1740-1790* (Cambridge: Cambridge University Press, 1986), 172).
148 Van der Laarse, 'Amsterdam en Oranje', 78–9, and see the map in Dessing, *De Amsterdamse buitenplaatsen*, 11.
149 Cited in Van der Laarse, 'Amsterdam en Oranje', 79.
150 Bourdieu, 'Social Space and Appropriated Physical Space', 108.
151 This is also what Duncan argues in his study of the city of Kandy in Sri Lanka: 'By becoming part of the everyday, the taken-for-granted, the objective, and the natural, the landscape masks the artifice and ideological nature of its form and content. Its history as a social construction is unexamined.' (James S. Duncan, *The City as Text: The Politics of Landscape Interpretation in the Kandy Kingdom* (Cambridge: Cambridge University Press, 1990), 19).
152 Bourdieu, 'Social Space and Appropriated Physical Space', 107 speaks of 'the effect of naturalization'.
153 See also Charles Tilly, 'What Good Is Urban History?', *Journal of Urban History* 22 (1996): 711.
154 Bourdieu, 'Social Space and Appropriated Physical Space', 112, and above, chapter 2, section 1.

Chapter 4

1 Ephemeral forms of appropriating urban space play an important role in Michel de Certeau, *The Practice of Everyday Life* (Berkeley: University of California Press, 1984), but his bipolar model of society, in which powerful individuals and institutions (producers of space) stand in opposition to the virtually powerless users of that space, is not in keeping with the interpretation of power used in this study. Here, after all, power is seen as a relational effect of social interaction, with the context in which that interaction takes place largely determining the balance of power (see the introduction). Criticism of De Certeau's bipolar model of society in John Frow,

Cultural Studies and Cultural Value (Oxford: Clarendon Press, 1995), 47-59, and Tony Bennett, *Culture. A Reformer's Science* (London: Sage, 1998), 174-88.

2   Richard Sennett, *Together: The Rituals, Pleasures, and Politics of Cooperation* (New Haven: Yale University Press, 2012), 89-93, distinguishes three building blocks of ritual: repetition; the transformation of objects, gestures and words into symbols; and thirdly dramatic expression. All these elements can be found in the violent appropriation of urban space that is the focus of this chapter. For rituals, see also David I. Kertzer, *Ritual, Politics, and Power* (New Haven: Yale University Press, 1988), chapter 1, and Edward Muir, *Rituals in Early Modern Europe* (Cambridge: Cambridge University Press, 1997), Introduction. The theatrical nature of violence receives much attention in Antoon Vrints, *Het theater van de straat. Publiek geweld in Antwerpen tijdens de eerste helft van de twintigste eeuw* (Amsterdam: Amsterdam University Press, 2011).

3   A survey of political manifestations with a ritual character in early modern cities in Maartje van Gelder, 'Street Politics', in *Early Modern Streets. A European Perspective*, ed. Danielle van den Heuvel (Abingdon, Oxon: Routledge, 2022).

4   'die menselijke handeling, die erop gericht is de fysieke integriteit van personen of groepen aan te tasten en die tot doel heeft de gedragsalternatieven van personen of groepen te beperken' (Piet van Reenen, *Overheidsgeweld; een sociologische studie van de dynamiek van het geweldsmonopolie* (Alphen aan den Rijn: Samson, 1979), 18).

5   Violent damage to objects is explicitly included in the more general definition of violence borrowed by Achterhuis from Boeykens: 'the more or less intentional infliction or threat of inflicting damage to people or objects' (Hans Achterhuis, *Met alle geweld. Een filosofische zoektocht* (Rotterdam: Lemniscaat, 2008), 78).

6   Van Reenen, *Overheidsgeweld*, 19. The latter we also see in states where the government uses terror to stay in power. This violent form of exercising power also has its limits, though. See for this ibid., 20-1.

7   Michel Foucault, *Discipline and Punish. The Birth of the Prison* (New York: Vintage books, 1995), 3-6, for a much more comprehensive and detailed description of the execution.

8   Pieter Spierenburg, *The Spectacle of Suffering. Executions and the Evolution of Repression: From a Preindustrial Metropolis to the European Experience* (Cambridge: Cambridge University Press, 1984), 73-4, for more examples and see for more information about the 1746 murder case the description in Jacob Bicker Raije's chronicle (Machiel Bosman, *De polsslag van de stad. De Amsterdamse kroniek van Jacob Bicker Raije (1732-1772)*) (Amsterdam: Athenaeum - Polak & Van Gennep, 2009), 93-7. Breaking on the wheel 'from below' means that the victim was not first killed before the bones were smashed with an iron bar.

9   For the following, see Sjoerd Faber, *Strafrechtspleging en criminaliteit in Amsterdam, 1680-1811. De nieuwe menslievendheid* (Arnhem: Gouda Quint, 1983), 154-8; Spierenburg, *The Spectacle of Suffering*, 66-77, and Florike Egmond, 'Fragmentatie, rechtsverscheidenheid en rechtsongelijkheid in de Noordelijke Nederlanden tijdens de zeventiende en achttiende eeuw', in *Nieuw licht op oude justitie. Misdaad en straf ten tijde van de Republiek*, ed. Sjoerd Faber (Muiderberg: Dick Coutinho, 1989).

10 Because a great deal of research has been done into criminal justice in Amsterdam, much of what follows will refer to legal practice in that city.

11 Spierenburg, *The Spectacle of Suffering*, 68, and see for an eyewitness account from 1827 Herman Franke, *De dood in het leven van alledag. Twee eeuwen*

rouwadvertenties en openbare strafvoltrekkingen in Nederland (Den Haag: Nijgh & Van Ditmar, 1985), 99, where the number of sixty is mentioned.

12 'met de strop om den hals onder de galg en met het pistool boven zijn hoofd gegeeselt' (Jori Zijlmans, 'In handen van justitie', in *Den Haag. Geschiedenis van de stad*, vol. 2, *De tijd van de Republiek*, ed. Th. Wijsenbeek (Zwolle: Waanders, 2005), 124).

13 For branding, see also C. L. ten Cate, *Tot glorie der gerechtigheid. De geschiedenis van het brandmerken als lijfstraf in Nederland* (Amsterdam: Wetenschappelijke Uitgeverij, 1975). Recidivism was an important factor in determining the sentence (Egmond, 'Fragmentatie', 14–15).

14 Maarten Müller, *Misdaad en straf in een Hollandse stad: Haarlem, 1245-1615* (Hilversum: Verloren, 2017), 62. It is noteworthy that a few decades earlier in Haarlem there had been an increase in this type of punishment. Local factors could thus apparently strongly influence the practice of criminal law in the short term (ibid., 90). For the situation in Amsterdam, see Jan Wagenaar, *Amsterdam, in zyne opkomst, aanwas, geschiedenissen, voorregten, koophandel, gebouwen, kerkenstaat, schoolen, schutterye, gilden en regeeringe* (Amsterdam: Isaak Tirion, 1760-1767), part VII, book I, 314.

15 Faber, *Strafrechtspleging en criminaliteit*, 157. As in Germany and England public scaffold punishments in Holland also had the purpose of dishonouring the convict (Richard J. Evans, *Rituals of Retribution. Capital Punishment in Germany 1600-1987* (Oxford: Oxford University Press, 1996), 53–6, and Martin Ingram, 'Shame and Pain: Themes and Variations in Tudor Punishments', in *Penal Practice and Culture, 1500-1900. Punishing the English*, ed. Simon Devereaux and Paul Griffiths (Houndmills: Palgrave MacMillan, 2004)).

16 Also depicted here is the *Roede van Justitie* (Rod of Justice), which was stuck out the window of Amsterdam's town hall during the execution of punishments.

17 A spindle (*spinrok*) is the stick on which the wool or flax to be spun is put.

18 Foucault, *Discipline and Punish*, 34–5.

19 Wagenaar, *Amsterdam, in zyne opkomst*, part VII, book I, 314.

20 In Wagenaar's time the city government of Amsterdam apparently deployed soldiers at executions. Elsewhere, maintaining order at public executions was mainly a task of the civic militia.

21 Wagenaar, *Amsterdam, in zyne opkomst*, part VII, book I, 318, and Spierenburg, *The Spectacle of Suffering*, 59.

22 For the ritualistic and theatrical nature of public punishment in Germany, see Evans, *Rituals of Retribution*, chapter 2, and for the in some respects very similar procedure during the Spanish *autos-de-fe* Ruiz, *Spanish Society*, 155–60.

23 In Haarlem, public prayers for forgiveness (kneeling and bare headed) were part of the repertoire of punishments (Müller, *Misdaad en straf, 1245-1615*, 101).

24 Nicholas Terpstra, 'Theory into Practice: Executions, Comforting, and Comforters in Renaissance Italy', in *The Art of Executing Well. Rituals of Execution in Renaissance Italy*, ed. Nicholas Terpstra (Kirksville: Truman State University Press, 2008), 122–5. In Italy, those sentenced to death were not assisted by clergymen, but by lay brotherhoods known as conforteries (ibid., 1).

25 Spierenburg, *The Spectacle of Suffering*, 64–5.

26 For the numbers of property crimes and their punishments, see tables 10–12 in Faber, *Strafrechtspleging en criminaliteit*.

27 'had bij voorbaat een slechte naam' (Egmond, 'Fragmentatie', 14).

28 Egmond, 'De boeven van Coornhert', in *Scherp toezicht; van 'Boeventucht' tot 'Samenleving en criminaliteit'*, ed. Cyrille Fijnaut and Pieter Spierenburg (Arnhem: Gouda Quint, 1990), 105, and see also Faber, *Strafrechtspleging en criminaliteit*, 266.
29 Spierenburg, *The Spectacle of Suffering*, 157–8. As in Holland, in Germany too there was a clear connection between the status of a person and the nature of the scaffold punishment (Evans, *Rituals of Retribution*, 53–64).
30 In Rome, convicted aristocrats were spared the humiliation of public execution. Rebecchini argues that this was not only to protect the honour of their families, but also – and possibly more importantly – to prevent a public undermining of the existing social hierarchy (Guido Rebecchini, 'Rituals of Justice and the Construction of Space in Sixteenth-Century Rome', *I Tatti Studies in the Italian Renaissance* 16 (2013): 157). More research is needed to establish whether this was also an argument in allowing financial settlements in Holland.
31 Zijlmans, 'In handen van justitie', 124–6.
32 'strafrechtelijk onheil' (Faber, *Strafrechtspleging en criminaliteit*, 300, 321). That the possession of cultural and social capital made a difference is also shown by the fact that during the 1696 Aansprekersoproer, a boy 'from a good family' who had been sentenced to death was released through the intercession of clergymen (Joris Craffurd, 'Een generaal en kort verhaal (Aansprekersoproer 1696)', in *Oproeren in Holland gezien door tijdgenoten. Ooggetuigenverslagen van oproeren in de provincie Holland ten tijde van de Republiek (1690-1750)*, ed. R. M. Dekker (Assen: Van Gorcum, 1979), 85).
33 Calculated on the basis of Spierenburg, *The Spectacle of Suffering*, 82, table 1.
34 In Amsterdam, in the years 1693–1766, 57 per cent of the bodies of those executed were exhibited on Volewijk, the gallows field of Amsterdam (H. G. Jelgersma, *Galgebergen en galgevelden in West- en Midden Nederland* (Zutphen: De Walburg Pers, 1978), 31).
35 A non-exhaustive overview of gallows fields in Holland can be found in ibid., and see also Spierenburg, *The Spectacle of Suffering*, 57–8.
36 Spierenburg, *The Spectacle of Suffering*, 58–9, 97–8.
37 Foucault, *Discipline and Punish*, 6–7, the quotation on page 8.
38 Ibid., 9.
39 Herman Franke, 'Opkomst en neergang van eenzame opsluiting. Historisch-sociologische verklaringen en lange-termijn ontwikkelingen binnen het gevangeniswezen in de westerse wereld', in *Scherp toezicht; van 'Boeventucht' tot 'Samenleving en criminaliteit'*, ed. Cyrille Fijnaut and Pieter Spierenburg (Arnhem: Gouda Quint, 1990), 169–70.
40 Ibid., 175; Sjoerd Faber, 'Een zachte botsing. Celstraf en schavot te Amsterdam in 1854', in *Criminaliteit in de negentiende eeuw*, ed. Sjoerd Faber et al. (Hilversum: Verloren, 1989), 69, and Pieter Spierenburg, 'Boeventucht en vrijheidsstraffen. Coornherts betekenis voor het ontstaan en de ontwikkeling van het gevangeniswezen in Nederland', in *Scherp toezicht; van 'Boeventucht' tot 'Samenleving en criminaliteit'*, ed. Cyrille Fijnaut and Pieter Spierenburg (Arnhem: Gouda Quint, 1990). The empirical critique of Foucault's *Discipline and punish* is in line with Elden's conclusion that the significance of Foucault's work lies not so much in the concrete analysis of historical developments, but in the concepts he developed and the themes he called attention to (Stuart Elden, *Foucault. The Birth of Power* (Cambridge: Polity, 2017), 188). See also Evans, *Rituals of Retribution*, 880–91, for a critique of *Discipline and Punish* and a reflection on the intellectual, social and political context in which that book was written.

41 Spierenburg, *The Spectacle of Suffering*, chapter 1 and the conclusion, and also the pages 77–80, and Franke, *De dood in het leven van alledag*, 87 and 155.
42 Norbert Elias, *The Civilizing Process. Sociogenetic and Psychogenetic Investigations* (Oxford: Blackwell, 1994).
43 Ibid., part II, in particular the synopsis 'Towards a theory of civilizing processes'.
44 Spierenburg, *The Spectacle of Suffering*, ix.
45 Evans, *Rituals of Retribution*, 891–4, for a critical evaluation of the work of Elias and Spierenburg.
46 Müller, *Misdaad en straf, 1245-1615*, 88.
47 Ibid., 89–90. In a more recent publication the author seeks an explanation for the trend in Haarlem in urban corporatism and evolutionary psychology (*Misdaad en Straf in een Hollandse Stad: Haarlem, 1673-1811* (Hilversum: Verloren, 2022), 85–8).
48 Guy Geltner, *Flogging Others: Corporal Punishment and Cultural Identity from Antiquity to the Present* (Amsterdam: Amsterdam University Press, 2014), 9 and 62–3.
49 Ibid., 12.
50 Evans, *Rituals of Retribution*, 895, and see also for example Robert B. Shoemaker, 'Streets of Shame? The Crowd and Public Punishments in London, 1700-1820', in *Penal Practice and Culture, 1500-1900. Punishing the English*, ed. Simon Devereaux and Paul Griffiths (Houndmills: Palgrave MacMillan, 2004).
51 Evans, *Rituals of Retribution*, 901.
52 Shoemaker, 'Streets of Shame?', 241. For the situation in England, see also Paul Griffiths, 'Introduction: Punishing the English', In *Penal Practice and Culture, 1500-1900. Punishing the English*, ed. Simon Devereaux and Paul Griffiths (Houndmills: Palgrave MacMillan, 2004), 1–35. The thinking on penal policy during the Enlightenment and the influence of Cesare Beccaria is discussed in Evans, *Rituals of Retribution*, 127–33, and in Randall McGowan, 'The Problem of Punishment in Eighteenth-Century England', in *Penal Practice and Culture, 1500-1900. Punishing the English*, ed. Simon Devereaux and Paul Griffiths (Houndmills: Palgrave MacMillan, 2004).
53 Shoemaker explains the latter by the growing importance of pamphlets/printing as a means of damaging reputations (Shoemaker, 'Streets of Shame?', 247–53). Evans, *Rituals of Retribution*, 903 points to Germany's transition from a traditional 'society of orders', in which honour and status were central, to a class society in which these lost significance and the public disgrace of the convicted person's body '[was] placed out as ineffective and unnecessary'.
54 For the discussion at that time on the desirability and effect of imprisonment, see Franke, 'Opkomst en neergang', and also the contributions by Diederiks, Faber and Franke in Sjoerd Faber et al., eds, *Criminaliteit in de negentiende eeuw* (Hilversum: Verloren, 1989).
55 Franke, *De dood in het leven van alledag*, 94.
56 Ibid., 130–8.
57 Ibid., 105.
58 Ibid., 105, 135–7, 151.
59 'het indrukwekkende aanzien van het schavot, als zijnde in rouwfloers gehuld'. Quoted in ibid., 140, and see ibid. 109 for the number of people attending public punishments in Amsterdam.
60 Ibid., and see also Faber, 'Een zachte botsing', 80.
61 Franke, *De dood in het leven van alledag*, 142.

62 Maarten Prak, 'Corporate Politics in the Low Countries. Guilds as Institutions, 14th-18th Centuries', in *Craft Guilds in the Early Modern Low Countries. Work, Power, and Representation*, ed. Maarten Prak et al. (Aldershot: Ashgate, 2006), 88–9 and 104–6.
63 For a more detailed description of these processions in Amsterdam, see A. J. M. Brouwer Ancher, *De gilden* (Den Haag: Loman & Funke, 1895), 228–32.
64 M. Carasso-Kok, 'Der stede scut. De schuttersgilden in de Hollandse steden tot het einde der zestiende eeuw', in *Schutters in Holland. Kracht en zenuwen van de stad*, ed. M. Carasso-Kok and J. Levy-van Halm (Zwolle: Waanders, 1988), 23–5.
65 Ibid., 23, and Knevel, *Burgers in het geweer*, chapter 1 and especially 47.
66 Carasso-Kok, 'Der stede scut', 23–9, and Knevel, *Burgers in het geweer*, chapter 6.
67 In The Hague, the social distinction within the militia-guilds was demonstrated by the exemption of nobles from the obligation to wear the prescribed clothing (Jeanne Verbij-Schillings and Monique van Veen, 'Cultuur, literatuur en onderwijs', in *Den Haag. Geschiedenis van de stad*, vol. 1, *Vroegste tijd tot 1574*, ed. J. G. Smit (Zwolle: Waanders, 2004)), 330.
68 'felle, agressieve kleuren'(Carasso-Kok, 'Der stede scut', 23).
69 Knevel, *Burgers in het geweer*, chapters 2 and 3; Marc Boone and Maarten Prak, 'Rulers, Patricians and Burghers: The Great and the Little Traditions of Urban Revolt in the Low Countries', in *A Miracle Mirrored. The Dutch Republic in European Perspective*, ed. Karel Davids and Jan Lucassen (Cambridge: Cambridge University Press, 1995), 113–16.
70 Knevel, *Burgers in het geweer*, 93–4.
71 For the organizational structure of the civic militia, see ibid., chapter 4. Only a part of the citizenry was actually active in the militia. Especially the more affluent citizens bought off their obligations and others were exempted from active service (ibid., 189–90).
72 M. Carasso-Kok and J. Levy-van Halm, eds, *Schutters in Holland. Kracht en zenuwen van de stad* (Zwolle: Waanders, 1988), 214 and 235. The militarization of the militias is also expressed in the *schuttersstukken* (group portraits of the militias). After 1580, they show much more weapons and also the position of persons on the canvas reflects the hierarchical structure of the organization (J. B. Kist and J. P. Puype, 'Wapens op schutterstukken', in *Schutters in Holland. Kracht en zenuwen van de stad*, ed. M. Carasso-Kok and J. Levy-van Halm (Zwolle: Waanders, 1988), 167).
73 The following is mainly based on Knevel, *Burgers in het geweer*, 271–81.
74 Based on W. F. van Zegveld, 'Zilveren schutterspenningen van Leiden', *Leids Jaarboekje* 80 (1988): 62. The map is the 1649 edition of Joan Blaeu.
75 The situation in Leiden differs from that in other cities because Leiden lacked a central square. Elsewhere, that was the designated location for the ceremonial part of the *optrek*. Comparison with Map A.15 in the appendix shows that the route of the militias passed the residences of the wealthiest inhabitants of Leiden.
76 Knevel, *Burgers in het geweer*, 273.
77 According to the caption of the print (not shown here), the five regiments presented themselves on that occasion to the 'Groot Agtb: Heeren Burgemeesteren' (very esteemed lords burgomasters) of Amsterdam. In the lower margin of the print are the names of the colonel and captains of each regiment (not shown here).
78 See Kertzer, *Ritual, Politics, and Power*, 179–80, for the importance of emotional involvement in political rituals.

79 Knevel, *Burgers in het geweer*, 274.
80 The presentation of the militia in front of the town hall on Dam square and its representation in prints such as Figure 4.5 obviously reinforced the symbolic significance of Dam square as the centre of political power in Amsterdam. In Venice, the Piazza San Marco (including the Piazzetta) played a central role in the important rituals (Edward Muir, *Civic Ritual in Renaissance Venice* (Princeton: Princeton University Press, 1981), the map on page 9 and chapters 5 and 6, and Maartje van Gelder, 'Protest in the Piazza. Contested Space in Early Modern Venice', in *Popular Politics in an Aristocratic Republic: Political Conflict and Social Contestation in Late Medieval and Early Modern Venice*, ed. Maartje van Gelder and Claire Judde de Larivière (London: Routledge, 2020)).
81 Knevel, *Burgers in het geweer*, 220–38, and for the situation in The Hague see also Wijsenbeek, 'Schutters', 149–62.
82 Complaints of misconduct by the militiamen in Knevel, *Burgers in het geweer*, 229–30.
83 The maps are included in the image collection of Erfgoed Leiden en omgeving (https://www.erfgoedleiden.nl/). The map shown here (signature PV_PV371.8) is the best preserved, but copy PV_PV373.2 contains in the lower margin additional information on the *loopplaatsen*.
84 Counted on the basis of information on *loopplaatsen* at Erfgoed Leiden en omstreken, image collection PV_PV373.2.
85 This is particularly clear at Rapenburg. The same strategy obviously worked when the city was invaded by enemy armies. Bridges were also of strategic importance during riots in other cities (see e.g. Craffurd, 'Een generaal en kort verhaal', 74).
86 'komen de schutters terstondt in de Wapenen, elck op sijn Wijck besetten de Wegen, stuyten het woedende Volck, ende met een vaendel Burghers bewaren sy 't Stadt-huys' (quoted in Paul Knevel, 'De kracht en zenuwen van de Republiek. De schutterijen in Holland, 1580-1650', in *Schutters in Holland. Kracht en zenuwen van de stad*, ed. M. Carasso-Kok and J. Levy-van Halm (Zwolle: Waanders, 1988), 44).
87 Dekker, *Oproeren in Holland* and idem, *Holland in beroering*.
88 Craffurd, 'Een generaal en kort verhaal', 51 and 65.
89 'van boven tot beneden schrickelijck met bloed bespat ende besoetelt [was]. Het vloeijde langhs de trappen en op de vloer als water ...' (ibid., 75–6). The bloody action of the militia is also mentioned in a letter from 1696 from Lijsbet Heere to her son-in-law in Haarlem (Dekker, *Oproeren in Holland*, 116).
90 Craffurd, 'Een generaal en kort verhaal', 78.
91 'om de beveelen van de heeren van de magistraat punctelijck op te volgen ...' (ibid., 79).
92 'groote schrick en vrees onder het gemeen' (ibid., 82) and see also Dekker, *Oproeren in Holland*, 78 and 116 for this equestrian force.
93 'het gemeen seer omsigtig weezen [deed] en een ijder wierd als met schrick bevangen ...' (Craffurd, 'Een generaal en kort verhaal', 82).
94 'de Raet van Amsterdam / vereert Haere Burgers deese Penningh / tot vergeldingh van Haer Oude Dueght / en Bevonde Trouheyt. The text on the medal is included on the print commemorating the Aansprekersoproer (figure 4.6).
95 "t Roofgierig graauw, belust op Burger-buyt'. The quotation is in the text box at the bottom right of the print. See also Knevel, *Burgers in het geweer*, 242–3, for this print.
96 'de geheele stad een algemene plundering zoude overstroomt hebben' (Craffurd, 'Een generaal en kort verhaal', 77).

97 Carasso-Kok, 'Der stede scut', 31.
98 For the system of farmed taxes, see J. A. F. de Jongste, *Onrust aan het Spaarne. Haarlem in de jaren 1747-1751* (Amsterdam: De Bataafsche Leeuw, 1984), 42–5.
99 'dat zij zich voor geen pachter in enig gevaar wilden begeven of zich daarvoor in de waagschaal stellen'; 'dat zij niet voor de pachters zouden in de bres springen ofte voor haar huizen staan, ja veel minder haar te salveren van verdere onheilen' (quoted in Dekker, *Holland in beroering*, 103). For Haarlem, see also De Jongste, *Onrust aan het Spaarne*, 180–4.
100 Dekker, *Holland in beroering*, 103.
101 Boone and Prak, 'Rulers, Patricians and Burghers', 119, and Knevel, *Burgers in het geweer*, 337.
102 Boone and Prak, 'Rulers, Patricians and Burghers', 99–101.
103 For this theme, see also Van Nierop, 'Popular Participation'.
104 Dekker, *Holland in beroering*, 104, and for the relation between the Orange-stadtholders and the militia in The Hague, see also Zijlmans, 'In handen van justitie'.
105 On this insurgency, see Dekker, *Holland in beroering*, 42–4, and Knevel, *Burgers in het geweer*, 324–6.
106 For the activities of the militias in The Hague and the murder of the De Witt brothers, see Wijsenbeek, 'Schutters', and Zijlmans, 'In handen van justitie', 128–30.
107 Knevel, *Burgers in het geweer*, 346, note 101 and see 348–50 for the 'battle' between the militias and the burgomasters about the control of the city keys.
108 See Maarten Prak, 'Burgers in beweging. Ideaal en werkelijkheid van de onlusten te Leiden in 1748', *Bijdragen en Mededeelingen betreffende de Geschiedenis der Nederlanden* 16 (1991): 365–93.
109 Prak, 'Burgers in beweging', 383–90, and Boone and Prak, 'Rulers, Patricians and Burghers', 118.
110 Boone and Prak, 'Rulers, Patricians and Burghers', 121, and Remieg Aerts, 'Een staat in verbouwing. Van republiek naar constitutioneel koninkrijk, 1780-1848', in *Land van kleine gebaren. Een politieke geschiedenis van Nederland 1780-1990*, ed. Remieg Aerts et al. (Nijmegen: SUN, 1999), 19.
111 'de boodschap van het deugd- en verdraagzaam, productief en maatschappelijk betrokken burgerschap' (Aerts, 'Een Staat in Verbouwing', 24).
112 'Wapent Ulieden allen' (quoted in H. L. Zwitzer, 'De militaire dimensie van de patriottenbeweging', in *Voor vaderland en vrijheid. De revolutie van de patriotten*, ed. F. Grijzenhout, W. W. Mijnhardt and N. C. F. van Sas (Amsterdam: De Bataafsche Leeuw, 1987), 33–9, and Aerts, 'Een staat in verbouwing', 28–30).
113 For the problematic state of the militia in Haarlem around the middle of the eighteenth century, see De Jongste, *Onrust aan het Spaarne*, 153–4.
114 For the composition of the patriot movement, see F. Grijzenhout and N. C. F. van Sas, *Voor vaderland en vrijheid. Revolutie in Nederland 1780-1787* (Utrecht: Centraal Museum Utrecht, 1987), 8, and Aerts, 'Een staat in verbouwing', 29–30. The presence of the working classes in the Patriot movement is evidenced by the social composition of some refugee communities after the restoration of 1787, which came about with Prussian military aid (A. Doedens, 'De patriotse vluchtelingen', in *Voor vaderland en vrijheid. De revolutie van de patriotten*, ed. F. Grijzenhout, W. W. Mijnhardt and N. C. F. van Sas (Amsterdam: De Bataafsche Leeuw, 1987), 164–5).
115 F. Grijzenhout, 'De patriotse beeldenstorm', ibid., 138–46, and Grijzenhout and Van Sas, *Voor vaderland en vrijheid*, 32–3. In this appropriation, they consciously followed the tradition of the militias (Knevel, *Burgers in het geweer*, 373–4).

116 Indeed, in the Southern Low Countries, where middle classes had considerably more influence on the urban administration, this influence did not lead to fundamentally different power relations, but to what Blondé et al. call the Low Countries Paradox: 'strong middle classes reproduce social inequality' (Blondé et al., 'The Low Countries' Paradox').
117 Aerts, 'Een staat in verbouwing', 33–8.
118 Paul Knevel, 'Epiloog. De schutterijen na 1650', in *Schutters in Holland. Kracht en zenuwen van de stad*, ed. M. Carasso-Kok and J. Levy-van Halm (Zwolle: Waanders, 1988). For the problems of the militia in the 1840s and proposals to transform it into an elite corps, see R. van der Wal, *Of geweld zal worden gebruikt. Militaire bijstand bij de handhaving en het herstel van de openbare orde, 1840-1920* (Hilversum: Verloren, 2003), 80–1.
119 See for the history of the Dutch police Cyrille Fijnaut, *De geschiedenis van de Nederlandse politie. Een staatsinstelling in de maalstroom van de geschiedenis* (Amsterdam: Boom, 2007).
120 Max Weber, *Economy and Society. An Outline of Interpretive Sociology*, vol. II, ed. Guenther Roth and Claus Wittich (Berkeley: University of California Press, 1978), 997. The degree of bureaucratization in the Dutch Republic was relatively low. See Jos Gabriëls, 'Patrizier und Regenten: städtische Eliten in den Nördlichen Niederlanden 1500-1800', in *Bürgerliche Eliten in den Niederlanden und in Nordwestdeutschland*, ed. H. Schilling and H. A. Diederiks (Köln: Böhlau, 1985), 48, and especially Paul Knevel, *Het Haagse Bureau. Zeventiende-eeuwse ambtenaren tussen staatsbelang en eigenbelang* (Amsterdam: Prometheus; Bert Bakker, 2001), Introduction and 171.
121 See Max Weber, *Economy and Society. An Outline of Interpretive Sociology*, vol. I, ed. Guenther Roth and Claus Wittich (Berkeley: University of California Press, 1978), 220–1, and Idem, *Economy and Society*, vol. II, 956–63, for a more detailed description.
122 Weber, *Economy and Society*, vol. I, 225. The rise of these bureaucratic organizations was, according to Weber, a consequence of the fact that in the execution of their task they were superior to all other forms of organization in accuracy, speed, knowledge, continuity, discipline and reliability (ibid., 223, and Idem, *Economy and Society*, vol. II, 973–4).
123 In Thelle, 'Crowding as Appropriation', the 'bodily presence of the crowd' and appropriation of urban space in Copenhagen is studied for the period after the liberal constitution of 1849. Small-scale riots and urban space in the Middle Ages are addressed in Hannah Serneels, 'Making Space for Resistance: The Spatiality of Popular Protest in the Late Medieval Southern Low Countries', *Urban History* 48 (2021): 1–16 and see the historiographical survey in Justine Firnhaber-Baker, 'Introduction. Medieval Revolt in Context', in *The Routledge History Handbook of Medieval Revolt*, ed. Justine Firnhaber-Baker and Dirk Schoenaers (London: Routledge, 2017), which is also relevant to the early modern period.
124 See also chapter 1.
125 Dekker, *Holland in beroering*, 74.
126 E. P. Thompson, 'The Moral Economy of the English Crowd in the Eighteenth Century', *Past and Present* 50 (1971): 76–9. An introduction to Thompson's work (and life) in Marc Edelman, 'E. P. Thompson and Moral Economies', in *A Companion to Moral Anthropology*, ed. Didier Fassin (Chichester: Wiley-Blackwell, 2012) and for the use of the term 'moral economy' in the period before Thompson's article see

Norbert Götz, '"Moral Economy": Its Conceptual History and Analytical Prospects', *Journal of Global Ethics* 11 (2015): 148-51.
127 Thompson, 'The Moral Economy' 88, 98.
128 Ibid., 112-14, and for *taxation populaire* George Rudé, *Paris and London in the Eighteenth Century. Studies in Popular Protest* (London: Lawrence and Wishart, 1970), 19. Related to the concept of the moral economy, but with a clear element of revenge and physical violence against persons is what Beik in his research on violence in pre-modern France calls the 'culture of retribution' (William Beik, 'The Violence of the French Crowd from Charivari to Revolution', *Past and Present* 197 (2007): 76-7).
129 Dekker, *Holland in beroering*, 23-4; T. Tromp, '"De gesteldheid van den publieken geest" (in Noord-Holland)', in *Autoriteit en strijd*, ed. A. Doedens (Amsterdam: VU Uitgeverij, 1981), 89, and A. Doedens, 'Collectief verzet in de Nederlanden 1813-1848: een terreinverkenning', *Autoriteit en strijd*, ed. A. Doedens (Amsterdam: VU Uitgeverij, 1981), 194-5.
130 Dekker, *Holland in beroering*, 26.
131 Ibid.
132 Ibid., 28-38.
133 These farmed taxes were replaced in 1750 by a system in which excise duties were collected by officials.
134 'De heren handelen met ons als canaille en dan zullen wij voor burgemeesteren spelen en wij zullen de zaken dan wel schikken' (quoted in Dekker, *Holland in beroering*, 78).
135 'En zo hebben zij rechtgesproken en daarop ging men plunderen'. Quoted in L. Fuks, ed., *De Zeven Provinciën in beroering. Hoofdstukken uit een Jiddische kroniek over de jaren 1740-1752 van Abraham Chaim Braatbard* (Amsterdam: J. M. Meulenhoff, 1960), 49, and see Dekker, *Holland in beroering*, 78-9, for these and more examples.
136 Dekker, *Holland in beroering*, 79.
137 Wagenaar, *Amsterdam, in zyne opkomst*, part II, book 22, 711-20, and see for the course of this insurrection also Craffurd, 'Een generaal en kort verhaal' and Dekker, *Holland in beroering*, 32-5.
138 Wagenaar, *Amsterdam, in zyne opkomst*, part II, book 22, 713. Wagenaar speaks of a white coffin. This is presumably a cheap coffin made of pinewood.
139 Bos, *Waarachtige volksvrienden*, 30, and a similar 'strategy' in London (Robert B. Shoemaker, *The London Mob. Violence and Disorder in Eighteenth-Century England* (London: Hambledon and London, 2004) 122-3). For the smashing of windows as a means of dishonouring residents, see Daniel Jütte, 'Smashed Panes and "Terrible Showers": Windows, Violence, and Honor in the Early Modern City', *West 86th: A Journal of Decorative Arts, Design History, and Material Culture* 22 (2015): 131-56 particularly 147-51. In the context of gender and honour in early modern Rome, Cohen speaks of 'the practice of house scorning' (Elizabeth S. Cohen, 'Honor and Gender in the Streets of Early Modern Rome', *Journal of Interdisciplinary History* 22 (1992): 598).
140 Dekker, *Holland in beroering*, 86.
141 This was also generally the case in England and France (Rudé, *Paris and London*, 27-8). Incidentally, Shoemaker (*The London Mob*, 144-8) shows that in the second half of the eighteenth century, riots and the suppression of riots in London became much more violent.

142 In water-rich Amsterdam and other cities in Holland, household goods were often thrown in the canals; in London, household goods were destroyed by burning them in the streets (Shoemaker, *The London Mob*, 130-1 and illustration 14).
143 Fuks, *De Zeven Provinciën in beroering*, 49, and for more examples of the structured and ritualistic nature of looting, see Dekker, *Holland in beroering*, 87-92.
144 Rudé, *Paris and London*, 31, and see also his *The Crowd in History. A Study of Popular Disturbances in France and England, 1730-1848* (London: Lawrence and Wishart, 1981), 224-5.
145 Hans Achterhuis, 'Verslaafd aan geweld', *NRC-Handelsblad, Opinie & Debat*, 14 August 2021, 4-5 speaks of the addictive effect of violence. In addition, those temporarily present in a city may have been less sensitive to the moral economy of the working classes in that specific city. It is striking, for instance, that among the 51 persons arrested during the Aansprekersoproer, sailors were by far the largest occupational group, and of these sixteen sailors, only two came from the Dutch Republic (Dekker, *Holland in beroering*, 183-4).
146 E. J. Hobsbawn, 'Cities and Insurrections', in *Revolutionaries. Contemporary Essays*, ed. E. J. Hobsbawn (London: Weidenfeld and Nicolson, 1973), 222-3.
147 Quoted in Dekker, *Holland in beroering*, 55. The adoption of a military title by insurgents was apparently not unusual, for in 1629, during a food riot in Maldon, England, Ann Carter called on supporters to follow her as their 'Captain' (John Bohstedt, *The Politics of Provisions: Food Riots, Moral Economy, and Market Transition in England, c. 1550-1850* (London: Routledge, 2016), 26).
148 See for more examples Dekker, *Holland in beroering*, 53-7 and 77, and for a broad overview of the role of women in riots Van Gelder, 'Street Politics'. Note that the militias were also equipped with drums and banners. In London too, drums and banners were used to mobilize a crowd (Shoemaker, *The London Mob*, 116-17).
149 'trocken zoo met een zeer groot gedruijs door veele straaten en langs burgwallen. Haare hoop groeijden geweldig aan, ja namen de stoutheijt om in zulcke gestalte over den Dam en onder het stadhuijs door te trecken'; 'Dit huijs is te huur. Terstond in te vaaren' (Craffurd, 'Een generaal en kort verhaal', 48).
150 Ibid., 48, and see also 59-60. Almost two hundred years later (in 1885), the town hall of Amsterdam, by then the Royal Palace, was symbolically expropriated and put up for rent by socialists in a similar way (Piet de Rooy, *Een revolutie die voorbij ging. Domela Nieuwenhuis en het Palingoproer* (Bussum: Fibula-Van Dishoeck, 1971), 27).
151 The relatively strong orientation of working-class women towards their own neighbourhood is also evident in Pierik, 'Urban Life on the Move', 55-72. That these intensive neighbourhood contacts could also lead to tensions becomes clear in Olga Ruitenbeek, 'Niet zonder kleerscheuren. Criminaliteitspatroon, eergevoel en het gebruik van fysiek geweld door Amsterdamse volksvrouwen (1811-1838)', *Jaarboek Amstelodamum* 102 (2010): 63-85.
152 'Weet je 't al, vader! wat ik in de kommenij gehoord heb? . . . Buurvrouw Grietje heeft van buurvrouw Stijntje vernomen, dat buurman Pieter een gedrukt briefje op den weg gevonden heeft . . .' (quoted in Bos, *Waarachtige volksvrienden*, 32). In London, from the first half of the eighteenth century, printed handbills were used to recruit supporters and call for protest (Shoemaker, *The London Mob*, 263-4).
153 Delft, as was established in chapter 3, had enough space to accommodate the population for centuries after the large city extension of 1355.
154 Bos, *Waarachtige volksvrienden*, 28-9.

155 Hobsbawn, 'Cities and Insurrections', 222.
156 These are the Meuse/Merwede for Dordrecht, the Meuse for Rotterdam and the IJ for Amsterdam.
157 Van Gelder, 'Protest in the Piazza', in particular 129 and 148.
158 More specifically, I used the segment angular analysis available in DepthMap (version 10.14.00b) where street segments are used as the unit of analysis because long streets with many side streets disproportionately affect the analysis. For each street segment it is determined how easy it is to reach all other street segments within a certain radius. The unit of calculation is the angle needed to get from one segment to the next. According to Hillier et al. the results of this *segment angular analysis* show the most similarity to the way in which people move through a city in practice (Bill Hillier, Tao Yang and Alasdair Turner, 'Normalising Least Angle Choice in Depthmap and How It Opens up New Perspectives on the Global and Local Analysis of City Space', *Journal of Space Syntax* 3 (2012): 156).
159 I have used the street pattern of the cities as depicted in the 1832 *Minuutplans* of the land registry.
160 Not unimportant in times of upheaval was that the ring of canals was sandwiched between the centre with Dam square and a poor population in its numerous alleys, and poor working-class neighbourhoods like the Jordaan on the outskirts of the city. See also map 4.7.
161 Hobsbawn, 'Cities and Insurrections', 222.
162 Bos, *Waarachtige volksvrienden*, 28–9. Anti-Semitism in Amsterdam and the dependence of the Jewish community on the goodwill of the city government undoubtedly played a role as well. For the spatially confined character of the Jewish community, see also Pierik, 'Urban Life on the Move', 78–82.
163 This may also explain the fierce Orange-mindedness of the inhabitants of the Oostelijke Eilanden (A. J. Deurloo, 'Bijltjes en klouwers. Een bijdrage tot de geschiedenis der Amsterdamse scheepsbouw, in het bijzonder in de tweede helft der achttiende eeuw', *Economisch- en Sociaal-Historisch Jaarboek* 34 (1971): 54–65).
164 The quotation in Dekker, *Holland in beroering*, 55, and see also 100–1 and 140.
165 Thompson, 'The Moral Economy', 78.
166 Charles Tilly, Louise Tilly and Richard Tilly, *The Rebellious Century 1830-1930* (Cambridge, MA: Harvard University Press, 1975), 50, 241. E. J. Hobsbawn (*Primitive Rebels. Studies in Archaic Forms of Social Movement in the 19th and 20th Centuries* (1959; Manchester: Manchester University Press, 1974), 7, 110) characterizes this type of popular riot as 'the most primitive and pre-political of the movements of the urban poor'. That these riots were pre-political is firmly denied in Tilly, Tilly and Tilly, *The Rebellious Century*, 289–90, but much, of course, depends on how the term 'political' is defined. Thompson, 'The Moral Economy', 79, argues that the 'moral economy of the crowd' was not political 'in any advanced sense', but neither was it a-political because it contained notions of the common good that partly matched those of the authorities.
167 Tilly, Tilly and Tilly, *The Rebellious Century*, 49, 249–50. Rudé, *Paris and London*, 31–2, makes a similar distinction and speaks of 'indigenous motives' and 'derived motives'.
168 Tilly, Tilly and Tilly, *The Rebellious Century*, 49, 253–4. On page 263, the authors speak of the contrast between 'communal groups acting on a small, local scale' and 'associational groups acting on a large, national scale'.
169 Ibid., 49, 263.

170 For those critical statements about social and economic inequality in Holland, see Dekker, *Holland in beroering*, 139–41.
171 'die hunne belangen zullen behartigen, en alzoo middelen zullen beramen om in dit algemeen belang hun lot te verbeteren'. Quoted in Bos, *Waarachtige volksvrienden*, 37, and see 17–53 for an extensive description and analysis of the riot. See also M. J. F. Robijns, *Radicalen in Nederland (1840-1851)* (Leiden: Universitaire Pers Leiden, 1967), chapter 7.
172 Bos, *Waarachtige volksvrienden*, 49.
173 The riot and looting came to an end on Kaasmarkt (present Thorbeckeplein).
174 Bos, *Waarachtige volksvrienden*, 349–51, and see also for example De Rooy on the Palingoproer of 1886 (De Rooy, *Een revolutie die voorbij ging*, 56 ff.).
175 See also Hobsbawm, *Primitive Rebels*, 124. Old and new forms of collective action came together as late as 1917 in the Aardappeloproer (Potato Riot) in Amsterdam (Rudolf M. Dekker, 'Women in Revolt: Popular Protest and Its Social Basis in Holland in the Seventeenth and Eighteenth Centuries', *Theory and Society* 16 (1987): 354).
176 See for this development in Amsterdam Wagenaar, *Amsterdam 1876-1914*, chapters 5 and 7, and for The Hague Schmal, *Den Haag of 's-Gravenhage?*, chapters 3 and 4.
177 E. J. Hobsbawm, *Revolutionaries. Contemporary Essays* (London: Weidenfeld and Nicolson, 1973), 224, and see also *Primitive Rebels*, 124.
178 In the period before gentrification, the Jordaan district in Amsterdam was a good example of such a working-class neighbourhood, I know from my own observation. A nice description of a twentieth-century working-class neighbourhood and its inhabitants in Diederick Klein Kranenburg, *'Samen voor ons eigen'. De geschiedenis van een Nederlandse volksbuurt: de Haagse Schilderswijk 1920-1985* (Hilversum: Verloren, 2013).
179 For Copenhagen in the decades around 1900, Thelle notes a long-term effect of the 'agency of the crowd' on urban space, but he emphasizes that this was then a relatively recent phenomenon (Thelle, 'Crowding as Appropriation', 276 and 290).

Chapter 5

1 By discursive, I mean that the texts, maps and images discussed in this chapter are part of and contribute to a discourse on the social relations in the cities of Holland.
2 Allen, *Lost Geographies of Power*, chapter 7.
3 Ibid., 160. Of course, complete displacement is not possible and Allen therefore devotes considerable attention to the appropriation of space by those who do their work almost invisibly (ibid., 163–6).
4 Van Leeuwen, *The Logic of Charity*, 43, table 2.2; De Vries, *Electoraat en elite*, 28–31, and Giele and Van Oenen, 'Theorie en Praktijk'. It will be clear that the sources used and views on the social structure influence these figures, but the percentages given can certainly serve as a rough indication.
5 Clé Lesger, 'Stagnatie en stabiliteit. De economie tussen 1730 en 1795', in *Geschiedenis van Amsterdam. Zelfbewuste stadstaat 1650-1813*, ed. Willem Frijhoff and Maarten Prak (Amsterdam: SUN, 2005), 259, and H. A. Diederiks, 'Beroepsstructuur en sociale stratificatie in Leiden in het midden van de achttiende eeuw', in *Armoede en sociale spanning. Sociaal-historische studies over Leiden in de achttiende eeuw*, ed. H. A. Diederiks, D. J. Noordam and H. D. Tjalsma (Hilversum: Verloren, 1985), 57–8.

6 The literature on itinerant trade is extraordinarily vast and diverse. For good introductions, see Melissa Calaresu and Danielle van den Heuvel, 'Introduction: Food Hawkers from Representation to Reality', in *Food Hawkers. Selling in the Streets from Antiquity to the Present*, ed. Melissa Calaresu and Danielle van den Heuvel (London: Routledge, 2016) and Danielle van den Heuvel, 'Selling in the Shadows. Peddlers and Hawkers in Early Modern Europe', in *Working on Labor: Essays in Honor of Jan Lucassen*, ed. Leo Lucassen and Marcel van der Linden (Leiden: Brill, 2012).

7 Jeroen Salman, '"Vreemde loopers en kramers". De ambulante boekhandel in de achttiende eeuw', *Jaarboek voor Nederlandse Boekgeschiedenis* 8 (2001): 81, 92–3, and Idem, *'Zijn Marsie, en zijn stok, Aanschouwer sta wat stil'. Ontmoetingen met rondtrekkende boekverkopers* (Leiden: Stichting Neerlandistiek Leiden, 2006), 17. See also Clé Lesger, 'Spaces and Places', in *A Cultural History of Shopping in the Age of Enlightenment*, ed. Ilja van Damme (London: Bloomsbury Academic, 2022), 44–52. In Venice, the Rialto Bridge fulfilled a similar function (Rosa M. Salzberg, 'The Margins in the Centre. Working around Rialto in Sixteenth-Century Venice', in *The Place of the Social Margins, 1350-1750*, ed. Andrew Spicer and Jane L. Stevens Crawshaw (New York: Routledge, 2017)).

8 Leontine Buijnsters-Smeets, *Straatverkopers in beeld. Tekeningen en prenten van Nederlandse kunstenaars circa 1540-1850* (Nijmegen: Vantilt, 2012), Introduction; Salman, 'Vreemde loopers', 83, 96; V. R. A. D. Huberts, *De Amsterdamse venters. Een sociografische monografie* (Amsterdam: Van Campen, 1940), 172–5.

9 'Eene aanstotelijke menigte van blinden, kreupelen, verminkten en anderen, uit de schamele gemeente, krielde, eertijds, door de gansche stad. Men ontmoette dezelve, vooral, op de Sluizen of Bruggen, ook langs de Straaten, daar zij de ooren der Voorbygangeren, door hun jammergeluid, bijkans ondraaglijk vielen, en door stoute bedelaary, den voortgang, gestadig, afsneeden' (quoted in Pieter Vlaardingerbroek, 'Architectuur en tekening', in *Kijk Amsterdam 1700-1800: de mooiste stadsgezichten*, ed. Bert Gerlagh (Bussum: Thoth; Amsterdam: Stadsarchief Amsterdam, 2017), 70). Similar texts on the presence and obtrusiveness of the poor in London in Marriott, 'The Spatiality of the Poor', 124.

10 Good introductions to the genre of city descriptions can be found in Eddy Verbaan, *De woonplaats van de faam. Grondslagen van de stadsbeschrijving in de zeventiende-eeuwse Republiek* (Hilversum: Verloren, 2011), introduction and conclusion; Raingard Esser, *The Politics of Memory. The Writing of Partition in the Seventeenth-Century Low Countries* (Leiden: Brill, 2012), introduction, and Boudewijn Bakker, 'Het imago van de stad: Zelfportret als propaganda', in *Het aanzien van Amsterdam. Panorama's, plattegronden en profielen uit de Gouden Eeuw*, ed. Boudewijn Bakker and Erik Schmitz (Bussum: Thoth; Amsterdam: Stadsarchief Amsterdam, 2007), 57–9. An almost exhaustive list of published city descriptions can be found in Maud C. M. Lankester-Marcus, 'Stedentrots & stedenpracht: kunstenaarsvermeldingen in stadsbeschrijvingen van Noord-Nederlandse steden 1600-1850', *RKD Studies (online)* (2020). http://stedentrots.rkdmonographs.nl/ (last consulted 10 May 2023). For Amsterdam, the city for which by far the largest number of city descriptions have been published, J. van der Zande, 'Amsterdamse stadsgeschiedschrijving vóór Wagenaar', *Holland* 17 (1985): 218–30 and E. O. G. Haitsma Mulier, 'De zeventiende-eeuwse stadsbeschrijvingen van Amsterdam', *Maandblad Amstelodamum* 85 (1998): 107–15 are important.

11 A Dutch translation of his work appeared in 1612 by Cornelis Kiliaan, with additions by Petrus Montanus: Lodovico Guicciardini, *Beschryvinghe van alle de Nederlanden; anderssins ghenoemt Neder-Duytslandt* (Amsterdam: Wilem Jansz., 1612).

12 An overview in Verbaan, *De woonplaats van de faam*, 292 ff. A Dutch translation of the 1611 city description written in Latin by Pontanus appeared in 1614: Pontanus, *Historische beschrijvinghe*.
13 Van der Zande, 'Amsterdamse stadsgeschiedschrijving', 221.
14 Verbaan, *De woonplaats van de faam*, 281, and Esser, *The Politics of Memory*, 328.
15 For this section I consulted the following city descriptions: for Amsterdam Pontanus, *Historische Beschrijvinghe*; Melchior Fokkens, *Beschrijvinge der wijdtvermaarde koop-stadt Amstelredam, van haar eerste beginselen, oude voor-rechten . . . en, haar tegenwoordigen standt* (Amsterdam: Abraham and Jan de Wees, 1662); Filips von Zesen, *Beschreibung der Stadt Amsterdam . . . vor augen gestellet werden* (Amsterdam: Joachim Nosche, 1664) and Tobias van Domselaer, *Beschryvinge van Amsterdam, haar eerste oorspronk . . . tot dezen tegenwoordige jare 1665, is voorgevallen* (Amsterdam: Marcus Willemsz. Doornick, 1665). For Leiden Orlers, *Beschrijvinge der stad Leyden*, for Delft Dirk Evertsz. van Bleyswijck, *Beschryvinge der stadt Delft, betreffende des selfs situatie, oorsprong en ouderdom . . . Tot bericht, nut, ende gerief van alle soo tegenwoordige als nakomende burgeren der selver stad* (Delft: Arnold Bon, 1667) and Boitet, *Beschryving der stadt Delft*. For The Hague Jacob van der Does, *'s Graven-Hage, met de voornaemste plaetsen en vermaecklijckheden* (Den Haag: Hermanus Gael, 1668) and Gysbert de Cretser, *Beschryvinge van 's Gravenhage: behelsende desselfs eerste opkomste, stichtinge en vermakelyke situatie . . . wandelingen en buytenwegen* (Amsterdam: Jan ten Hoorn, 1711), for Haarlem Schrevelius, *Harlemias*, and for Alkmaar Cornelis van der Woude, *Kronijcke van Alckmaer met zijn dorpen . . . van 't beginsel der bouwinge der voorsz. stadt Alckmaer, tot den jare Christi 1658* (Alkmaar: Symon Cornelisz. Brekegeest, 1658).
16 Bleyswijck, *Beschryvinge der stadt Delft*, 629. For early modern Venice, Van Gelder and De Vivo observe that the authorities did not include any reference to riots and other forms of protest in official documents. In this context, the authors speak of 'archival suppression' (Maartje van Gelder and Filippo de Vivo, 'Papering over Protest: Contentious Politics and Archival Suppression in Early Modern Venice', *Past and Present* 258 (2023): 44–78).
17 'de Heeren ende Regeerders deser Stede, als mede hare Innewoonderen ende Borgeren' take care that 'de bedroefde, ellendige, en van Godt so hooch bevolen Armen, Weduwen, Wesen ofte Vaderloose kinderen, en andere ghebreckelicke persoonen, ten vollen mochten werden onderhouden ende van alle tijdelicke havenisse versien' (Orlers, *Beschrijvinge der stad Leyden*, 91).
18 'oft hy heeft eñ vercrijcht hulpe ende assistentie in sijne armoede' (ibid., 104).
19 'een goede somme gelts bedraecht' (ibid., 103).
20 Ibid., 105.
21 Ibid., 104–5.
22 'na gelegentheydt van persoonen en saecken' (Bleyswijck, *Beschryvinge der stadt Delft*, 505).
23 Pontanus, *Historische beschrijvinghe*, 132–7, 306–9.
24 Bleyswijck, *Beschryvinge der stadt Delft*, 536–40.
25 See also Esser, *The Politics of Memory*, 59.
26 See for the Amsterdam Rasphuis Sjoerd Faber, 'Het Rasphuis: wat was dat eigenlijk?', in *Scherp toezicht; van 'Boeventucht' tot 'Samenleving en criminaliteit'*, ed. Cyrille Fijnaut and Pieter Spierenburg (Arnhem: Gouda Quint, 1990).
27 Verbaan, *De woonplaats van de faam*, 258–62.

28 De Cretser, *Beschryvinge van 's Gravenhage*. See about this city description Thera Wijsenbeek, 'Inleiding: Den Haag in beeld en geschrift', in *Den Haag. Geschiedenis van de Stad*, vol. 2, *De Tijd van de Republiek*, ed. Th. Wijsenbeek (Zwolle: Waanders, 2005), 11–12.
29 'onder 't geruysch en de beweginge van de bladeren'; 'aan wederzyden zeer aanzienelyke huizen, waar van sommige wel Paleysen konnen genoemt worden' (De Cretser, *Beschryvinge van 's Gravenhage*, 49–51).
30 'en waar inne geen een Huis van neringe te vinden is' (ibid., 55).
31 Van der Does, *'s Graven-Hage*, XIII, and see also Wijsenbeek, 'Inleiding', 11–12.
32 'de aanzienlijkste en heerlijkste Gebouwen der Stadt, en hier woonen de Rijkste en Voornaamste Kooplieden; geen huyzen der Winkeliers ziet men hier met open winkels, al de Gebouwen zijn hier hoogh, en net, als uyt een handt getimmert' (Fokkens, *Beschrijvinge der wijdt-vermaarde koop-stadt Amstelredam*, 68–9).
33 Von Zesen, *Beschreibung der Stadt Amsterdam*, 355–6.
34 Fokkens, *Beschrijvinge der wijdt-vermaarde koop-stadt Amstelredam*, 90, and Von Zesen, *Beschreibung der Stadt Amsterdam*, 210–12.
35 Fokkens, *Beschrijvinge der wijdt-vermaarde koop-stadt Amstelredam*, 88.
36 H.Tj. Dijkhuis, 'De Jordaan. De ontwikkeling van een volkswijk in een grote stad', *Economisch-Historisch Jaarboek* 21 (1940): 15.
37 Von Zesen, *Beschreibung der Stadt Amsterdam*, 221.
38 'krielen en grimmelen van alderley handtwerks volk' (Van Domselaer, *Beschryvinge van Amsterdam*, book III, 251).
39 'zo grouzamen menichte van gemeen varendt, en handtwerks volk, 't welk met de scheepstimmerwerven en vaarten, hun kost wint, ja wel vier huys gezinnen zomtijdts in een huys, als in de voorhuyzen, achterhuyzen, kelders, voor, en achter-kamers, dat het ongeloofelijk is' (ibid., book III, 239 and see also 244 and 251).
40 Unlike, for instance, descriptions of Naples in the eighteenth century, Van Domselaer's descriptions of Amsterdam's working-class neighbourhoods are not an expression of a romantic interest in the picturesque nature of these neighbourhoods and their inhabitants. For the representation of Naples and the Neapolitans, see Melissa Calaresu, 'From the Street to Stereotype: Urban Space, Travel and the Picturesque in Late Eighteenth-Century Naples', *Italian Studies* 62 (2007): 189–203.
41 A short summary of the development of Dutch historiography can be found in E. O. G. Haitsma Mulier, 'Geschiedschrijving in het vroegmoderne Nederland (16e-18e eeuw)', *Holland* 17 (1985): 185–99. On the access to and the use of sources, see the Preface to Wagenaar, *Amsterdam, in zyne opkomst*, II-III and the numerous copies of official documents he included as appendices in his city description. See also Van der Zande, 'Amsterdamse stadsgeschiedschrijving', 218–19.
42 Lankester-Marcus, 'Stedentrots & stedenpracht', Conclusions: http://stedentrots.rkdmonographs.nl/.
43 'Door alle tydvakken heeft *Delft* nooit zo treurig geweest als nu ...' (Rs. Bakker, *Den opkomst, bloei, verval en tegenwoordigen toestand der stad Delft, in derzelver fabryken en trafyken* (Delft: Rs. Bakker, n.d. (*c.*1800)), 32–3).
44 C. van der Vijver, *Wandelingen in en om Amsterdam* (Amsterdam: J. C. van Kesteren, 1829).
45 'de zindelijkheid der schaduwrijke breede gracht, en de regelmatigheid der trotsche en prachtige gebouwen'; 'breede, zindelijke en fraai bebouwde straat' (ibid., 262 and 332–3).

46 'De kerk verlaten hebbende, wandelden wij voorwaarts, zonder acht te slaan op de *Markensteeg* en *Marken*' (ibid., 183).
47 'afschuwelijke vuilnishoopen en vuilnisvaten die . . . eene verpestende lucht uitwasemden'; 'een afzigtelijke gracht . . . die niets dan een weemoedig gevoel kan opwekken' (ibid., 357).
48 Systematic attention to the well-being of the working classes and the housing and living conditions in poor neighbourhoods was paid in the so-called *Geneeskundige plaatsbeschrijvingen* (medical city descriptions) that were published from the second decade of the nineteenth century onwards, but these publications were mainly read by doctors and not by the general public. For the readers of the Amsterdam medical city description, see the list of subscribers in C. J. Nieuwenhuijs, *Proeve eener geneeskundige plaatsbeschrijving (topographie) der stad Amsterdam*, vol. 4 (Amsterdam: Johannes van der Hey, 1820).
49 Only on Amsterdam's Herengracht and Keizersgracht was this made impossible by building regulations.
50 'want het zoude te verdrietig zijn, die alle te noemen' (Fokkens, *Beschrijvinge der wijdt-vermaarde koop-stadt Amstelredam*, 91).
51 See Chapter 2 and the appendix.
52 For the following, see Stephen Daniels and Denis Cosgrove, 'Introduction: Iconography and Landscape', in *The Iconography of Landscape : Essays on the Symbolic Representation, Design and Use of Past Environments*, ed. Denis Cosgrove and Stephen Daniels (Cambridge: Cambridge University Press, 1988), introduction, and Peter Burke, *Eyewitnessing. The Uses of Images as Historical Evidence* (London: Reaktion Books, 2001), chapter 2. A general treatise on images (and language) in W. J. T. Mitchell, *Iconology. Image, Text, Ideology* (Chicago: University of Chicago Press, 1986), especially Chapter 1.
53 Quoted in Daniels and Cosgrove, 'Introduction', 2, and see also Burke, *Eyewitnessing*, 36. For this approach to images, see also Roelof van Straten, *Inleiding in de iconografie. Enige theoretische en praktische kennis* (Bussum: Coutinho, 2002).
54 A summary of the criticism of Panofsky's approach in Burke, *Eyewitnessing*, 40–2.
55 For the early history of the genre of city maps and city profiles, see Deirdre Carasso, 'Kroniek van het Amsterdamse stadsportret 1540-1740', in *Het aanzien van Amsterdam. Panorama's, plattegronden en profielen uit de Gouden Eeuw*, ed. Boudewijn Bakker and Erik Schmitz (Bussum: Thoth; Amsterdam: Stadsarchief Amsterdam, 2007), 42–5; Boudewijn Bakker, 'De stad in beeld. Het stadsportret als genre in de beeldende kunst', ibid., 10–13, and Jelle De Rock, *The Image of the City in Early Netherlandish Painting (1400-1550)* (Turnhout: Brepols, 2019), where chapter V argues that in urban iconography in the fifteenth and sixteenth centuries there was a 'gradual evolution towards a more realistic, autonomous, secularised, and multifunctional image' (298).
56 Marc Hameleers, *Kaarten van Amsterdam 1538-1865* (Bussum:Thoth; Amsterdam: Gemeentearchief Amsterdam, 2013), 25, and for the use of perspective by mapmakers Bakker, 'De stad in beeld', 13–17.
57 Bakker, 'Het imago van de stad', 56.
58 Elizabeth A. Sutton, *Capitalism and Cartography in the Dutch Golden Age* (Chicago: The University of Chicago Press, 2015), 26. The 1703 reissue of the Map Figurative of Delft in four sheets was sold for 2 guilders (W. F. Weve and H. W. van Leeuwen,

'De dateringen van de plattegrond en de randprenten van de Kaart Figuratief'), in *De Kaart Figuratief van Delft*, ed. H. L. Houtzager et al. (Rijswijk: Elmar, 1997), 37.
59 Hubert Nusteling, *Welvaart en werkgelegenheid in Amsterdam 1540-1860. Een relaas over demografie, economie en sociale politiek van een wereldstad* (Amsterdam: De Bataafsche Leeuw, 1985), Appendix 5.1, and L. Noordegraaf, *Daglonen in Alkmaar 1500-1650* (Historische Vereniging Holland, 1980), table B.7.
60 Here I join Harley who states that maps 'exert a social influence through their omissions as much as by the features they depict and emphasise' (J. B. Harley, 'Maps, Knowledge, and Power', in *The Iconography of Landscape: Essays on the Symbolic Representation, Design and Use of Past Environments*, ed. Denis Cosgrove and Stephen Daniels (Cambridge: Cambridge University Press, 1988), 290). So, unlike in Vannieuwenhuyze and Vernackt, this section is not about uncovering the many layers of meaning in historic maps and cityscapes (Bram Vannieuwenhuyze and Elien Vernackt, 'The Digital Thematic Deconstruction of Historic Town Views and Maps', in *Portraits of the City. Representing Urban Space in Later Medieval and Early Modern Europe*, ed. Katrien Lichtert, Jan Dumolyn and Maximiliaan P. J. Martens (Turnhout: Brepols, 2014)).
61 Similarly, the 1609 bird's eye view map of Paris by Benedit de Vassallieu (dit Nicolay) largely omits the 'formless suburban sprawl' on the Right Bank (Ballon, *The Paris of Henri IV*, 222–3, 227).
62 For the following, see also B. J. M. Speet, 'Een stad raakt verstopt. Ruimtelijke ontwikkelingen in de 16de eeuw', in *Woelige tijden. Amsterdam in de eeuw van de Beeldenstorm*, ed. Margriet de Roever and Boudewijn Bakker (Amsterdam: De Bataafsche Leeuw, 1987) and Ben Speet, 'Verstening, verdichting en vergroting', in *Geschiedenis van Amsterdam. Een stad uit het niets (tot 1578)*, ed. Marijke Carasso-Kok (Amsterdam: SUN, 2004). A detailed treatment of this map in Hameleers, *Kaarten van Amsterdam 1538-1865*, catalogue numbers 1 and 2.
63 J. B. Harley in 'Silences and Secrecy: The Hidden Agenda of Cartography in Early Modern Europe', *Imago Mundi* 40 (1988): 57–8, speaks of 'cartographic silence'.
64 A. J. M. Brouwer Ancher and J. C. Breen, 'De doleantie van een deel der burgerij van Amsterdam tegen den Magistraat dier stad in 1564 en 1565', *Bijdragen en Mededeelingen van het Historisch Genootschap* 24 (1903): 188–96, and see also the appendix below.
65 Ibid., 190–1, 195.
66 'veel ende diversche oude ende schamele luyden huyskens' (quoted in ibid., 196).
67 Harley, 'Maps, Knowledge, and Power', 292 and see also his 'Silences and Secrecy' and 'Deconstructing the Map, in *The Map Reader: Theories of Mapping Practice and Cartographic Representation*, ed. Martin Dodge, Rob Kitchin and Chris Perkins (Chichester: John Wiley & Sons, 2011).
68 Hameleers, *Kaarten van Amsterdam 1538-1865*, 31. The gallows field (Volewijck) in the lower right corner of the map indicates that Amsterdam possessed *halsrecht*, that is the right to pronounce and execute death sentences. At the same time, this element can also be interpreted as a symbol of firm governance.
69 Ibid., catalogue numbers 45, 79 and 88. The reputation of Goudsbloemgracht in Dijkhuis, 'De Jordaan', 15.
70 Only on the very large (*c.* 140*165 cm) and extremely detailed map by Balthasar Florisz. van Berckenrode from 1625 are walled-in houses in inner courtyards depicted (see Chapter 3, Map 3.10). However, this map too, is not a 'neutral' cartographic representation, but a celebration of Amsterdam's relatively recent

position as one of the major trading centres of Europe (Boudewijn Bakker and Erik Schmitz, eds, *Het Aanzien van Amsterdam. Panorama's, plattegronden en profielen uit de Gouden Eeuw* (Bussum: Thoth; Amsterdam: Stadsarchief Amsterdam, 2007), 103).

71 'gammele houten krotjes' (Van der Wulp, 'Het stadsbeeld van Delft', 32) and see also Wijsenbeek-Olthuis, *Achter de gevels van Delft*, 152-3.

72 H. W. van Leeuwen, 'Dirck van Bleyswijck, de geschiedschrijver en het Delft van zijn tijd', in *De Kaart Figuratief van Delft*, ed. H. L. Houtzager et al. (Rijswijk: Elmar, 1997), 14-15.

73 De Wit's atlas of cities has been digitized in its entirety and is accessible via https://www.kb.nl (Stedenatlas De Wit).

74 'actief beleefd burgerschap' (Bakker, 'De stad in beeld', 23).

75 Harley, 'Maps, Knowledge, and Power', 302-3, states that cartography 'remains a teleological discourse, reifying power, reinforcing the status quo, and freezing social interaction within charted lines'.

76 For the international diffusion of this genre see, among others, Burke, *Eyewitnessing*, 84, and Cynthia Lawrence, *Gerrit Adriaensz. Berckheyde (1638-1698). Haarlem Cityscape Painter* (Doornspijk: Davaco, 1991), Chapters 5 and 6. A quantitative approach to cityscape analysis in Jelle De Rock, 'The Image of the City Quantified: The Serial Analysis of Pictorial Representations of Urbanity in Early Netherlandish Art (1420-1520)', in *Portraits of the City. Representing Urban Space in Later Medieval and Early Modern Europe*, ed. Katrien Lichtert, Jan Dumolyn and Maximiliaan P. J. Martens (Turnhout: Brepols, 2014) and a historiographical overview of urban iconography in Jelle de Rock, *The Image of the City*, Introduction.

77 B. Haak, R. J. Wattenmaker and B. Bakker, 'Foreword', in *Opkomst en bloei van het Noordnederlandse stadsgezicht in de 17de eeuw / the Dutch Cityscape in the 17th Century and Its Sources*, ed. B. Haak, R. J. Wattenmaker and B. Bakker (Bentveld-Aerdenhout: Landshoff, 1977), 10. For the related streetscapes, see Melissa Calaresu, 'Representing the Street', in *Early Modern Streets. A European Perspective*, ed. Danielle van den Heuvel (Abingdon, Oxon: Routledge, 2022).

78 R. J. Wattenmaker, 'Introduction', in *Opkomst en bloei van het Noordnederlandse stadsgezicht in de 17de eeuw / the Dutch Cityscape in the 17th Century and Its Sources*, ed. B. Haak, R. J. Wattenmaker and B. Bakker (Bentveld-Aerdenhout: Landshoff, 1977), 18 and B. Haak, 'The City Portrayed', ibid., 190.

79 Boudewijn Bakker, 'Maps, books and prints', ibid., 66, and see also Christopher Brown, *Dutch Townscape Painting. Themes and Painters in the National Gallery* (London: National Gallery, 1972).

80 R. Fritz, *Das Stadt- und Strassenbild in der holländischen Malerei des 17. Jahrhunderts* (Berlin, 1932), 64-96, and Bakker, 'Maps, books and prints', 73-4.

81 Brown, *Dutch Townscape Painting*, 8-10; Bakker, 'Maps, books and prints', 74-5; Haak, 'The City Portrayed', 194-5; Lawrence, *Gerrit Adriaensz. Berckheyde*, 8-11, and Leonore Stapel, *Perspectieven van de stad. Over bronnen, populariteit en functie van het zeventiende-eeuwse stadsgezicht* (Hilversum: Verloren, 2000), 46-55.

82 Boudewijn Bakker, 'Cornelis Ploos van Amstel en het stadsgezicht als kunst', in *Kijk Amsterdam 1700-1800: de mooiste stadsgezichten*, ed. Bert Gerlagh (Bussum: Thoth; Amsterdam: Stadsarchief Amsterdam, 2017), 21, 32-3, and Lawrence, *Gerrit Adriaensz. Berckheyde*, 8.

83 Wattenmaker, 'Introduction', 15, and Bert Gerlagh, ed., *Kijk Amsterdam 1700-1800: de mooiste stadsgezichten* (Bussum: Thoth; Amsterdam: Stadsarchief Amsterdam, 2017), 6: 'Het gedetailleerd en waarheidsgetrouw uitbeelden van de omgeving ...'.

84 Fritz, *Das Stadt- und Strassenbild*, 11. Gombrich distinguishes between the evocative and informative qualities of images and states that it is primarily on the basis of the evocative qualities that an image is considered true (E. H. Gombrich, 'Standards of Truth: The Arrested Image and the Moving Eye', in *The Language of Images*, ed. W. J. T. Mitchell (Chicago: The University of Chicago Press, 1980), 211, 214). This also seems to play a role in pre-modern cityscapes; their power lies in the image they evoke rather than in the representation of a situation actually encountered.

85 B. Haak, R. J. Wattenmaker and B. Bakker, eds, *Opkomst en bloei van het Noordnederlandse stadsgezicht in de 17de eeuw / the Dutch Cityscape in the 17th Century and Its Sources* (Bentveld-Aerdenhout: Landshoff, 1977), catalogue numbers 52, 110 and 115.

86 Charles Dumas, *Haagse stadsgezichten 1550-1800. Topografische schilderijen van het Haags Historisch Museum* (Zwolle: Waanders, 1991), 12-13.

87 Haak, Wattenmaker and Bakker, eds, *Opkomst en bloei / the Dutch Cityscape*, catalogue numbers 55 and 102. Often, preliminary studies have no staffage at all (Gerlagh, ed., *Kijk Amsterdam*, 194).

88 Compare the illustrations of Prinsessegracht and Hofvijver in The Hague around 1760 by La Fargue (Dumas, *Haagse stadsgezichten*, 455-6 and 432-3).

89 Brown, *Dutch Townscape Painting*, 11; Dumas, *Haagse stadsgezichten*, 114; Lawrence, *Gerrit Adriaensz. Berckheyde*, 70-1, and more examples in Dumas, *Haagse stadsgezichten*, 27, 28 and 97-8.

90 Lawrence, *Gerrit Adriaensz. Berckheyde*, 11-12, 33, and Stapel, *Perspectieven van de stad*, 72, 75-6.

91 And just like the previously discussed city descriptions and city maps, it is also important with cityscapes to be on the lookout for things that are not depicted. See also Burke, *Eyewitnessing*, 187-8.

92 Lawrence, *Gerrit Adriaensz. Berckheyde*, 11, and see also Arthur K. Wheelock Jr., '"Worthy to Behold". The Dutch City and Its Image in the Seventeenth Century', in *Dutch Cityscapes of the Golden Age*, ed. Ariane van Suchtelen and Arthur K. Wheelock Jr. (Zwolle: Waanders, 2008) and Burke, *Eyewitnessing*, 84-5.

93 The Nieuwe Kerk, which represents the ecclesiastical power, is on the right in the background and seems further away from the town hall than it actually is. Due to the chosen position, the church is also largely hidden behind the weighing house.

94 Stapel, *Perspectieven van de stad*, 56-61, and Lawrence, *Gerrit Adriaensz. Berckheyde*, 49-56.

95 Bakker, 'Cornelis Ploos van Amstel', 27, and see also Calaresu, 'Representing the Street'.

96 For my argument about the appropriation of urban space, especially cityscapes are relevant. Therefore, the work of the Bamboccianti, images of professions by someone like Jan Luyken, images of folk figures by, for example, Gillis van Scheyndel, and images of pedlars and of market scenes fall outside the scope of this study. For the Bamboccianti, see Giuliano Briganti, Ludovica Trezzani and Laura Laureati, *The Bamboccianti. The Painters of Everyday Life in Seventeenth Century Rome* (Rome: Ugo Bozzi Editore, 1983) and David A. Levine and Ekkehard Mai, eds, *I Bamboccianti. Niederländische Malerrebellen im Rom des Barock* (Rome: Ugo Bozzi Editore, 1991). The popularity of images of Neapolitan pedlars, promoted in part by the Grand Tour, in Melissa Calaresu, 'Costumes and Customs in Print: Travel, Ethnography, and the Representation of Street-Sellers in Early Modern Italy', in *Not Dead Things: The Dissemination of Popular Print in England and Wales, Italy, and the Low Countries,*

1500-1820, ed. Roeland Harms, Joad Raymond and Jeroen Salman (Leiden: Brill, 2013) and an analysis of Dutch prints of pedlars in Karen Bowen, 'Peddling in Texts and Images. The Dutch Visual Perspective', ibid. For the interpretation of market scenes, see Elizabeth Alice Honig, 'Desire and Domestic Economy', *The Art Bulletin* 83 (2001): 294–315 and idem, *Painting & the Market in Early Modern Antwerp* (New Haven: Yale University Press, 1998).

97 Much has been written about the economic stagnation and decline of this period. See for instance P. C. Jansen, 'Poverty in Amsterdam at the Close of the 18th Century', *Acta Historiae Neerlandicae: Studies on the History of the Netherlands* 10 (1978): 98–114; Maarten Prak, 'Stad van tegenstellingen 1730-1795', in *Geschiedenis van Amsterdam. Zelfbewuste stadstaat 1650-1813*, ed. Willem Frijhoff and Maarten Prak (Amsterdam: SUN, 2005) and Van Leeuwen, *Bijstand in Amsterdam for Amsterdam*; Pot, *Arm Leiden for Leiden*; Nico Siffels and Willem van Spijker, 'Haarlemse paupers. Arbeidsmarkt, armoede en armenzorg in Haarlem in de eerste helft van de negentiende eeuw', *Tijdschrift voor Sociale Geschiedenis* 13 (1987): 458–93 for Haarlem; Wijsenbeek-Olthuis, *Achter de gevels van Delft* for Delft. In Amsterdam, the number of foundlings increased rapidly from the 1770s onwards (Nanda Geuzebroek, *Vondelingen. Het Aalmoezeniersweeshuis van Amsterdam), 1780-1830* (Hilversum: Verloren, 2020), Appendix, Table 1.
98 Compare this image with the very similar one of the mackerel-seller in the well-known series of prints of 'London Cries' by Francis Wheatley, reproduced in Sean Shesgreen, 'In Search of the Marginal and the Outcast: The "Lower Orders" in the Cries of London and Dublin', in *Others and Outcasts in Early Modern Europe. Picturing the Social Margins*, ed. Tom Nichols (Aldershot: Ashgate, 2007), figure 10.2.
99 Bakker, 'Maps, books and prints', 75.
100 Bert Gerlagh, 'Verandering en continuïteit in de topografie', in *Kijk Amsterdam 1700-1800: de mooiste stadsgezichten* ed. Bert Gerlagh (Bussum: Thoth; Amsterdam: Stadsarchief Amsterdam, 2017), 60.
101 Pieter Vlaardingerbroek, 'Architectuur en tekening', 67.
102 Because the larger collectors also commissioned artists, their influence on the genre was considerable. See Dumas, *Haagse stadsgezichten*, 41–2 and 434, and also Bakker, 'Cornelis Ploos van Amstel', 26. The illustrations in the *Tegenwoordige Staat der Nederlanden*, published between 1738 and 1803, exude a similar atmosphere of peace and prosperity. The dozens of pictures of cities and rural landscapes in this series have recently been brought together in Everhard Korthals Altes and Bram Vannieuwenhuyze, *Nederland op zijn mooist. De achttiende-eeuwse Republiek in kaart en beeld* (Bussum: Thoth, 2022).
103 See for the specific interpretation of the classicist ideal by an Amsterdam art collector Bakker, 'Cornelis Ploos van Amstel'.
104 A highly idealized version of reality can also be found in images of plantations and colonial society in the then Dutch colonies in the East and West Indies.
105 'De heer Whistler zei ons reeds in November op zijn eigenaardige sarcastische toon, dat de Hollandsche schilders niet wisten wat zij verzuimden door niets van hun wondervol Amsterdam te maken, de stad die hij mooier dan Venetië prees. En nu moest een vreemdeling, zeide hij, hier komen doen wat voor Hollanders zoo voor de hand zou liggen.' (quoted in J. F. Heijbroek, 'Holland vanaf het water. De bezoeken van James Abbott McNeill Whistler aan Nederland', *Bulletin van het Rijksmuseum* 36 (1988): 245). Elsewhere in Europe, already from the end of the

eighteenth century, there was a growing interest in popular culture, the working classes and street life (Burke, *Popular Culture*, chapter 1, and Calaresu, 'From the Street to Stereotype').

106 Wagenaar, *Stedebouw en burgerlijke vrijheid*, 10–14. Early photographs of working-class neighbourhoods can be found in Paul Hefting, *De foto's van Breitner* (Den Haag: SDU, 1989), 51–3, and Kees Nieuwenhuijzen, ed., *De vroegste foto's van Amsterdam* (Amsterdam: Van Gennep, 1974).

Conclusion

1 See Pierre Bourdieu, *Outline of a Theory of Practice* (Cambridge: Cambridge University Press, 1977), 86, where he writes: 'the habitus could be considered as a subjective but not individual system of internalized structures, schemes of perception, conception, and action common to all members of the same group or class'.
2 Muir (*Rituals in Early Modern Europe*, 6) specifically points to the effect of rituals on habitus.
3 Pierre Bourdieu, *The Logic of Practice* (Stanford: Stanford University Press, 1990), 56.
4 See also Wacquant, 'Pierre Bourdieu', 221, where he quotes Bourdieu who defines habitus as 'the product of structure, producer of practice, and reproducer of structure'.
5 For the distinction between primary and additional/secondary habitus, see Loïc Wacquant, 'Homines in Extremis: What Fighting Scholars Teach Us About Habitus', *Body & Society* 20 (2014): 6–8.
6 Pierre Bourdieu, *Pascalian Meditations* (Stanford: Stanford University Press, 2000), 161, and see also 'Habitus', in *Habitus: A Sense of Place*, ed. Jean Hillier and Emma Rooksby (Aldershot: Ashgate, 2005).
7 Van der Woud, *Koninkrijk van sloppen*, chapter 4, and the changes in Amsterdam after the mid-nineteenth century in Wagenaar, *Amsterdam 1876-1914* and Piet de Rooy, 'De geest van omverwerping 1851-1876', in *Geschiedenis van Amsterdam 1813-1900. Hoofdstad in aanbouw*, ed. Remieg Aerts and Piet de Rooy (Amsterdam: SUN, 2006).
8 For the political field in Bourdieu's work, see Thompson, 'Editor's Introduction', 26–9, and for a model of political change in line with Bourdieu's field theory, Marcos Ancelovici, 'Bourdieu in Movement: Toward a Field Theory of Contentious Politics', *Social Movement Studies* 20 (2021): 155–73. A broad perspective on the modernization of the Dutch economy in this period can be found in Jan Luiten van Zanden and Arthur van Riel, *The Strictures of Inheritance: The Dutch Economy in the Nineteenth Century*, The Princeton Economic History of the Western World (Princeton: Princeton University Press, 2004).

Appendix: Patterns of residential differentiation in the cities of Holland, fourteenth–nineteenth centuries

1 J. Aalbers, *De Republiek en de vrede van Europa. De buitenlandse politiek van de republiek der Verenigde Nederlanden na de vrede van Utrecht (1713), voornamelijk gedurende de jaren 1720-1733* (Groningen: Wolters-Noordhoff, 1980), chapter 3 on

the disputes between the cities of Holland and the long and difficult history of this redress of the *verponding*.
2   Ibid., 126.
3   The charter and the instruction are also included in the records of the *verponding* of Delft (Nationaal Archief, 3.01.29 (Financie van Holland), inv.no. 492).
4   'getauxeert sullen werden alle Huisen, klein of groot, publicque of andere, daar Huur of Profijt af komt'.
5   I owe many thanks to George Buzing, who used his great knowledge of the topography of Delft to map the houses in the 1730 tax register. The map presented here is also the result of his efforts. For residential patterns in Delft, see also Lesger, Van Leeuwen and Buzing, 'Residentiële segregatie in Delft'.
6   Van der Vlis, *Leven in armoede*, 89–95. Due to removals, no less than 1158 addresses are known of the 656 households that received poor relief.
7   Kees van der Wiel, 'Zicht op Delft in de 17de en 18de eeuw', in *De Snijkunst verbeeld. Delftse anatomische lessen nader belicht. Beschrijving van de vier Delftse anatomische lessen en een overzicht van de gezondheidszorg in Delft en haar beoefenaren in de zeventiende en achttiende eeuw*, ed. Hans Houtzager and Michiel Jonker (Zwolle: Waanders, 2002), 15–17 and in particular figure 9.
8   To arrive at these percentages, Van der Wiel related the number of taxpayers in the 1674 *Groot Familiegeld* to the number of houses in the 1732 *verponding* tax. Because the number of houses at that time may have been lower than at the end of the seventeenth century, these percentages may have been slightly inflated.
9   This is the area where Grijzenhout on Vlamingstraat locates the house and blind alley (Penspoort), which is depicted in the famous painting by Johannes Vermeer (Frans Grijzenhout, *Vermeer's Little Street. A View of the Penspoort in Delft* (Amsterdam: Rijksmuseum Amsterdam, 2015) and idem, 'Vermeer's the Little Street Revisited', *Bulletin KNOB* 117 (2018): 1–13).
10 When analysing this register, I was allowed to use a digital version that Gerrit Verhoeven made available to me. I am of course very grateful for that.
11 A detailed consideration of the source in Gerrit Verhoeven, *Het eerste kohier van de tiende penning van Delft (1543)* (Dordrecht: Historische Vereniging Holland; Hilversum: Verloren, 1999), Introduction. See also J. A. M. Y. Bos-Rops, 'De kohieren van de gewestelijke belastingen in Holland, 1543-1579', *Holland* 29 (1997): 18–36 and the contribution of the same author to G. A. M. van Synghel, ed., *Bronnen betreffende de registratie van onroerend goed in middeleeuwen en ancien régime*, Broncommentaren, vol. 4 (Den Haag: Instituut voor Nederlandse Geschiedenis, 2001).
12 For the great city fire that reduced two thirds of the city to ashes, see Weve, *Huizen in Delft*, 17–23, and Verhoeven, *De derde stad*, 187–93.
13 See Verhoeven, *Het Eerste Kohier*, 91–107. Only in the eleventh section (south-western part of the city) and the sixteenth section (mainly cheap houses with weekly rents outside the city walls) did it prove impossible to reconstruct the route of the tax-collectors. Of necessity, I have placed the rental values in clusters there.
14 D. E. H. de Boer, 'Delft omstreeks 1400', in *De stad Delft. Cultuur en maatschappij*, vol. 1, *Tot 1572*, ed. I. V. T. Spaander and R. A. van Leeuw (Delft: Delft Stedelijk Museum 'Het Prinsenhof', 1979). At the time of his research, the *Kerkgeld* registers were still in the Haarlem Bishop's Archive, but today they are in the collection of Stadsarchief Delft, Archief Delftse parochiekerken (435), inv. nos. 55-6.
15 Ibid., 93, table 1.
16 For the location of these streets, see Map A.1.

17 De Boer was able to trace almost 60 per cent of the bailiffs and aldermen in the registers of the *Kerkgeld*. The remaining 40 per cent also included the bailiffs and aldermen who lived in the parish of the Nieuwe Kerk.
18 De Boer, 'Delft omstreeks 1400', 94.
19 Verhoeven, *De derde stad*, 285.
20 Ibid., 284–6.
21 For the wealth of Delft's elite in the eighteenth century, see Wijsenbeek-Olthuis, *Achter de gevels van Delft*, chapter IV. A map with the location of breweries and earthenware factories can be found in Verhoeven, *De derde stad*, 362.
22 Verhoeven, *De derde stad*, 314.
23 Similar changes within a relatively stable residential structure at the macro-level have also been observed for Bruges (Deneweth, Leloup and Speecke, 'Een versteende ruimte?', 36).
24 Wijsenbeek-Olthuis, *Achter de gevels van Delft*, 154.
25 Lourens and Lucassen, *Inwonertallen van Nederlandse steden*, 58–9, and for 1569 Boschma-Aarnoudse, *Tot verbeteringe van de neeringe*, 425–6.
26 Herman Rijswijk was kind enough to provide me with a digital version of the *redres van de verponding* and Corrie Boschma-Aarnoudse helped reconstruct the tax collector's route through the city. I would like to thank them both for that.
27 In addition, Alva introduced taxes on the sale of movable property and the sale of real estate. For these taxes, see Bos-Rops, 'De kohieren van de gewestelijke belastingen', 21.
28 For this source, see Boschma-Aarnoudse, *Tot verbeteringe van de neeringe*, appendix 2. Herman Rijswijk has also provided me with a digital version of this tax register, and again Corrie Boschma-Aarnoudse has helped me reconstruct the tax collector's routes. Possible inaccuracies and errors in the use and interpretation of this source are of course entirely my responsibility.
29 Edam received permission to reinforce the city with fortifications in 1513. Before that time, the city was virtually unprotected from enemy armies (Speet, *Edam*, 26–7).
30 Van Deventer's map is included in chapter 3. For this map, see also http://bdh-rd.bne.es/viewer.vm?pid=d-2685031 and Reinout Rutte, Bram Vannieuwenhuyze and Yvonne van Mil, *Stedenatlas Jacob van Deventer: 226 stadsplattegronden uit 1545-1575 - schakels tussen verleden en heden* (Bussum: Thoth; Tielt: Lannoo, 2018). The map by Taems Sijmonsz. is reproduced in Speet, *Edam*, 286, and Boschma-Aarnoudse, *Tot verbeteringe van de neeringe*, 318–19. For cartographic material on Edam, see also Hulskemper, *500 jaar Edamse cartografie*.
31 Boschma-Aarnoudse, *Edam, behouden stad*, 88.
32 Ibid., 72–5.
33 A detailed introduction to this source can be found in J. Sparreboom, 'Twee fiscale bronnen uit het stadsarchief van Edam, circa 1462', *Holland* 13 (1981): 146–64 and in Boschma-Aarnoudse, *Tot verbeteringe van de neeringe*, appendices 1 and 2. Incidentally, Sparreboom (159) wrongly assumes that the impecunious and the poor were not included in the *schotgeld* tax (see Boschma-Aarnoudse, *Tot verbeteringe van de neeringe*, 404–5).
34 These figures, as well as those on which the maps are based, are taken from Boschma-Aarnoudse, *Tot verbeteringe van de neeringe*, overzichtstabellen C1.a-f. The *verndel* (a quarter of a Holland pound) is the currency used in the *schotgeld* registers (ibid., 407).
35 These maps show the infrastructure of 1562 for reference.

36 This was still the case in the seventeenth century (Boschma-Aarnoudse, *Edam, behouden stad*, 192).
37 'met een bequamen bloem ende cruijtthuijn, mitsgaders een boomgaert daer achteraen, wel voorsien van veel schoone boomen en wijngaarden, omheijnt met een cierlijke heijninge van doornen gevlochte ...' (ibid., 173). The description of the house and interior is taken from an auction deed of 1655.
38 Ibid., 234–7.
39 Lourens and Lucassen, *Inwonertallen van Nederlandse steden*, 54–5, and Herman Kaptein, 'Kaasstad van Holland. Een markt- en verzorgingscentrum van naam', in *Geschiedenis van Alkmaar*, ed. Diederik Aten et al. (Zwolle: Waanders, 2007), 228.
40 The location of residential houses within the block faces cannot be determined exactly. For the purpose for which the maps are used here, this is not a major problem.
41 The data on which this map is based were also taken from the 'Historisch Kadaster Alkmaar' by Willem van den Berg. I am very grateful that I was allowed to use these data. For residential patterns in Alkmaar, see also Van den Berg, Van Leeuwen and Lesger, 'Residentiële segregatie in Hollandse steden'.
42 Bitter, 'Ommuurd, volgebouwd en uitgelegd', 77.
43 Until the sixteenth century, most houses in Alkmaar probably had their own alley to the rear yard, where independent 'camers' could be built and rented out (Peter Bitter, 'Huis, erf en straat. Woningen en werkplaatsen, leven en werken in Alkmaar', in *Geschiedenis van Alkmaar*, ed. Diederik Aten, Jan Drewes, Joop Kila and Harry de Raad (Zwolle: Waanders, 2007), 85, and idem, 'De stad versteent. Huizen, woninginrichting en hygiëne', in *Geschiedenis van Alkmaar*, ed. Diederik Aten, Jan Drewes, Joop Kila and Harry de Raad (Zwolle: Waanders, 2007), 213, 216).
44 The register of the *haardstedegeld* of 1492, for instance, is not very useful for measuring residential differentiation, because the indication of wealth – the number of fireplaces – is almost always one (Regionaal Archief Alkmaar, Collection of acquisitions 1412-1984, inv. no. NL-AmRAA-95.001).
45 Bitter, 'Ommuurd, volgebouwd en uitgelegd', 69–71.
46 The following is based on Peter Bitter, 'Van nederzetting tot handelsplaats. Resultaten van archeologisch onderzoek', in *Geschiedenis van Alkmaar*, ed. Diederik Aten et al. (Zwolle: Waanders, 2007), 31–8.
47 Bitter, 'Ommuurd, volgebouwd en uitgelegd', 68.
48 See Kees Stal, 'Een plaets so magnifycq van gebouwen', in *Den Haag. Geschiedenis van de stad*, vol. 2, *De tijd van de Republiek*, ed. Th. Wijsenbeek (Zwolle: Waanders, 2005), 53–4, 59–60; Wijsenbeek, 'Schutters, gilden en buurten', 169, and idem, 'Wooncultuur en sociale verschillen', in *Den Haag. Geschiedenis van de stad*. vol. 2, *De tijd van de Republiek*, ed. Th. Wijsenbeek (Zwolle: Waanders, 2005), 259, 272. The boundary of the Hofbuurt is based on Pieter Wagenaar, 'Haagse bestuurders en ambtenaren', ibid., 91.
49 Stal, 'Een plaets so magnifycq van gebouwen', 54, and also the *redres van de verponding* from 1731 mentions remarkably many houses in *poorten*, that is alleys and blind alleys (Nationaal Archief, 3.01.29 (Financie van Holland), inv. no. 513).
50 When entering the data into the computer, I not only used the original register (Nationaal Archief, Staten van Holland voor 1572, inv.no. 1269) but also the transcription of this source available at the Haags Gemeentearchief (Library, Gg-73). I thank Mr Kersing for drawing my attention to the existence of this transcription. The very detailed map in Ter Meer Derval proved very useful in establishing the boundaries of the built-up area in those years (A. Ter Meer Derval, 'Een kaart van

's-Gravenhage van omstreeks 1560-1570', *Jaarboek Die Haghe* (1932): 1–20). The individual data points are evenly distributed over street segments separated by side streets and, of course, objects without a residential function or with a subordinate residential function are excluded.

51 Kees Stal and Victor Kersing, 'Ruimtelijke ontwikkeling in de late middeleeuwen', in *Den Haag. Geschiedenis van de stad*, vol. 1, *Vroegste tijd tot 1574*, ed. J. G. Smit (Zwolle: Waanders, 2004), 54.
52 De Klerk, *Bouwen aan de hofstad*, 15.
53 Ibid., 11 and 15.
54 Stal and Kersing, 'Ruimtelijke ontwikkeling', 59, from which I also derive the term 'backyard' (*achtertuin*).
55 Ibid., 67, and Stal, 'Een plaets so magnifycq van gebouwen', 40.
56 Wijsenbeek, 'Wooncultuur', 283–4.
57 Ibid., 253, 258 and 285, and also Thera Wijsenbeek, 'Epiloog - gespleten stad', in *Den Haag. Geschiedenis van de stad*, vol. 2, *De tijd van de Republiek*, ed. Th. Wijsenbeek (Zwolle: Waanders, 2005), 331–2.
58 Wijsenbeek, 'Wooncultuur', 272.
59 This database and the associated metadata have been made available via the website of the KNAW institute DANS (https://dans.knaw.nl). A detailed introduction to and analysis of this source can be found in Diederiks, Noordam and Tjalsma, eds, *Armoede en sociale spanning*.
60 For the location and names of these *bonnen*, see for instance Gerrit Jan Peltjes, *Leidse lasten. Twee belastingkohieren uit 1674* (Leiden: Nederlands Historisch Data Archief, 1995), 21. In Diederiks, Noordam and Tjalsma, eds, *Armoede en sociale spanning* a different number of *bonnen* is mentioned, but that is because there also mills and the outlying area are considered as *bonnen*.
61 I will come back to this later, but this interpretation is supported by the fact that the coefficient of variation of the assessments in the *verponding* tax for the Noord-Rapenburg *bon* is the highest of all *bonnen*: 1.38.
62 These percentages are taken from H. D. Tjalsma, 'Een karakterisering van Leiden in 1749', in *Armoede en sociale spanning. Sociaal-historische studies over Leiden in de achttiende eeuw*, ed. H. A. Diederiks, D. J. Noordam and H. D. Tjalsma (Hilversum: Verloren, 1985), table 2.32.
63 Ibid., table 2.3, and see also Ronald Sluijter and Ariadne Schmidt, 'Sociale verhoudingen en maatschappelijke zorg', in *Leiden. De geschiedenis van een Hollandse stad*, vol. 2, *1574-1795*, ed. S. Groenveld (Leiden: Stichting Geschiedschrijving Leiden, 2003), 117.
64 A digital version of this tax roll is also available via DANS.nl.
65 In 1675 there were about 65,000 people living in Leiden and in 1699 about 12,500 households (Dirk Jaap Noordam, 'Demografische ontwikkelingen', in *Leiden. De geschiedenis van een Hollandse Stad*, vol. 2, *1574-1795*, ed. S. Groenveld (Leiden: Stichting Geschiedschrijving Leiden, 2003), 44).
66 See the map in Peltjes, *Leidse lasten*, 22.
67 This last addition is important because the members of the city government are listed at the beginning of the tax roll and without their place of residence. Within the streets, the locations are evenly distributed, but when streets intersect several *bonnen*, the boundaries of the *bonnen* have obviously been taken into account.
68 That 'fraeije huijsen met hare erven' has changed into 'vuile ongesonde gaten en krotten; ende dese soo schoone stad vervuldt werd ... met altijds ontuchtige, ende kijffachtige poortjens' (quoted in Taverne, *In 't land van belofte*, 212).

69 A digital version of this register, edited by D. J. Noordam, is available on the website of the Vereniging Oud Leiden. Arie van Steensel allowed me to use an updated version of this file, for which I am very grateful, of course. In making the interpolation map, I have split up entries that consisted of several residential units and removed the very expensive residential/business properties of brewers from the dataset. The data points were distributed evenly across the streets, obviously taking into account the boundaries of the *bonnen*.
70 See also the illustrative graph based on data for 1558 in A. J. Brand, 'Sociale omstandigheden en charitatieve zorg', in *Leiden. De geschiedenis van een Hollandse Stad*, vol. 1, *Leiden tot 1574*, ed. J. W. Marsilje (Leiden: Stichting Geschiedschrijving Leiden, 2002), 126.
71 N. W. Posthumus, *De geschiedenis van de Leidsche lakenindustrie*, vol. I, *De middeleeuwen (veertiende tot zestiende eeuw)* (Den Haag: Martinus Nijhoff, 1908), 386 ff., and see for a more recent use of this source Tim Bisschops, 'Ruimtelijke vermogensverhoudingen in Leiden (1438–1561). Een pleidooi voor een perceelsgewijze analyse van steden en stedelijke samenlevingen in de Lage Landen', *Stadsgeschiedenis* 2 (2007): 121–38. A digital version of this tax roll is available on the websites of Historisch Leiden in Kaart and of DANS. I thank Arie van Steensel for his support in my research on the residential patterns in Leiden.
72 In calculating the average wealth, I used the data on the amount actually paid and not the assessment established by the *bon*-masters, because the former gives a more realistic picture of the financial resources, especially of the less well-off. See also Brand, 'Sociale omstandigheden', 121.
73 This is not to say, however, that there could not have been considerable differences within the same street. See for instance Stadsarchief Leiden I, Stadsbestuur, inv. no. 578, folios 65v. and 66.
74 Bisschops, 'Ruimtelijke vermogensverhoudingen in Leiden', 125.
75 The remarkably high contributions in the *bon* Rapenburg, in 1498 one of the poorest districts, cannot easily be accounted for. Possibly the number of observations there is very small. For the spatial distribution of wealth in Leiden between 1438 and 1561, see the cartographic representation in ibid., figure 1.
76 Van der Vlist, 'De stedelijke ruimte', 22, 26, 51–2. For the spatial development of the count's court in Leiden, see idem, 26–32 and also H. A. van Oerle, *Leiden. Een multidisciplinaire benadering van het proces der stadwording en de ontwikkeling van het oudste stadsgebied in de middeleeuwen* (Leiden: Brill, 1974), 62, figure 71. For the location of Breestraat and Langebrug, see map A.16 in this appendix.
77 Compare Maps A.16 and A.17 and see also D. J. Noordam, 'Leiden in last. De financiële positie van de Leidenaren aan het einde van de middeleeuwen', *Jaarboek Dirk van Eck* (2001): 17–40: table 4, and Brand, 'Sociale omstandigheden', 125–6.
78 R. C. J. van Maanen, 'De vermogensopbouw van de Leidse bevolking in het laatste kwart van de zestiende eeuw', *Bijdragen en Mededelingen betreffende de Geschiedenis der Nederlanden* 93 (1978): 35.
79 Again, it must be emphasized that the residences of the members of the city government are not mentioned in this tax register and they are therefore not included in this analysis.
80 Van Maanen, 'Stadsbeeld en ruimtelijke ordening', 41. The map of Leiden by Joan Blaeu, published in 1649 but made around 1646, still depicts blocks of small houses west of Rapenburg.
81 For the tax register of 1733, I made use of a digital version available at Stadsarchief Amsterdam as well as a concordance to current addresses. The latter made it

possible to map the exact location of almost 12,000 of the approximately 23,500 inhabited objects listed in the tax roll. I thank Stadsarchief Amsterdam for making this information available. In determining the 250 Amsterdam residents with the highest incomes, use was made of the 1742 register of the Personele Quotisatie. This source is published in Oldewelt, *Kohier van de Personeele Quotisatie*. I thank Caitlin Schouten for allowing me to use the maps in her master's thesis on the residences of Amsterdam's elites during the early modern period.

82 The tax register is published in J. G. Frederiks and P. J. Frederiks, *Kohier van den tweehonderdsten penning voor Amsterdam en onderhoorige plaatsen over 1631* (Amsterdam: Ten Brink & De Vries, 1890). As is often the case with this type of tax roll, the members of the city government are listed at the top without address. To the extent that they were among the top 250 taxpayers, I have retrieved their addresses from Elias, *De vroedschap van Amsterdam*.

83 The value of the assets as declared to the tax-collectors was often considerably less than the actual value. See J. G. van Dillen, ed., *Bronnen tot de geschiedenis van het bedrijfsleven en het gildewezen van Amsterdam*, vol. II, *1612-1632*, Rijks Geschiedkundige Publicatiën (Grote Serie), 78 (Den Haag: Martinus Nijhoff, 1933), XXXVIII-XLIV for a more detailed analysis of this tax roll.

84 'En alle deze straten krielen en grimmelen van alderley handtwerks volk' (Van Domselaer, *Beschryvinge van Amsterdam*, book III, 251).

85 Dijkhuis, 'De Jordaan', 16.

86 See the images of these maps in the image collection of the Stadsarchief Amsterdam and Hameleers, *Kaarten van Amsterdam 1538-1865*, 67-71. These very large and extremely detailed maps by Balthasar Florisz. van Berckenrode are, to my knowledge, the only ones on which walled-in housing is depicted in a recognizable manner (see Chapter 3, Map 3.10).

87 'grouzamen menichte van gemeen varendt, en handtwerks volk' (Van Domselaer, *Beschryvinge van Amsterdam*, book III, 239).

88 I would like to thank my colleague Gabri van Tussenbroek for providing the data file of the city *intra muros* (see also Van Tussenbroek, 'Geografie van arm en rijk'). I added the houses in the outlying area. For the location of these houses, I used the maps in Pontanus' city descriptions from the years 1611-14 (printed in Hameleers, *Kaarten van Amsterdam 1538-1865*, 52-5). The location of *'t Eijlant* proved impossible to establish. The houses registered there were placed in a square north of the city. Obviously, the analysis is limited to the buildings with a residential function and does not include commercial buildings, charitable institutions, public buildings and monasteries.

89 J. G. Kam, *Waar was dat huis in de Warmoesstraat* (Amsterdam: Dienst der Publieke Werken, 1968) and Van der Leeuw-Kistemaker, *Wonen en werken in de Warmoesstraat*, 7.

90 For the situation in 1585, see Bart Reuvekamp, 'De Amsterdamse rijken in 1585. Belastingadministratie als demografische bron', *Amstelodamum* 108 (2021): 13-25.

91 Brouwer Ancher and Breen, 'De doleantie', 191, 196, 125-6.

92 The recent state of knowledge can be found in Gawronski, 'Ontstaan uit een storm' and Jayasena, 'Amsterdam 1200-1300'. The continuity in the city's spatial structure was facilitated by the fact that after city fires and also during the 'petrification' of the city (from the second quarter of the sixteenth century onwards) rebuilding took place house by house and large-scale interventions in the urban landscape were absent (kind communication by Gabri van Tussenbroek).

93 Jayasena, 'Amsterdam 1200-1300' and Speet, 'Verstening, verdichting en vergroting'.

94 Speet, 'Verstening, verdichting en vergroting', 86.

Bibliography

Aalbers, Johan. *De Republiek en de vrede van Europa. De buitenlandse politiek van de republiek der Verenigde Nederlanden na de vrede van Utrecht (1713), voornamelijk gedurende de jaren 1720-1733.* Groningen: Wolters-Noordhoff, 1980.

Abrahamse, Jaap Evert. *Metropolis in the Making. A Planning History of Amsterdam in the Dutch Golden Age.* Turnhout: Brepols, 2019.

Abrahamse, Jaap Evert, Menne Kosian, Reinout Rutte, Otto Diesfeldt, Iskandar Pané, Yvonne van Mil, Thomas van den Brink and Arnoud de Waaijer. 'Water System and Urban Form in Holland. A Survey in Maps: 1575, 1680, 1900 and 2015'. *OverHolland* 21 (2021): 46-121.

Achterhuis, Hans. *Met alle geweld. Een filosofische zoektocht.* Rotterdam: Lemniscaat, 2008.

Achterhuis, Hans. 'Verslaafd aan geweld'. *NRC-Handelsblad, Opinie & Debat*, 14 August 2021: 4-5.

Aerts, Remieg. 'Een staat in verbouwing. Van republiek naar constitutioneel koninkrijk, 1780-1848'. In *Land van kleine gebaren. Een politieke geschiedenis van Nederland 1780-1990*, edited by Remieg Aerts, Herman de Liagre Böhl, Piet de Rooy and Henk te Velde, 13-95. Nijmegen: SUN, 1999.

Alfani, Guido and Wouter Ryckbosch. 'Growing Apart in Early Modern Europe? A Comparison of Inequality Trends in Italy and the Low Countries, 1500-1800'. *Explorations in Economic History* 62 (2016): 143-53.

Allen, John. *Lost Geographies of Power.* Oxford: Blackwell, 2003.

Allen, John. 'The Whereabouts of Power: Politics, Government and Space'. *Geografiska Annaler, Series B* 86 (2004): 19-32.

Ancelovici, Marcos. 'Bourdieu in Movement: Toward a Field Theory of Contentious Politics'. *Social Movement Studies* 20 (2021): 155-73.

Angermuller, Johannes 'Discourse Studies'. In *International Encyclopedia of the Social & Behavioral Sciences*, edited by James D. Wright, 510-15. Amsterdam: Elsevier, 2015.

Archer, Ian W. 'Responses to Alien Immigrants in London, c.1400-1650'. In *Le Migrazioni in Europa secc. XIII-XVIII*, edited by Simonetta Cavaciocchi, 755-74. Prato: Le Monnier, 1994.

Aristotle. *Aristotle's Politics.* Translated by Benjamin Jowett. New York: Random House, 1943.

Baart, Jan. 'De materiële stadskultuur'. In *De Hollandse stad in de dertiende eeuw*, edited by E. H. P. Cordfunke, F. W. N Hugenholtz and K. Sierksma, 93-112. Zutphen: De Walburg Pers, 1988.

Baart, Jan. 'De ontstaansgeschiedenis van Amsterdam'. In *Van stadskern tot stadsgewest. Stedebouwkundige geschiedenis van Amsterdam*, edited by Michiel Jonker, Leo Noordegraaf and Michiel Wagenaar, 15-34. Amsterdam: Verloren, 1984.

Backer, A. J. *Leidse wevers onder gaslicht. Schering en inslag van Zaalberg dekens onder gaslicht (1850-1915).* Leiden: N.V. Koninklijke Nederlandse Fabriek van Wollen Dekens, 1952.

Bairoch, Paul, Jean Batou and Pierre Chèvre. *La population des villes Européennes. Banque de données et analyse sommaire des résultats, 800-1850.* Genève: Droz, 1988.

Bakker, Boudewijn. 'Cornelis Ploos van Amstel en het stadsgezicht als kunst'. In *Kijk Amsterdam 1700-1800: De mooiste stadsgezichten*, edited by Bert Gerlagh, 20-33. Bussum: Thoth; Amsterdam: Stadsarchief Amsterdam, 2017.

Bakker, Boudewijn. 'De stad in Beeld. Het stadsportret als genre in de beeldende kunst'. In *Het aanzien van Amsterdam. Panorama's, plattegronden en profielen uit de Gouden Eeuw*, edited by Boudewijn Bakker and Erik Schmitz, 10-23. Bussum: Thoth; Amsterdam: Stadsarchief Amsterdam, 2007.

Bakker, Boudewijn. 'Het imago van de stad: Zelfportret als propaganda'. In *Het aanzien van Amsterdam. Panorama's, plattegronden en profielen uit de Gouden Eeuw*, edited by Boudewijn Bakker and Erik Schmitz, 56-78. Bussum: Thoth; Amsterdam: Stadsarchief Amsterdam, 2007.

Bakker, Boudewijn. 'Maps, Books and Prints'. In *Opkomst en bloei van het Noordnederlandse stadsgezicht in de 17de eeuw / the Dutch Cityscape in the 17th Century and Its Sources*, edited by B. Haak, R. J. Wattenmaker and B. Bakker, 66-75. Bentveld-Aerdenhout: Landshoff, 1977.

Bakker, Boudewijn and Erik Schmitz, eds. *Het aanzien van Amsterdam. Panorama's, plattegronden en profielen uit de Gouden Eeuw.* Bussum: Thoth; Amsterdam: Stadsarchief Amsterdam, 2007.

Bakker, Rs. *Den opkomst, bloei, verval en tegenwoordigen toestand der stad Delft, in derzelver fabryken en trafyken.* Delft: Rs. Bakker, n.d. (c.1800).

Ballon, Hilary. *The Paris of Henri IV. Architecture and Urbanism.* New York: The Architectural History Foundation; Cambridge, MA: The MIT Press, 1991.

Barry, Jonathan and Christopher Brooks, eds. *The Middling Sort of People. Culture, Society and Politics in England, 1550-1800.* Basingstoke: MacMillan, 1994.

Beik, William. 'The Violence of the French Crowd from Charivari to Revolution'. *Past and Present* 197 (2007): 75-110.

Bell, Nancy. 'Power, Alternative Theories of'. In *Encyclopedia of Violence, Peace, and Conflict*, edited by Lester Kurtz and Jennifer Turpin, 99-105. San Diego: Academic Press, 1999.

Bennett, Tony. *Culture. A Reformer's Science.* London: Sage, 1998.

Berry, Charlotte. *The Margins of Late Medieval London, 1430-1541.* London: University of London Press, 2022.

Besteman, Jan C. and A. J. Guiran. 'De middeleeuwse bewoningsgeschiedenis van Noord-Holland boven het IJ en de ontginning van de veengebieden. Opgravingen in Assendelft in perspectief'. In *Rotterdam Papers V, A Contribution to Prehistoric, Roman and Medieval Archeology*, edited by M. C. van Trierum and H. E. Henkes, 183-212. Rotterdam, 1986.

Bisschops, Tim. 'Ruimtelijke vermogensverhoudingen in Leiden (1438-1561). Een pleidooi voor een perceelsgewijze Analyse van steden en stedelijke samenlevingen in de Lage Landen'. *Stadsgeschiedenis* 2 (2007): 121-38.

Bitter, Peter. 'De stad versteent. Huizen, woninginrichting en hygiëne'. In *Geschiedenis van Alkmaar*, edited by Diederik Aten, Jan Drewes, Joop Kila and Harry de Raad, 210-25. Zwolle: Waanders, 2007.

Bitter, Peter. 'Huis, erf en straat. Woningen en werkplaatsen, leven en werken in Alkmaar'. In *Geschiedenis van Alkmaar*, edited by Diederik Aten, Jan Drewes, Joop Kila and Harry de Raad, 79-90. Zwolle: Waanders, 2007.

Bitter, Peter. 'Nederzetting op het zand. Landschappelijk dynamiek en menselijke bewoning'. In *Geschiedenis van Alkmaar*, edited by Diederik Aten, Jan Drewes, Joop Kila and Harry de Raad, 12-21. Zwolle: Waanders, 2007.

Bitter, Peter. 'Ommuurd, volgebouwd en uitgelegd. Ruimtelijke ontwikkeling van de middeleeuwse stad'. In *Geschiedenis van Alkmaar*, edited by Diederik Aten, Jan Drewes, Joop Kila and Harry de Raad, 64–77. Zwolle: Waanders, 2007.

Bitter, Peter. 'Van nederzetting tot handelsplaats. Resultaten van archeologisch onderzoek'. In *Geschiedenis van Alkmaar*, edited by Diederik Aten, Jan Drewes, Joop Kila and Harry de Raad, 31–8. Zwolle: Waanders, 2007.

Bitter, Peter, and Willem van den Berg. 'Historische gegevens over huizen en bedrijven, hun eigenaren en bewoners'. In *Afval van gorters, brouwers en een hospitaal. Archeologisch onderzoek van het Wortelsteegplein*, edited by S. Ostkamp, P. Bitter, R. Roedema and R. van Wilgen. Rapporten over de Alkmaarse monumentenzorg en archeologie, 6, 21–56. Alkmaar: Gemeente Alkmaar, 1998.

Blok, Josine. 'Hemelse rozen door 't wereldse leven. Sekse en de Nederlandse burgerij in de negentiende eeuw'. In *De stijl van de burger. Over Nederlandse burgerlijke cultuur vanaf de middeleeuwen*, edited by Remieg Aerts and Henk te Velde, 123–56. Kampen: Kok Agora, 1998.

Blondé, Bruno. 'The Low Countries' Paradox. Historical Perspectives on Inequality and the City'. In *Inequality and the City in the Low Countries (1200–2020)*, edited by Bruno Blondé, Sam Geens, Hilde Greefs, Wouter Ryckbosch, Tim Soens and Peter Stabel, 15–42. Turnhout: Brepols, 2020.

Blondé, Bruno, Sam Geens, Hilde Greefs, Wouter Ryckbosch, Tim Soens and Peter Stabel, eds. *Inequality and the City in the Low Countries (1200–2020)*. Turnhout: Brepols, 2020.

Boele, Anita. *Leden van één lichaam. Denkbeelden over armen, armenzorg en liefdadigheid in de Noordelijke Nederlanden 1300–1650*. Hilversum: Verloren, 2013.

Boerefijn, Wim. 'De totstandkoming van de stedelijke vorm'. In *Stadswording in de Nederlanden. Op zoek naar overzicht*, edited by Reinout Rutte and Hildo van Engen, 123–42. Hilversum: Verloren, 2008.

Bohstedt, John. *The Politics of Provisions: Food Riots, Moral Economy, and Market Transition in England, c. 1550–1850*. London: Routledge, 2016.

Boitet, Reinier. *Beschryving der stadt Delft, behelzende een zeer naaukeurige en uitvoerige verhandeling van deszelfs eerste oorsprong, benaming, bevolking ... en regeeringsvorm*. Delft: Reinier Boitet, 1729.

Bonke, Hans. *De kleyne mast van de Hollandse coopsteden. Stadsontwikkeling in Rotterdam 1572–1795*. Amsterdam: Historisch Seminarium van de Universiteit van Amsterdam, 1996.

Boone, Marc and Maarten Prak. 'Rulers, Patricians and Burghers: The Great and the Little Traditions of Urban Revolt in the Low Countries'. In *A Miracle Mirrored. The Dutch Republic in European Perspective*, edited by Karel Davids and Jan Lucassen, 99–134. Cambridge: Cambridge University Press, 1995.

Bos, Dennis. *Waarachtige volksvrienden. De vroege socialistische beweging in Amsterdam 1848–1898*. Amsterdam: Bert Bakker, 2001.

Bos-Rops, Jeannette A. M. Y. 'De kohieren van de gewestelijke belastingen in Holland, 1543–1579'. *Holland* 29 (1997): 18–36.

Boschma-Aarnoudse, Corrie. *Buitenplaatsen in de Purmer. Investeren en buiten leven in een Noord-Hollandse polder*. Stichting Uitgeverij Noord-Holland, 2016.

Boschma-Aarnoudse, Corrie. *Edam, behouden stad. Houten en stenen huizen 1500–1800*. Utrecht: Matrijs, 2007.

Boschma-Aarnoudse, Corrie. *Het Westeinde van Edam. Armoede en welvaren van een stadsbuurt. Een onderzoek naar wonen en werken aan de Lingerzijde en Schepenmakersdijk sinds 1560*. Edam: Hoogheemraadschap van Uitwaterende Sluizen, 1994.

Boschma-Aarnoudse, Corrie. *Tot verbeteringe van de neeringe deser stede. Edam en de Zeevang in de late middeleeuwen en de 16de eeuw*. Hilversum: Verloren, 2003.
Boschma-Aarnoudse, Corrie, Dick M. Bunskoeke and Jan Sparreboom. *Vestingwerken van Edam*. Edam: Vereniging Oud Edam, 1998.
Bosman, Machiel. *De polsslag van de stad. De Amsterdamse kroniek van Jacob Bicker Raije (1732-1772)*. Amsterdam: Athenaeum - Polak & Van Gennep, 2009.
Bourdieu, Pierre. 'The Forms of Capital'. In *Handbook of Theory and Research for the Sociology of Education*, edited by J. Richardson, 241-58. Westport: Greenwood, 1986.
Bourdieu, Pierre. 'Habitus'. In *Habitus: A Sense of Place*, edited by Jean Hillier and Emma Rooksby, 43-9. Aldershot: Ashgate, 2005.
Boudieu, Pierre. *Language and Symbolic Power*. Cambridge, MA: Harvard University Press, 1991.
Bourdieu, Pierre. *The Logic of Practice*. Stanford: Stanford University Press, 1990.
Bourdieu, Pierre. *Outline of a Theory of Practice*. Cambridge: Cambridge University Press, 1977.
Bourdieu, Pierre. *Pascalian Meditations*. Stanford: Stanford University Press, 2000.
Bourdieu, Pierre. 'Physischer, sozialer und angeeigneter physischer Raum'. In *Stadt-Räume: Die Zukunft des Städtischen*, edited by Martin Wentz, 25-34. Frankfurt am Main: Campus; Suhrkamp, 1991.
Bourdieu, Pierre. 'Social Space and the Genesis of Appropriated Physical Space'. *International Journal of Urban and Regional Research* 42 (2018): 106-14.
Bourdieu, Pierre. 'The Social Space and the Genesis of Groups'. *Theory and Society* 14 (1985): 723-44.
Bourdieu, Pierre. *The Social Structures of the Economy*. Cambridge: Polity Press, 2005.
Bowen, Karen. 'Peddling in Texts and Images. The Dutch Visual Perspective'. In *Not Dead Things: The Dissemination of Popular Print in England and Wales, Italy, and the Low Countries, 1500-1820*, edited by Roeland Harms, Joad Raymond and Jeroen Salman, 153-80. Leiden: Brill, 2013.
Brand, Hanno J. 'Sociale omstandigheden en charitatieve zorg'. In *Leiden. De geschiedenis van een Hollandse stad. Vol. 1. Leiden tot 1574*, edited by J. W. Marsilje, 113-50. Leiden: Stichting Geschiedschrijving Leiden, 2002.
Breen, Johannes C. 'De verordeningen op het bouwen te Amsterdam vóór de negentiende eeuw'. *Jaarboek Amstelodamum* 6 (1908): 107-48.
Briganti, Giuliano, Ludovica Trezzani and Laura Laureati. *The Bamboccianti. The Painters of Everyday Life in Seventeenth Century Rome*. Rome: Ugo Bozzi Editore, 1983.
Briggs, Charles L. 'Anthropology of Discourse'. In *International Encyclopedia of the Social & Behavioral Sciences*, edited by James D. Wright, 503-9. Amsterdam: Elsevier, 2015.
Brouwer Ancher, Aloysius J. M. *De gilden*. Den Haag: Loman & Funke, 1895.
Brouwer Ancher, Aloysius J. M., and J. C. Breen. 'De doleantie van een deel der burgerij van Amsterdam tegen den Magistraat dier stad in 1564 en 1565'. *Bijdragen en Mededeelingen van het Historisch Genootschap* 24 (1903): 59-200.
Brown, Christopher. *Dutch Townscape Painting*. Themes and Painters in the National Gallery. London: National Gallery, 1972.
Brugmans, Hendrik. *Geschiedenis van Amsterdam. Vol. 3, Bloeitijd 1621/1697*. Utrecht: Het Spectrum, 1973.
Buijnsters-Smeets, Leontine. *Straatverkopers in beeld. Tekeningen en prenten van Nederlandse kunstenaars circa 1540-1850*. Nijmegen: Vantilt, 2012.

Burgess, Ernest W. 'The Growth of the City: An Introduction to a Research Project'. In *The City*, edited by Robert E. Park, Ernest W. Burgess and Roderick D. MacKenzie, 47–62. Chicago: University of Chicago Press, 1925.
Burke, Peter. *Eyewitnessing. The Uses of Images as Historical Evidence*. London: Reaktion Books, 2001.
Burke, Peter. *History and Social Theory*. Cambridge: Polity Press, 2016.
Burke, Peter. 'The Language of Orders in Early Modern Europe'. In *Social Orders and Social Classes in Europe since 1500: Studies in Social Stratification*, edited by M. L. Bush, 1–12. London: Longman, 1992.
Burke, Peter. *Popular Culture in Early Modern Europe*. London: Temple Smith, 1979.
Burke, Peter. 'Some Reflections on the Pre-Industrial City'. *Urban History Yearbook* (1975): 13–21.
Burm, Paul and Guus J. Borger. 'De stichting van Friedrichstadt in 1621. Sociale segregatie in een geplande nederzetting'. *Bulletin KNOB* 102 (2003): 170–85.
Calaresu, Melissa. 'Costumes and Customs in Print: Travel, Ethnography, and the Representation of Street-Sellers in Early Modern Italy'. In *Not Dead Things: The Dissemination of Popular Print in England and Wales, Italy, and the Low Countries, 1500–1820*, edited by Roeland Harms, Joad Raymond and Jeroen Salman, 181–209. Leiden: Brill, 2013.
Calaresu, Melissa. 'From the Street to Stereotype: Urban Space, Travel and the Picturesque in Late Eighteenth-Century Naples'. *Italian Studies* 62 (2007): 189–203.
Calaresu, Melissa. 'Representing the Street in Words and Images'. In *Early Modern Streets. A European Perspective*, edited by Danielle van den Heuvel, 50–80. Abingdon, Oxon: Routledge, 2022.
Calaresu, Melissa and Danielle van den Heuvel. 'Introduction: Food Hawkers from Representation to Reality'. In *Food Hawkers. Selling in the Streets from Antiquity to the Present*, edited by Melissa Calaresu and Danielle van den Heuvel, 1–18. London: Routledge, 2016.
Carasso, Deirdre. 'Kroniek van het Amsterdamse stadsportret 1540–1740'. In *Het aanzien van Amsterdam. Panorama's, plattegronden en profielen uit de Gouden Eeuw*, edited by Boudewijn Bakker and Erik Schmitz, 42–55. Bussum: Thoth; Amsterdam: Stadsarchief Amsterdam, 2007.
Carasso-Kok, Marijke. 'Der stede scut. De schuttersgilden in de Hollandse steden tot het einde der zestiende eeuw'. In *Schutters in Holland. Kracht en zenuwen van de stad*, edited by M. Carasso-Kok and J. Levy-van Halm, 16–35. Zwolle: Waanders, 1988.
Carasso-Kok, Marijke and Koos Levy-van Halm, eds. *Schutters in Holland. Kracht en zenuwen van de stad*. Zwolle: Waanders, 1988.
Casson, Catherine and Mark Casson. 'Location, Location, Location? Analysing Property Rents in Medieval Gloucester'. *Economic History Review* 69 (2016): 575–99.
Clark, Peter. *European Cities and Towns 400-2000*. Oxford: Oxford University Press, 2009.
Cohen, Elizabeth S. 'Honor and Gender in the Streets of Early Modern Rome'. *Journal of Interdisciplinary History* 22 (1992): 597–625.
Colson, Justin and Arie van Steensel, eds. *Cities and Solidarities: Urban Communities in Pre-Modern Europe*. Abingdon, Oxon: Routledge, 2017.
Coquery, Natacha. 'Shopping Streets in Eighteenth-Century Paris. A Landscape Shaped by Historical, Economic and Social Forces'. In *The Landscape of Consumption. Shopping Streets and Cultures in Western Europe, 1600–1900*, edited by Jan Hein Furnée and Clé Lesger, 57–77. Houndmills: Palgrave Macmillan, 2014.

Craane, Marlous L. 'Spatial Patterns. The Late-Medieval and Early-Modern Economy of the Bailiwick of 's-Hertogenbosch from an Interregional, Regional and Local Spatial Perspective'. PhD thesis, Tilburg University, 2013.

Craffurd, Joris. 'Een generaal en kort verhaal (Aansprekersoproer 1696)'. In *Oproeren in Holland gezien door tijdgenoten. Ooggetuigenverslagen van oproeren in de provincie Holland ten tijde van de Republiek (1690-1750)*, edited by R. M. Dekker, 38-107. Assen: Van Gorcum, 1979.

Curdes, Gerhard. 'Spatial Organization of Towns at the Level of the Smallest Urban Unit: Plots and Buildings'. In *Urban Landscape Dynamics. A Multi-Level Innovation Process*, edited by Armando Montanari, Gerhard Curdes and Leslie Forsyth, 281-94. Aldershot: Avebury, 1993.

Daniels, Stephen and Denis Cosgrove. 'Introduction: Iconography and Landscape'. In *The Iconography of Landscape : Essays on the Symbolic Representation, Design and Use of Past Environments*, edited by Denis Cosgrove and Stephen Daniels, 1-10. Cambridge: Cambridge University Press, 1988.

Davids, Carolus A. 'De migratiebeweging in Leiden in de achttiende eeuw'. In *Armoede en sociale spanning. Sociaal-historische studies over Leiden in de achttiende eeuw*, edited by H. A. Diederiks, D. J. Noordam and H. D. Tjalsma, 137-56. Hilversum: Verloren, 1985.

De Boer, Dick E. H. 'Delft omstreeks 1400'. In *De stad Delft. Cultuur en maatschappij. Vol. 1, Tot 1572*, edited by I. V. T. Spaander and R. A. van Leeuw, 92-8. Delft: Delft Stedelijk Museum 'Het Prinsenhof', 1979.

De Boer, Dick E. H. '"Op weg naar volwassenheid". De ontwikkeling van produktie en consumptie in de Hollandse en Zeeuwse Steden in de dertiende eeuw'. In *De Hollandse stad in de dertiende eeuw*, edited by J. M. Baart, Dick E. H. de Boer , G. van Herwijnen, H. Janse, C. v.d. Kieft, C. I. Kruisheer, P. H. D. Leupen, H. H. van Regteren Altena and R. Rentenaar, 28-43. Zutphen: Walburg Pers, 1988.

De Certeau, Michel. *The Practice of Everyday Life*. Berkeley: University of California Press, 1984.

De Cretser, Gysbert. *Beschryvinge van 's Gravenhage: Behelsende desselfs eerste opkomste, stichtinge en vermakelyke situatie ... wandelingen en buytenwegen*. Amsterdam: Jan ten Hoorn, 1711.

De Jong, Joop. *Een deftig bestaan. Het dagelijks leven van regenten in de 17de en 18de eeuw*. Utrecht: Kosmos, 1987.

De Jongste, Jan A. F. *Onrust aan het Spaarne. Haarlem in de jaren 1747-1751*. Amsterdam: De Bataafsche Leeuw, 1984.

De Klerk, Arie. *Bouwen aan de hofstad. De geschiedenis van het bouwtoezicht in Den Haag 1250-1900, in sociaal en cultureel perspectief*. Delft: Delft University Press, 1998.

De Klerk, Len A. "Verscheydentheydt behaecht". Enige hoofdstukken uit de geschiedenis van het publieke domein'. In *De openbare ruimte van de stad*, edited by G. van der Plas, 13-30. Amsterdam: Genootschap Amstelodamum; Stadsuitgeverij, 1991.

De Munck, Bert. 'Diachrony, Synchrony and Modernity. How to Contribute to the Debate on Economic Inequality from an Historical Perspective?'. In *Inequality and the City in the Low Countries (1200-2020)*, edited by B. Blondé, Sam Geens, Hilde Greefs, Wouter Ryckbosch, Tim Soens and Peter Stabel, 377-96. Turnhout: Brepols, 2020.

De Rock, Jelle. *The Image of the City in Early Netherlandish Painting (1400-1550)*. Turnhout: Brepols, 2019.

De Rock, Jelle. 'The Image of the City Quantified: The Serial Analysis of Pictorial Representations of Urbanity in Early Netherlandish Art (1420-1520)'. In *Portraits of the City. Representing Urban Space in Later Medieval and Early Modern Europe*, edited by Katrien Lichtert, Jan Dumolyn and Maximiliaan P. J. Martens, 67–81. Turnhout: Brepols, 2014.

De Rooy, Piet. 'De geest van omverwerping 1851–1876'. In *Geschiedenis van Amsterdam 1813–1900. Hoofdstad in aanbouw*, edited by Remieg Aerts and Piet de Rooy, 341–431. Amsterdam: SUN, 2006.

De Rooy, Piet. *Een revolutie die voorbij ging. Domela Nieuwenhuis en het Palingoproer*. Bussum: Fibula-Van Dishoeck, 1971.

De Vries, Boudien. *Electoraat en elite. Sociale structuur en sociale mobiliteit in Amsterdam 1850–1895*. Amsterdam: De Bataafsche Leeuw, 1986.

De Vries, Jan. *Barges and Capitalism. Passenger Transportation in the Dutch Economy, 1632–1839*. Utrecht: HES Publishers, 1981.

De Vries, Jan. *European Urbanization 1500–1800*. Cambridge, MA: Harvard University Press, 1984.

De Vries, Jan and Ad van der Woude. *The First Modern Economy. Success, Failure, and Perseverance of the Dutch Economy, 1500–1815*. Cambridge: Cambridge University Press, 1997.

Dekker, Rudolf M. *Holland in beroering. Oproeren in de 17de en 18de eeuw*. Baarn: Ambo, 1982.

Dekker, Rudolf M. *Oproeren in Holland gezien door tijdgenoten. Ooggetuigenverslagen van oproeren in de provincie Holland ten tijde van de Republiek (1690–1750)*. Assen: Van Gorcum, 1979.

Dekker, Rudolf M. 'Women in Revolt: Popular Protest and Its Social Basis in Holland in the Seventeenth and Eighteenth Centuries'. *Theory and Society* 16 (1987): 337–62.

Deneweth, Heidi. 'Real Property, Speculation and Housing Inequality. Bruges, 1550-1670'. In *Inequality and the City in the Low Countries (1200-2020)*, edited by B. Blondé, Sam Geens, Hilde Greefs, Wouter Ryckbosch, Tim Soens and Peter Stabel, 251–68. Turnhout: Brepols, 2020.

Deneweth, Heidi, Ward Leloup and Mathijs Speecke. 'Een versteende ruimte? De impact van stedelijke veranderingsprocessen op de sociale geografie van Brugge, 1380–1670'. *Stadsgeschiedenis* 13 (2018): 19–40.

Dessing, René W.Chr. *De Amsterdamse buitenplaatsen. Een vergeten stadsgeschiedenis*. Utrecht: Matrijs, 2015.

Deurloo, A. J. 'Bijltjes en klouwers. Een bijdrage tot de geschiedenis der Amsterdamse scheepsbouw, in het bijzonder in de tweede helft der achttiende eeuw'. *Economisch- en Sociaal-Historisch Jaarboek* 34 (1971): 4–71.

Dickinson, Robert E. *The West European City. A Geographical Interpretation*. 1951. London: Routledge & Kegan Paul, 1962.

Diederiks, Herman A. 'Beroepsstructuur en sociale stratificatie in Leiden in het midden van de achttiende eeuw'. In *Armoede en sociale spanning. Sociaal-historische studies over Leiden in de achttiende eeuw*, edited by H. A. Diederiks, D. J. Noordam and H. D. Tjalsma, 45–67. Hilversum: Verloren, 1985.

Diederiks, Herman A. *Een stad in verval. Amsterdam omstreeks 1800: Demografisch, economisch, ruimtelijk*. Amsterdam: Historisch Seminarium van de Universiteit van Amsterdam, 1982.

Diederiks, Herman A., Dirk Jaap Noordam and Heiko D. Tjalsma, eds. *Armoede en sociale spanning. Sociaal-historische studies over Leiden in de achttiende eeuw*. Hilversum: Verloren, 1985.

Digeser, Peter. 'The Fourth Face of Power'. *The Journal of Politics* 54 (1992): 977–1007.

Dijkhuis, Henk Tj. 'De Jordaan. De ontwikkeling van een volkswijk in een grote stad'. *Economisch-Historisch Jaarboek* 21 (1940): 1-90.
Doedens, Anne. 'Collectief verzet in de Nederlanden 1813-1848: Een terreinverkenning'. In *Autoriteit en strijd*, edited by A. Doedens, 181-271. Amsterdam: VU Uitgeverij, 1981.
Doedens, Anne. 'De patriotse vluchtelingen'. In *Voor vaderland en vrijheid. De revolutie van de patriotten*, edited by F. Grijzenhout, W. W. Mijnhardt and N. C. F. van Sas, 156-75. Amsterdam: De Bataafsche Leeuw, 1987.
Dorren, Gabrielle. *Eenheid in verscheidenheid. De burgers van Haarlem in de Gouden Eeuw*. Amsterdam: Prometheus; Bert Bakker, 2001.
Dudok van Heel, Sebastien A. C. 'Regent Families and Urban Development in Amsterdam'. In *Rome - Amsterdam. Two Growing Cities in Seventeenth-Century Europe*, edited by Peter van Kessel and Elisja Schulte, 124-45. Amsterdam: Amsterdam University Press, 1997.
Dumas, Charles. *Haagse stadsgezichten 1550-1800. Topografische schilderijen van het Haags Historisch Museum*. Zwolle: Waanders, 1991.
Duncan, James S. *The City as Text: The Politics of Landscape Interpretation in the Kandy Kingdom*. Cambridge: Cambridge University Press, 1990.
Edelman, Marc. 'E.P. Thompson and Moral Economies'. In *A Companion to Moral Anthropology*, edited by Didier Fassin, 49-66. Chichester: Wiley-Blackwell, 2012.
Een-Amsterdammer. *Amsterdam en de Amsterdammers*. Deventer: A.J. van den Sigtenhorst, 1875.
Egmond, Florike. 'De boeven van Coornhert'. In *Scherp toezicht; van 'Boeventucht' tot 'Samenleving en criminaliteit'*, edited by Cyrille Fijnaut and Pieter Spierenburg, 99-111. Arnhem: Gouda Quint, 1990.
Egmond, Florike. 'Fragmentatie, rechtsverscheidenheid en rechtsongelijkheid in de Noordelijke Nederlanden tijdens de zeventiende en achttiende eeuw'. In *Nieuw licht op oude justitie. Misdaad en straf ten tijde van de Republiek*, edited by Sjoerd Faber, 9-23. Muiderberg: Dick Coutinho, 1989.
Elden, Stuart. *Foucault. The Birth of Power*. Cambridge: Polity, 2017.
Elias, Johan E. *De vroedschap van Amsterdam 1578-1795. 1903-1905*. Reprinted. Amsterdam: N. Israel, 1963.
Elias, Norbert. *The Civilizing Process. Sociogenetic and Psychogenetic Investigations*. Oxford: Blackwell, 1994.
Esser, Raingard. *The Politics of Memory. The Writing of Partition in the Seventeenth-Century Low Countries*. Leiden: Brill, 2012.
Evans, Richard J. *Rituals of Retribution. Capital Punishment in Germany 1600-1987*. Oxford: Oxford University Press, 1996.
Faber, Sjoerd. 'Een zachte botsing. Celstraf en schavot te Amsterdam in 1854'. In *Criminaliteit in de negentiende eeuw*, edited by S. Faber, J. E. A. Boomgaard and M. Carasso-Kok, 69-82. Hilversum: Verloren, 1989.
Faber, Sjoerd. 'Het Rasphuis: Wat was dat eigenlijk?'. In *Scherp toezicht; van 'Boeventucht' tot 'Samenleving en criminaliteit'*, edited by Cyrille Fijnaut and Pieter Spierenburg, 127-43. Arnhem: Gouda Quint, 1990.
Faber, Sjoerd. *Strafrechtspleging en criminaliteit in Amsterdam, 1680-1811. De nieuwe menslievendheid*. Arnhem: Gouda Quint, 1983.
Faber, Sjoerd, Johannes E. A. Boomgaard and Marijke Carasso-Kok, eds. *Criminaliteit in de negentiende eeuw*. Hilversum: Verloren, 1989.
Fijnaut, Cyrille. *De geschiedenis van de Nederlandse politie. Een staatsinstelling in de maalstroom van de geschiedenis*. Amsterdam: Boom, 2007.

Firnhaber-Baker, Justine. 'Introduction. Medieval Revolt in Context'. In *The Routledge History Handbook of Medieval Revolt*, edited by Justine Firnhaber-Baker and Dirk Schoenaers, 1–15. London: Routledge, 2017.
Fokkens, Melchior. *Beschrijvinge der wijdt-vermaarde koop-stadt Amstelredam, van haar eerste beginselen, oude voor-rechten . . . en, haar tegenwoordigen standt*. Amsterdam: Abraham and Jan de Wees, 1662.
Foucault, Michel. *Discipline and Punish. The Birth of the Prison*. New York: Vintage books, 1995.
Franke, Herman. *De dood in het leven van alledag. Twee eeuwen rouwadvertenties en openbare strafvoltrekkingen in Nederland*. Den Haag: Nijgh & Van Ditmar, 1985.
Franke, Herman. 'Opkomst en neergang van eenzame opsluiting. Historisch-sociologische verklaringen en lange-termijn ontwikkelingen binnen het gevangeniswezen in de westerse wereld'. In *Scherp toezicht; van 'Boeventucht' tot 'Samenleving en criminaliteit'*, edited by Cyrille Fijnaut and Pieter Spierenburg, 167–89. Arnhem: Gouda Quint, 1990.
Frederiks, Johannes G. and Pieter J. Frederiks. *Kohier van den tweehonderdsten penning voor Amsterdam en onderhoorige plaatsen over 1631*. Amsterdam: Ten Brink & De Vries, 1890.
Friedrichs, Christopher R. *The Early Modern City 1450–1750*. London: Longman, 1995.
Friedrichs, Christopher R. 'German Social Structure'. In *Germany. A New Social and Economic History*, edited by Bob Scribner, 233–58. London: Arnold, 1996.
Frijhoff, Willem and Marijke Spies. *1650. Bevochten eendracht. Nederlandse cultuur in Europese context*. Den Haag: Sdu Uitgevers, 1999.
Fritz, Rolf. *Das Stadt- und Strassenbild in der holländischen Malerei des 17. Jahrhunderts*. Berlin: 1932.
Frow, John. *Cultural Studies and Cultural Value*. Oxford: Clarendon Press, 1995.
Froy, Francesca 'Understanding the Spatial Organisation of Economic Activities in Early 19th Century Antwerp'. *Journal of Space Syntax* 6 (2016): 225–46.
Fruin, Jacobus A. 'Het oudste der tot dusver bekende keurboeken van Delft'. *Nieuwe bijdragen voor rechtsgeleerdheid en wetgeving, nieuwe reeks* 8 (1882): 277–356.
Fruin, Robert J. *Geschiedenis der staatsinstellingen in Nederland tot den val der Republiek*. 1901. Edited by H. T. Colenbrander. Den Haag: Martinus Nijhoff, 1980.
Fuks, Leo, ed. *De Zeven Provinciën in beroering. Hoofdstukken uit een Jiddische kroniek over de jaren 1740–1752 van Abraham Chaim Braatbard*. Amsterdam: J.M. Meulenhoff, 1960.
Gabriëls, Jos. 'Patrizier und Regenten: Städtische Eliten in den Nördlichen Niederlanden 1500–1800'. In *Bürgerliche Eliten in den Niederlanden und in Nordwestdeutschland*, edited by H. Schilling and H. A. Diederiks, 37–64. Köln: Böhlau, 1985.
Garrioch, David. *Neighbourhood and Community in Paris 1740–1790*. Cambridge: Cambridge University Press, 1986.
Gawronski, Jerzy. 'Ontstaan uit een storm. De vroegste geschiedenis van Amsterdam archeologisch en landschappelijk belicht'. *Jaarboek Amstelodamum* 109 (2017): 54–91.
Gelderblom, Oscar. 'From Antwerp to Amsterdam. The Contribution of Merchants from the Southern Netherlands to the Commercial Expansion of Amsterdam (c.1540–1609)'. *Review (Fernand Braudel Center)* 26 (2003): 247–82.
Geltner, Guy. *Flogging Others: Corporal Punishment and Cultural Identity from Antiquity to the Present*. Amsterdam: Amsterdam University Press, 2014.
Geremek, Bronisław. *Het Kaïnsteken. Het beeld van armen en vagebonden in de Europese literatuur van de 15e tot de 17e eeuw*. Baarn: Anthos, 1992.

Gerlagh, Bert, ed. *Kijk Amsterdam 1700–1800: De mooiste stadsgezichten*. Bussum: Thoth; Amsterdam: Stadsarchief Amsterdam, 2017.

Gerlagh, Bert. 'Verandering en continuïteit in de topografie'. In *Kijk Amsterdam 1700–1800: De mooiste stadsgezichten*, edited by Bert Gerlagh, 52–65. Bussum: Thoth; Amsterdam: Stadsarchief Amsterdam, 2017.

Geuzebroek, Nanda. *Vondelingen. Het Aalmoezeniersweeshuis van Amsterdam, 1780–1830*. Hilversum: Verloren, 2020.

Giddens, Anthony. *The Constitution of Society. Outline of the Theory of Structuration*. Oxford: Polity Press, 1984.

Giddens, Anthony. *A Contemporary Critique of Historical Materialism*. 1981. Stanford: Stanford University Press, 1995.

Giele, Jacques J. and Geert Jan van Oenen. 'Theorie en praktijk van het onderzoek naar de sociale structuur'. *Tijdschrift voor Sociale Geschiedenis* 5 (1976): 167–85.

Gombrich, Ernst H. 'Standards of Truth: The Arrested Image and the Moving Eye'. In *The Language of Images*, edited by W. J. T. Mitchell, 181–217. Chicago: The University of Chicago Press, 1980.

Götz, Norbert '"Moral Economy": Its Conceptual History and Analytical Prospects'. *Journal of Global Ethics* 11 (2015): 147–62.

Griffiths, Paul. 'Introduction: Punishing the English'. In *Penal Practice and Culture, 1500–1900. Punishing the English*, edited by Simon Devereaux and Paul Griffiths, 1–35. Houndmills: Palgrave MacMillan, 2004.

Grijzenhout, Frans. 'De patriotse beeldenstorm'. In *Voor Vaderland en vrijheid. De revolutie van de patriotten*, edited by F. Grijzenhout, W. W. Mijnhardt and N. C. F. van Sas, 131–55. Amsterdam: De Bataafsche Leeuw, 1987.

Grijzenhout, Frans. *Vermeer's Little Street. A View of the Penspoort in Delft*. Amsterdam: Rijksmuseum Amsterdam, 2015.

Grijzenhout, Frans. 'Vermeer's the Little Street Revisited'. *Bulletin KNOB* 117 (2018): 1–13.

Grijzenhout, Frans and Niek C. F. van Sas. *Voor Vaderland en vrijheid. Revolutie in Nederland 1780–1787*. Utrecht: Centraal Museum Utrecht, 1987.

Guicciardini, Lodovico. *Beschryvinghe van alle de Nederlanden; anderssins ghenoemt Neder-Duytslandt*. Amsterdam: Willem Jansz., 1612.

Haak, Bob. 'The City Portrayed'. In *Opkomst en bloei van het Noordnederlandse stadsgezicht in de 17de eeuw / the Dutch Cityscape in the 17th Century and Its Sources*, edited by B. Haak, R. J. Wattenmaker and B. Bakker, 190–6. Bentveld-Aerdenhout: Landshoff, 1977.

Haak, Bob, Richard J. Wattenmaker and Boudewijn Bakker. 'Foreword'. In *Opkomst en bloei van het Noordnederlandse stadsgezicht in de 17de eeuw / the Dutch Cityscape in the 17th Century and Its Sources*, edited by B. Haak, R. J. Wattenmaker and B. Bakker, 10–13. Bentveld-Aerdenhout: Landshoff, 1977.

Haak, Bob, Richard J. Wattenmaker and Boudewijn Bakker, eds. *Opkomst en bloei van het Noordnederlandse stadsgezicht in de 17de eeuw / the Dutch Cityscape in the 17th Century and Its Sources*. Bentveld-Aerdenhout: Landshoff, 1977.

Haitsma Mulier, Eco O. G. 'De zeventiende-eeuwse stadsbeschrijvingen van Amsterdam'. *Maandblad Amstelodamum* 85 (1998): 107–15.

Haitsma Mulier, Eco O. G. 'Geschiedschrijving in het vroegmoderne Nederland (16e-18e eeuw)'. *Holland* 17 (1985): 185–99.

Hameleers, Marc. *Kaarten van Amsterdam 1538–1865*. Bussum: Thoth; Amsterdam: Gemeentearchief Amsterdam, 2013.

Harley, John B. 'Deconstructing the Map'. 1989. In *The Map Reader: Theories of Mapping Practice and Cartographic Representation*, edited by Martin Dodge, Rob Kitchin and Chris Perkins, 56-64. Chichester: John Wiley & Sons, 2011.

Harley, John B. 'Maps, Knowledge, and Power'. In *The Iconography of Landscape: Essays on the Symbolic Representation, Design and Use of Past Environments*, edited by Denis Cosgrove and Stephen Daniels, 277-312. Cambridge: Cambridge University Press, 1988.

Harley, John B. 'Silences and Secrecy: The Hidden Agenda of Cartography in Early Modern Europe'. *Imago Mundi* 40 (1988): 57-76.

Harvey, David. *Social Justice and the City*. Baltimore: John Hopkins University Press, 1973.

Haugaard, Mark. 'Concerted Power over'. *Constellations* 22 (2015): 147-58.

Haugaard, Mark. *The Constitution of Power. A Theoretical Analysis of Power, Knowledge and Structure*. Manchester: Manchester University Press, 1997.

Haugaard, Mark. 'Power, Social and Political Theories of'. In *Encyclopedia of Violence, Peace, and Conflict*, edited by Lester Kurtz and Jennifer Turpin, 107-21. San Diego: Academic Press, 1999.

Haugaard, Mark. ed. *Power: A Reader*. Manchester: Manchester University Press, 2002.

Hayward, Katy. 'Conflict and Consensus'. In *International Encyclopedia of the Social & Behavioral Sciences*, edited by James D. Wright, 589-93. Amsterdam: Elsevier, 2015.

Hefting, Paul. *De foto's van Breitner*. Den Haag: SDU, 1989.

Heijbroek, Jan F. 'Holland vanaf het water. De bezoeken van James Abbott McNeill Whistler aan Nederland'. *Bulletin van het Rijksmuseum* 36 (1988): 225-56.

Hell, Maarten. *De Amsterdamse herberg 1450-1800. Geestrijk centrum van het openbare leven*. Nijmegen: Vantilt, 2017.

Hell, Maarten. 'De Oude Geuzen en de Opstand. Politiek en lokaal bestuur in tijd van oorlog en expansie 1578-1650'. In *Geschiedenis van Amsterdam. Centrum van de Wereld 1578-1650*, edited by Willem Frijhoff and Maarten Prak, 241-97. Amsterdam: SUN, 2004.

Herbert, David T. and Colin J. Thomas. *Cities in Space: City as Place*. London: David Fulton, 1997.

Hillier, Bill, Tao Yang and Alasdair Turner. 'Normalising Least Angle Choice in Depthmap and How It Opens up New Perspectives on the Global and Local Analysis of City Space'. *Journal of Space Syntax* 3 (2012): 155-93.

Hindess, Barry. *Discourses of Power: From Hobbes to Foucault*. Oxford: Blackwell, 1996.

Hobsbawn, Eric J. 'Cities and Insurrections'. In E. J. Hobsbawn, *Revolutionaries. Contemporary Essays*, 220-33. London: Weidenfeld and Nicolson, 1973.

Hobsbawn, Eric J. *Primitive Rebels. Studies in Archaic Forms of Social Movement in the 19th and 20th Centuries*. 1959. Manchester: Manchester University Press, 1974.

Hobsbawn, Eric J. *Revolutionaries. Contemporary Essays*. London: Weidenfeld and Nicolson, 1973.

Hoekveld, Gerard A. *Baarn. Schets van de ontwikkeling van een villadorp*. Baarn: Bosch & Keuning, 1964.

Hoekveld, Gerard A. 'Over de voorspelbaarheid van ruimtelijke patronen: Areale modellen van de Noordwest-Europese stad, 1300-heden'. *Historisch-Geografisch Tijdschrift* 8 (1990): 1-23.

Hoeufft, Johannes D. and Johannes C. R. van Hoorn van Burgh. *Kadastrale uitkomsten van Noord- en Zuid-Holland 1832*. 1832. Reissue with an introduction by W. J. van Den Berg en Ph. Kint. Dordrecht: Historische Vereniging Holland, 1993.

Hofland, Peter. *Leden van de Raad. De Amsterdamse gemeenteraad 1814–1941.* Amsterdam: Gemeentearchief Amsterdam; H.J. Duyvisfonds, 1998.
Honig, Elizabeth Alice. 'Desire and Domestic Economy'. *The Art Bulletin* 83 (2001): 294–315.
Honig, Elizabeth Alice. *Painting & the Market in Early Modern Antwerp.* New Haven: Yale University Press, 1998.
Hoppenbrouwers, Peter C. M. 'Van Waterland tot stedenland. De Hollandse economie c. 975-c. 1570'. In *Geschiedenis van Holland tot 1572*, edited by Thimo de Nijs and Eelco Beukers, 103–48. Hilversum: Verloren, 2002.
Huberts, Veronica R. A. D. *De Amsterdamse venters. Een sociografische monografie.* Amsterdam: Van Campen, 1940.
Hulskemper, Kees, ed. *500 Jaar Edamse cartografie. Plattegronden, landmeters en kaarttekenaars sinds 1540 (met een genealogische bijdrage van Jan Doets).* Edam: Vereniging Oud Edam, 1993.
IJsselstijn, Marcel and Reinout Rutte. 'Meer dan honderdtwintig steden en ruim veertig mislukkingen. Vijfhonderd jaar stadsworting in Nederland (elfde-vijftiende eeuw)'. *Amstelodamum* 109 (2017): 10–53.
Ingram, Martin. 'Shame and Pain: Themes and Variations in Tudor Punishments'. In *Penal Practice and Culture, 1500–1900. Punishing the English*, edited by Simon Devereaux and Paul Griffiths, 36–62. Houndmills: Palgrave MacMillan, 2004.
Jansen, Peter C. 'Poverty in Amsterdam at the Close of the 18th Century'. *Acta Historiae Neerlandicae: Studies on the History of the Netherlands* 10 (1978): 98–114.
Jayasena, Ranjith. 'Amsterdam 1200–1300, stadsworting aan de monding van de Amstel'. *Jaarboek Amstelodamum* 109 (2017): 113–49.
Jelgersma, Hendrik C. *Galgebergen en galgevelden in West- en Midden Nederland.* Zutphen: De Walburg Pers, 1978.
Jenkins, Richard. *Pierre Bourdieu.* Key Sociologists. London: Routledge, 1992.
Jenner, Mark. 'Circulation and Disorder. London Streets and Hackney Coaches, c.1640-c.1740'. In *The Streets of London; from the Great Fire to the Great Stink*, edited by Tim Hitchcock and Heather Shore, 40–53. London: Rivers Oram Press, 2003.
Jensen, Sune Qvotrup 'Othering, Identity Formation and Agency'. *Qualitative Studies* 2 (2011): 63–78.
Johnston, Ron J. *City and Society. An Outline for Urban Geography.* London: Hutchinson, 1984.
Jones, Emrys. 'London in the Early Seventeenth Century: An Ecological Appraoch'. *The London Journal* 6 (1980): 123–33.
Jütte, Daniel. 'Smashed Panes and 'Terrible Showers': Windows, Violence, and Honor in the Early Modern City'. *West 86th: A Journal of Decorative Arts, Design History, and Material Culture* 22 (2015): 131–56.
Kam, Jan G. *Waar was dat huis in de Warmoesstraat.* Amsterdam: Dienst der Publieke Werken, 1968.
Kaptein, Herman. 'Kaasstad van Holland. Een markt- en verzorgingscentrum van naam'. In *Geschiedenis van Alkmaar*, edited by Diederik Aten, Jan Drewes, Joop Kila and Harry de Raad, 226–51. Zwolle: Waanders, 2007.
Keene, Derek J. 'Suburban Growth'. In *The English Medieval Town. A Reader in English Urban History*, edited by Richard Holt and Gervase Rosser, 97–119. London: Longman, 1990.
Kertzer, David I. *Ritual, Politics, and Power.* New Haven: Yale University Press, 1988.

Kettering, Sharon. *French Society 1589-1715*. A Social History of Europe. Harlow: Longman, 2001.
Keverling Buisman, Frank and E. Muller. *"Kadaster-Gids"*. *Gids voor de raadpleging van hypothecaire en kadastrale archieven uit de 19e en de eerste helft van de 20e eeuw*. Den Haag: Rijksarchiefdienst, 1979.
Kilian, Ted. 'Public and Private, Power and Space'. In *Philosophy and Geography II. The Production of Public Space*, edited by Andrew Light and Jonathan M. Smith, 115-34. Lanham: Rowman & Littlefield, 1998.
Kist, J. Bas and Jan P. Puype. 'Wapens op schutterstukken'. In *Schutters in Holland. Kracht en zenuwen van de stad*, edited by M. Carasso-Kok and J. Levy-van Halm, 16-35. Zwolle: Waanders, 1988.
Klein Kranenburg, Diederick. *'Samen voor ons eigen'. De geschiedenis van een Nederlandse volksbuurt: De Haagse Schilderswijk 1920-1985*. Hilversum: Verloren, 2013.
Kloek, Els. 'De vrouw'. In *Gestalten van de Gouden Eeuw. Een Hollands groepsportret*, edited by H. M. Beliën, A. Th. van Deursen and G. J. van Setten, 241-79. Amsterdam: Bert Bakker, 1995.
Knevel, Paul. *Burgers in het geweer. De schutterijen in Holland, 1550-1700*. Dordrecht: Historische Vereniging Holland; Hilversum: Verloren, 1994.
Knevel, Paul. 'De kracht en zenuwen van de Republiek. De schutterijen in Holland, 1580-1650'. In *Schutters in Holland. Kracht en zenuwen van de stad*, edited by M. Carasso-Kok and J. Levy-van Halm, 37-53. Zwolle: Waanders, 1988.
Knevel, Paul. 'Een kwestie van overleven. De kunst van het samenleven'. In *Geschiedenis van Holland*, edited by Thimo de Nijs and Eelco Beukers, 217-54. Hilversum: Verloren, 2002.
Knevel, Paul. 'Epiloog. De schutterijen na 1650'. In *Schutters in Holland. Kracht en zenuwen van de stad*, edited by M. Carasso-Kok and J. Levy-van Halm, 172-4. Zwolle: Waanders, 1988.
Knevel, Paul. *Het Haagse Bureau. Zeventiende-eeuwse ambtenaren tussen staatsbelang en eigenbelang*. Amsterdam: Prometheus; Bert Bakker, 2001.
Korthals Altes, Everhard and Bram Vannieuwenhuyze. *Nederland op zijn mooist. De achttiende-eeuwse Republiek in kaart en beeld*. Bussum: Thoth, 2022.
Kuijpers, Erika. *Migrantenstad. Immigratie en sociale verhoudingen in 17e-eeuws Amsterdam*. Hilversum: Verloren, 2005.
Kuijpers, Erika and Maarten Prak. 'Burger, ingezetene, vreemdeling: Burgerschap in Amsterdam in de 17e en 18e eeuw'. In *Burger*, edited by Joost Kloek and Karin Tilmans, 113-32. Amsterdam: Amsterdam University Press, 2002.
Kuijpers, Erika, and Maarten Prak. 'Gevestigden en buitenstaanders'. In *Geschiedenis van Amsterdam. Centrum van de wereld 1578-1650*, edited by Willem Frijhoff and Maarten Prak, 189-239. Amsterdam: SUN, 2004.
Künzel, Rudi. *Beelden en zelfbeelden van middeleeuwse mensen. Historisch-antropologische studies over groepsculturen in de Nederlanden*. Nijmegen: SUN, 1997.
Langton, John. 'Residential Patterns in Pre-Industrial Cities: Some Case Studies from Seventeenth-Century Britain'. *Transactions of the Institute of British Geographers* 65 (1975): 1-27.
Lankester-Marcus, Maud C. M. 'Stedentrots & stedenpracht: Kunstenaarsvermeldingen in stadsbeschrijvingen van Noord-Nederlandse steden 1600-1850'. *RKD Studies (online)* (2020).

Lara-Hernandez, Jose Antonio. 'General Introduction'. In *Temporary Appropriation in Cities: Human Spatialisation in Public Spaces and Community Resilience*, edited by Alessandro Melis, Jose Antonio Lara-Hernandez and James Thompson, 1–9. Cham: Springer International Publishing, 2020.

Lawrence, Cynthia. *Gerrit Adriaensz. Berckheyde (1638–1698). Haarlem Cityscape Painter*. Doornspijk: Davaco, 1991.

Le Bon, Gustave. *The Crowd: A Study of the Popular Mind*. 1895. London: T.F. Unwin, 1908.

Lesger, Clé. 'De wereld als horizon. De economie tussen 1578 en 1650'. In *Geschiedenis van Amsterdam. Centrum van de wereld 1578–1650*, edited by Willem Frijhoff and Maarten Prak, 102–87. Amsterdam: SUN, 2004.

Lesger, Clé. 'Economic Growth, Social Differentiation and the Reshaping of the Urban Landscape in Amsterdam During Its Golden Age'. In *The English Urban Renaissance Revisited*, edited by John Hinks and Catherine Armstrong, 188–210. Cambridge Scholars, 2018.

Lesger, Clé. *Huur en conjunctuur. De woningmarkt in Amsterdam, 1550–1850*. Amsterdam: Historisch Seminarium van de Universiteit van Amsterdam, 1986.

Lesger, Clé. *Hoorn als stedelijk knooppunt. Stedensystemen tijdens de late middeleeuwen en vroegmoderne tijd*. Dordrecht: Historische Vereniging Holland; Hilversum: Verloren, 1990.

Lesger, Clé. *The Rise of the Amsterdam Market and Information Exchange; Merchants, Commercial Expansion and Change in the Spatial Economy of the Low Countries, c.1550–1630*. Aldershot: Ashgate, 2006.

Lesger, Clé. *Shopping Spaces and the Urban Landscape in Early Modern Amsterdam, 1550–1850*. Amsterdam: Amsterdam University Press, 2020.

Lesger, Clé. 'Spaces and Places'. In *A Cultural History of Shopping in the Age of Enlightenment*, edited by Ilja van Damme, 43–63. London: Bloomsbury Academic, 2022.

Lesger, Clé. 'Stagnatie en stabiliteit. De economie tussen 1730 en 1795'. In *Geschiedenis van Amsterdam. Zelfbewuste stadstaat 1650-1813*, edited by Willem Frijhoff and Maarten Prak, 219–65. Amsterdam: SUN, 2005.

Lesger, Clé and Marco H. D. van Leeuwen. 'Residential Segregation from the Sixteenth to the Nineteenth Century. Evidence from the Netherlands'. *Journal of Interdisciplinary History* XLII, no. 3 (2012): 333–69.

Lesger, Clé, Marco H. D. van Leeuwen and George Buzing. 'Residentiële segregatie in Delft. Een verkenning van ruimtelijke patronen in 1832'. In *Tijd en ruimte. Nieuwe toepassingen van GIS in de alfawetenschappen*, edited by Onno Boonstra and Anton Schuurman, 52–61. Utrecht: Matrijs, 2009.

Lesger, Clé, Marco H. D. van Leeuwen and Bart Vissers. 'Residentiële segregatie in vroegmoderne steden. Amsterdam in de eerste helft van de negentiende eeuw'. *Tijdschrift voor Sociale en Economische Geschiedenis* 10 (2013): 102–32.

Levine, David A. and Ekkehard Mai, eds. *I Bamboccianti. Niederländische Malerrebellen im Rom des Barock*. Rome: Ugo Bozzi Editore, 1991.

Lis, Catharina and Hugo Soly. *Worthy Efforts: Attitudes to Work and Workers in Pre-Industrial Europe*. Leiden: Brill, 2012.

Looijesteijn, Henk, Sanne Muurling, Anne Petterson, Tim de Ridder and Ad van der Zee, eds. 'Het ontstaan van het graafschap Holland'. *Holland* 50 (2018).

Lourens, Piet and Jan Lucassen. *Inwonertallen van Nederlandse steden ca.1300–1800*. Amsterdam: NEHA, 1997.

Lukes, Steven. *Power. A Radical View*. 1974. Basingstoke: Palgrave, 2005.

Maclot, Petra. 'A Portrait Unmasked: The Iconology of the Birds'-Eye View of Antwerp by Virgilius Bononiensis (1565) as a Source for Typological Research of Private Buildings in Fifteenth- and Sixteenth-Century Antwerp'. In *Portraits of the City. Representing Urban Space in Later Medieval and Early Modern Europe*, edited by Katrien Lichtert, Jan Dumolyn and Maximiliaan P. J. Martens, 33–47. Turnhout: Brepols, 2014.

Marriott, John. 'The Spatiality of the Poor in Eighteenth-Century London'. In *The Streets of London; from the Great Fire to the Great Stink*, edited by Tim Hitchcock and Heather Shore, 119–34. London: Rivers Oram Press, 2003.

Marx, Karl and Friedrich Engels. *The Communist Manifesto*. 1848. London: Pluto Press, 2008.

Materiële Welvaart in Nederland 2020. Den Haag: Centraal Bureau voor Statistiek, 2020.

Mayne, Alan. 'Representing the Slum'. *Urban History Yearbook* 17 (1990): 66–83.

McCants, Anne E. C. *Civic Charity in a Golden Age. Orphan Care in Early Modern Amsterdam*. Urbana: University of Illinois Press, 1997.

McCants, Anne E. C. 'Goods at Pawn. The Overlapping Worlds of Material Possessions and Family Finance in Early Modern Amsterdam'. *Social Science History* 31 (2007): 213–38.

McGowan, Randall. 'The Problem of Punishment in Eighteenth-Century England'. In *Penal Practice and Culture, 1500-1900. Punishing the English*, edited by Simon Devereaux and Paul Griffiths, 210–31. Houndmills: Palgrave MacMillan, 2004.

Medema, Geert. *Achter de façade van de Hollandse stad. Het stedelijk bouwbedrijf in de achttiende eeuw*. Nijmegen: Vantilt, 2011.

Meijer Drees, Marijke. '"Burgerlijke" zeventiende-eeuwse literatuur'. In *Burger*, edited by Joost Kloek and Karin Tilmans, 133–53. Amsterdam: Amsterdam University Press, 2002.

Meischke, Rudolph. 'Städtischer Parzellenzuschnitt und Wohnhaustypen nach 1400'. In *Hausbau in den Niederlanden*. Jahrbuch für Hausforschung, 9–20. Marburg: Jonas Verlag, 1990.

Meyer, Han. 'Het bouwblok als microkosmos van de stad'. In *Atlas van het Hollandse bouwblok*, edited by Susanne Komossa, Han Meyer, Max Risselada, Sabien Thomaes and Nynke Jutten, 251–8 Bussum: Thoth, 2002.

Miller, Seumas 'Foucault on Discourse and Power'. *Theoria: A Journal of Social and Political Theory* 76 (1990): 115–25.

Mitchell, William J. T. *Iconology. Image, Text, Ideology*. Chicago: University of Chicago Press, 1986.

Mol, Hans. 'Het Napoleontisch kadaster van Holland in GIS: Belang en perspectieven'. *Holland* 52 (2020): 20–8.

Muir, Edward. *Civic Ritual in Renaissance Venice*. Princeton: Princeton University Press, 1981.

Muir, Edward. *Rituals in Early Modern Europe*. Cambridge: Cambridge University Press, 1997.

Müller, Maarten. *Misdaad en straf in een Hollandse stad: Haarlem, 1245-1615*. Hilversum: Verloren, 2017.

Müller, Maarten. *Misdaad en straf in een Hollandse stad: Haarlem, 1673-1811*. Hilversum: Verloren, 2022.

Mumford, Lewis. *The City in History. Its Origins, Its Transformations, and Its Prospects*. 1961. London: Penguin Books, 1966.

Nevola, Fabrizio. *Street Life in Renaissance Italy*. New Haven: Yale University Press, 2020.
Nichols, Tom. 'The Vagabond Image: Depictions of False Beggars in Northern Art of the Sixteenth Century'. In *Others and Outcasts in Early Modern Europe. Picturing the Social Margins*, edited by Tom Nichols, 37-60. Aldershot: Ashgate, 2007.
Nieuwenhuijs, Christianus J. *Proeve eener geneeskundige plaatsbeschrijving (topographie) der stad Amsterdam*, Vol. 4. Amsterdam: Johannes van der Hey, 1820.
Nieuwenhuijzen, Kees, ed. *De vroegste foto's van Amsterdam*. Amsterdam: Van Gennep, 1974.
Noordam, Dirk Jaap. 'Demografische ontwikkelingen'. In *Leiden. De geschiedenis van een Hollandse stad. 1574-1795*, Vol. 2, edited by S. Groenveld, 43-53. Leiden: Stichting Geschiedschrijving Leiden, 2003.
Noordam, Dirk Jaap. 'Leiden in last. De financiële positie van de Leidenaren aan het einde van de middeleeuwen'. *Jaarboek Dirk van Eck* (2001): 17-40.
Noordegraaf, Leo. *Daglonen in Alkmaar 1500-1650*. Historische Vereniging Holland, 1980.
Nusteling, Hubert. 'De homeostatische bevolkingsreeks voor Amsterdam in 1586-1865 toegelicht en getoetst'. *Tijdschrift voor Sociale en Economische Geschiedenis* 15 (2018): 31-65.
Nusteling, Hubert. *Welvaart en werkgelegenheid in Amsterdam 1540-1860. Een relaas over demografie, economie en sociale politiek van een wereldstad*. Amsterdam: De Bataafsche Leeuw, 1985.
Oldewelt, Willem F. H., ed. *Kohier van de Personeele Quotisatie te Amsterdam over het jaar 1742*. Amsterdam: Genootschap Amstelodamum, 1945.
Olsen, Donald J. *The City as a Work of Art*: London, Paris, Vienna and New Haven: Yale University Press, 1986.
Olsen, Donald J. *The Growth of Victorian London*. London: Batsford, 1976.
Orlers, Jan. *Beschrijvinge der stad Leyden. Inhoudende 't begin, den voortgang, ende den wasdom der selver ... met groote moeijten, uyt verscheyden schriften ende papieren by een vergadert, ende beschreven door I.I. Orlers*. Leiden: Henrick Haestens, Jan Orlers and Jan Maire, 1614.
Orsel, Edwin D. 'Hausbau in Leiden'. In *Hausbau in Holland. Baugeschichte und Stadtentwicklung*, edited by Gabri van Tussenbroek. Jahrbuch für Hausforschung, 243-65. Marburg: Jonas Verlag, 2010.
Orsel, Edwin D. 'Zijn er nog 'veel' middeleeuwse huizen in Leiden?'. In *Dwars door de stad. Archeologische en bouwhistorische ontdekkingen in Leiden*, edited by Chrystel R. Brandenburgh, 114-34. Leiden: Primavera Pers; Dienst Bouwen en Wonen, 2007.
Pahl, Raymond E. *Whose City? And Further Essays on Urban Society*. Harmondsworth: Penquin Books, 1975.
Patroon: Lineaire, hiërarchische structuren en (gesloten) bouwblokken. Bouwprincipes historische stad. Rotterdam: FlexusAWC, 2008.
Peltjes, Gerrit Jan. *Leidse lasten. Twee belastingkohieren uit 1674*. Leiden: Nederlands Historisch Data Archief, 1995.
Peteri, Willem B. *Overheidsbemoeiingen met de stedebouw tot aan de vrede van Münster*. Alkmaar: W.B., 1913.
Phillips, Derek. *Well-Being in Amsterdam's Golden Age*. Amsterdam: Amsterdam University Press, 2008.
Pierik, Bob. 'Urban Life on the Move. Gender and Mobility in Early Modern Amsterdam'. PhD thesis, Universiteit van Amsterdam, 2022.

Pollmann, Judith. 'Eendracht maakt macht. Stedelijke cultuuridealen en politieke werkelijkheid in de Republiek'. In *Harmonie in Holland. Het poldermodel van 1500 tot nu*, edited by Dennis Bos, Maurits Ebben and Henk te Velde, 134–51. Amsterdam: Bert Bakker, 2007.

Pontanus, Johannes Isacius. *Historische beschrijvinghe der seer wijt beroemde coopstadt Amsterdam: waer inne benevens de eerste beginselen ende opcomsten der stadt, verscheyden privilegien . . . in Nederduyts overgheset door Petrvm Montanvm*. Amsterdam: Jodocus Hondius, 1614.

Pooley, Colin G. 'Patterns on the Ground: Urban Form, Residential Structure and the Social Construction of Space'. In *The Cambridge Urban History of Britain*, edited by Martin Daunton, 429–66. Cambridge: Cambridge University Press, 2000.

Posthumus, Nicolaas W. *De geschiedenis van de Leidsche lakenindustrie. Vol. I, De middeleeuwen (veertiende tot zestiende eeuw)*. Den Haag: Martinus Nijhoff, 1908.

Pot, Gerardus P. M. *Arm Leiden. Levensstandaard, bedeling en bedeelden, 1750–1854*. Hilversum: Verloren, 1994.

Pot, Gerardus P. M. 'Het beleid ten aanzien van bedelaars, passanten en immigranten te Leiden, 1700–1795'. *Leids Jaarboekje* 79 (1987): 82–95.

Prak, Maarten. 'Burgers in beweging. Ideaal en werkelijkheid van de onlusten te Leiden in 1748'. *Bijdragen en Mededeelingen betreffende de Geschiedenis der Nederlanden* 16 (1991): 365–93.

Prak, Maarten. 'Corporate Politics in the Low Countries. Guilds as Institutions, 14th–18th Centuries'. In *Craft Guilds in the Early Modern Low Countries. Work, Power, and Representation*, edited by Maarten Prak, Catharina Lis, Jan Lucassen and Hugo Soly, 74–106. Aldershot: Ashgate, 2006.

Prak, Maarten. 'Individu, corporatie en samenleving. De retoriek van de Amsterdamse gilden in de 18de eeuw'. In *Werelden van verschil. Ambachtsgilden in de Lage Landen*, edited by Catharina Lis and Hugo Soly, 293–319. Brussel: VUB Press, 1997.

Prak, Maarten. 'Stad van tegenstellingen 1730–1795'. In *Geschiedenis van Amsterdam. Zelfbewuste stadstaat 1650-1813*, edited by Willem Frijhoff and Maarten Prak, 267–307. Amsterdam: SUN, 2005.

Prak, Maarten. 'Velerlei soort van volk. Sociale verhoudingen in Amsterdam in de zeventiende eeuw'. *Jaarboek Amstelodamum* 91 (1999): 29–54.

Prak, Maarten and Jan Luiten van Zanden. *Nederland en het poldermodel. Sociaaleconomische geschiedenis van Nederland, 1000–2000*. Amsterdam: Bert Bakker, 2013.

Price, John L. 'De regent'. In *Gestalten van de Gouden Eeuw. Een Hollands groepsportret*, edited by H. M. Beliën, A. Th. van Deursen and G. J. van Setten, 25–62. Amsterdam: Bert Bakker, 1995.

Raben, Remco. 'Colonial Shorthand and Historical Knowledge: Segregation and Localisation in a Dutch Colonial Society'. *Journal of Modern European History* 18 (2020): 177–93.

Radford, John P. 'Testing the Model of the Pre-Industrial City. The Case of Ante-Bellum Charleston, South Carolina'. *Transactions of the Institute of British Geographers* 4 (1979): 392–410.

Raue, J. J. *De stad Delft: Vorming en ruimtelijke ontwikkeling in de late middeleeuwen. Interpretatie van 25 Jaar binnenstadsonderzoek*. Delft: Delftse Universitaire Pers, 1982.

Rebecchini, Guido 'Rituals of Justice and the Construction of Space in Sixteenth-Century Rome'. *I Tatti Studies in the Italian Renaissance* 16 (2013): 153–79.

Renes, Hans. 'De stad in het landschap'. In *Stadswording in de Nederlanden. Op zoek naar overzicht*, edited by Reinout Rutte and Hildo van Engen, 15-46. Hilversum: Verloren, 2008.
Rentenaar, Rob. 'De oudste stedelijke toponymie in het graafschap Holland'. In *De Hollandse stad in de dertiende eeuw*, 65-78. Zutphen: Walburg Pers, 1988.
Reuvekamp, Bart. 'De Amsterdamse rijken in 1585. Belastingadministratie als demografische bron'. *Amstelodamum* 108 (2021): 13-25.
Robijns, Marinus J. F. *Radicalen in Nederland (1840-1851)*. Leiden: Universitaire Pers Leiden, 1967.
Rudé, George. *The Crowd in History. A Study of Popular Disturbances in France and England, 1730-1848*. London: Lawrence and Wishart, 1981.
Rudé, George. *Paris and London in the Eighteenth Century. Studies in Popular Protest*. London: Lawrence and Wishart, 1970.
Ruitenbeek, Olga. 'Niet zonder kleerscheuren. Criminaliteitspatroon, eergevoel en het gebruik van fysiek geweld door Amsterdamse volksvrouwen (1811-1838)'. *Jaarboek Amstelodamum* 102 (2010): 63-85.
Ruiz, Teofilo F. *Spanish Society, 1400-1600*. A Social History of Europe. Harlow: Longman, 2001.
Rutte, Reinout. *Stedenpolitiek en stadsplanning in de Lage Landen (12de-13de eeuw)*. Zutphen: Walburg Pers, 2002.
Rutte, Reinout and Jaap Evert Abrahamse, eds. *Atlas of the Dutch Urban Landscape. A Millennium of Spatial Development*. Bussum: Thoth, 2016.
Rutte, Reinout and G. A. Hoekveld. 'Stadswording en machtspolitiek. Vergelijkend onderzoek met een modelmatige benadering'. *Historisch-Geografisch Tijdschrift* 21 (2003): 77-92.
Rutte, Reinout, Bram Vannieuwenhuyze and Yvonne van Mil. *Stedenatlas Jacob van Deventer: 226 stadsplattegronden uit 1545-1575 - schakels tussen verleden en heden*. Bussum: Thoth; Tielt: Lannoo, 2018.
Rutte, Reinout, Ko Visser and Wim Boerefijn. 'Stadsaanleg in de late middeleeuwen. Over bouwpercelen, straten en standaardmaten in Elburg en enige andere steden'. *Bulletin KNOB* 102 (2003): 122-37.
Ryckbosch, Wouter. 'Economic Inequality and Growth before the Industrial Revolution: The Case of the Low Countries (Fourteenth to Nineteenth Centuries)'. *European Review of Economic History* 20 (2015): 1-22.
Salman, Jeroen. '"Vreemde loopers en kramers". De ambulante boekhandel in de achttiende eeuw'. *Jaarboek voor Nederlandse Boekgeschiedenis* 8 (2001): 73-97.
Salman, Jeroen. *"Zijn Marsie, en zijn stok, Aanschouwer sta wat stil". Ontmoetingen met rondtrekkende boekverkopers*. Leiden: Stichting Neerlandistiek Leiden, 2006.
Salzberg, Rosa M. 'The Margins in the Centre. Working around Rialto in Sixteenth-Century Venice'. In *The Place of the Social Margins, 1350-1750*, edited by Andrew Spicer and Jane L. Stevens Crawshaw, 135-52. New York: Routledge, 2017.
Santing, Catrien. 'Tegen ledigheid en potverteren. De habitus van de laatmiddeleeuwse stadsburger'. In *De stijl van de burger. Over Nederlandse burgerlijke cultuur vanaf de middeleeuwen*, edited by Remieg Aerts and Henk te Velde, 28-59. Kampen: Kok Agora, 1998.
Sarfatij, Herbert. 'Dutch Towns in the Formative Period (Ad 1000-1400). The Archaeology of Settlement and Building'. In *Medieval Archaeology in the Netherlands. Studies Presented to H.H. van Regteren Altena*, edited by J. C. Besteman, J. M. Bos and H. A. Heidinga, 183-98. Assen: Van Gorcum, 1990.

Schmal, Henk. 'De trek naar buiten. De opkomst van het forensisme'. In *Amsterdam in kaarten. Verandering van de stad in vier eeuwen cartografie*, edited by W. F. Heinemeijer and M. F. Wagenaar, 164–7. Ede: Zomer & Keuning, 1987.

Schmal, Henk. *Den Haag of 's-Gravenhage? De 19de-eeuwse gordel, een zone gemodelleerd door zand en veen*. Utrecht: Matrijs, 1995.

Schoorl, Henk. 'Het Hollandse kustgebied tussen Helinium en Vlie vanaf de Romeinse tijd tot 1421'. In *Holland en het water in de middeleeuwen*, edited by J. J. J. M. Beenakker, J. C. Besteman, D. E. H. de Boer, G. J. Borger, P. A. Henderikx, H. Schoorl, C. L. Verkerk and K. Vlierman, 9–19. Hilversum: Verloren, 1997.

Schrevelius, Theodorus. *Harlemias, ofte, om beter te seggen, de eerste stichtinghe der Stadt Haerlem, het toe-nemen en vergrootinge der selfden . . . de oeffeninghe van de Inghesetenen, in alle Wetenschap, Kunst ende Gheleertheydt, Neeringhe en Hanteringe, en wat dies meer is*. Haarlem: Thomas Fonteyn, 1648.

Sennett, Richard. *Authority*. New York: Vintage Books, 1981.

Sennett, Richard. *Together: The Rituals, Pleasures, and Politics of Cooperation*. New Haven: Yale University Press, 2012.

Serneels, Hannah. 'Making Space for Resistance: The Spatiality of Popular Protest in the Late Medieval Southern Low Countries'. *Urban History* 48 (2021): 1–16.

Shesgreen, Sean. 'In Search of the Marginal and the Outcast: The "Lower Orders" in the Cries of London and Dublin'. In *Others and Outcasts in Early Modern Europe. Picturing the Social Margins*, edited by Tom Nichols, 215–39. Aldershot: Ashgate, 2007.

Shoemaker, Robert B. 'The London "Mob" in the Early Eighteenth Century'. In *The Eighteenth-Century Town. A Reader in English Urban History 1688–1820*, edited by Peter Borsay, 188–222. London: Longman, 1990.

Shoemaker, Robert B. *The London Mob. Violence and Disorder in Eighteenth-Century England*. London: Hambledon and London, 2004.

Shoemaker, Robert B. 'Streets of Shame? The Crowd and Public Punishments in London, 1700–1820'. In *Penal Practice and Culture, 1500–1900. Punishing the English*, edited by Simon Devereaux and Paul Griffiths, 232–57. Houndmills: Palgrave MacMillan, 2004.

Siffels, Nico and Willem van Spijker. 'Haarlemse paupers. Arbeidsmarkt, armoede en armenzorg in Haarlem in de eerste helft van de negentiende eeuw'. *Tijdschrift voor Sociale Geschiedenis* 13 (1987): 458–93.

Sjoberg, Gideon. *The Pre-Industrial City. Past and Present*. New York: The Free Press, 1960.

Sluijter, Ronald, and Ariadne Schmidt. 'Sociale verhoudingen en maatschappelijke zorg'. In *Leiden. De geschiedenis van een Hollandse stad. 1574-1795*, Vol. 2, edited by S. Groenveld, 108–25. Leiden: Stichting Geschiedschrijving Leiden, 2003.

Soltow, Lee and Jan Luiten van Zanden. *Income and Wealth Inequality in the Netherlands, 16th–20th Century*. Amsterdam: Het Spinhuis, 1998.

Soutendam, Jan. 'Het oudste keurboek van Delft'. *Nieuwe bijdragen voor rechtsgeleerdheid en wetgeving*, nieuwe reeks 2/3 (1876): 393–432, 81–555.

Soutendam, Jan. *Keuren en ordonnantiën der stad Delft van den aanvang der XVIe eeuw tot het jaar 1536*. Delft: J.H. Molenbroek, 1870.

Sparreboom, Jan. 'Twee fiscale bronnen uit het stadsarchief van Edam, circa 1462'. *Holland* 13 (1981): 146–64.

Speet, Ben J. M. 'Een stad raakt verstopt. Ruimtelijke ontwikkelingen in de 16de eeuw'. In *Woelige tijden. Amsterdam in de eeuw van de Beeldenstorm*, edited by Margriet de Roever and Boudewijn Bakker, 31–43. Amsterdam: De Bataafsche Leeuw, 1987.

Speet, Ben J. M. *Edam. Duizend jaar geschiedenis van een stad*. Zwolle: Waanders 2007.

Speet, Ben J. M. 'Verstening, verdichting en vergroting'. In *Geschiedenis van Amsterdam. Een stad uit het niets (tot 1578)*, edited by Marijke Carasso-Kok, 75–107. Amsterdam: SUN, 2004.

Spence, Craig. *London in the 1690s. A Social Atlas*. London: Centre for Metropolitan History, University of London, 2000.

Spierenburg, Pieter. 'Boeventucht en vrijheidsstraffen. Coornherts betekenis voor het ontstaan en de ontwikkeling van het gevangeniswezen in Nederland'. In *Scherp toezicht; van 'Boeventucht' tot 'Samenleving en criminaliteit'*, edited by Cyrille Fijnaut and Pieter Spierenburg, 11–30. Arnhem: Gouda Quint, 1990.

Spierenburg, Pieter. *The Spectacle of Suffering. Executions and the Evolution of Repression: From a Preindustrial Metropolis to the European Experience*. Cambridge: Cambridge University Press, 1984.

Stal, Kees. 'Een plaets so magnifycq van gebouwen'. In *Den Haag. Geschiedenis van de stad. De tijd van de Republiek*, Vol. 2, edited by Th. Wijsenbeek, 23–56. Zwolle: Waanders, 2005.

Stal, Kees and Victor Kersing. 'Ruimtelijke ontwikkeling in de late middeleeuwen'. In *Den Haag. Geschiedenis van de stad. Vroegste tijd tot 1574*, Vol. 1, edited by J. G. Smit, 27–76. Zwolle: Waanders, 2004.

Stapel, Leonore. *Perspectieven van de stad. Over bronnen, populariteit en functie van het zeventiende-eeuwse stadsgezicht*. Hilversum: Verloren, 2000.

Stenvert, Ronald. 'Enkhuizen: Morphologie einer schrumpfenden vormodernen Stadt'. In *Hausbau in Holland. Baugeschichte und Stadtentwicklung*, edited by Gabri van Tussenbroek. Jahrbuch für Hausforschung, 215–40. Marburg: Jonas Verlag, 2010.

Summerson, John. *Georgian London*. London: Barrie & Jenkins, 1988.

Sutton, Elizabeth A. *Capitalism and Cartography in the Dutch Golden Age*. Chicago: The University of Chicago Press, 2015.

Swartz, David. *Culture & Power. The Sociology of Pierre Bourdieu*. Chicago: The University of Chicago Press, 1997.

Sweezy, Paul, Maurice Dobb, Kohachiro Takahashi, Rodney Hilton, Christopher Hill, Henri Lefebvre, Giuliano Procacci, Eric Hobsbawn and John Merrington, eds. *The Transition from Feudalism to Capitalism*. London: NLB, 1976.

't Hart, Marjolein. 'Polderen en ploeteren. Een debat over geschiedenis, continuïteit en Nederlandse identiteit'. In *Vroegmoderne geschiedenis in actuele debatten*, edited by Hans Cools and Jasper van de Steen, 17–38. Leuven: Leuven University Press, 2020.

Taverne, Ed. *In 't land van belofte: in de nieue stadt. Ideaal en werkelijkheid van de stadsuitleg in de Republiek 1580–1680*. Maarssen: Gary Schwartz, 1978.

Te Velde, Henk. 'Het poldermodel. Een introductie'. In *Harmonie in Holland. Het poldermodel van 1500 tot nu*, edited by Dennis Bos, Maurits Ebben and Henk te Velde, 9–29. Amsterdam: Bert Bakker, 2007.

Ten Cate, C. L. *Tot glorie der gerechtigheid. De geschiedenis van het brandmerken als lijfstraf in Nederland*. Amsterdam: Wetenschappelijke Uitgeverij, 1975.

Ten Cate, T. 'De topografie van de "Oude Zijde" van Amsterdam in de 14e eeuw. Onderzoekingen naar de bruikbaarheid en de waarde van het middeleeuwse oorkondenmateriaal als bron voor topografisch onderzoek'. MA dissertation, Universiteit van Amsterdam, 1989.

Ter Meer Derval, Adrianus. 'Een kaart van 's-Gravenhage van omstreeks 1560–1570'. *Jaarboek Die Haghe* (1932): 1–20.

Terpstra, Nicholas. 'Theory into Practice: Executions, Comforting, and Comforters in Renaissance Italy'. In *The Art of Executing Well. Rituals of Execution in Renaissance*

Italy, edited by Nicholas Terpstra, 118-58. Kirksville: Truman State University Press, 2008.

Thelle, Mikkel. 'Crowding as Appropriation: Voting, Violence and Bodies in a Nineteenth-Century Urban Space'. *Distinktion: Journal of Social Theory* 17 (2016): 276-93.

Thompson, Edward P. 'The Moral Economy of the English Crowd in the Eighteenth Century'. *Past and Present* 50 (1971): 76-136.

Thompson, John B. 'Editor's Introduction'. In *Language and Symbolic Power*, edited by Pierre Boudieu, 1-31. Cambridge, MA: Harvard University Press, 1991.

Tilly, Charles. 'Demographic Origins of the European Proletariat'. In *Proletarianization and Family History*, edited by David Levine, 1-85. Orlando: Academic Press, 1984.

Tilly, Charles. 'What Good Is Urban History?'. *Journal of Urban History* 22 (1996): 702-19.

Tilly, Charles, Louise Tilly and Richard Tilly. *The Rebellious Century 1830-1930*. Cambridge MA: Harvard University Press, 1975.

Tjalsma, Heiko D. 'Een karakterisering van Leiden in 1749'. In *Armoede en sociale spanning. Sociaal-historische studies over Leiden in de achttiende eeuw*, edited by H. A. Diederiks, D. J. Noordam and H. D. Tjalsma, 17-44. Hilversum: Verloren, 1985.

Tromp, T. '"De gesteldheid van den publieken geest" (in Noord-Holland)'. In *Autoriteit en strijd*, edited by A. Doedens, 81-100. Amsterdam: VU Uitgeverij, 1981.

Unger, Richard W. *A History of Brewing in Holland 900-1900: Economy, Technology and the State*. Leiden: Brill, 2001.

Van Bleyswijck, Dirk Evertsz. *Beschryvinge der stadt Delft, betreffende des selfs situatie, oorsprong en ouderdom . . . Tot bericht, nut, ende gerief van alle soo tegenwoordige als nakomende burgeren der selver stad*. Delft: Arnold Bon, 1667.

Van Dam, Peter, Jouke Turpijn and Bram Mellink, eds. *Onbehagen in de polder. Nederland in conflict sinds 1795*. Amsterdam: Amsterdam University Press, 2014.

Van de Kieft, Co. 'Perspectief van de Hollandse stad'. In *De Hollandse stad in de dertiende eeuw*, edited by E. H. P. Cordfunke, F. W. N Hugenholtz and K. Sierksma, 113-20. Zutphen: Walburg Pers, 1988.

Van den Berg, Willem J. and Phil Kint. 'Inleiding'. In *Kadastrale uitkomsten van Noord- en Zuid-Holland 1832. Heruitgave ingeleid door W.J. van Den Berg en Ph. Kint*, edited by J. D. Hoeufft and J. C. R. van Hoorn van Burgh, 9-49. Dordrecht: Historische Vereniging Holland, 1993.

Van den Berg, Willem J. and Jan Luiten van Zanden. 'Vier eeuwen welstandsongelijkheid in Alkmaar, ca 1530-1930'. *Tijdschrift voor Sociale Geschiedenis* 19 (1993): 193-215.

Van den Berg, Willem J., Marco H. D. van Leeuwen and Clé Lesger. 'Residentiële segregatie in Hollandse steden. Theorie, methodologie en empirische bevindingen voor Alkmaar en Amsterdam, 16e-19e eeuw'. *Tijdschrift voor Sociale Geschiedenis* 24 (1998): 402-36.

Van den Heuvel, Danielle. 'Selling in the Shadows. Peddlers and Hawkers in Early Modern Europe'. In *Working on Labor: Essays in Honor of Jan Lucassen*, edited by Leo Lucassen and Marcel van der Linden, 125-51. Leiden: Brill, 2012.

Van der Borch tot Verwolde-Swemle, Evelyn C. 'Wonen in Delft'. In *De stad Delft. Cultuur en maatschappij, tot 1572*, edited by I. V. T. Spaander and R. A. van Leeuw, 123-7. Delft: Delft Stedelijk Museum 'Het Prinsenhof', 1979.

Van der Does, Jacob. *'s Graven-Hage, met de voornaemste plaetsen en vermaecklijckheden*. Den Haag: Hermanus Gael, 1668.

Van der Gaag, Stef. *Historische atlas van Delft. Stad van ambacht en techniek*. Nijmegen: Vantilt, 2015.

Van der Krogt, Peter C. J. *Geschiedenis en verklaring van de straatnamen in Delft*. Den Haag: Kruseman, 1985.
Van der Laarse, Rob. 'Amsterdam en Oranje: De politieke cultuur van kasteel en buitenplaats in Hollands Gouden Eeuw'. In *Buitenplaatsen in de Gouden Eeuw: De rijkdom van het buitenleven in de Republiek*, edited by Y. Kuiper, B. Olde Meierink and E. Storms-Smeets, 66–95. Hilversum: Verloren, 2015.
Van der Leeuw-Kistemaker, Renée E. *Wonen en werken in de Warmoesstraat van de 14de tot het midden van de 16de eeuw*. Amsterdam: Historisch Seminarium van de Universiteit van Amsterdam, 1974.
Van der Linden, Hendrik. 'Het platteland in het noordwesten met nadruk op de occupatie circa 1000–1300'. In *Algemene Geschiedenis der Nederlanden*. Vol. 2, 48–82. Haarlem: Fibula-Van Dishoeck, 1982.
Van der Schoor, Arie. *Het ontstaan van de middeleeuwse stad Rotterdam. Nederzettingsgeschiedenis in het Maas-Merwedegebied van ca. 400-1400*. Canaletto, 1992.
Van der Vijver, Cornelis. *Wandelingen in en om Amsterdam*. Amsterdam: J.C. van Kesteren, 1829.
Van der Vlis, Ingrid. *Leven in armoede. Delftse bedeelden in de zeventiende eeuw*. Amsterdam: Prometheus; Bert Bakker, 2001.
Van der Vlist, Ed. 'De stedelijke ruimte en haar bewoners'. In *Leiden. De geschiedenis van een Hollandse stad*. Vol. 1, Leiden tot 1574, edited by J. W. Marsilje, 15–57. Leiden: Stichting Geschiedschrijving Leiden, 2002.
Van der Wal, Ronald. *Of geweld zal worden gebruikt. Militaire bijstand bij de handhaving en het herstel van de openbare orde, 1840-1920*. Hilversum: Verloren, 2003.
Van der Wiel, Kees. 'Zicht op Delft in de 17de en 18de eeuw'. In *De snijkunst verbeeld. Delftse anatomische lessen nader belicht. Beschrijving van de vier Delftse anatomische lessen en een overzicht van de gezondheidszorg in Delft en haar beoefenaren in de zeventiende en achttiende eeuw*, edited by Hans Houtzager and Michiel Jonker, 8–31. Zwolle: Waanders, 2002.
Van der Woud, Auke. *Koninkrijk van sloppen. Achterbuurten en vuil in de negentiende eeuw*. Amsterdam: Bert Bakker, 2010.
Van der Woude, Adrianus M. 'Demografische ontwikkeling van de Noordelijke Nederlanden 1500-1800'. In *Algemene Geschiedenis der Nederlanden*. Vol. 5, 102–68. Haarlem: Fibula-Van Dishoeck, 1980.
Van der Woude, Cornelis. *Kronijcke van Alckmaer met zijn dorpen . . . van 't beginsel der bouwinge der voorsz. stadt Alckmaer, tot den jare Christi 1658*. Alkmaar: Symon Cornelisz. Brekegeest, 1658.
Van der Wulp, Bas. 'Het stadsbeeld van Delft tijdens het leven van Vermeer: Delft in Hollands verband'. In *De Hollandse samenleving in de tijd van Vermeer*, edited by Donald Haks and Marie Christine van der Sman, 32–51. Zwolle: Waanders, 1996.
Van der Zande, J. 'Amsterdamse stadsgeschiedschrijving vóór Wagenaar'. *Holland* 17 (1985): 218–30.
Van Deursen, Arie Th. *Het kopergeld van de Gouden Eeuw. Volk en overheid*, Vol. III. Assen: Van Gorcum, 1979.
Van Dillen, Johannes G., ed. *Bronnen tot de geschiedenis van het bedrijfsleven en het gildewezen van Amsterdam. 1612-1632*, Vol. II, Rijks Geschiedkundige Publicatiën (Grote Serie), 78. Den Haag: Martinus Nijhoff, 1933.
Van Domselaer, Tobias. *Beschryvinge van Amsterdam, haar eerste oorspronk . . . tot dezen tegenwoordige jare 1665, is voorgevallen*. Amsterdam: Marcus Willemsz. Doornick, 1665.

Van Gelder, A. Margaretha. *Amsterdamsche straatnamen geschiedkundig verklaard.* Amsterdam: P.N. van Kampen & Zoon, 1913.
Van Gelder, Herman A. Enno. *De Levensbeschouwing van Cornelis Pieterszoon Hooft, Burgemeester van Amsterdam 1547-1626.* 1918. Utrecht: HES, 1982.
Van Gelder, Herman A. Enno, ed. *Memoriën en adviezen van Cornelis Pietersz. Hooft.* Werken uitgegeven door het Historisch Genootschap, 3e serie, 48. Utrecht, 1925.
Van Gelder, Maartje. 'Protest in the Piazza. Contested Space in Early Modern Venice'. In *Popular Politics in an Aristocratic Republic: Political Conflict and Social Contestation in Late Medieval and Early Modern Venice*, edited by Maartje van Gelder and Claire Judde de Larivière, 129-57. London: Routledge, 2020.
Van Gelder, Maartje. 'Street Politics'. In *Early Modern Streets. A European Perspective*, edited by Danielle van den Heuvel, 111-33. Abingdon, Oxon: Routledge, 2022.
Van Gelder, Maartje and Filippo de Vivo. 'Papering over Protest: Contentious Politics and Archival Suppression in Early Modern Venice'. *Past and Present* 258 (2023): 44-78.
Van Kooten, Rogier. 'Antwerpen 1584. Oorlog en ongelijkheid in de stedelijke ruimte'. PhD thesis, Universiteit Antwerpen, 2020.
Van Kooten, Rogier. 'Levelling through Space? The Redistributive Capacity of Demographic Decline in Antwerp's Darkest Hour (1584-1586)'. In *Inequality and the City in the Low Countries (1200-2020)*, edited by B. Blondé, Sam Geens, Hilde Greefs, Wouter Ryckbosch, Tim Soens and Peter Stabel, 231-49. Turnhout: Brepols, 2020.
Van Leeuwen, Daan. 'Lepra en de bouw van leprosaria. Ziekte en segregatie in middeleeuws Holland'. *Holland* 51 (2019): 168-74.
Van Leeuwen, Henry W. 'Dirck van Bleyswijck, de geschiedschrijver en het Delft van zijn tijd'. In *De Kaart Figuratief van Delft*, edited by H. L. Houtzager, G. C. Klapwijk, H. W. van Leeuwen, M. A. Verschuyl and W. F. Weve, 10-22. Rijswijk: Elmar, 1997.
Van Leeuwen, Marco H. D. *Bijstand in Amsterdam, ca.1800-1850. Armenzorg als beheersings- en overlevingsstrategie.* Zwolle: Waanders; Amsterdam: Gemeentearchief Amsterdam, 1992.
Van Leeuwen, Marco H. D. *The Logic of Charity: Amsterdam, 1800-1850.* Houndmills: MacMillan, 2000.
Van Leeuwen, Marco H. D. and James E. Oeppen. 'Reconstructing the Demographic Regime of Amsterdam 1681-1920'. *Economic and Social History in the Netherlands* 5 (1993): 61-102.
Van Lennep, Frans J. E. *Late regenten.* Haarlem: H.D. Tjeenk Willink, 1962.
Van Maanen, Rudolf C. J. 'De vermogensopbouw van de Leidse bevolking in het laatste kwart van de zestiende eeuw'. *Bijdragen en Mededelingen betreffende de Geschiedenis der Nederlanden* 93 (1978): 1-42.
Van Maanen, Rudolf C. J. 'Stadsbeeld en ruimtelijke ordening'. In *Leiden. De geschiedenis van een Hollandse stad. 1574-1795*, Vol. 2, edited by S. Groenveld, 16-41. Leiden: Stichting Geschiedschrijving Leiden, 2003.
Van Nierop, Hendrik F. K. 'Popular Participation in Politics in the Dutch Republic'. In *Resistance, Representation and Community*, edited by Peter Blickle, 272-90. Oxford: Clarendon Press, 1997.
Van Nierop, Hendrik F. K. *Van ridders tot regenten. De Hollandse adel in de zestiende en de eerste helft van de zeventiende eeuw.* Amsterdam: De Bataafsche Leeuw, 1984.
Van Oerle, Hugo A. *Leiden. Een multidisciplinaire benadering van het proces der stadwording en de ontwikkeling van het oudste stadsgebied in de middeleeuwen.* Leiden: Brill, 1974.

Van Oers, Ron. *Dutch Town Planning Overseas During VOC and WIC Rule (1600–1800)*. Zutphen: Walburg Pers, 2000.
Van Oosten, Roos and Sanne Muurling. 'Smelly Business. De clustering en concentratie van vieze en stinkende beroepen in Leiden in 1581'. *Holland* 51 (2019): 128–32.
Van Ravesteyn Jr, Willem. *Onderzoekingen over de economische en sociale ontwikkeling van Amsterdam gedurende de 16de en het eerste kwart der 17de eeuw*. Amsterdam: S.L. van Looy, 1906.
Van Reenen, Piet. *Overheidsgeweld; een sociologische studie van de dynamiek van het geweldsmonopolie*. Alphen aan den Rijn: Samson, 1979.
Van Straten, Roelof. *Inleiding in de iconografie. Enige theoretische en praktische kennis*. Bussum: Coutinho, 2002.
Van Synghel, Geertrui A. M., ed., *Bronnen betreffende de registratie van onroerend goed in de negentiende en twintigste eeuw*. Broncommentaren. Vol. 3. Den Haag: Instituut voor Nederlandse Geschiedenis, 1997.
Van Synghel, Geertrui A. M., ed., *Bronnen betreffende de registratie van onroerend goed in middeleeuwen en ancien régime*. Broncommentaren. Vol. 4. Den Haag: Instituut voor Nederlandse Geschiedenis, 2001.
Van Tussenbroek, Gabri. 'Geografie van arm en rijk. Het kohier van de tiende penning van Amsterdam (1562) in GIS'. *Tijdschrift voor Historische Geografie* 3 (2018): 242–55.
Van Tussenbroek, Gabri. 'Voor de grote uitleg. Stedelijke transformatie en huisbouw in Amsterdam, 1452–1578'. *Stadsgeschiedenis* 10 (2015): 1–23.
Van Uytven, Raymond. 'Sociaal-economische evoluties in de Nederlanden voor de revoluties (14e-16e eeuw)'. *Bijdragen en Mededelingen betreffende de Geschiedenis der Nederlanden* 87 (1972): 60–93.
Van Zanden, Jan Luiten and Arthur van Riel. *The Strictures of Inheritance: The Dutch Economy in the Nineteenth Century*. The Princeton Economic History of the Western World. Princeton: Princeton University Press, 2004.
Vance Jr., James E. 'Land Assignment in the Pre-Capitalist, Capitalist and Post-Capitalist City'. *Economic Geography* 47 (1971): 101–20.
Vandermeersch, P., Bruno Blondé and R. Marynissen. 'Typologie sociale du parc de logements à Anvers basée sur la Cadastre de 1834'. In *Nouvelles approches concernant la culture de l'habitat / New Approaches to Living Patterns*, edited by R. Baetens and B. Blondé, 49–67. Turnhout: Brepols, 1991.
Vanneste, Dominique. *De pré-industriële Vlaamse stad: Een sociaal-economische survey. Interne differentiatie te Gent en te Kortrijk op het einde van de 18e eeuw*. Leuven: Geografisch Instituut Katholieke Universiteit te Leuven, 1987.
Vannieuwenhuyze, Bram and Elien Vernackt. 'The Digital Thematic Deconstruction of Historic Town Views and Maps'. In *Portraits of the City. Representing Urban Space in Later Medieval and Early Modern Europe*, edited by Katrien Lichtert, Jan Dumolyn and Maximiliaan P. J. Martens, 9–31. Turnhout: Brepols, 2014.
Veldhorst, Wini D. M. 'Het Nederlandse vroeg-19e-eeuwse kadaster als bron voor andersoortig onderzoek, een verkenning'. *Historisch-Geografisch Tijdschrift* 9 (1991): 8–27.
Verbaan, Eddy. *De woonplaats van de faam. Grondslagen van de stadsbeschrijving in de zeventiende-eeuwse Republiek*. Hilversum: Verloren, 2011.
Verbij-Schillings, Jeanne and Monique van Veen. 'Cultuur, literatuur en onderwijs'. In *Den Haag. Geschiedenis van de stad*, edited by J. G. Smit, 271–330. Zwolle: Waanders, 2004.
Verhoeven, Gerrit. *De derde stad van Holland. Geschiedenis van Delft tot 1795*. Zwolle: WBooks, 2015.

Verhoeven, Gerrit. *Het eerste kohier van de tiende penning van Delft (1543)*. Dordrecht: Historische Vereniging Holland; Hilversum: Verloren, 1999.
Verschuur-Stuip, Gerdy and Hans Renes. 'Hollandse buitenplaatsenlandschappen. Buitenplaatsen en hun relatie met het landschap (1609-1672)'. In *Buitenplaatsen in de Gouden Eeuw: De rijkdom van het buitenleven in de Republiek*, edited by Y. Kuiper, B. Olde Meierink and E. Storms-Smeets, 42-65. Hilversum: Verloren, 2015.
Vis, Jurjen. 'Chirurgijns, aalmoezeniers en weesmeesters. Welzijn, armoede en gezondheidszorg'. In *Geschiedenis van Alkmaar*, edited by Diederik Aten, Jan Drewes, Joop Kila and Harry de Raad, 277-300. Zwolle: Waanders, 2007.
Visser, Jacobus C. 'Het Delftse stadsplan'. In *Delftse studiën. Een bundel historische opstellen over de stad Delft geschreven voor dr. E.H. Ter Kuile naar aanleiding van zijn afscheid als hoogleraar in de geschiedenis van de Bouwkunst*, 1-19. Assen: Van Gorcum, 1967.
Vlaardingerbroek, Pieter. 'Architectuur en tekening'. In *Kijk Amsterdam 1700-1800: De mooiste stadsgezichten*, edited by Bert Gerlagh, 66-77. Bussum: Thoth; Amsterdam: Stadsarchief Amsterdam, 2017.
Von Zesen, Filips. *Beschreibung der Stadt Amsterdam ... vor augen gestellet werden*. Amsterdam: Joachim Nosche, 1664.
Vrints, Antoon. *Het theater van de straat. Publiek geweld in Antwerpen tijdens de eerste helft van de twintigste eeuw*. Amsterdam: Amsterdam University Press, 2011.
Wacquant, Loïc. 'Homines in Extremis: What Fighting Scholars Teach Us About Habitus'. *Body & Society* 20 (2014): 3-17.
Wacquant, Loïc J. D. 'Pierre Bourdieu'. In *Key Sociological Thinkers*, edited by Rob Stones, 215-29. Houndmills: MacMillan, 1998.
Wagenaar, Jan. *Amsterdam, in zyne opkomst, aanwas, geschiedenissen, voorregten, koophandel, gebouwen, kerkenstaat, schoolen, schutterye, gilden en regeeringe*. 2 vols, Amsterdam: Isaak Tirion, 1760-1767.
Wagenaar, Michiel. *Amsterdam 1876-1914. Economisch herstel, ruimtelijke expansie en de veranderende ordening van het stedelijk grondgebruik*. Amsterdam: Historisch Seminarium, Universiteit van Amsterdam, 1990.
Wagenaar, Michiel. *Stedebouw en burgerlijke vrijheid. De constrasterende carrières van zes Europese hoofdsteden*. Bussum: Thoth, 1998.
Wagenaar, Pieter. 'Haagse bestuurders en ambtenaren'. In *Den Haag. Geschiedenis van de stad. De tijd van de Republiek*, Vol. 2, edited by Th. Wijsenbeek, 90-120. Zwolle: Waanders, 2005.
Walle, Kees. *Buurthouden. De geschiedenis van burengebruiken en buurtorganisaties in Leiden (14e-19e eeuw)*. Leiden: Ginkgo, 2005.
Walzer, Michael. *Spheres of Justice. A Defense of Pluralism and Equality*. New York: Basic Books, 1983.
Wattenmaker, Richard J. 'Introduction'. In *Opkomst en bloei van het Noordnederlandse stadsgezicht in de 17de eeuw / the Dutch Cityscape in the 17th Century and Its Sources*, edited by B. Haak, R. J. Wattenmaker and B. Bakker, 14-50. Bentveld-Aerdenhout: Landshoff, 1977.
Weber, Max. *Economy and Society. An Outline of Interpretive Sociology*. Vol. I, edited by Guenther Roth and Claus Wittich. Berkeley: University of California Press, 1978.
Weber, Max. *Economy and Society. An Outline of Interpretive Sociology*. Vol. II, edited by Guenther Roth and Claus Wittich. Berkeley: University of California Press, 1978.
Weber, Max. 'Wirtschaft und Gesellschaft'. In *Max Weber-Gesamtausgabe digital*, edited by Knut Borchardt, Edith Hanke and Wolfgang Schluchter. Unvollendet, 1919-1920.

Wedman, Homme. 'Socialisme en burgerlijke cultuur in Nederland'. In *De stijl van de burger. Over Nederlandse burgerlijke cultuur vanaf de middeleeuwen*, edited by Remieg Aerts and Henk te Velde, 218–45. Kampen: Kok Agora, 1998.

Weve, Wim F., and Henry W. van Leeuwen. 'De dateringen van de plattegrond en de randprenten van de Kaart Figuratief'. In *De Kaart Figuratief van Delft*, edited by H. L. Houtzager, G. C. Klapwijk, H. W. van Leeuwen, M. A. Verschuyl and W. F. Weve, 37–8. Rijswijk: Elmar, 1997.

Weve, Wim. *Huizen in Delft in de 16de en 17de eeuw*. Zwolle: WBooks, 2013.

Wheelock Jr., Arthur K. '"Worthy to Behold". The Dutch City and Its Image in the Seventeenth Century'. In *Dutch Cityscapes of the Golden Age*, edited by Ariane van Suchtelen and Arthur K. Wheelock Jr., 14–33. Zwolle: Waanders, 2008.

White, Paul. *The West European City. A Social Geography*. London: Longman, 1984.

Wijbenga, Douwe. *Delft. Een verhaal van de stad en haar bewoners. Van de vroegste tijd tot het jaar 1572*, Vol. I. Rijswijk: Elmar, 1984.

Wijbenga, Douwe. *Delft. Een verhaal van de stad en haar bewoners. Van 1572 tot het jaar 1700*. Vol. II. Rijswijk: Elmar, 1986.

Wijsenbeek-Olthuis, Thera. *Achter de gevels van Delft. Bezit en bestaan van rijk en arm in een periode van achteruitgang (1700–1800)*. Hilversum: Verloren, 1987.

Wijsenbeek, Thera. 'Economisch leven'. In *Den Haag. Geschiedenis van de stad. De tijd van de Republiek*, Vol. 2, edited by Th. Wijsenbeek, 57–89. Zwolle: Waanders, 2005.

Wijsenbeek, Thera. 'Epiloog - Gespleten stad'. In *Den Haag. Geschiedenis van de stad. De tijd van de Republiek*, Vol. 2, edited by Th. Wijsenbeek, 331–4. Zwolle: Waanders, 2005.

Wijsenbeek, Thera. 'Inleiding: Den Haag in beeld en geschrift'. In *Den Haag. Geschiedenis van de stad. De tijd van de Republiek*, Vol. 2, edited by Th. Wijsenbeek, 11–17. Zwolle: Waanders, 2005.

Wijsenbeek, Thera. 'Schutters, gilden en buurten'. In *Den Haag. Geschiedenis van de stad. De tijd van de Republiek*, Vol. 2, edited by Th. Wijsenbeek, 149–76. Zwolle: Waanders, 2005.

Wijsenbeek, Thera. 'Wooncultuur en sociale verschillen'. In *Den Haag. Geschiedenis van de stad. De tijd van de Republiek*, Vol. 2, edited by Th. Wijsenbeek, 252–86. Zwolle: Waanders, 2005.

Willemsen, René T. H. *Enkhuizen tijdens de Republiek. Een economisch-historisch onderzoek naar stad en samenleving van de 16e tot de 19e eeuw*. Hilversum: Verloren, 1988.

Woolf, Stuart. 'Order, Class and the Urban Poor'. In *Social Orders and Social Classes in Europe since 1500: Studies in Social Stratification*, edited by M. L. Bush, 185–98. London: Longman, 1992.

Yntema, Richard. 'The Brewing Industry in Holland, 1300–1800: A Study in Industrial Development'. PhD thesis, University of Chicago, 1992.

Yntema, Richard. 'Een kapitale nering. De brouwindustrie in Holland tussen 1500 en 1800'. In *Bier! Geschiedenis van een volksdrank*, edited by R. E. Kistemaker and V. T. van Vilsteren, 72–81. Amsterdam: De Bataafsche Leeuw, 1994.

Zandvliet, Kees. *De 250 rijksten van de Gouden Eeuw. Kapitaal, macht, familie en levensstijl*. Amsterdam: Nieuw Amsterdam, 2006.

Zandvliet, Kees. *De 500 rijksten van de Republiek. Rijkdom, geloof, macht & cultuur*. Zutphen: Walburg Pers, 2018.

Zegveld, W. F. van. 'Zilveren schutterspenningen van Leiden'. *Leids Jaarboekje* 80 (1988): 51–67.

Zemon Davis, Natalie. 'The Rites of Violence: Religious Riots in Sixteenth-Century France'. *Past and Present* 59 (1973): 51–91.
Zijlmans, Jori. 'In handen van justitie'. In *Den Haag. Geschiedenis van de stad. De tijd van de Republiek*, Vol. 2, edited by Th. Wijsenbeek, 121–48. Zwolle: Waanders, 2005.
Zwitzer, Hans L. 'De militaire dimensie van de patriottenbeweging'. In *Voor vaderland en vrijheid. De revolutie van de patriotten*, edited by F. Grijzenhout, W. W. Mijnhardt and N. C. F. van Sas, 27–51. Amsterdam: De Bataafsche Leeuw, 1987.

Index

Abrahamse, Jaap Evert   57
Abu-Lughod, Janet L.   30
Alkmaar   12–13, 19, 35–40, 65, 89, 118, 123, 128–31, 140, 148, 186–90
  residential appropriation, c. 1830   38–40
  residential appropriation, genesis and continuity   65, 89
  residential patterns, fourteenth-nineteenth centuries   186–90
Allen, John   63, 72, 144, 153, 165, 168
  on power   2–4
  on smothering   139
alliances, web of   6–9, 19–22, 27, 108–9, 112–19, 137, 167, 169
Alva, Duke of   181
Ambrose   23
Amsterdam   6, 12–16, 19–20, 22, 25–7, 35–6, 50, 55, 80, 89–94, 98–103, 108–9, 112, 114, 116, 123–4, 128–35, 140–50, 153–5, 157–63, 167, 173, 190
  residential appropriation, c. 1830   47–9
  residential appropration, genesis and continuity   69–78, 83–6
  residential patterns, fourteenth-nineteenth centuries   200–6
Anthonisz, Cornelis   77, 147–50
Antwerp   12, 141
Aquinas, Thomas   15
Arendt, Hannah   3, 72
Aristotle   15
Augsburg   147

Baarn   7
Bakker, Rs.   146–8
Bambuccianti   156
Belgium   12, *see also* Antwerp; Leuven (Louvain); Southern Low Countries
Berckheyde, Gerrit   153–5
Bisschops, Tim   181

Blaeu, Joan   79, 153
Blaeu, Willem Jansz.   203
block (of houses) formation   74–82, 166
Bloemendaal   7
Boele, Anita   23
Boone, Marc   117, 120
Bos, Dennis   128, 133, 135
Boschma-Aarnoudse, Corrie   183
Bourdieu, Pierre   7–8, 15–17, 21, 29–30, 34, 51–3, 80, 91, 94–5, 140, 165–71
  on appropriated physical space   29–30
  on capital   4
  on classes   5
  on fields   4–5
  on habitus   5, 171
  on language   15
  on symbolic violence   95
Braatbard, Abraham Chaim   124
Breitner, George Hendrik   163

capital
  economic, social and cultural capital   4–8, 11, 14–15, 18–19, 29–31, 34, 38, 45, 51, 59, 61, 63, 67, 69–73, 80–3, 95, 102–3, 153, 165–9
  symbolic capital   4, 19, 21, 112
Carasso-Kok, Marijke   109
Casson, Catherine and Mark   81
Cats, Jacob   18–19
cities and insurrections   116–37
cities and townspeople, selective view of
  in city descriptions   141–7, 168–70
  in city maps   147–53, 168–70
  in cityscapes   153–63, 168–70
cities in Holland
  built-up area   36, 128–9
  city extensions   35, 61, 65–7, 71–3, 76–8, 82–3, 87, 100, 128–31, 141, 166, 179, 190, 204
  population density   129
  population figures   36, 190
  settlement history   56–9, 64–70

civilizing process   104–7
collective action, reactive and proactive forms of   134–7
Coornhert, Dirk Volkertsz.   24–5, 104, 142
Cosimo III de' Medici   94
country houses   94–5
Craffurd, Joris   16–17, 22, 114–17, 127

De Barbari, Jacopo   147
De Boer, Dick E.H.   178–9
De Cretser, Gysbert   144–6, 191–2
De Klerk, Len A.   54
De la Court, Pieter   197
De Ram, Johannes   150–1
De Wit, Frederik   37, 79, 153
De Witt, Johan and Cornelis   118
Dekker, Rudolf M.   114, 123–4
Delft   12–13, 25, 35–6, 50, 128–9, 141–3, 146, 151, 153, 160
   residential appropriation, c. 1830   40–3
   residential appropriation, genesis and continuity   57–64, 75–6, 88
   residential patterns, fourteenth-nineteenth centuries   173–80
Den Haag, *see* The Hague
Dordrecht   20, 80, 91, 109, 128–9, 140
Du Jardin, Karel   203
Dutch Revolt   6, 18, 25, 110, 117, 170

Edam   6, 12, 35–6, 50
   residential appropriation, c. 1830   35–8
   residential appropriation, genesis and continuity   67–9, 78–80, 89–91
   residential patterns, fourteenth-nineteenth centuries   180–6
Egmond, Florike   102
Elias, Norbert   106–7
England   7, 86, 117–20, 123, 126, 134, *see also* Gloucester; London
Enkhuizen   19, 118
enlightenment thinking   107
Evans, Richard J.   106–7
exclusive elite neighbourhoods, desire for   55, 74, 83–95, 167, 179–80, 186–8, 193–4, 200, 206
externalities   73, 83, 94, 97, 166
   definition of   51

Faber, Sjoerd   99, 103
Fabritius, Carel   153
Faucher, Leon   104
fields, *see also* Bourdieu
   definition of   4–5
   and habitus   5
Flinck, Govert Teunisz.   203
Florisz. van Berckenrode, Balthasar   78, 203
Fokkens, Melchior   144–6
Foucault, Michel   15, 17, 98, 100, 104
France   23, 86, 106, 135, *see also* Paris; Versailles
Franke, Herman   104, 107
Friedrich III, Duke of Schleswig-Holstein and Oldenburg   91
Friedrichs, Christopher R.   54
Friedrichstadt   91–2
Fritz, Rolf   154

Geltner, Guy   107
Germany   12, 91, 107, 135, 147, *see also* Augsburg; Oldenburg
Giddens, Anthony   2–3
Gloucester   81
Gouda   23, 60, 107
Grotius (Hugo de Groot)   18
Guicciardini, Ludovico   141
guilds   18–20, 31–2, 109
   militia-guilds   109–11, 117

Haarlem   16, 23, 25, 27, 60, 100, 106–7, 114, 117–18, 123, 128–9, 154, 160
habitus   9, 171–2, *see also* Bourdieu
   definition of   5
   primary and additional   171
The Hague   12, 14, 20, 35–6, 49–50, 55, 117–18, 123, 128–9, 131, 140, 144, 146, 152–3, 156, 173
   residential appropriation, c. 1830   45–7
   residential appropriation, genesis and continuity   64–5, 88–9
   residential patterns, fourteenth-nineteenth centuries   190–4
Harley, John B.   149
Haugaard, Mark   2
Havard, Henry   163
Heemstede   7

Hobsbawn, Eric J. 126, 129, 132, 136, 169
Hoekveld, Gerard A. 53
Holland, physical-geography and reclamation 56–7, 75
Hooft, Cornelis Pietersz. 19, 22
Huygens senior, Christiaan 194

iconography and iconology 147
IJsselstijn, Marcel 70
industries, location of 38–51, 59–67, 70–3, 82, 88, 144, 166, 179, *see also* tanneries
inequality 1, 8–15, 80, 93–4, 102, 126, 135, 139, 164, 167
Italy 135, 147, *see also* Naples; Venice

Jayasena, Ranjith 70
Jensen, Sune Qvotrup 28
Johnston, Ron J. 51

Kam, Jan G. 204
Kilian, Ted 2

La Fargue, Maria Margaretha 157
Lamberts, Gerrit 161
Le Bon, Gustave 22
Leiden 12–13, 26, 35–6, 50, 92, 107–8, 111, 114, 117–18, 123, 128–31, 140–2, 190, 193
  residential appropriation, c. 1830 43–5
  residential appropriation, genesis and continuity 66–7, 86–8
  residential patterns, fourteenth-nineteenth centuries 194–200
Leuven (Louvain) 148
Lievens, Jan 203
Lis, Catharina and Hugo Soly 22–3
London 6–7, 82–6, 107, 129–31, 139
  the City 83–4, 139 (*see also* smothering)
Louis XIV 117
Louis XV 98
Luttenberg, Gerrit 26

Margaret of Parma 149, 204
Marx, Karl 5
Mary of Hungary 176

McCants, Anne E.C. 20
McNeill Whistler, James 163
militias (middle classes) 1–2, 6, 9, 19–21, 69, 97, 108–21, 123–6, 130–8, *see also* guilds (militia guilds)
  middle-class riots and revolts 19, 97, 117–21, 170
  night watch 109, 112–14, 168–70
  optrek 111–13, 132, 168–70
Monet, Claude 163
Montague, William 99
moral economy 122–3, 136, 167–70
Müller, Maarten 106
Mumford, Lewis 53

Naples 6
Netherlands, *see also* Alkmaar; Amsterdam; Baarn; Bloemendaal; Delft; Dordrecht; Edam; Enkhuizen; Gouda; Haarlem; Heemstede; Holland; Leiden; Purmerend; Rotterdam; Schiedam; Schoonhoven; Texel; The Hague; Wassenaar
nobility 6–7, 16, 82, 120
Norway 12

Oldenburg 91
Orange, House of 14
  prince Maurice 110
  stadtholder William III 117
  stadtholder William IV 119
  stadtholder William V 120
  Wilhelmina of Prussia (wife of king William I) 46
  William of Orange 69
Orlers, Jan Jansz. 13, 141–2, 153
Othering, definition of 28

Palladio, Andrea 94
Panofsky, Erwin 147
Paris 6, 82–6, 98, 104, 129–31
Peltjes, Gerrit Jan 196
Philip II of Spain 181
Pontanus, Johannes 141–3, 153
poor, the
  beggars 23–7, 140–3, 156, 158–9, 170
  poor relief 13, 23–7, 142, 164, 168, 175

shamefaced poor   26–7
true and false poor   24, 142–3, 170
views on   22–8
Posthumus, Nicolaas W.   198
Pot, Gerardus P.M.   26
power
   associational power   3–4, 72, 86, 93
   definition of   2
   instrumental power   3–4, 63, 166
   modalities of   3–4, 20–1, 51–2, 63, 69, 98, 103, 108, 112, 119, 126, 166–8
   theory of   2–4
power relations
   continuity of   1–2, 5, 8–9, 20, 53, 95–6, 104, 120, 137, 141, 147, 153, 165, 171
   definition of   3
Prak, Maarten   117, 120
Pronk, Cornelis   160
property market
   fragmentation of private land ownership   82, 166–7
   in Holland   81–2
public scaffold punishments
   (authorities)   98–108, *see also* state formation; civilizing process
   ceremonial character of   100–2, 108
   selectivity of   102–3
Purmerend   118

Rembrandt   203
residential differentiation
   basic patterns in Holland   54–5, 165–6
   explanations   80–3
   macro-level   43, 49–50, 54–74, 81, 175, 182, 191, 206
   meso-level   33, 39, 42–51, 54–5, 74–80, 92–4, 175, 178–82, 187–8, 191–201, 204
   micro-level   32–3
   as symbolic violence   95
   theory of   30–4, 49–51, 165–6
resources, *see* capital; power (theory of)
riots and revolts (working classes), *see also* militias
   Aansprekersoproer (1696)   16, 19, 22, 114–17, 124–7
   Costerman oproer (1690)   126, 134

Damoproer (1848)   128, 133, 135–6
   ritual character of looting   124–6, 135
   role of women and children   22, 126–8, 134
Rotterdam   126–9, 134, 140, 173
Rudé, George   123, 126
Rudolf, abbot of the monastery Saint Truiden   22
Rutte, Reinout   70

Sarfatij, Herbert   75
Schiedam   173
Schleswig-Holstein   91–2, *see also* Friedrichstadt
Schoonhoven   123
Schouten, Herman   160
Schrevelius, Theodorus   16–18, 27, 114
Shoemaker, Robert B.   107
Sijmonsz., Taems   181
Sjoberg, Gideon   8, 29–39, 45, 47–53, 55, 81, 89, 166, 188
smothering   139, 141, 144, 153, 163–4, 168, *see also* Allen
social classes, size and composition of   7–8, 22, 140, *see also* Bourdieu; social hierarchy
social hierarchy   17, 28, 51, 80, 92, 144–7, 158, 169–70
   views on   16–17
society, consensual and conflictual model of   1, 5, 165
Soly, Hugo   22–3
Sonoy, Diederick   69
South Africa   13
Southern Low Countries   62, 109, 147
Space Syntax Analysis   130–4
Spierenburg, Pieter   103–6
Stal, Kees   191
state formation   7, 104–7, 135, 168, 190, *see also* civilizing process
   authority apparatus   121–2, 168
street networks, *see also* block (of houses) formation
   genesis and structure of   74–5
   and residential differentiation   81–2, 166
street vendors   140
Swartz, David   5

tanneries   38–49, 51, 62, 67, 69, 145, 160
taxation populaire   123
Temple, William   20
Ten Compe, Jan   156
Terpstra, Nicholas   102
Texel   63
Thompson, Edward P.   5, 122–3, 134, 208
Tilly, Charles   22
Tilly, Charles, Louise and Richard
    134–5, 170
Toren, Hendrik   126, 134

United Kingdom   12
United States   12–13

Van Bleyswijck, Dirk Evertsz.   142, 151
Van de Velde, Adriaan   154
Van den Berg, Laurens Ph.C.   26
Van den Berg, Willem   11, 186
Van den Vondel, Joost   22, 155
Van der Capellen tot den Pol, Joan
    Derk   120
Van der Does, Jacob   144
Van der Heyden, Jan   153–4, 158, 160
Van der Leeuw-Kistemaker, Renée
    E.   204
Van der Vijver, Cornelis   146
Van der Vlis, Ingrid   175
Van der Wiel, Kees   175
Van der Woud, Auke   171
Van Deventer, Jacob   79, 148, 181
Van Domselaer, Tobias   144–5, 203–4
Van Hout, Jan   67, 93

Van Huchtenburgh, Jan   154
Van Laer, Pieter   156
Van Leeuwen, Marco H.D.   26
Van Nierop, Hendrik F.K.   6
Van Oldenbarnevelt, Johan   194
Van Reenen, Piet   97–8
Van Uytven, Raymond   54
Van Zanden, Jan Luiten   11, 13
Vance Jr., James E.   8, 29–34, 39–40,
    49–53, 81, 166, 178, 197
Venice and the Veneto   94, 130, 147, 150,
    163
Verhoeven, Gerrit   176–7
Vermeer, Johannes   153
Versailles   84
Veth, Jan   163
violence
    definition of   97–8
    symbolic violence (*see* Bourdieu)
Visscher, Nicolaes   151
Vives, Juan Luis   24, 142
Von Zesen, Filips   144–5
Vosmaer, Jacob Woutersz.   153

Wagenaar, Jan   100–1
Wassenaar   7
Wattenmaker, Richard J.   154
Weber, Max   3, 121
Wenckebach, Willem   163
Wijsenbeek-Olthuis, Thera   180, 191
Witsen, Willem   163

Zandvliet, Kees   14

www.ingramcontent.com/pod-product-compliance
Lightning Source LLC
Chambersburg PA
CBHW071804300426
44116CB00009B/1195